THE DISNEY SONG
ENCYCLOPEDIA

THE DISNEY SONG ENCYCLOPEDIA

Updated Edition

Thomas S. Hischak
and
Mark A. Robinson

TAYLOR TRADE PUBLISHING
Lanham • New York • Boulder • Toronto • Plymouth, UK

Published by Taylor Trade Publishing
An imprint of The Rowman & Littlefield Publishing Group, Inc.
4501 Forbes Boulevard, Suite 200, Lanham, Maryland 20706
www.rowman.com

10 Thornbury Road, Plymouth PL6 7PP, United Kingdom

Distributed by National Book Network

British Library Cataloguing in Publication Information Available

Library of Congress Cataloging-in-Publication Data

Hischak, Thomas S.
   The Disney song encyclopedia / Thomas S. Hischak and Mark A. Robinson. —
Updated edition.
      pages ; cm
   Annotated bibliography of songs from Disney films, television, Broadway, and
theme parks from the 1930s to the present day. It also contains Alternate song titles;
Songwriters directory; Sources and songs; Guide to recordings, videos, and DVDs;
Academy Awards for Disney songs and scores, and Glossary of song terms.
   Includes bibliographical references and index.
   ISBN 978-1-58979-713-0 (pbk. : alk. paper)
   1. Popular music—Bibliography. 2. Walt Disney Company—Bibliography.
I. Robinson, Mark A., 1973– II. Title.
   ML128.P63H58 2012
   016.78242164—dc23

                                                                              2012025836

∞™ The paper used in this publication meets the minimum requirements of
American National Standard for Information Sciences—Permanence of Paper for
Printed Library Materials, ANSI/NISO Z39.48-1992.

Printed in the United States of America

For the Bleemer family, devoted Disney fans
—T.S.H.

For Dorothy and Robert VanWagenen, the closest thing to a
Disney "happily-ever-after" that I know
—M.A.R.

When Walt Disney (at head of the table) drew this sketch circa 1941, his company had already introduced several unforgettable characters, many still familiar icons today. Seated around the table, clockwise, are Mickey Mouse, Ferdinand the Bull, Pluto, the Three Little Pigs, Jiminy Cricket, Pinocchio, Donald Duck (sporting a Pinocchio hat), Snow White, Dopey, and Minnie Mouse, with the Blue Fairy casting a spell on the whole ensemble. (Walt Disney/Photofest)

CONTENTS

Preface   vii

Acknowledgments   xi

A Brief History of Disney Music   xiii

Songs   1

Appendix A: Alternate Song Titles   261

Appendix B: Songwriters Directory   265

Appendix C: Sources and Songs   285

Appendix D: Guide to Recordings, Videos, and DVDs   309

Appendix E: Academy Awards for Disney Songs and Scores   335

Glossary of Song Terms   339

Bibliography   343

Index   347

About the Authors   375

PREFACE

There's a terrific power to music. You can run any of these pictures and they'd be dragging and boring, but the minute you put music behind them, they have life and vitality they don't get any other way.

—Walt Disney

Songs written for Disney productions over the decades have become a potent part of American popular culture. Since most Americans first discovered these songs in their youth, they hold a special place in their consciousness. Yet there have been few serious studies of these beloved songs. The purpose of this book is to describe and discuss hundreds of famous and not-so-famous songs from Disney films, television, Broadway productions, records, and theme parks, from the 1930s to the present day. The goal is not only to inform readers about these many songs but also to rekindle memories that readers have associated with them.

What is a Disney song? For the purposes of this book, it is any new song written for a Disney product, be it a feature or short film, a Broadway musical, a television show or special, a made-for-video production, a Disney record, or a theme park. But a Disney song is also a state of mind, a lyrical and musical expression of an idea that harkens to the simple but potent premise that first distinguished Walt Disney more than nine decades ago. Whether it is an animated fairy tale, a live-action adventure, a silly sitcom, or a Disneyland attraction, a Disney production is distinguished by its fine craftsmanship, ambitious goals, and generally optimistic view of life. The same can be said for most of the songs created for these productions. The variety of songs is impressive, from sunny kids' songs and heartfelt blues numbers to rustic folk songs and pulsating rock numbers. Yet there is something positive in the outlook of all of these. The Disney experience is basically a hopeful one. The productions affirm life and avoid cynicism and despair. Even when the Disney artists tackle disturbing issues, such as racial inequality and the destruction of the environment, the tone is one of hope. A Disney song, regardless of the many and diverse forms it may take, is a small musical affirmation of what makes life worth living.

We have selected 1,115 songs and given them individual entries presented in alphabetical order. The songwriters and original singers are identified, as well as the source (film, television, theatre, theme park, record) of the song and other venues in which it might have been used over the years. Notable recordings of the song are also listed. But most important, an effort has been made to describe each song and explain what makes it memorable. The goal is to provide not a reference list but a true encyclopedia of Disney songs. Both short and feature films are covered, as are movies made for television. While the Disney company also releases films and television programs under the banner of Touchstone, Hollywood, and Caravan Pictures, these are included here only if it is felt they are truly in the Disney tone. Full-length and short video productions are covered, as are all the Broadway musicals produced by Disney. The company has long been active in recordings, starting with Disney Records, and introduced many new songs in that venue; a sampling of these is included. Walt Disney was among the first Hollywood producers to branch out into television. In programs such as *The Mickey Mouse Club*, *Disneyland*, *Walt Disney's Wonderful World of Color*, and those many shows on the Disney Channel, hundreds of songs have been written and presented. We have attempted to provide a wide and representative selection of these from the 1950s to the present day.

A brief history of Walt Disney's interest in music is offered to introduce the reader to the special relationship the studio has always had with soundtrack scores as well as songs. Because song terminology varies in its meaning, a glossary of popular music terms is included to define the parts and kinds of songs as used in this book. Following the entries is a listing of alternate song titles to help the reader locate songs that are known by different titles. There is also a directory of all the songwriters mentioned in the book with lists of the Disney productions that utilize their work. The listing of sources and songs will help the reader locate which songs came from which production. A guide to recordings, videos, and DVDs; a list of all Academy Award nominations and wins for Disney songs; and a selected bibliography of books dealing with Disney and Disney music are also included.

Finally, it should be pointed out again that a Disney song in this book is one written for a Disney production and not just interpolated into the presentation. Disney has used classical music, Tin Pan Alley standards, traditional folk songs, and pop songs from the charts in the company's productions. Unless they were translated or largely reconfigured for the Disney presentation, they are not included here.

ACKNOWLEDGMENTS

We would like to express our thanks to Michael and Dottie Sills; Jack, Julie, and Susannah Carr; Cathy Hischak; Kim Cargen; Amy Johnson; Robbie Rozelle; Ron Mandelbaum at Photofest; Bill Whiting; and the people at Scarecrow Press for their valuable assistance in the preparation of this book. We hope they enjoy the results of their efforts, just as we hope this encyclopedia will interest and please all lovers of Disney magic.

A BRIEF HISTORY
OF DISNEY MUSIC

A great deal has been written about the evolution of American musical theatre, pinpointing the Rodgers and Hammerstein classic *Oklahoma!* as the first integrated musical in which the music and lyrics augment the plot, allowing the story to grow and characters to develop through the score. Richard Rodgers and Oscar Hammerstein were pioneers in the field of the stage musical. *Oklahoma!* opened in 1943, and musical theatre changed forever. But when did this change happen in Hollywood *movie* musicals, and who was instrumental in finding a way to use music to tell the story and deepen our understanding of the characters? It seems that one of the greatest proponents of this evolution of the film musical is Walt Disney.

Disney had a deep respect for the power of music in storytelling and it is not surprising that some of his initial animated efforts are told predominantly through song. The studio's first talkie, the Mickey Mouse short *Steamboat Willie* (1928), not only used music as well as sound but made a conscious effort to coordinate the onscreen movement and sound effects with the music on the soundtrack. Such Silly Symphonies as *The Pied Piper* (1933) and *The Golden Touch* (1935) took their cue from the popular operetta form by singing through most of the story. In the most successful Silly Symphony short, *The Three Little Pigs* (1933), the breakout hit song "Who's Afraid of the Big Bad Wolf?" managed to create a satiric and emotional resonance with listeners, becoming a symbolic laugh in the face of the Great Depression. The popularity and sheet music sales of this song did not go unnoticed by Disney, and it is clear that he made very calculated choices regarding the music in his projects from this point forward.

When Disney began preparing for his first feature-length animated film, he was chided by many in Hollywood who thought audiences would never sit and watch a cartoon that was any longer than ten or twelve minutes. *Snow White and the Seven Dwarfs* (1937) proved the skeptics wrong, becoming the top grossing film to date. It would hold that record for one year until the monumental run of Metro-Goldwyn-Mayer's *Gone with the Wind* absconded with the title. *Snow White and the Seven Dwarfs* is a visual masterpiece of storytelling, yet the score by Frank Churchill and Larry Morey emerged as highly singable to the American public and is perhaps a major reason the movie held the audience's interest for eighty-three minutes. The score was nominated for an Oscar, and many of the titles—including "Some Day My Prince Will Come," "Whistle While You Work," and "Heigh-Ho"— became radio standards. Disney entered into this project with the idea that he wanted the music to be part of the storytelling—not just in an expository or narrative way as it had in the Silly Symphonies, but as an emotional outgrowth and understanding of the characters' feelings. The film audience was to be privy to the internalized monologues of characters, allowing us to feel with them instead of merely observing their story.

Snow White changed the way Hollywood viewed the feature-length animated film, but the road ahead was a rough one. World War II changed the international film market, limiting the studio's potential for distribution and financial growth. The cost of making animated features was high, and in the coming years the studio would not turn a profit on many films until their subsequent re-release. However, during this time, Disney Studios produced superb and beguiling work. *Pinocchio* (1940), *Dumbo* (1941), and *Bambi* (1942) offer some of the lushest songs in the Disney canon. *Pinocchio*'s "When You Wish Upon a Star" brought an Academy Award to the songwriting team of Leigh Harline and Ned Washington. The songs "Baby Mine" from *Dumbo* and "Love Is a Song" from *Bambi* were both nominated for Oscars.

In the late 1940s Disney had to resort to less expensive projects, such as the animated anthologies *Make Mine Music* (1946), *Fun and Fancy Free* (1947), *Melody Time* (1948), and *The Adventures of Ichabod and Mr. Toad* (1949). To appeal to the South American market and to replace the loss of European ticket buyers during World War II, Disney produced the Latin-flavored *Saludos Amigos* (1942) and *The Three Caballeros* (1944). These, as well as two traditional films, *Song of the South* (1946) and *So Dear to My Heart* (1948), employed a clever mixture of live action and animation.

Song of the South also garnered the studio its second Oscar for best song with "Zip-a-Dee-Doo-Dah." In all of these cases, music played a major role in the storytelling.

As the financially fraught 1940s ended, the studio needed a hit and it found one in *Cinderella* (1950) by returning to the formula that was successful in *Snow White and the Seven Dwarfs*: a maiden in distress, a handsome prince, a wicked stepmother as a villain, and help from enthusiastic animal friends. The movie hit pay dirt. More importantly, it marked a return to the style of storytelling that used a musical score, in this case by Mack David, Jerry Livingston, and Al Hoffman. Disney hired these Tin Pan Alley composers to create his first musical score that was more in step with those of the modern musical theatre. The result was a hit score that included "A Dream Is a Wish Your Heart Makes," "The Work Song," and the Oscar-nominated "Bibbidi-Bobbidi-Boo." *Cinderella* marked the first time Walt Disney took control of the recording and distribution of a film's music; thus Disney Records was born and a long tradition of bringing music and storytelling to families began.

The 1950s saw the rise of television as a new venue for Disney Studios, and music was a regular requirement of this emerging art form. Disney began hosting his own program, entitled *Disneyland*, which debuted in 1954. The following year, *The Mickey Mouse Club* made its debut. From these two popular shows, legions of new songs were introduced to the American public, especially within *The Mickey Mouse Club*'s variety show format. Television proved to be a potent place for Disney to exercise his ideas for family entertainment. The studio has upheld this tradition over the years, and in the 1980s it spawned its own network in the form of the Disney Channel. More TV shows meant more theme songs, so there are literally hundreds of Disney songs ingrained in our collective psyche through the availability and affordability of television entertainment.

In 1955 the Disneyland theme park opened in Anaheim, California, and with it came dozens of Disney attractions, shows, and parades full of original songs. Later, other Disney parks would spring up in Florida, France, Japan, and China, each utilizing the ever-growing list of popular Disney musical numbers, including "It's a Small World," "Grim Grinning Ghosts," and "There's a Great Big Beautiful Tomorrow." Walt Disney World in Florida is currently the most-visited attraction in the world, with millions of patrons passing through the gates each year, all of them entertained by delightful Disney music.

The 1960s found Disney stretching himself with new musical storytelling ideas, experimenting with new forms of music, and perhaps finding the apex of his artistic vision with *Mary Poppins* (1964), a mixture of live action and animation that is the studio at its finest. The production values, special effects, and casting are near perfection, and the score by Richard and Robert Sherman is quite possibly the most evocative, colorful and at times haunting one to be written for a Disney film. A highlight, "Chim Chim Cher-ee," won an Academy Award for Best Song, but it was the wistful "Feed the Birds" that would be Walt Disney's favorite song to come from any of his films. *The Jungle Book* (1967) was the last animated film directly supervised by Disney, and the music has a succinctly new flavor for a Disney film. The score has a jazz and blues sound, quite unlike any of the previous scores written for animated features. The song "The Bare Necessities" was nominated for an Oscar. Disney never got to hear or see the final product before he passed away in 1966, but his vision for both art and music would live long beyond his lifetime.

After Disney's death, the studio seemed to lose heart for a while. The movie products turned out during the time from 1967 to the mid-1970s range from uninspired to mildly entertaining, frequently missing Walt Disney's magical touch. It is not until the studio regrouped in the late 1980s that the magic seemed to return through the music of the composing team of Alan Menken and Howard Ashman. *The Little Mermaid* (1989) was so well received that Disney Studios emerged once again as the top producer of family entertainment and, for our purposes, songs. Two songs from *The Little Mermaid* were nominated for Oscars, with "Under the Sea" bringing home the prize. Menken and Ashman's next endeavor, *Beauty and the Beast* (1991), produced three Oscar-nominated songs, with the title tune fetching the statue. *Beauty and the Beast* also holds the distinction of being the only animated film to be nominated for Best Picture. Sadly, Howard Ashman passed away from AIDS while working on his next animated feature, *Aladdin* (1992), but his efforts at the Disney studio opened the door for many musicals to come. *The Lion King* (1994), *Pocahontas* (1995), *The Hunchback of Notre Dame* (1996), and *Tarzan* (1999) proved that the Disney movie musical was alive and well.

During the 1990s, Disney branched into two new areas of entertainment: the Broadway musical and direct-to-home-video markets. As its maiden voyage, Disney Theatrical Productions produced a stage adaptation of its hit animated film *Beauty and the Beast* in 1994. Composer Alan Menken returned to the project and teamed with lyricist Tim Rice to create several new songs to flesh out the existing score from the original feature. Although it was not critically well received, the piece was an audience favorite and ran for thirteen years, paving the way for other Disney musicals on Broadway, including the critically acclaimed *The Lion King* (1997), the original musical *Aida* (2000), *Tarzan* (2006), *Mary Poppins* (2006), and *The Little Mermaid* (2008). The critics have been reticent to embrace Disney as an artistic presence on Broadway, but the audiences have had their say, flocking to the family-friendly entertainments in droves. Each of these productions carried with it new songs, creating a fully realized theatrical score.

With the advent of home video and DVDs, Disney cornered another market of family entertainment. Originally creating direct-to-video sequels to beloved classics and then imagining original works for this medium, the company has introduced a barrage of new songs into the lexicon of popular music. Video and DVD sales of both classic and new films have made Disney entertainment accessible to myriad households and families around the world. The music heard in these productions has become a part of our everyday culture. The overwhelming success and evolution of the Disney song experience has become available to every man, woman, and child. To have the Disney experience is to have a musical one.

"Absalom, My Absalom" is the stinging song of regret and loss from the biblical concert *King David* (1997) which was presented on Broadway to open Disney's newly restored New Amsterdam Theatre. When Absalom (Anthony Galde), the son of King David (Marcus Lovett), enacts a revolt against his father's army, he is killed in the conflict. David mourns for his son despite their estrangement and pours out his emotion in this song, sung over the body of Absalom. The number starts out gentle and somber, then builds to a volcanic eruption of anger, pain, and regret. Alan Menken composed the distraught melody and Tim Rice provided the tumultuous lyrics.

"Adventure Is a Wonderful Thing" is the rousing, parade-like song written by Michael Abbott and Sarah Weeks for the made-for-video film *Pooh's Grand Adventure: The Search for Christopher Robin* (1997). When Winnie the Pooh and his friends decide they must go on an expedition to save Christopher Robin, Owl (voice of Andre Stojka) creates a map and sings this patriotic-sounding song of encouragement, praising the glories of adventure even if it includes quicksand and fearsome creatures. As Owl describes the types of adventures the group will have, the characters are seen on a three-dimensional version of the map as they meet with different kinds of dangers.

"Adventures in Wonderland" is the electronic-sounding, disco-flavored theme song for the live-action television series *Disney's Adventures in Wonderland* (1992) about a contemporary Alice who enters a magical other world. The vibrating song is sung by Sarah Taylor over the opening sequence in which Alice (Elisabeth Harnois) floats across a surreal landscape and meets characters from the Lewis Carroll books.

"A-E-I-O-U" is the musical mantra of the mysterious Caterpillar (voice of Richard Haydn) in the animated film fantasy *Alice in Wonderland* (1951). Oliver Wallace wrote the short and exotic song, which the Caterpillar sings as he blows smoke from his hookah in the form of the vowels he chants. The number is sometimes listed as "The Caterpillar Song."

"After Today" is the slightly rocking song in which various teenagers look forward to summer vacation in the animated film *A Goofy Movie* (1995). Tom Snow (music) and Jack Feldman (lyric) wrote the rhythmic number and it is sung by high-schooler Max (singing voice of Aaron Lohr) who vows to no longer be such a goof and to win the heart of the pretty coed Roxanne. Students on the bus, the sports field, and in school join in singing the catchy song as they make their own plans for the day after school lets out.

"The Age of Not Believing" is the Oscar-nominated ballad about the loss of a child's innocence that Richard M. and Robert B. Sherman wrote for the musical film fantasy *Bedknobs and Broomsticks* (1971). The friendly witch Miss Eglantine Price (Angela Lansbury) and her youthful evacuees Carrie (Cindy O'Callaghan) and Paul (Roy Snart) prepare a magic flying bed for travel, but the eldest youth, Charlie (Ian Weighill), who is eleven going on twelve years old, doubts her powers of sorcery. So Miss Price sings of the age when a child starts to question everything and make-believe is coming to an end. The music from the song is used throughout the movie every time the magical bed travels. Christine Ebersole made a distinctive recording of the bittersweet ballad in 2003.

"A La Nanita Nana" is a traditional Spanish folk song that was adapted and arranged by David Lawrence for the television musical sequel *The Cheetah Girls 2* (2006). At a restaurant in Barcelona, the American singing stars Galleria (Raven-Symoné), Chanel (Adrienne Bailon), Aqua (Kiely Williams), and Dorinda (Sabrina Bryan) listen to a guitarist play the gentle and flowing lullaby and they sing it in Spanish from their tables with the singer Belinda.

"Alice" is the haunting, New Age song composed and performed by Avril Lavigne for *Alice in Wonderland* (2010), conceived and directed by Tim Burton as a film sequel to the Lewis Carroll stories *Alice's Adventures in Wonderland* and *Through the Looking Glass*. Lavigne, as composer/lyricist and performer, puts herself in the place of the young woman Alice as she returns to the fantasy world of her youth for another round of frightful and illogical adventures. The piece has a spooky musical quality with lyrics that make reference to falling and picking oneself up again, exactly what Alice does each time she enters the rabbit hole.

"Alice in Wonderland" is the dreamy title number sung by a chorus on the soundtrack at the beginning and end of the 1951 animated film fantasy. Sammy Fain composed the warm music and Bob Hilliard wrote the chorale-like lyric, which lists the virtues of Wonderland and all the things Alice will find there. Rosemary Clooney made an effective recording of the ballad combined with "The Unbirthday Song" from the same film, and years later Michael Feinstein included it in a medley of songs he recorded from the movie.

"Alice's Theme" is the insistent and mystical theme song written by Danny Elfman for Tim Burton's 2010 film adaptation of *Alice in Wonderland*. The piece is used as a recurring motif throughout the movie, almost like a constant beckoning from beyond that invites Alice to return to the Wonderland of her youth. The choral piece is performed by a choir of spectral-like voices asking questions and inviting the now grown-up Alice to cast aside logic and once again join in the madness.

"All for Love" is the rock ballad from the adventure film *The Three Musketeers* (1993) that celebrates the dedication and valor of the three heroes, particularly their devotion to true love. Bryan Adams, Robert John Lange, and Michael Kamen wrote the number, which is a variation on the musketeer trio's watch cry "All for one and one for all." It is sung by Adams, Sting, and Rod Stewart on the soundtrack over the closing credits of the movie.

"All for One" is the feel-good finale for the television movie *High School Musical 2* (2007), a song of togetherness written by Matthew Gerrard and Robbie Nevil. Teenagers Troy (Zac Efron), Gabriella (Vanessa Anne Hudgens), Sharpay (Ashley Tisdale), Ryan (Lucas Grabeel), Chad (Corbin Bleu), Taylor (Monique Coleman), and others who have worked at the country club for the summer gather together around the pool and have one last celebration of their fun in the sun by singing the spirited pop song.

"All in a Golden Afternoon" is the operetta-like choral number that various flowers sing in the animated movie *Alice in Wonderland* (1951). Sammy Fain (music) and Bob Hilliard (lyric) wrote the lyrical number in which the various flora celebrate their beauty in front of Alice, who they think is also a flower. Barbara Hendricks and the Abbey Road Ensemble made a pleasing recording of the song.

"All the Cats Join In" is a visually and musically swinging sequence from the animated anthology film *Make Mine Music* (1946). Alec Wilder, Ray Gilbert, and Eddie Sauter wrote the vivacious bebop music and it is performed by clarinetist Benny Goodman and his orchestra while bobby-soxers from all over town drop what they are doing and rush down to the malt shop, where they engage in furious dancing. The ingenious animation keeps pace with the music, the animator's pencil furiously drawing objects as quickly as they are needed to tell the story.

"Almost There" is the Oscar-nominated jazzy "I am" song for the heroine Tiana (voice of Anika Noni Rose) in the animated movie *The Princess and the Frog* (2009). As Tiana works hard and saves her money so that she can someday open her own restaurant, she sings to her friends about how she is almost to the point of achieving her dream. Randy Newman's music has a Dixieland style, and his lyric is hopeful and upbeat.

"Although I Dropped $100,000 (I Found a Million Dollars in Your Smile)" is a dandy pastiche of a Depression-era song of optimism that Richard M. and Robert B. Sherman wrote for a 1962 segment on the television program *Walt Disney's Wonderful World of Color*. In the segment, *A Symposium on Popular Songs*, Professor Ludwig von Drake (voice of Paul Frees) holds a symposium in his mansion, and he introduces this song to demonstrate the Depression chasers of the 1930s. It is then sung by a cut-out animated crooner (also Frees) with a megaphone, imitating the period singer Ted Lewis. Interestingly, the father of the Sherman brothers, songwriter Al Sherman, wrote several similar kinds of songs in the Depression, some of them sung by Lewis. The music has the sound of a moaning ballad while the lyric is filled with hyperbole, arguing that a sweetheart's smile is worth much more than all the money the singer lost in the stock market crash. The song is sometimes listed by an even longer title: "Although I

Dropped $100,000 in the Market, Baby (I Found a Million Dollars in Your Smile.)"

"Always" is the Polynesian narrative ballad written by Jeanine Tesori (music) and Alexa Junge (lyric) for the video sequel *Lilo and Stitch 2: Stitch Has a Glitch* (2005). The Hawaiian girl Lilo (voice of Dakota Fanning) searches all over the island for a song to use in a hula competition and discovers this melodic piece about the beauty of love. The number tells the mythological tale of the Hawaiian goddess Hi'iaka, who is the patron of the island. Hi'iaka falls in love with a young native chief named Lahaiu and sacrifices many things for his safety.

"Always Know Where You Are" is the pulsating rock song written by John Rzeznik for the animated adventure film *Treasure Planet* (2002), a space-age version of Robert Louis Stevenson's *Treasure Island*. Rzeznik sings the driving number on the soundtrack, revealing the thoughts of Jim Hawkins. The song is a musical vow to never forget a friend, referring to the cyborg cook John Silver, who has taken the young Jim under his care.

"Always There" is the heartwarming song about family written by Melissa Manchester and Norman Gimbel for the animated video sequel *Lady and the Tramp II: Scamp's Adventure* (2001). Having run away from home, the young canine Scamp (singing voice of Roger Bart) mourns the loss of his home and family, while the stray dog Angel (Susan Egan) longs for the family she never had. Back at home, Lady (Jodi Benson) and Tramp (Jeff Bennett) sing about how much they miss and worry about Scamp, the four voices combining in a gentle and moving quartet.

"American Dragon" is the hard-rock number by Perry LaMarca that serves as the theme song for the second and succeeding seasons of the animated adventure series *American Dragon: Jake Long* (2005). It replaced "The Chosen One," the series' original theme song. The Jonas Brothers sing the repetitive song about the Asian American Jake, that can transform himself into a tough, swift, and fearless dragon that defends the city from evil. The Jonas Brothers also made a music video of the number in 2006.

"Amigas Cheetahs" is the disco-flavored rock song by Will Robinson and Jamie Houston that is sung by the American teens Galleria (Raven-Symoné), Chanel (Adrienne Bailon), Aqua (Kiely Williams), and Dorinda (Sabrina Bryan) when they are in Barcelona in the TV movie sequel *The*

Cheetah Girls 2 (2006). During a concert in the Spanish city, the four sing-ing stars sing about how they are friends to everyone in Barcelona and how they have embraced the city during their stay.

"Anastasia's Theme" is the tender song of longing written by Alan Zachary and Michael Weiner for the animated video sequel *Cinderella III: A Twist in Time* (2007). The Evil Stepmother has used magic to erase the prince's memory of Cinderella and arranges a marriage between him and her daugh-ter Anastasia (singing voice of Lesli Margherita). Although Anastasia sees her dream coming true, she questions in this reflective number the validity of a love forced by magic and wishes the prince loved her for herself.

"And Now to Sleep" is the soothing lullaby written by George Bruns (music) and Winston Hibler (lyric) for the nature film *Perri* (1957) about a female squirrel and her first year of life in the forest. An unidentified female singer on the soundtrack sings the number, which comforts a young one and encourages sleep. Nature footage of mother and baby animals snuggling together in the night accompanies the song, which is also titled "Lullaby of the Wildwood."

"And Son" is the Italian-flavored duet, complete with concertina accom-paniment, that Stephen Schwartz wrote for the television musical *Geppetto* (2000) which looks at the Pinocchio tale from the toymaker's point of view. After the Blue Fairy brings the puppet Pinocchio (Seth Adkins) to life, the proud Geppetto (Drew Carey) takes his new "son" through the village, proclaiming him perfect and their relationship ideal. Yet their optimism is damped by Pinocchio's naive actions, which indicate that not all is perfect.

"Another Believer" is the hopeful song by Rufus Wainwright (music and lyric) and Marius De Vries (music) from the animated film *Meet the Rob-insons* (2007). While Lewis works on a time machine to take him back to his birth year, where he hopes to convince his birth mother not to abandon him, Wainwright sings this wistful number about believing that the future will bring a better life.

"Another Part of Me" is the climactic celebration number written and performed by Michael Jackson in the 3-D movie *Captain EO* at the Journey into Imagination attraction at Epcot in 1986. Having conquered the evil tyrant Supreme Leader (Anjelica Huston), Captain EO (Jackson) sings of one's interconnectedness as a member of a shared world and the number explodes into the final dance segment of the seventeen-minute film. Jackson recorded the song for his 1987 album *Bad*. The *Captain EO* film was also seen at Disneyland in California and at Disneyland Resort Paris.

"Another Pyramid" is a song of exposition by Elton John (music) and Tim Rice (lyric) for the Broadway musical *Aida* (2000). The Egyptian prime minister Zoser (John Hickok) welcomes his son Radames (Adam Pascal) back from the war with Nubia and informs him that the pharaoh is near death, his pyramid tomb is nearly completed, and it is time for Radames to wed the dying king's daughter Amneris. Other ministers of the court join Zoser in urging Radames to make Egypt greater by building more and more pyramids. The song was recorded by Sting before the musical opened on Broadway.

"Any Fool Can See" is a riveting song of transformation written by Marvin Hamlisch (music) and Allee Willis (lyric) for the modern movie fantasy *The Devil and Max Devlin* (1981). Shy Stella Summers (Julie Budd) wants to be a singing star but lacks confidence until the devil's assistant Max (Elliott Gould) uses his magic on her. She starts out singing the number as a mousy no-talent, but during the song Stella grows in power and explodes with passion, becoming a belting superstar by the end.

"Anything Can Happen (If You Let It)" is the optimistic song of self-fulfillment written by George Stiles and Anthony Drewe for the 2004 London stage version of *Mary Poppins*. Nanny Mary Poppins (Laura Michelle Kelly) sings the up-tempo number to the Banks household near the end of the show, arguing that your dreams will come true only if you believe in yourself and set out to win. Soon the family and the servants join in on the cheery song, and the entire cast reprises it at the end of the musical. Ashley Brown played Mary in the 2006 Broadway version and led the cast in singing the song.

"Anything Can Happen Day" is the zesty theme song used for Wednesdays on the television series *The Mickey Mouse Club* (1955). The Mouseketeers announce in song that Wednesday is a day for surprises and that there will be unexpected thrills on that day's show. The bouncy number then leads into a roll call in which each Mouseketeer is called by name and enters dressed as a particular kind of person (ballerina, fireman, and so on) or an animal. Adult Mouseketeer host Jimmie Dodd wrote the happy number and usually led the cast in singing it.

"Anytime You Need a Friend" is the pop ballad about devotion to a friend sung by the Beu Sisters over the final credits of the animated movie *Home on the Range* (2004). Alan Menken (music) and Glenn Slater (lyric) wrote the rockabilly number, which is one of two songs heard during the final credits. The other is "Wherever the Trail May Lead."

"The Apple Dumpling Gang" is the hootin' and hollerin' Western-style title song written by Shane Tatum for the 1975 movie comedy about three orphans who go out West and get involved with a pair of bumbling crooks. The feisty campfire song, complete with "yeehaws," tells the story of the young trio and is sung by Randy Sparks and the Back Porch Majority over the opening credits of the film. The melody is also heard in the sequel *The Apple Dumpling Gang Rides Again* (1979).

"The Apple Song" is a merry list song written by Kim Gannon and Walter Kent for the "Johnny Appleseed" section of the animated movie anthology *Melody Time* (1948). Young Johnny Appleseed (voice of Dennis Day) is persuaded to go out West and plant apple trees by his guardian angel (also voiced by Day), who lists all the uses for apples and how the growing country is waiting for him to bring the fruit trees to the new land.

"Appreciate the Lady" is the bluesy ballad written by Jim Stafford for the animated film *The Fox and the Hound* (1981). The wise old owl Big Mama (voice of Pearl Bailey) sings the smooth number to the fox Tod (Mickey Rooney) about how to woo the pretty vixen Vixey (Sandy Duncan).

"Arabian Nights" is the exotic opening number written by Alan Menken (music) and Howard Ashman (lyric) for the animated movie *Aladdin* (1992). A Middle Eastern merchant, voiced by Robin Williams, introduces the film, but Bruce Adler provides the singing voice as the sly salesman croons about the enchanted land of many stories. Because some moviegoers took offense at Ashman's lyric about the barbaric tendency to cut off one's nose if they didn't like your face, the lyric was changed to references about the flat terrain and the intense heat when the movie was released on video. The number serves as the theme song for the animated television series *Aladdin* (1994) and is reprised by Adler in the animated video sequel *Aladdin and the King of Thieves* (1995).

"Are We Dancing?" is the waltzing love song for the Philadelphian Cordelia Biddle (Lesley Ann Warren) and the New Yorker Angie Duke

(John Davidson) in the movie musical *The Happiest Millionaire* (1967). The two lovers first meet at a party in New Jersey and dance out onto the terrace to sing this entrancing number appropriate for the 1916 period of the film. Richard M. and Robert B. Sherman wrote the flowing music and the romantic lyric, which takes the form of a series of questions. Tami Tappan and David Burnham made a playful duet recording of the song in 2003.

"Are You In or Out?" is the jazzy, upbeat number about a sinister conspiracy from the animated video sequel *Aladdin and the King of Thieves* (1995). Randy Petersen and Kevin Quinn wrote the arresting number, which is sung by the thief Sa'luk (voice of Jerry Orbach) as he tries to convince some of his fellow outlaws to overtake Aladdin's father Cassim and make Sa'luk the king of the Forty Thieves. Among the voices featured as the fellow thieves are those of Jeff Bennett, Guy Stroman, Scott Barnes, Paul Kandel, Gordon Stanley, David Friedman, Merwin Foard, Rob Paulsen, Jess Harnell, and Clyde Kusatsu.

"The Aristocats" is the Gallic-sounding title song by Richard M. and Robert B. Sherman for the 1970 animated film, sung on the soundtrack by Maurice Chevalier, the last time the beloved French entertainer was heard in a movie musical. Chevalier came out of retirement to sing (in English and French) over the opening credits. The number has the style of a French café song as it describes the upper-class felines of Paris.

"As Long as I'm Here with You" is the gentle ballad about friendship written by Mark Watters (music) and Lorraine Feather (lyric) for the made-for-video film *Pooh's Heffalump Halloween Movie* (2005). During the final credits of the film, Joseph Lawrence sings on the soundtrack the folk ballad about braving all of life's difficulties as long as one's friend is near.

"As Long as There's Christmas" is the seasonal song of hope written by Rachel Portman (music) and Don Black (lyric) for the made-for-video animated musical *Beauty and the Beast: The Enchanted Christmas* (1997). Although Belle (voice of Paige O'Hara) is trapped in the Beast's castle, she believes there is still hope for a merry Christmas as she sings this flowing ballad with Mrs. Potts (Angela Lansbury), Cogsworth (David Ogden Stiers), Lumière (Jerry Orbach), and the other enchanted objects. Later in the film, when the Beast casts Belle into the dungeon for trying to celebrate Christmas, the song is reprised by Belle and the French tree ornament Angelique

(Bernadette Peters). During the final credits, a duet version of the song is sung on the soundtrack by Roberta Flack and Peabo Bryson.

"At the Ball" is the clever song of exposition by Alan Zachary and Michael Weiner in which two mice reenact the tale of Cinderella in the animated video sequel *Cinderella III: A Twist in Time* (2007). A spell has caused the prince to lose all memory of Cinderella, so her rodent friends Gus (Corey Burton) and Jaq (Rob Paulsen) act out in song and dance how the prince first met Cinderella at the ball, using a wind-up music box with a ballet dancer on it to play the role of Cinderella.

"Athena's Song" is the pleasing lullaby written by Jeanine Tesori for the animated made-for-video prequel *The Little Mermaid: Ariel's Beginning* (2008). The mermaid queen Athena (singing voice of Andrea Robinson) sings the gentle ballad about love and happiness under an endless sky to her daughters at bedtime. The melody is put into a magical music box King Triton gives to his wife, and the song is heard throughout the movie whenever the music box is opened. The song is also listed as "Endless Sky."

B

"Babes in the Woods" is the operatic title song for the 1932 Silly Symphony film short loosely based on *Hansel and Gretel*. Bert Lewis wrote the number, which is sung by an uncredited voice on the soundtrack, telling how two Dutch children are captured by an evil witch and almost added to her collection of humans turned into spiders and rats, but are rescued by a band of forest elves.

"Baby Mine" is the heartbreaking lullaby ballad written by Frank Churchill (music) and Ned Washington (lyric) for the animated circus tale *Dumbo* (1941). Betty Noyes sings the number on the soundtrack as young Dumbo is comforted by his mother, who is locked up as dangerous and can touch him only with her outstretched trunk. Les Brown (vocal by Betty Bonney) and Jane Froman both had popular records of the Oscar-nominated song and years later Barbara Cook, Ashley Brown, Kerry Butler, Steve Tyrell, Paige Morehead, Michael Crawford, and Bette Midler each made a heartfelt recording of the lullaby.

"Back in Business" is a bouncy pastiche number written by Stephen Sondheim in the 1930s Depression-be-damned style for the film *Dick Tracy* (1990), where it was sung by a line of nightclub chorines during a montage showing Big Boy Caprice's illegal enterprises booming. Sondheim's energetic melody and dancing lyric are somewhat lost in the busy editing, but the song has resurfaced on several occasions. Julie Andrews, Stephen Collins, Christopher Durang, Michael Rupert, and Rachel York sang it in the Off-Broadway revue *Putting It Together* (1993); Liza Minnelli and Billy Stritch sang and recorded the number in the 1992 *Sondheim: A Celebration at Carnegie Hall*; and Alet Oury made a complete recording (verse and refrains) with Julie Alderfer, Farah Alvin, Heidi Godt, Kelli Shrewsbury, and Gretchen Weiss in 1997. Madonna, who was in *Dick Tracy* but didn't sing the number, later recorded it.

"Back to Tennessee" is an impassioned tribute to the U.S. state of its title, performed by Billy Ray Cyrus in the 2009 film *Hannah Montana: The Movie*. The stirring ballad, written by Cyrus, Tamara Dunn, and Matthew Wilder, was released before the movie opened on Cyrus's album *Back to Tennessee* as an early promotion for the film. In the movie, the song is performed at a hoedown fundraiser aimed to raise cash to keep the Tennessee countryside from being developed into a shopping mall.

"The Backson Song" is the ominous song about the mysterious creature called the "Backson" in the 2011 animated film *Winnie the Pooh*. The menagerie of the Hundred Acre Wood believes that the Backson has kidnapped their dear friend Christopher Robin, so Owl (voice of Craig Ferguson) leads the band of stuffed animals in singing this determined march about retrieving their kindly owner from the beast. The number was written by Robert Lopez and Kristen Anderson-Lopez.

"Baia" is the enticing ballad about the Brazilian resort city that is used so effectively in the animated travelogue *The Three Caballeros* (1944). Ary Barroso (music) and Ray Gilbert (lyric) wrote the Portuguese song, which is sung by the parrot Joe Carioca (singing voice of Nestor Amoral) as the port city is seen silhouetted in the red sunset.

"The Ballad of Bullwhip Griffin" is a mock-heroic song about the brave and legendary Eric Griffin (Roddy McDowall), who is really a very stuffy Boston butler with a great deal of luck out West in the film *The Adventures of Bullwhip Griffin* (1967). George Bruns and Mel Leven wrote the tongue-in-cheek ballad, which is heard over the opening credits and throughout the film as a running wry commentary on Griffin's misadventures.

"The Ballad of Davy Crockett" was one of the few chart hits to come out of television in the 1950s. The song was written by George Bruns (music) and Tom Blackburn (lyric) for the popular adventure series *Davy Crockett* (1954) featured on the weekly *Disneyland* show, and soon everyone was singing it and buying imitation raccoon-skin hats. The number is a narrative ballad that relates the history of Crockett with more legends than facts, such as his killing a bear when he was only a young child. Fess Parker plays Davy and sings the song over the credits of the television show, then reprises his performance as Crockett and sings it in the feature films *Davy Crockett, King of the Wild Frontier* (1955) and *Davy Crockett and the River Pirates* (1956). New lyrics were written for the two feature films, and the song, performed by a male chorus on the soundtrack, is used as a narrative link for the different episodes. Parker, Bill Hayes, and Tennessee Ernie Ford each recorded the song, and each version sold more than a million discs. By the end of the decade there were twenty-three different recordings made, selling more than ten million copies. There was even a jazz version of the song recorded by Louis Armstrong. Surprisingly, this all-American tune was an international bestseller as well. There were records made in several countries, including more than twenty different versions in France, and it was the top-selling song in Japan for a while. Billy Cotton, the Cliff Adams Singers, Eddie Fisher, the Wellingtons, Eddy Arnold, the Kentucky Headhunters, the Four Mosquitoes, and Mannheim Steamroller were among the others who recorded the ballad in the States. The audio-animatronic bear Henry and a raccoon cap named Sammy sing "The Ballad of Davy Crockett" as part of the Country Bear Jamboree attraction seen in the Disney theme parks. Disney legend has it that Bruns and Blackburn quickly wrote the song at the last minute because the television episode was running short and they needed something to make the show fit into the scheduled time slot.

"The Ballad of Smith and Gabriel Jimmyboy" is the folk ballad written by Bob Russell for the movie *Smith!* (1969), about a western rancher who defends a Native American youth. Songwriter Russell sings the narrative number over the opening credits of the film, telling the tale of the Indian boy Gabriel Jimmyboy, who is falsely accused of murder, and the cattleman Smith, who comes to his defense. The seemingly genial song has a dark undercurrent of foreboding in the music, which foreshadows the disturbing events of the movie.

"The Bare Necessities" is the Oscar-nominated song of the low-down, low-key philosophy by Terry Gilkyson that was featured in the animated movie *The Jungle Book* (1967). Baloo the Bear (voice of Phil Harris) sings to the man-cub Mowgli (Bruce Reitherman) about taking the easy road in life and looking for creature comforts as the two friends cavort through the Indian jungle. The lively number is in the form of a Dixieland jazz tune and is filled with opportunities for vocal and instrumental improvisation. Harris's recording enjoyed some popularity, as did one by Louis Armstrong, and years later there were notable records by Harry Connick Jr. in 1995, the Jazz Networks in 1996, Bowling for Soup in 2005, Steve Tyrell in 2006, and Kerry Butler in 2008. A bluegrass rendition of the song was recorded by Mike Toppins, Glen Duncan, Billy Troy, Jim Brown, James Freeze, and David Chase. The song is heard in the animated television series *Jungle Cubs* (1996), and in the video sequel *The Jungle Book 2* (2003), it is reprised by Baloo (voice of John Goodman), Mowgli (Haley Joel Osment), and Shanti (Mae Whitman).

"Barking at the Moon" is a country-flavored song about finding happiness with the home you have, written by Rilo Kiley for the animated movie *Bolt* (2008). While the television canine star Bolt travels across the country with the alley cat Mittens and the hamster Rhino, Jenny Lewis sings the song on the soundtrack. The clever montage shows Mittens teaching Bolt how to behave like a normal pet as the lyric expresses contentment with an everyday dog's life.

"Be a Star" is the disco-flavored song about shining bright and getting noticed, sung on the soundtrack by Tyra Banks during the final scene of the television movie *Life-Size* (2000). George Blondheim and Mark Rosman wrote the splashy song while the teenager Casey (Lindsay Lohan) and her real-life fashion doll Eve (Tyra Banks) cause a sensation at a fashion show.

"Be Our Guest" is the Busby Berkeley–like production number in the animated movie *Beauty and the Beast* (1991) that affectionately spoofs the Hollywood musicals of the past. The enchanted candelabra Lumière (voice of Jerry Orbach) leads the silverware, plates, and other kitchen paraphernalia in the pseudo–French music hall number about the joy of dining. Alan Menken composed the can-can-like melody, Howard Ashman wrote the slapstick lyric, and the merry list song was nominated for an Oscar. In the 1994 Broadway version of *Beauty and the Beast*, the number was led by Gary Beach as Lumière and the song was given a satiric Ziegfeld Follies–like staging. A bluegrass rendition of the song was recorded in 1998 by Mike Toppins, Glen Duncan, Billy Troy, Jim Brown, James Freeze, and David Chase.

The Lion King (1994) remains one of the Disney Company's greatest screen successes, matched by its popularity on Broadway beginning in 1997. The young lion cubs Simba and Nala look forward to a fun-filled future with the song "I Just Can't Wait to Be King." Little do they know their future is going to be far from merry. (Walt Disney/Photofest)

"Be Prepared" is a sinister call to arms written by Elton John (music) and Tim Rice (lyric) for the animated film *The Lion King* (1994), in which the scheming lion Scar (voice of Jeremy Irons) urges the hyenas to aid him in overthrowing the lion king Mufasa and putting himself on the throne. While the three main hyenas, Shenzi (Whoopi Goldberg), Banzai (Cheech Marin), and Ed (Jim Cummings), provide the comic element in the number, the song is actually a Fascist promise of a new age that is chilling. In the 1997 Broadway version of *The Lion King*, the number was sung by John Vickery as Scar, and Tracy Nicole Chapman, Stanley Wayne Mathis, and Kevin Cahoon as the featured hyenas.

"Be True to Your Groove" is the pulsating rock song about finding your own worth heard at the beginning and end of the animated made-for-video sequel *The Emperor's New Groove 2: Kronk's New Groove* (2005). Peter Lurye, who wrote the disco-like number, sings it on the soundtrack with Sandy Barber when all the villagers are urging the chef Kronk to trust in himself.

"Bear Band Serenade" is a vigorous hoedown number by Henry D. Haynes (music) and Xavier Atencio (lyric) that starts the show by introducing the bear members of the band at the theme park attraction Country Bear

Jamboree, which premiered at the Disney World Magic Kingdom in 1971. The song, heard on the speaker system, is sung by a male country-western vocalist who introduces the five audio-animatronic bear characters, telling their names and describing which instruments they play in the jug band.

"Bear in the Big Blue House Theme Song" is the cheerful welcome song by Tyler Bunch that opens each episode of the children's television series *Bear in the Big Blue House* (1997). After a blue dollhouse opens up and releases various Muppet creatures, the oversized Bear (voice of Noel MacNeal) leads the cast in this mildly rocking number that greets the viewers and promises fun.

"Beautiful Beulah" is not a love song about a girl but a tribute to the small town of Beulah, Maine, which Richard M. and Robert B. Sherman wrote for the film musical *Summer Magic* (1963). Young Bostonian Nancy Carey (Hayley Mills) has written the gentle ragtime song about the town and she sings it to her mother (Dorothy McGuire) and younger brother Peter (Jimmy Mathers) while her elder brother Gilly (Eddie Hodges) accompanies her on the piano.

"The Beautiful Briny" is the carefree song about traveling underwater that was used in a mixed animation and live-action sequence in the movie fantasy *Bedknobs and Broomsticks* (1971). The harmless witch Miss Eglantine Price (Angela Lansbury) and her friend Professor Emelius Brown (David Tomlinson) sing the bubbly song as they travel below the surface on a magical bed with three children (Roy Snart, Ian Weighill, and Cindy O'Callaghan) and observe the animated flowers and sea life. The scene climaxes with an acrobatic dance at the Beautiful Briny Ballroom where Miss Price and the professor win a trophy for their fancy footwork. Richard M. and Robert B. Sherman originally wrote the jovial song, having fun with "b" alliteration in the lyric, for a sequence in the earlier film *Mary Poppins* (1964), but it was cut. The *Bedknobs and Broomsticks* scene is similar to a superior one in *Mary Poppins* in which the governess Mary (Julie Andrews), her pal Bert (Dick Van Dyke), and two children (Karen Dotrice and Matthew Garber) enter an animated world and win a trophy for a horse race. Yet "The Beautiful Briny" has a charm all its own, and the scene is perhaps the finest in the film.

"Beauty and the Beast" is the entrancing title ballad from the 1991 animated film. The teapot Mrs. Potts (voice of Angela Lansbury) sings the gentle number while the Beast and Belle dance in the castle ballroom. The song is also reprised at the end of the film with a choral version as Belle and the transformed prince dance in the same ballroom. Alan Menken composed the flowing music and Howard Ashman wrote the simple but affecting lyric about how two tentative hearts are united in love. A record three songs from the movie were nominated for the Best Song Oscar, and this one won. Peabo Bryson and Céline Dion sing a duet version of the ballad over the closing credits of the movie, and their recording was very popular. Among the other versions recorded were those by flutist James Galway, jazz musician Earl Rose, harpist Carmen Dragon, the Jazz Networks, Barbara Cook, Steve Tyrell, Paige O'Hara, Debbie Shapiro Gravitte, the group Jump 5, and Barbara Hendricks and the Abbey Road Ensemble. In the 1994 Broadway version of *Beauty and the Beast*, Beth Fowler was Mrs. Potts and sang the number.

"Behind the Clouds" is the optimistic country-western song written by Brad Paisley and Frank Rogers for the computer-animated film *Cars* (2006). Paisley sings the laid-back number on the soundtrack, reminding one that even on dark, cloudy days, the sun is still shining above those clouds.

"Being Mrs. Banks" is the revealing character song written by George Stiles and Anthony Drewe for the stage version of *Mary Poppins*, which opened in London in 2004. The former actress Winifred Banks (Linzi Hateley) is having difficulty fitting into the strict upper middle class of London society and wonders if her role in life is to be nothing more than an organizer of the house. She reprises the number later in the show when her husband is having financial difficulty and she assures him that her primary job as Mrs. Banks is to love and support him. When *Mary Poppins* opened on Broadway in 2006, Rebecca Luker played Mrs. Banks and sang the song.

"Bella Notte" is the warm serenade written by Sonny Burke and Peggy Lee for the animated canine movie *Lady and the Tramp* (1955). Restaurateur Tony (voice of George Givot) sings the romantic number during the film's most affecting scene, the spaghetti dinner shared by the streetwise mutt Tramp and the refined cocker spaniel Lady as they dine in the alley behind Tony's restaurant. Tony accompanies himself on the concertina and his waiter Joe plays the mandolin. The lyric is in English except for the Italian title phrase for "beautiful night" and the music has a gentle but very Italianate flavor. A studio chorus sings the song on the soundtrack over the opening credits of the movie. Among the artists to record the ballad are Bryn Terfel, folk singer Marylee, Steve Tyrell, and Barbara Hendricks and the Abbey Road Ensemble. There was a jazz rendition by Earl Rose and a quartet version by Meredith Inglesby, Andy Karl, Tyler Maynard, and Keewa Nurullah. The song is sung by Joy Enriquez and Carlos Ponce on the soundtrack during the end credits for the video sequel *Lady and the Tramp II: Scamp's Adventure* (2001). The number is sometimes listed as "This Is the Night."

"Belle" is the extended musical sequence by Alan Menken (music) and Howard Ashman (lyric) that opens the story proper in the animated fairy-tale movie *Beauty and the Beast* (1991). As the French country girl Belle (voice of Paige O'Hara) sings about the predictable ways of the townsfolk and dreams of something better for herself, the villagers comment on the beautiful but odd girl who doesn't seem to fit in. In a masterful interplay of song and dialogue reminiscent of the best Broadway musicals, characters are introduced and attitudes established. The arrival of the thickheaded Gaston (Richard White) in the sequence is particularly effective as he bounds onto the scene and sings of his wish to marry Belle. Belle reprises the song later in the film after turning down Gaston's crude marriage proposal, and she wonders if she will ever find happiness in such a place. Ashman's lyric is a triumph of storytelling and character development, and Menken's music has the classical air of a sprightly period minuet. The Oscar-nominated song was sung by Susan Egan and the ensemble in the 1994 Broadway version of *Beauty and the Beast*.

"The Bells of Notre Dame" is the prologue number for *The Hunchback of Notre Dame* (1996), one of the most complex musical sequences ever devised for an animated film. The narrator Clopin (voice of Paul Kandel) relates in song and storytelling the history of the hunchback Quasimodo: how he was born and nearly killed, how he was hidden away, and how Paris has become subject to the powerful judge Frollo. Alan Menken composed the vivid, urgent music and Stephen Schwartz penned the lyric that even utilizes sections of Latin religious texts. The song is reprised briefly by Clo-pin and the citizens of Paris at the very end of the film.

"Berrily We Roll Along" is the brief but catchy number written by Patty and Michael Silversher for the holiday video *Winnie the Pooh: Seasons of Giving* (1999). Sent by Rabbit to collect cranberries for Thanksgiving din-ner, Tigger (voice of Jim Cummings) and Eeyore (Peter Cullen) stumble through the Hundred Acre Wood as Tigger sings this peppy number about all the kinds of berries one can find if you put your mind to it.

"The Best Christmas of All" is the gentle and reflective holiday song about friends and family being the only things necessary for a special Christmas, written by Randy Petersen and Kevin Quinn for the made-for-video film *Mickey's Magical Christmas* (2001). Gathered together at the House of Mouse for a yuletide celebration, Mickey, Peter Pan, Cinderella, Belle, the Beast, and many others sing the warm carol at the end of the video.

"Best of Both Worlds" is the rocking theme song for the television series *Hannah Montana* (2006) about an ordinary California teenager (Miley Cyrus) who has a secret life as a singing superstar. Matthew Gerrard and Robbie Nevil wrote the pop-rock song about a girl who gets to be both a regular teen and a celebrity, and it is sung over the opening credits by Cyrus, who also made a music video of the number. Cyrus reprised the song in the feature film *Hannah Montana: The Movie* (2009).

"Best of Friends" is the breezy ballad by Richard O. Johnston (music) and Stan Fidel (lyric) about an unlikely friendship in the animated movie *The Fox and the Hound* (1981). The wise old owl Big Mama (voice of Pearl Bailey) sings the poignant number about Tod the fox and Copper the hound dog as the two young friends play together, unaware that they are supposed to be enemies.

"The Best Time of Your Life" is the catchy march song that was written by Richard M. and Robert B. Sherman to replace their "There's a Great Big Beautiful Tomorrow" as the theme song for the Carousel of Progress attraction when it was re-created for Disney World in 1975. The original number proclaimed the philosophy of General Electric, who had sponsored the exhibit at the 1964 New York World's Fair. The new song, which cheerfully announces that there is no time better than the present, is more in keeping with the Disney philosophy. Yet the earlier song was so popular with visitors to the theme parks that it was reinstated when Carousel of Progress was revamped in 1997. The number is sometimes listed as "Now Is the Time."

"Bet on It" is the revealing character song for a teenager who realizes he has made some wrong choices in the television film sequel *High School Musical 2* (2007). Antonina Armato and Tim James wrote the angst-ridden ballad, which is sung by the once-popular Troy (Zac Efron), who realizes he has alienated his friends and his girlfriend with his self-centered behavior.

"Between Two Worlds" is the pop ballad written by Stacy Widelitz and Blaise Tosti for the made-for-video animated sequel *Pocahontas II: Journey to a New World* (1998). Judy Kuhn (singing voice for Pocahontas) and Billy Zane (voice for John Rolfe) sing the romantic song, about how faith and love can overcome any differences between two people, on the soundtrack during the end credits of the video.

"Beware the Jabberwock" is a silly but highly literate song written by Don Raye (music) and Gene de Paul (lyric) in 1947 for an animated sequence in the film *Alice in Wonderland* (1951), but it was not used. Based on Lewis Carroll's famous poem "Jabberwocky," the jazzy number is meant as a warning for Alice against the monster that inhabits the Tulgy Wood, using some of Carroll's made-up words and adding a few invented by de Paul. A demo recording of the two songwriters singing the song was included as an extra when the film was released on DVD.

"Beyond My Wildest Dreams" is the gleeful song of discovery written by Alan Menken (music) and Glenn Slater (lyric) for the 2008 Broadway version of *The Little Mermaid*. After Ariel (Sierra Boggess) has become human, she sings to herself (because she has given her public voice to the sea witch) about how the human world is even better than she anticipated. The song has a busy lyric listing the many wonders of life on land, and the music is equally rapid and bouncy.

"Beyond the Laughing Sky" is the unused dreamy "I am" song written by Sammy Fain (music) and Bob Hilliard (lyric) for the title heroine of the animated movie *Alice in Wonderland* (1951). Alice lets her imagination run free and pictures marvelous things in far-off places, the music soaring gently and the lyric filled with poetic images. The ballad was cut when it was deemed too low-key for the character and because Kathryn Beaumont, who provided the voice of Alice, had trouble singing it. The number was replaced by the more lively "In a World of My Own," but the melody's refrain shows up as "The Second Star to the Right" in *Peter Pan* (1953).

"Bibbidi-Bobbidi-Boo" is the gleeful nonsense song the Fairy Godmother (voice of Verna Felton) sings in the animated film *Cinderella* (1950) to cheer up the title orphan while demonstrating her magical powers. Al Hoffman, Jerry Livingston (music), and Mack David (lyric) wrote the sparkling number, and Perry Como had a hit recording of it. The Oscar-nominated ditty was also recorded by such artists as Louis Armstrong, Dinah Shore, Ilene Woods, Brooke Allison, Barbara Hendricks and the Abbey Road Ensemble, Mary Martin, and Gordon MacRae and Jo Stafford in a duet version. Bobby McFerrin sang the song in a 1995 recording of the complete *Cinderella* score. The number, sometimes listed as "Put It Together" or "The Magic Song," is reprised, with a slightly altered lyric, by Michael Bradford in the animated video sequel *Cinderella II: Dreams Come True* (2002), where it is given a hip-hop treatment and is sung by Brooke Allison over the closing credits.

"Biddle-Dee-Dee" is the lighthearted nonsense song from the movie *Toby Tyler* (1960). Diane Lampert and Richard Loring wrote the carefree number, which is in keeping with the nature of the title character, an independent orphan boy who runs away to join the circus.

"Bill Nye, the Science Guy" is the repetitive yet memorable title song for the 1993 television series hosted by unconventional scientist Bill Nye. Mike Greene wrote the simple jazz number, which is sung over the opening credits as Nye is seen floating through a montage of science images. The lyric mostly repeats the title of the show, which comes across as a bass rhythm line, and the number is punctuated by repeating the word "Bill" as a percussive shout.

"Bill of Sale" is the hillbilly romp written by Al Kasha and Joel Hirschhorn for the partially animated film *Pete's Dragon* (1977). When the backwoods Gogan family (Shelley Winters, Jeff Conaway, Charles Tyner, and Gary Morgan) find the runaway orphan Pete (Sean Marshall) living with the lighthouse keeper, Lampie (Mickey Rooney), and his daughter, Nora (Helen Reddy), they produce a bill of sale that says the boy belongs to them. In counterpoint to their jaunty song, Nora sings her observations of the disreputable Gogans and charges them with cruelty and abuse.

"The Bird and the Cricket and the Willow Tree" is the frothy list song about melody written by Paul Francis Webster (music) and Sonny Burke (lyric) for the film short *Adventures in Music: Melody* (1953), the first 3-D animated movie ever made. Professor Owl (voice of Bill Thompson) instructs his classroom full of birds on how to find melody in nature. Sung by the Disney Studio Chorus over a sequence showing animated birds chirping, crickets rubbing their legs together, and wind blowing through a willow tree, the song has a pleasant tune and lyrics that are simply a list of these musical nature sounds. Parts of the movie, sometimes listed as *Melody (Adventures in Music)*, were used in the 1956 film *3D Jamboree* that was shown at the Fantasyland Theater in Disneyland. Although 3-D movies did not catch on as Hollywood had hoped, this short film was a popular attraction at the theme park for many years. It was part of a planned series of movie shorts about music, but only one other one, *Toot, Whistle, Plunk and Boom* (1953), was made.

"Blame It on the Samba" is the Latin number the Dinning Sisters sing on the soundtrack of the anthology film *Melody Time* (1948). During the musical sequence, Donald Duck and his parrot pal Joe Carioca, reunited from *The Three Caballeros* (1944), dance and frolic while a live-action Ethel Smith plays the organ. Ernesto Nazareth composed the exotic music for the original Brazilian song and Ray Gilbert provided the nimble English lyric for the film, describing the ingredients that go into the samba. The song sequence was re-released as a movie short in 1955.

"Bless Us All" is the harmonic song of thanksgiving the Cratchit family sings in the holiday movie *The Muppet Christmas Carol* (1992). Paul Williams wrote the warm and gentle number and it is sung by Bob Cratchit, played by Kermit the Frog (voice of Steve Whitmire), Mrs. Cratchit, played by Miss Piggy (Frank Oz), Tiny Tim (Jerry Nelson), and other members of the family as they sit around the table and share their humble Christmas feast.

"Blow Me Down" is the oddball "I am" song for the sailor Popeye (Robin Williams) in the movie musical *Popeye* (1980). Harry Nilsson wrote the unusual number capitalizing on the cartoon's famous catchphrase and Popeye sings it when he arrives at the seaside town of Sweethaven looking for his long-lost Pappy. Everyone in the village is eccentric and ignores the gruff sailor, but he takes it all in stride, confident that he can be happy here despite the offbeat citizens.

"Bluddle-Uddle-Um-Dum" is the tuneful charm song written by Frank Churchill (music) and Larry Morey (lyric) for the dwarfs in the groundbreaking animated movie *Snow White and the Seven Dwarfs* (1937). Told by Snow White to wash up before dinner, the seven dwarfs gather outside at the water trough where Doc (voice of Roy Atwell) urges them to lather up with this fun song that imitates the sounds of washing, yodeling, and blubbering. The number is punctuated by snide comments by Grumpy (Pinto Colvig) until the six others force him to wash as well. The number is sometimes listed as "The Dwarfs' Washing Song."

"Blue Bayou" is the atmospheric number by Bobby Worth (music) and Ray Gilbert (lyric) that provided the background music for a lyrical sequence in the animated anthology movie *Make Mine Music* (1946). The Ken Darby Chorus sings the song on the soundtrack during a "tone poem" in which an egret stops at a bayou to rest, finds a companion, and the two fly off toward the moon that is reflected in the water. The poetic animation was originally created for a sequence in *Fantasia* (1940) and was set to Claude Debussy's "Clair de Lune," but was abandoned when the movie got too long.

"Blue Beyond" is the lullaby-like song about trusting in friends written by Gordon Kennedy and Blair Masters for the made-for-video animated sequel *The Fox and the Hound 2* (2006). Trisha Yearwood sings the gentle ballad on the soundtrack after the friends Copper and Tod have a falling out and are not speaking to each other. The lyric is about longing for a friend who will follow you anywhere you go.

"Blue Shadows on the Trail" is the pleasing cowboy ballad sung by Bob Nolan and the Sons of the Pioneers on the soundtrack of the "Pecos Bill" segment of the animated anthology film *Melody Time* (1948). Eliot Daniel (music) and Johnny Lange (lyric) wrote the bucolic song that describes the atmosphere of the desert at night. While the singers are live action, sitting around a campfire, the desert around them and the night animals are animated. Roy Rogers, Bing Crosby, and Vaughn Monroe and his Orchestra each had successful recordings of the song.

"The Boatniks" is the bebopping title song for the 1970 movie comedy about a bumbling Coast Guard captain and a gang of equally incompetent jewel thieves. Bruce Belland and Robert F. Brunner wrote the pop number about the intrepid Coast Guard, which is "nautical but nice," and it is sung by a studio chorus over the opening credits.

"Bon Voyage" is the perky and insistent title song for the 1962 film comedy. Richard M. and Robert B. Sherman wrote the list song, which is sung by a chorus over the credits, about the preparations to be made and places to visit when the Willard family goes on a vacation to Europe. A portion of the song is sung in French. The number is reprised over the closing credits of the movie.

"Bonkers" is the frantic title song by Mark Watters for the 1993 animated television series about the crazy Hollywood cop Bonkers D. Bobcat. The rapid jazz number, which invites viewers to join the cat-cop on the beat and to go bonkers with him, is sung over the action-packed opening sequence, in which Bonkers wildly bounces from one misadventure to another.

"Boo Bop Bopbop Bop (I Love You, Too)" is the happy nonsense song that illustrates the affection between the orphan Pete (Sean Marshall) and his pal, the dragon Elliott (voice of Charlie Callas), in the partially animated movie musical *Pete's Dragon* (1977). Al Kasha and Joel Hirschhorn wrote the saccharine but bouncy number in which the two friends find comradeship and love even though they are so different.

"The Boogie Beagle Blues" is the farcical rock-and-roll spoof written by Michael and Patty Silversher for a 1989 episode of the animated television series *DuckTales* (1990). A gang of canine crooks boast that they have broken out of prison and are on a crime spree, proud of their mug shots put out by the FBI. The song pastiches rock icons from the 1950s and 1960s, with references to blue suede shoes and a howling harmony stolen from the Beatles.

"The Boogie Woogie Bakery Man" is a spoof of an Andrews Sisters number from the 1940s that Richard M. and Robert B. Sherman wrote for *A Symposium on Popular Songs*, a musical short that was first shown on the television program *Walt Disney's Wonderful World of Color* in 1962. A trio of animated harmony singers (voices of Betty Allen, Diane Pendleton, and Gloria Wood), who look very much like the Andrews Sisters, sing the boogie-woogie number about a Chinese man who bakes the best fortune cookies in town. The lyric refers to the baker as a "sentimental Oriental," and the animation employs Asian stereotypes that many might find offensive today. Yet the amusing song is making fun of the boogie-woogie style of popular song and not any ethnic group.

"Boom Shakalaka" is the silly tribal chant in the film *Muppet Treasure Island* (1996) that spoofed tropical island movies. Barry Mann and Cynthia Weil wrote the rhythmic ditty which is sung by the cloth natives of a Caribbean island, preparing the entrance of their tribal princess Benjamina

Gunn, played by Miss Piggy (voice of Frank Oz). The nonsense lyric repeats itself and the accompaniment is mostly hyperactive drumming.

"Bop to the Top" is the pseudo-Latin number the conceited Sharpay Evans (Ashley Tisdale) and her spineless brother Ryan (Lucas Grabeel) perform at the callback auditions in the television movie *High School Musical* (2006). Randy Petersen and Kevin Quinn wrote the silly number filled with Spanish phrases, and the sister-brother team, used to getting all the leads in the school's musicals, perform it with relentless energy and self-devotion.

"'Bout Time" is the casual but heartfelt love song written by Richard M. and Robert B. Sherman for the film musical *The One and Only, Genuine, Original Family Band* (1968). Young lovers Joe Carder (John Davidson) and Alice Bower (Lesley Ann Warren) agree that they have put off talking about and expressing the love they have only written about to each other in letters. In a bucolic setting in the hills of Dakota, the two declare their love in the fervent but lighthearted song. Joe and Alice reprise the number briefly at the end of the movie. Louis Armstrong made a vivacious recording of the song.

"A Boy Needs a Dog" is the saccharine song of canine devotion that is used satirically in the animated movie *Teacher's Pet* (2004), based on the 2000 television series. Kevin Quinn and Randy Petersen wrote the number about how everyone needs a best friend and a dog is the ideal friend. It was used throughout the film as a kind of leitmotif. The boy, Leonard Helperman (voice of Shaun Fleming), sings it to his pet dog, Spot (Nathan Lane), whenever he wants to remind the canine that he is a dog, and each sings it separately when the two are separated later in the story.

"The Boys Are Back" is the vivacious number by Matthew Gerrard and Robbie Nevil about how childhood resurfaces in grown-up males when they are faced with uncertainty, as heard in the film sequel *High School Musical 3: Senior Year* (2008). Best friends and high school seniors Troy Bolton (Zac Efron) and Chad Danforth (Corbin Bleu) sit in a junkyard wondering and worrying about life after graduation. In a bonding moment, the two revert back to their childhood and the games of spies and superheroes they played in that very junkyard. The joyous number is filled with energy that captures the playfulness of two little boys. Soon they use the various objects around the junkyard as percussion instruments, much as in the Off-Broadway show *Stomp*.

"Brand New Day" is the lively ensemble number that is sung during the first major musical sequence in the 2010 made-for-TV film *Camp Rock 2: The Final Jam*. With music and lyrics by Kara DioGuardi and Mitch Allan, the pop-rock piece is sung by Demi Lovato as Mitchie Torres, leading the cast in the optimistic number that finds the teenagers looking forward to another summer at Camp Rock.

"Brave Together" is the happy march song written by Michael and Patty Silversher for the video feature film *Pooh's Heffalump Halloween Movie* (2005). The young kangaroo Roo (voice of Jimmy Bennett) and his pal Lumpy the elephant (Kyle Stanger) sing the confident song about their combined courage as they set off to trap the spooky Gobloon on Halloween. The number is reprised during the end credits of the film.

"Bravo, Stromboli!" is the mock operatic aria sung by the villain in the live-action television musical *Geppetto* (2000). The evil puppeteer Stromboli (Brent Spiner) learns that his star attraction, Pinocchio, has run away but he vows, with comedic brio, to take revenge on the boy and to use the stringless puppet to make his fortune. Stephen Schwartz wrote the brash character song in the style of a Rossini aria, with delightfully comic lyrics to match.

"Brazil" is the durable samba number that has remained a Latin standard over the decades. Ary Barroso wrote the music and the original Portuguese lyric (the title then was "Aquarela do Brasil" or "Watercolor of Brazil"), then Bob Russell provided an English lyric when the song was interpolated into the animated film travelogue *Saludos Amigos* (1942). Aloysio de Oliveira sings the rhythmic number on the soundtrack with Eddy Duchin and His Orchestra, while a paintbrush creates watercolor scenes of the flora and fauna of Brazil. The catchy song was also featured in the movie *The Gang's All Here* (1943), where it was sung by Carmen Miranda, Oliveira, and the chorus; in *Jam Session* (1944), where it was sung by Nan Wynn; and by big bands in *Road to Rio* (1948) and *The Eddy Duchin Story* (1956). Both Xavier Cugat (vocal by the band members themselves) and Jimmy Dorsey (vocal by Bob Eberle and Helen O'Connell) had best-selling records of the serenade, and Les Paul recorded a unique version using multitrack guitars. The song was a hit once again in 1975 with a top-selling disco version by the Richie Family. "Brazil" inspired three film titles, and it was played on the soundtrack of each movie: the 1943 Roy Rogers western, the 1944 Tito Guizar–Virginia Bruce musical, and the 1985 sci-fi satire.

"Brazzle Dazzle Day" is the infectious song of joy written by Al Kasha and Joel Hirschhorn for the partially animated film *Pete's Dragon* (1977). The lighthouse keeper, Lampie (Mickey Rooney); his daughter, Nora (Helen Reddy); and the runaway youth, Pete (Sean Marshall), celebrate a bright and glorious day that reflects their friendship as they cavort around the lighthouse while the camera takes in both the characters and the landscape.

"Break of Day" is the flowing ballad that a studio chorus sings on the soundtrack at the beginning of the nature adventure movie *Perri* (1957). George Bruns (music), Ralph Wright (lyric), and Winston Hibler (lyric) wrote the number about how nature refreshes itself and begins life anew with each new day. The footage accompanying the song is of a spring dawn in the forest, with the morning mist rising over mountains, valleys, and streams.

"Breakaway" is the pop ballad by Matthew Gerrard, Bridget Benenate, and Avril Lavigne that is used to illustrate a new adventure for the heroine in the film sequel *The Princess Diaries 2: Royal Engagement* (2004). Kelly Clarkson sings the number, about learning to fly, traveling to new places, and taking chances, on the soundtrack as the recent college grad Mia Thermopolis (Anne Hathaway) goes to Europe for the next stage of her life. Clarkson's recording was a pop hit in Great Britain and she also made a music video of the song.

"Breaking Free" is the soaring and emotionally charged love ballad written by Jamie Houston for the television movie *High School Musical* (2006). The basketball jock Troy Bolton (Zac Efron, with singing assist by Andrew Seeley) and the mathematics whiz Gabriella Montez (Vanessa Anne Hudgens) rehearse the song given to them for the callbacks for the school's "Spring Musicale." The lyric, about breaking free of stereotypes and seeing a whole new version of themselves that they are starting to like, parallels their own recent history.

"Brimstone and Treacle" is the sadistic character song for the evil nanny Miss Andrew (Rosemary Ashe) in the 2004 London stage version of *Mary Poppins*. George Stiles and Anthony Drewe wrote the harsh song in which George Banks's old nanny comes to Cherry Tree Lane to take charge of the children, Jane and Michael. The old crone describes her method for child rearing, which consists of dosages of cod liver oil and bitter treacle, scrubbing with carbonic soap, and severe punishment for whimpering and thumb sucking. The number is reprised later in the show by Mary Poppins (Laura Michelle Kelly), who returns to the Banks household, stands up to Miss Andrew, and sends her on her way. In the 2006 Broadway version of *Mary Poppins*, the number was sung by Ruth Gottschall as Miss Andrew and reprised by Ashley Brown as Mary Poppins.

"Bubba Duck Theme" is the driving rock song by Michael and Patty Silversher that sings the praise of a prehistoric "cave duck" in the animated television series *DuckTales* (1990). Bubba Duck is transported from the past to the present by Scrooge McDuck and the miser's three nephews bring the friendly visitor to school with them. There the duck demonstrates that rock and roll is not new, and the students cheer Bubba in this 1960s-style tribute, complete with "hubba hubba" and other rocking expressions.

"Bug-A-Boo" is the peppy and silly disco song by Larry Groce that encourages kids to dance like bugs. The vivacious number was written for the 1979 Disney Records album *Mickey Mouse Disco* but was cut before the record was put to vinyl. The song was included in the Disney aerobics album *Mousercise* (1982) and then was later used on occasion in the television exercise program *Mousercise* (1983).

"Bunnytown" is the sunny title song for the 2007 television series that utilizes puppets to play all the citizens of the kooky little town. A children's chorus sings the simple ditty on the soundtrack during a montage in which colorful bunnies go about their daily lives working, playing, driving cars, and acting like humans in a normal town.

"Butterfly Fly Away" is the tender duet between father and daughter in the film *Hannah Montana: The Movie* (2009). Miley Stewart's (Miley Cyrus) devoted father (Billy Ray Cyrus) ends his relationship with a woman he's falling for in order to keep his daughter's secret that she is the alter ego of pop sensation Hannah Montana. The girl feels bad that he makes the sacrifice and sings this loving duet with him about how little girls rely on their daddies. The understated, intimate number was written by Alan Silvestri and Glen Ballard.

"Bye-Yum Pum Pum" is the lighthearted tango number written by Richard M. and Robert B. Sherman for the movie musical *The Happiest Millionaire* (1967). Philadelphia heiress Cordelia Biddle (Lesley Ann Warren) asks her finishing school roommate Rosemary (Joyce Bulifant) for lessons in how to flirt with men, and Rosemary obliges with this silly Latin number about how to be alluring. The song soon turns into a duet in which the two girls do a wild Spanish-flavored dance in their dorm room. The music from the tango is then heard at the dance where the two try out their flirtation techniques.

C

"Cabin Fever" is the farcical song-and-dance number written by Barry Mann and Cynthia Weil for the film *Muppet Treasure Island* (1996). Adrift in the Atlantic Ocean for weeks without a breeze to propel their sails, the crew of the *Hispaniola* is going stir crazy and breaks out into a rousing number that moves from calypso to square dancing to a conga. The sailors get so carried away that some of the cloth and human characters dress up like Carmen Miranda and cut loose before a wind comes along and everyone returns to their senses.

"The Cabin Raising Song" is the homespun list song by Richard M. and Robert B. Sherman that is used in a folksy scene of friendship in the film *Those Calloways* (1965). Vermont homesteader Cam Calloway (Brian Keith) has spent so much of his time building a duck sanctuary in the marshes that the construction of his own home for his wife and child is far behind. But the Calloways' friends and neighbors, including Alf Simes (Walter Brennan), Ed Parker (Ed Wynn), Jim Mellott (John Larkin), and Bridie Mellott (Linda Evans), show up ready to lend a hand. As the townsfolk build the cabin, they sing the vigorous number with lyrics that list all of the things that will be accomplished by sunset.

"California Gold" is the catchy frontier song performed by a band of street musicians that is used to lure potential miners and prospectors to seek their fortune in the Gold Rush in the period movie *The Adventures of Bullwhip Griffin* (1967). Richard M. and Robert B. Sherman wrote the number, which entices young Jack Flagg (Bryan Russell) to run away from his Boston home and strike it rich out West. The song is also listed as "Cal-I-For-Nee Gold."

"The Call" is the haunting, dreamlike song by Regina Spektor that is used so effectively at the end of the film *The Chronicles of Narnia: Prince Caspian* (2008). After the lion Aslan informs the Pevensie siblings that they have become mature and that this will be their last visit to the enchanted land of Narnia, they magically disappear through an arbor of trees. Spektor is heard on the soundtrack singing the moving ballad about promising to return if one is called, so farewells are not needed.

"Call Me a Princess" is the sarcastic, vampy number written by Alan Menken (music) and Howard Ashman (lyric) for the animated film *Aladdin* (1992), but it was cut early on in the production process. The spoiled princess Jasmine confesses in song that she knows she is obsessed with clothes, her hair, and other superficialities, but she likes being in the upper class and always getting her own way. The song was discarded when the characterization of Jasmine changed to a restless young woman who wants to escape her royal lifestyle. Kerry Butler made a playful recording of the song in 2008.

"Call Me, Beep Me" is the Motown-flavored theme song written by Cory Lerios and George Gabriel for the animated television series *Kim Possible* (2002) about a teen girl who has a secret life going on missions to save the world from evil. Christina Milian sings the rhythm-and-blues number over the opening sequence, urging listeners to give her a call if there is trouble and she will not fail them. Sometimes listed as "The Kim Possible Song," the number is also heard in the various made-for-television movies featuring the female superhero.

"Calling All Munchkins" is a silly call to arms song that Rizzo the Rat (voice of Steve Whitmire) sings with the other rats dressed as Munchkins in the television movie *The Muppets' Wizard of Oz* (2005). Michael Giacchino, Debra Frank, and Steve L. Hayes wrote the short march, which is sung every time the Munchkins come to the rescue and help Dorothy and her friends.

"Can I Have This Dance?" is the waltzing love song written by Adam Anders and Nikki Hassman for the film sequel *High School Musical 3: Senior Year* (2008). High school senior Troy Bolton (Zac Efron) has asked his girlfriend, Gabriella (Vanessa Anne Hudgens), to the senior prom, which has the theme "The Last Waltz." Troy doesn't know how to waltz, so Gabriella teaches him on the roof of the high school building, and the two sing this lovely duet as they dance together. A thunderclap sounds and soon the pair are dancing and twirling in the rain.

"Can Love Stand the Test" is the country-western song by John Hiatt that provides a romantic moment in the satiric film *The Country Bears* (2002). Bear singer Tennessee O'Neal (voice of Toby Huss) has been jilted by his longtime sweetheart Trixie (Candy Ford) but when they meet up at a country music bar, they listen to the humans Don Henley and Bonnie Raitt sing this affecting love song and the two bears are soon back together.

"Can You Feel the Love Tonight?" is the Oscar-winning love song by Elton John (music) and Tim Rice (lyric) from the animated film *The Lion King* (1994). On the soundtrack, Joseph Williams and Sally Dworsky sing the thoughts of lions-in-love Simba and Nala while meerkat Timon (voice of Nathan Lane) and warthog Pumbaa (Ernie Sabella) make comments on the side about how love will destroy their trio. Although the song is a traditional pop ballad in music and words, the African tribal accompaniment gives the number a distinctive and haunting tone. The ballad is reprised over the closing credits of the film with a slightly altered lyric. Elton John's recording was a best seller, and there were also versions by Michael Crawford, Elliott Yamin, Paul Fried, John Barrowman, S-Club, Sara Paxton, jazz musician Earl Rose, pianists Jim Buchanan and John Bayless, and flutist John Galway with Mike Mower. The song is also used in the film *My Best Friend's Wedding* (1997) and in the made-for-video sequel *The Lion King 1½* (2004). In the 1997 Broadway version of *The Lion King*, the number was sung by Jason Raize and Heather Headley as Simba and Nala with commentary by Max Casella and Tom Alan Robbins as Timon and Pumbaa.

"Candle on the Water" is the heart-tugging ballad written by Al Kasha and Joel Hirschhorn for the part-animated, part-live-action musical film *Pete's Dragon* (1977). Lighthouse keeper's daughter Nora (Helen Reddy) sings the number as she looks out to the ocean from the lighthouse tower and prays that her sailor-fiancé Paul, who has been lost at sea, will return.

Reddy's recording of the Oscar-nominated song enjoyed some popularity. Anneliese van der Pol also recorded the ballad, in 2006.

"Can't Back Down" is the song of solidarity and protest sung by the campers of Camp Rock in the 2010 made-for-TV movie *Camp Rock 2: The Final Jam*. Faced with the possibility that their camp might be closed down and that they might be sent home early, the teenagers are led by Mitchie (Demi Lovato) in singing about their need to come together to save their summer haunt. With music and lyrics by Tim James, Antonina Armato, and Thomas Sturges, the number also features performers Alyson Stoner, Anna Maria Perez de Tagle, Jasmine Richards, and the Jonas Brothers.

"Carrying the Banner" is the rousing song of pride written by Alan Menken (music) and Jack Feldman (lyric) for the period movie musical *Newsies* (1992). The newsboys who sell the *World* on New York City street corners in 1899 wake up before dawn, wearily singing of their tough life. But as the sun rises and they hit the streets, the "newsies" come alive, proud to "carry the banner," and even break into a vigorous dance. The song is reprised in the closing sequence of the film as the boys celebrate their victory over Joseph Pulitzer in a newsboy strike.

"Casey Junior" is the rhythmic train song written by Frank Churchill (music) and Ned Washington (lyric) for the animated movie *Dumbo* (1941). A studio chorus on the soundtrack sings the chugging number about the little engine Casey Junior, who diligently pulls the circus train loaded with elephants and other heavy cargo. The title is a reference to the legendary train engineer Casey Jones.

"Casey, the Pride of Them All" is the adoring ballad about the mighty baseball player in the "Casey at the Bat" sequence in the animated movie anthology *Make Mine Music* (1946). Ray Gilbert, Ken Darby, and Eliot Daniel wrote the rousing song of affection that is sung by the crowd before and after the famous poem "Casey at the Bat" is narrated by Jerry Colonna. Although the action of the tale is animated, the song is illustrated with a series of Currier and Ives–like stills showing the crowd gathering at the ballpark.

"The Castaways Theme" is a torchy lullaby sung by Mary Grant (Hayley Mills) in the adventure film *In Search of the Castaways* (1962). Richard M. and Robert B. Sherman wrote the lovely song about hope for castaways of all kinds, and Mary sings it about her father, a skipper who was lost at sea near New Zealand.

"The Caucus Race" is a farcical list song written by Sammy Fain (music) and Bob Hilliard (lyric) for the animated fantasy movie *Alice in Wonderland* (1951). On a seashore, the Dodo (voice of Bill Thompson) organizes a method to get dry. While he stands on a rock dictating instructions, various sea creatures race around him and sing about getting dry. Soon they are exhausted and a wave washes over the ensemble, so the whole experiment is a failure.

"A Change in Me" is a moving ballad by Alan Menken (music) and Tim Rice (lyric) that was added to the 1994 stage version of *Beauty and the Beast* after it had been running on Broadway for four years. When singing star Toni Braxton took over the role of Belle in 1998, the songwriters provided this delicate song in which the heroine notices that she is a different and better person having known and fallen in love with the Beast. Susan Egan and Ashley Brown each made a poignant recording of the ballad.

"Charleston Charlie" is a parody of a Roaring Twenties dance song that was used on a special segment on the television program *Walt Disney's Wonderful World of Color* in 1962. Professor Ludwig von Drake (voice of Paul Frees) introduces the pastiche number as part of *A Symposium on Popular Songs*, and the number is sung by an animated flapper (voice of Gloria Wood) who sounds very much like the 1920s songstress Helen Kane, the "Boop boop de doop" girl. Richard M. and Robert B. Sherman wrote the eccentric number about a raccoon coat–wearing college guy who dances the charleston with the flapper, who thinks he's the cat's meow.

"Cheetah Sisters" is the lite-rock number by Jamie Houston that serves as the theme song for the four teen singers in the made-for-TV musical *The Cheetah Girls* (2003) and its sequel *The Cheetah Girls 2* (2006). Galleria (Raven-Symoné), Chanel (Adrienne Bailon), Aqua (Kiely Williams), and Dorinda (Sabrina Bryan) come from different races and backgrounds, but they consider themselves sisters, as they profess in this sassy, proud song.

"Cherish the Moment" is the pop ballad about remembering a special day, sung by the teen singing stars Galleria (Raven-Symoné), Chanel (Adrienne Bailon), Aqua (Kiely Williams), and Dorinda (Sabrina Bryan) in the television sequel *The Cheetah Girls 2* (2006). David Lawrence and Faye

Greenberg wrote the slightly rocking number, and the Cheetah Girls sing it on the soundtrack during a wedding scene.

"Cherry Tree Lane" is one of the new songs written by George Stiles and Anthony Drewe for the stage version of *Mary Poppins*, which opened in London in 2004. The number is sung by Mr. Banks (David Haig), who demands order and precision in his home; Mrs. Banks (Linzi Hateley), who tries (unsuccessfully) to provide that order; and the housekeeper Mrs. Brill (Jenny Galloway), who wryly comments on the chaos in the household. The expositional number is reprised twice in the show by the same characters to illustrate the reactions to events that occur after Mary Poppins (Laura Michelle Kelly) arrives. In the 2006 Broadway version of *Mary Poppins*, the number was sung by Daniel Jenkins as Mr. Banks, Rebecca Luker as Mrs. Banks, and Jane Carr as Mrs. Brill.

"Children" is an energetic list song about the difficulties of parenthood written by Harry Nilsson for the surreal musical *Popeye* (1980). When sailor Popeye (Robin Williams) and his long-lost Pappy (Ray Walston) are finally reunited, the old commodore launches into this patter song listing all the difficulties of raising children, who never appreciate your efforts.

"Chim Chim Cher-ee" is the Oscar-winning ditty by Richard M. and Robert B. Sherman that is used effectively in the movie musical *Mary Poppins* (1964). The melody is first heard as sidewalk artist Bert (Dick Van Dyke), as a one-man band, performs it for a small crowd gathered in a London park. Later he sings the number to cheer up the glum siblings Jane (Karen Dotrice) and Michael Banks (Matthew Garber), with Mary Poppins (Julie Andrews) joining him in the song. Although the lyric is in the vein of a nonsense song, the music has a haunting quality and the number takes on an almost reverent mood at times. The New Christy Minstrels and Burl Ives each had successful records of the song, which in the original screenplay was titled "Pavement Artist." Louis Prima and Gia Maione recorded it as a duet, and in 1996 the number got a new interpretation by the Jazz Networks. Other recordings were made by such artists as Louis Armstrong, Kahorn Nakasone, Barbara Hendricks and the Abbey Road Ensemble, the Boston Pops, and a bluegrass rendition by Mike Toppins, Glen Duncan, Billy Troy, Jim Brown, James Freeze, and David Chase. In the 2006 Broadway version of *Mary Poppins*, Gavin Lee played Bert and sang the number, as he had in the original London production in 2004.

"Chip 'n Dale Rescue Rangers Theme Song" is the disco-flavored number by Mark Mueller for the popular 1989 Disney television animated series. The rhythmic rock song is sung over the opening credits of the show, boasting that no espionage job is too big or too small for the chipmunk secret agents, comparing them to Holmes and Watson. Throughout the number, the word "chip" is repeated in the lyric as an effective musical punctuation.

"The Chosen One" is the driving rock number by Billy Lincoln, Kat Green, and Michael Gurley that served as the original theme song for the animated television series *American Dragon: Jake Long* (2005), about an Asian American teen who can transform into a dragon that helps stop crime. The song is performed by pop singer Mavin on the soundtrack and reveals the thoughts of Jake, who vows to travel the land and destroy evil. After the first season, the number was replaced by the song "American Dragon."

"Chow Down" is the sinister yet comic character song for the three hyenas in the 1997 Broadway version of *The Lion King*. Elton John (music) and Tim Rice (lyric) wrote the gluttonous number, which Shenzi (Tracy Nicole Chapman), Banzai (Stanley Wayne Mathis), and Ed (Kevin Cahoon) sing as they lick their chops and prepare to eat the young lion cub Simba (Scott Irby-Ranniar).

"Cinderella" is the enchanting title song written by Mack David, Jerry Livingston, and Al Hoffman for the 1950 animated fairy tale movie. The Disney Studio Chorus sings the dreamy number over the opening credits of the movie, promising Cinderella that she will live happily ever after if she gives her heart over to the possibility of such happiness.

"Cinderella" is the pulsating rock number written by Lindy Robins and Kevin Savigar for the made-for-television movie *The Cheetah Girls* (2003). Rehearsing in an empty theatre, the teenagers Galleria (Raven-Symoné), Chanel (Adrienne Bailon), Aqua (Kiely Williams), and Dorinda (Sabrina Bryan) sing about the fairy tales their mothers once read to them as children. They are self-empowered girls now and are not waiting for any prince; they vow to rescue themselves from any dragons that appear.

"Cinderella Work Song" is the busy character number written by Mack David, Jerry Livingston, and Al Hoffman for the title heroine in the animated movie *Cinderella* (1950), but it was cut from the final script. An early concept in the film had Cinderella, after being promised she could go to the ball if her chores are done, imagining herself multiplying into several girls in order to get the work completed. The frantic, repetitive melody evokes the circles Cinderella is going in and the lyric is a tongue twister of addition and multiplication as the heroine imagines transforming from one scullery maid into a regiment of housekeepers. Both the concept and song were later eliminated, but bits of the idea can be found in "The Work Song."

"The Circle of Life" is the stirring song about the mysterious ways of nature that opens the animated film *The Lion King* (1994). As the various animals on the savanna gather to pay tribute to the future Lion King named Simba, Carmen Twillie sings the entrancing number on the soundtrack with assist by Lebo M, whose African chanting made the Elton John (music) and Tim Rice (lyric) song soar to an almost spiritual level. John's recording, less reverent and more pop in flavor, was a major success. Other recordings were

After the success of *Mary Poppins* (1964), Disney and other studios tried to re-create the special magic of that blockbuster. *The Happiest Millionaire* (1967) was one of their most costly attempts. Songwriters Richard M. and Robert B. Sherman wrote the score with Rex Harrison in mind, but Walt Disney preferred his favorite, Fred MacMurray (far right). Hermione Baddeley is the housekeeper doing the Irish jig and she is applauded by Lesley Ann Warren and Tommy Steele. (Walt Disney/Photofest)

made by Michael Crawford, Roan Keating, John Bayless, Oliver Shanti, Barbara Hendricks and the Abbey Road Ensemble, and Magpie. In the 1997 Broadway version of *The Lion King*, the narrator Rafiki (Tsidii Le Loka) led the ensemble in the stunning opening number, and the song was used again in the made-for-video sequel *The Lion King 1½* (2004).

"Circus Day" is the carnival-like theme song used for Thursdays on the television series *Mickey Mouse Club* (1955). Adult host Jimmie Dodd wrote the lively song about Thursdays having a circus theme on the show, and he sings it with the Mouseketeers, dressed as big-top performers, sideshow attractions, and animal trainers. The number then turns into a roll call in which each cast member shouts his or her name and demonstrates a circus feat.

"The Climb" is the touching song of self-realization written by Jessi Alexander and Jon Mabe for the film *Hannah Montana: The Movie* (2009). When Miley Stewart (Miley Cyrus) finally reveals to the world that she is the pop star Hannah Montana, she sings this song about how the destinations in life are not as important as the journey (or the climb) to get there. The number is performed at a benefit concert being sponsored by Hannah/Miley as a fundraiser to help stop real-estate developers from turning the beautiful Tennessee meadows of her childhood into a shopping mall.

"Climb the Mountain" is the lighthearted march number by Franklyn Marks and By Dunham that is used throughout the adventure film *Third Man on the Mountain* (1959). The melodious number is reminiscent of Kenneth Alford's "Colonel Bogey March" from *The Bridge on the River Kwai* (1957). It is about scaling the heights and is the theme song for the ambitious young climber Rudi Matt (James MacArthur), who is determined to reach the top of the treacherous Citadel, the Alpine peak on which his father died. The song accompanies Rudi's practice climbs, is whistled by Rudi and his girlfriend, Lizbeth (Janet Munro), and becomes a soaring instrumental piece in the film's finale.

"Colonel Hathi's March" is the comic military number for a line of elephants in the animated movie *The Jungle Book* (1967). Richard M. and Robert B. Sherman wrote the playful march in which the head elephant, Colonel Hathi (voice of J. Pat O'Malley), leads his pack in military maneuvers, his forgetfulness often causing collisions and pileups. Joining in the march and the song are the colonel's wife, Winifred (Verna Felton); his son, Junior (Clint Howard); and the young man-cub Mowgli (Bruce Reitherman). In the video sequel *The Jungle Book 2* (2003), the song is reprised by a quartet of elephants voiced by Bob Joyce, Rick Logan, Guy Maeda, and Jerry Whitman. The number is sometimes listed as "The Elephant Song."

"Colors of the Wind" is the Oscar-winning song of inspiration about nature and racial tolerance written by Alan Menken (music) and Stephen Schwartz (lyric) for the animated film *Pocahontas* (1995). (It was Menken's fourth Best Song Oscar in six years.) The Native American girl Pocahontas (singing voice of Judy Kuhn) shows Captain John Smith the wonders of the land in the New World, arguing that it must be preserved to be understood, and tells him he must walk in the footsteps of the Native American in order to understand her people. Menken's expansive music and Schwartz's vivid imagery keep the song potent without being preachy. Vanessa Williams reprises the ballad during the end credits of the movie, and her recording was a popular favorite. It was also recorded by such artists as Harajuku, Kaitlin Hopkins, Vanessa Anne Hudgens, Michael Crawford, Christy Carlson Romano, Ashanti featuring Lil Shi Shi, Sara Ramirez, Kerry Butler, and Earl Rose, who made a pleasing jazz version of the song.

"Come Meet Santa" is the satirical song about commercializing Christmas written by Michael Lembeck for the film comedy *The Santa Clause 3: The Escape Clause* (2006). After Jack Frost (Martin Short) usurps Santa and turns the North Pole into a theme park, he sings this hyperbolic number about the terrific rides and attractions that are waiting for you if you are willing to pay.

"Comforting to Know" is the reassuring lullaby written by Carly Simon for the animated film *Piglet's Big Movie* (2003). Simon sings the affecting song, promising to remain by one's side and protect one from any harm, with Ben Taylor on the soundtrack. The number is reprised during the end credits of the movie.

"The Computer Wore Tennis Shoes" is the piquant title song written by Robert Brunner and Bruce Belland for the 1969 movie comedy about a college student computer whiz. Over the opening credits of the film, a bebopping male chorus, sounding much like the Beach Boys, sings the pop number about a computer that smiles and has other human characteristics.

"Cory in the House" is the rhythm-and-blues title song for the 2007 television series about Cory Baxter (Kyle Massey), who moves into the White

House when his father is hired as the new chef for the president. Matthew Gerrard and Robbie Nevil wrote the pulsating number, which warns everyone that now that Cory is in the White House, he's going to shake things up. Massey made a music video of the number as a promotion for the series, which was a spin-off of the popular sitcom *That's So Raven* (2003).

"County Fair" is the happy song about a rural Indiana fair in 1903, where young Jeremiah Kincaid (Bobby Driscoll) brings his pet ram hoping to win a prize, in the film *So Dear to My Heart* (1948). Mel Tormé and Robert Wells wrote the number, and Ken Carson sings it on the soundtrack during an animated sequence showing scenes from the fair.

"The Court of Miracles" is the pounding song of menace written by Alan Menken (music) and Stephen Schwartz (music) for the animated movie *The Hunchback of Notre Dame* (1996). The captain Phoebus (voice of Kevin Kline) and the hunchback Quasimodo (Tom Hulce) are ambushed in the sewers of Paris by a mob of outlaws led by Clopin (Paul Kandel) and are to be judged by the Court of Miracles. Clopin sings the Halloween-like number about the kangaroo court, which gets its name from the fact that it is a miracle if anyone is ever found innocent.

"A Cowboy Needs a Horse" is the lazy, western-flavored title song written by Paul Mason Howard and Billy Mills for the 1956 film short. A young boy dressed in cowboy gear rides his rocking horse and drifts off to sleep, fantasizing about all his Wild West adventures. A studio chorus sings the song on the soundtrack, the clip-clop accompaniment reminiscent of a horse's slow gait and the melody inspiring memories of Roy Rogers's riding song, "Happy Trails." The song is often used in Frontierland in the Disney theme parks.

"Crazier" is a melancholy country ballad sung by Taylor Swift in the 2009 film *Hannah Montana: The Movie*. At a fundraising hoedown to raise money to fight off wealthy land developers, the country star takes her turn at the microphone to sing the heartfelt song about the things your mind fools you with when you are in love. The number is written by Swift and Robert Ellis Orrall.

"Cruella De Vil" is the jazzy tribute to the villainess of the animated movie *One Hundred and One Dalmatians* (1961). Mel Leven wrote the catchy number, which the songwriter Roger Radcliffe (voice of Ben Wright) improvises when his wife's school friend Cruella De Vil comes to pay a visit. The song paints a silly picture of a devious, scary creature, but when the real Cruella arrives it is clear that she is even worse than described. Near the end of the film, the song is heard on the radio as the Radcliffes prepare for a dismal Christmas without their pet dalmatians. A version sung by Bill Lee is heard on the soundtrack of the made-for-video animated sequel *101 Dalmatians II: Patch's London Adventure* (2003). Recordings of the song were made by Hayden Panettiere, Steve Tyrell, Lalaine, Barbara Hendricks and the Abbey Road Ensemble, Selena Gomez, and a bluegrass rendition was made by Mike Toppins, Glen Duncan, Billy Troy, Jim Brown, James Freeze, and David Chase.

"A Cut Above the Rest" is the bouncy trio written by Rachel Portman (music) and Don Black (lyric) for the made-for-video animated musical *Beauty and the Beast: The Enchanted Christmas* (1997). The clock Cogsworth (voice of David Ogden Stiers) and the candelabra Lumière (Jerry Orbach) argue over which of them is the best at preparing for Christmas until Belle (Paige O'Hara) points out that when they put their two heads together they are above all others in talent.

D

"Dakota" is the fervent song of praise for the Dakota Territory in the movie musical *The One and Only, Genuine, Original Family Band* (1968). Newspaperman Joe Carder (John Davidson) urges the citizens of a Nebraska town to move north and settle in the rolling hills of Dakota, and the crowd soon joins in, singing about the land of opportunity soon to be admitted to the union. The Richard M. and Robert B. Sherman number is similar to Rodgers and Hammerstein's song "Oklahoma!" in spirit and style.

"Dalmatian Plantation" is the jaunty ditty songwriter Roger Radcliffe (voice of Ben Wright) improvises when he comes up with the idea of buying a farm to house all the dogs in the animated movie *One Hundred and One Dalmatians* (1961). Mel Leven wrote the short, sprightly number, which concludes the film on a silly and joyful note. The song is reprised by Anita (Jodi Benson) in the made-for-video animated sequel *101 Dalmatians II: Patch's London Adventure* (2003) as she packs up the family's belongings to move to a bigger house in the country.

"Dance of the Robe" is the musical plea for help the Nubians sing to the captive princess Aida (Heather Headley) in the Broadway musical *Aida* (2000). Elton John (music) and Tim Rice (lyric) wrote the rock anthem in which the Nubian slaves urge Aida to lead them in revolt against their captors, the Egyptians. She takes up their cause and joins them in the vibrant song and dance.

"Dance with Me" is the musical invitation by Ray Cham and Char Licera that is heard while teen stars Galleria (Raven-Symoné), Chanel (Adrienne Bailon), Aqua (Kiely Williams), and Dorinda (Sabrina Bryan) dance with some dashing young Spanish men in the television sequel *The Cheetah Girls 2* (2006). In a rehearsal hall in Barcelona, the four American girls go through some elegant Spanish dance footwork, but the song Andrew Seeley and Belinda sing on the soundtrack is more lite-rock than Latin.

"Dancing on a Cloud" is the waltzing love song that Mack David, Jerry Livingston, and Al Hoffman wrote for the animated film *Cinderella* (1950), but it was eliminated during the production process. Walt Disney was fascinated with the idea of animating a sequence in which two lovers dance on the clouds. He decided to put this idea to the test while assembling his story boards for *Cinderella*. The song was written with the image in mind and recorded by Ilene Woods as Cinderella and Mike Douglas as the Prince. The song has a haunting melody and a transporting lyric for the two to sing upon their first meeting, and soon the twosome waltz through the stars atop a dance floor of clouds. It is unclear why Disney scrapped the idea, but the number was replaced by the gentle "So This Is Love," which kept the lovers earthbound. The visual idea did not reach fruition until the finale of the animated movie *Sleeping Beauty* in 1959.

"Daring to Dance" is the urgent ballad sung by the mermaid Ariel (voice of Jodi Benson) in one of the episodes of the animated television series *The Little Mermaid* (1992). In the song of yearning, Ariel dreams of dancing to the songs that are in her heart, knowing she would be a wonderful dancer if only she had legs. Later in the episode she reprises the number with the mute mermaid Gabriella, who uses sign language to express her thoughts about dancing.

"Darkwing Duck Theme" is the pulsating jazz song written by Steve Nelson and Thomas Richard Sharp for the 1991 animated television series about the everyday duck Drake Mallard, who becomes the crime fighter Darkwing Duck when he dons a mask and cape. The theme song, sung by a chorus over the opening credits, celebrates the master of disguise who protects the city of St. Canard. After the first season, the song was altered a bit to give it a more heavy metal sound that was more in keeping with the sometimes dark and violent series.

"Daughters of Triton" is the minuet-like number sung by the mermaid princesses in the animated film *The Little Mermaid* (1989). Sebastian the Crab has staged a performance for King Triton and the royal sisters sing about who they are, all mermaids whose names begin with an A. When they introduce Ariel, the youngest princess is not there, and both the king and Sebastian are furious. In the 2008 Broadway version of *The Little Mermaid*, the song, by Alan Menken (music) and Howard Ashman (lyric), was also performed by the mermaids (or mersisters).

"The Death of Saul" is the requiem-like number written by Alan Menken (music) and Tim Rice (lyric) for the Broadway concert *King David* (1997). King Saul (Martin Vidnovic) loses his kingdom because he did not follow the word of the Lord, and the chorus, led by Samuel (Peter Samuel) and Jonathan (Roger Bart), sings this high-powered number in judgment of their former king.

"Deep Deep Water" is the pop ballad written by Dan Sawyer, Kristyn Osborn, and Linda Garvey for the animated film *Doug's 1st Movie* (1999), based on the popular television series. The song, about the anxiety of love being like swimming in deep water, is heard briefly at the Valentine's Day disco dance and is performed on the soundtrack by Sawyer and his band. During the movie's ending credits it is given a slower and more emotional rendition by Shedaisy.

"Delivering Christmas" is a merry song by Paul Williams about the joys of sending letters and packages at Christmastime, performed in the television special *A Muppets Christmas: Letters to Santa* (2008). A post-office employee (Jesse L. Martin), Kermit the Frog (voice of Steve Whitmire), friends, and postal workers sing and dance to the jolly rhythmic number in the back room of a New York City post office.

"Der Fuehrer's Face" is a highly satiric song of nationalism written by Oliver Wallace for the Donald Duck film short *Donald Duck in Nutzi Land*, but the mock anthem became so popular before the movie's release that the short was retitled *Der Fuehrer's Face* (1943). Donald (voice of Clarence Nash) dreams that he works in a munitions factory in Nazi Germany, where he is bombarded by the patriotic song that hails Hitler every time he turns around. He finally awakes to find himself in the shadow of the Statue of Liberty, thrilled to be an American citizen. The John Scott Trotter Orchestra, with trombonist Spike Jones, recorded the song while the film was in production, but Jones thought the rendition too tame. He formed his own band, the City Slickers, and they made a raucous recording of their own. Carly Grayson and Willie Spicer handle the vocals on the record, doing a "Bronx cheer" every time the dictator's name is mentioned, and Jones fills the recording with odd sound effects and incongruous musical notes to create a chaotic effect. The disc sold a million and a half copies and launched Jones's career. Renowned lyricist Oscar Hammerstein is quoted as saying that the number was "the great psychological song of the war."

"Destino" is the eerie and surreal title song from the mesmerizing and surreal film short Walt Disney and artist Salvador Dali collaborated on in the 1940s but was not completed until sixty years later. Armando Dominguez wrote the chanting, nearly wordless song about fate, and it is sung on the soundtrack by Dora Luz while a female figure pursues a male statue over a landscape of surreal monuments and shadows. Although work began on the movie in 1946, it was abandoned by the end of the decade, and it was Roy E. Disney who years later completed the small, weird masterwork and had it shown at an international film festival in 2003.

"Detroit" is the musical tribute to the city where the automobile is king, as expressed by the car-loving New Yorker Angie Duke (John Davidson) in the period musical *The Happiest Millionaire* (1967). Richard M. and Robert B. Sherman wrote the march-tempo number, which Angie sings to his sweetheart, Cordelia (Lesley Ann Warren), as they ride in his new 1916 automobile, confessing his dream of going to Detroit someday and making his name. She reprises the number a bit later in the film, reminding Angie of his dream, and the two of them sing parts of the song again when they decide to elope and go to Detroit.

"Different" is the musical first encounter between Tarzan (Josh Strickland) and Jane Porter (Jenn Gambatese) in the 2006 Broadway version of *Tarzan*. While the two make awkward and tentative attempts to communicate, Tarzan's thoughts are revealed: This new creature is not only different from any other he has encountered, but it is causing his heart to beat faster. Phil Collins wrote the clever duet, which is as funny as it is romantic.

"Dig It" is the plodding rhythm-and-blues number about continuing to search and not giving up, as featured in the movie *Holes* (2003). Young inmates Armpit (Bryan Cotton), Zigzag (Max Kasch), X-Ray (Brenden Jefferson), Zero (Khleo Thomas), and Stanley (Shia LaBeouf) are forced by the warden at the desert detention center Camp Green Lake to continually dig holes, and they sing this pulsating number as they dig in the sand for seemingly no reason. The song, written by Mickey Petralia and the five cast members, has an improvised yet rhythmic pattern that is very effective. The group D-Tent Boyz made a music video of the number.

"Dig a Little Deeper" is the rousing gospel hymn that the voodoo sorceress Mama Odie (voice of Jenifer Lewis) sings in the animated feature *The Princess and the Frog* (2009). Randy Newman wrote the lively number about going below the surface to find out what you really need in life. The aged, blind Odie "sees" right through Tiana and Prince Naveen and tells them to search within themselves to discover the truth about their dreams. Lewis performs the zesty song in a Cajun accent and is backed by the Pinnacle Gospel Choir.

"Digga Tunnah" is the satirical work song from the animated made-for-video sequel *The Lion King 1½* (2004) that spoofs the sound of the original *The Lion King* film. Timon (voice of Nathan Lane) and all the meerkats dig tunnels under the African savanna and sing the chantlike number that echoes the rhythmic arrangement of "The Circle of Life." Martin Erskine and Seth J. Friedman wrote the catchy, silly number, using the vocal background sounds Lebo M and Johnny Clegg created for the original *The Lion King* (1994).

"Dirty Bill" is the jolly song about the joy of not washing written by Frank Churchill for the Silly Symphony movie short *The Robber Kitten* (1935). The kitten Ambrose, who likes to pretend to be a Wild West outlaw, runs away from home at bath time and meets the real bandit Dirty Bill (voice of Billy Bletcher). When Ambrose asks Bill if he ever bathes, the outlaw answers with this merry ditty, a pledge to remain forever unwashed, and Ambrose joins in singing the number.

"Disney Afternoon Theme" is the calypso-sounding theme song for *The Disney Afternoon* (1990), a two-hour block of animated television series that featured such programs as *DuckTales*, *Disney's Adventures of the Gummi Bears*, *Bonkers*, *Darkwing Duck*, *Aladdin*, and others. Tom

Snow (music) and Dean Pitchford (lyric) wrote the rhythmic song, which promises thrills, chills, and spills in the action-packed cartoons to follow. It is sung by male voices on the soundtrack while the animation introduces some of the characters from the different series, each one coming to life as the artist's paintbrush gives it color.

"Don't Fall in Love" is the harsh song of warning written by Rachel Portman (music) and Don Black (lyric) for the made-for-video animated sequel *Beauty and the Beast: The Enchanted Christmas* (1997). The sinister pipe organ Forte (voice of Tim Curry) wants to remain as he is and tries to dissuade the Beast from having tender feelings for Belle by singing this heavy number. The music is a pastiche of a ponderous baroque organ piece, and the lyric argues that it is best to be alone and not emotionally involved with anything or anyone.

"Don't Walk Away" is the optimistic, country-pop ditty that Miley Stewart (Miley Cyrus) sings while collecting eggs from the henhouse in the 2009 film *Hannah Montana: The Movie*. Written by Cyrus, John Shanks, and Hillary Lindsey, the song is about determination and hanging in there, no matter how complicated things can be. It is heard during a humorous montage that features Miley overcoming her problems getting the chickens to give up their wares.

"The Doodlebops" is the lite-rock title song by Carl Lenox for the 2005 television series about a trio of pop singers who don colorful and exaggerated clothes, hair, and makeup. Rooney (Chad McNamara), Deedee (Lisa Lennox), and Moe Doodle (Jonathan Wexler) sing the peppy number at the opening of each show, introducing themselves and inviting viewers to join them for musical adventure.

"Doug's Theme" is the happy-go-lucky musical signature for the animated television series that was known by three different titles. Fred Newman and Dan Sawyer wrote the lyric-less number filled with easygoing scat singing, vocal sounds, whistling, and even everyday sound effects. It was written for the Nickelodeon series *Doug*, which premiered in 1991. When the series returned as a Disney show on ABC-TV in 1996, it was retitled *Brand Spanking New! Doug* and the theme song was retained. When the series was syndicated in 1998, the title was changed to *Disney's Doug*. In 1999 the song was heard over the opening credits in the feature film *Doug's 1st Movie* and in the Disney World musical show *Disney's Doug Live!*

"Down in New Orleans" is the Oscar-nominated blues number about the magic and joy of the Louisiana city, written by Randy Newman for the animated film *The Princess and the Frog* (2009). A quiet version of the song is briefly sung by Tiana (voice of Anika Noni Rose) in the movie's prologue, then Dr. John is heard singing an intoxicating, up-tempo rendition while both the rich and poor sections of New Orleans are shown. Tiana reprises the number at the end of the film when she finally opens her restaurant and sings that dreams do come true in New Orleans.

"Down to Earth" is the environment-friendly ballad by Peter Gabriel and Thomas Newman that is heard over the closing credits of the computer-animated film *WALL-E* (2008) about a robot who tries to single-handedly clean up the trash-ridden planet Earth. Songwriter Gabriel sings the gentle Oscar-nominated pop song on the soundtrack, pleading for people to stop taking the planet for granted and to make an effort to save the environment.

"Down to the Sea" is the extended musical sequence written by Michael and Patty Silversher for the opening of the animated video sequel *The Little Mermaid II: Return to the Sea* (2000). On the day that her baby daughter, Melody, is to be presented to King Triton and other inhabitants of the sea, Ariel (voice of Jodi Benson) sings a lullaby to the child, then her husband Prince Eric (Rob Paulsen) takes them both aboard a ship for the ceremony. Both humans and land and sea creatures prepare for the festivities in song, and the crab Sebastian (Samuel E. Wright) leads them all in this calypso-flavored number about everyone gathering together to cheer the baby princess.

"Dream" is the country-flavored ballad written by John Shanks and Kara DioGuardi for the 2009 film *Hannah Montana: The Movie*. Performed by Miley Cyrus as the character Miley Stewart, the number is used as background music for a montage featuring the teenager going horseback riding, swimming, and rebuilding a chicken coop with the farm boy Travis Brody (Lucas Till), with whom she is having burgeoning romantic feelings. The song is a gentle reminder to embrace one's dreams and to be open to new things.

"A Dream Is a Wish Your Heart Makes" is the flowing ballad heard near the beginning of the animated film *Cinderella* (1950) when the title heroine (voice of Ilene Woods) sings as she awakes from dreaming of a better life. Mack David, Jay Livingston, and Al Hoffman collaborated on the ballad, and Perry Como's recording was very popular. Michael Bolton's record in 1995 was also a success, and the next year Linda Ronstadt recorded the song (and much of the rest of the score) in both Spanish and English. Other recordings were made by Annette Funicello, Stacy Sullivan, Marjorie Hughes, Barbara Hendricks and the Abbey Road Ensemble, Christa Moore, Daniel Bedingfield, Kimberly Locke, David Benoit and David Sanborn, Ashley Brown with Andrew Samonsky, Barbara Cook, Donna McElroy, Nikki Blonsky, Steve Tyrell, and others.

"The Drinking Song" is the rousing song of celebration written by George Bruns for the adventure film *The Fighting Prince of Donegal* (1966) about the sixteenth-century Irish hero "Red Hugh" O'Donnell. After O'Donnell (Peter McEnery) has driven his English foes out of the castle and sent them back to Dublin, his loyal supporter Lord Sweeney (Andrew Keir) leads the Irish in this boastful number. Although the lusty ditty is inspired by the Irish folk song "O'Donnell Aboo," it is more reminiscent of a Sigmund Romberg operetta than an authentic Hibernian ballad.

"Drummin' Drummin' Drummin'" is the narrative ballad about a Civil War drummer boy that Richard M. and Robert B. Sherman wrote for the period movie musical *The One and Only, Genuine, Original Family Band* (1968). Grandpa Bower (Walter Brennan) sings the rhythmic number to the children in a one-room schoolhouse, beating out the pattern with his hands on the desks and telling the tale of the brave youth who kept beating his drum throughout the battle.

"DuckTales Theme" is the catchy title song for the 1987 animated television series featuring Donald Duck's three nephews. Mark Mueller wrote the bouncy pop-rock song about how every day in Duckburg brings a new adventure, and it is sung on the soundtrack over the opening sequence of each show.

"Dumbo's Circus" is the happy title song by Phillip Baron for the 1985 television series that used "puppetronics" to bring the popular characters from the film *Dumbo* (1941) into a lively children's show. The merry circuslike number, welcoming everyone to a show like no other, is sung by a chorus over the opening sequence in which larger-than-life puppets of Dumbo and his friends arrive in circus wagons and set up for a new episode.

"The Dwarfs' Yodel Song" is the rompish but charming nonsense number that Frank Churchill (music) and Larry Morey (lyric) wrote for the first animated feature film, *Snow White and the Seven Dwarfs* (1937). The seven little men sing, dance, and accompany themselves on makeshift instruments as they entertain Snow White in their cottage after dinner. The song consists of jokes with no meaning, sing-along sections, and high-flying yodeling. The number is also listed as "The Silly Song" and sometimes as "Isn't This a Silly Song?"

E

"Easter Day with You" is the happy march-tempo song by John Kava-naugh about how the holiday of Easter is best if shared with friends, heard three times in the animated video *Winnie the Pooh: Springtime with Roo* (2004). Tigger (voice of Jim Cummings) sings the number to the kangaroo Roo (Jimmy Bennett), who is too young to remember his first Easter. Roo later reprises the song, at a slower tempo, as he sits in bed and makes an Easter card for Rabbit. At the end of the film, Rabbit (Ken Sansom) and the other characters in the Hundred Acre Wood sing it once again after Rabbit has learned that the holiday is about having fun, not about having Easter rules.

"Easy as Life" is a fervent character song for the Nubian princess Aida (Heather Headley) written by Elton John (music) and Tim Rice (lyric) for the Broadway musical *Aida* (2000). Although she loves the Egyptian captain Radames (Adam Pascal), Aida knows she must work to help free her fellow Nubians from Egyptian slavery. Forgetting him will be easy, she argues, until she thinks of how much she loves Radames. Tina Turner recorded the song before *Aida* opened on Broadway.

"Eating the Peach" is the playful, British music hall–style number writ-ten by Randy Newman for the live-action, stop-motion film *James and the Giant Peach* (1996). The orphaned James (Paul Terry) is flying over the ocean on a giant peach with his friends, the Grasshopper (voice of Simon Callow), Earthworm (David Thewlis), Lady Bug (Jane Leeves), Spider (Susan Sarandon), Centipede (Richard Dreyfuss), and Glow Worm (Miriam Margolyes), and they begin to panic when they think they are going to starve to death. James points out that they are, in fact, riding on their dinner, and all sing this jolly list song about their favorite foods as they munch on the peach.

"Edge of the Edge of the Sea" is the driving ballad from an episode of the animated television series *The Little Mermaid* (1992). Angry with her overprotective father, King Triton, Ariel (voice of Jodi Benson) plans to run away and sings this determined song to her sea horse, Stormy, vowing to swim beyond the confines of her father's kingdom and explore the world.

"The Edison Twins" is the energetic title song for the 1984 television series about a brainy brother and sister who solve mysteries by using science. The happy bluegrass number, complete with whistling and rhythmic guitar, is sung by a male trio over the opening credits. The lyric introduces the twins and argues that life is a learning game, so viewers should use their heads like the twins do.

"Eglantine" is the musical tribute to the friendly witch Miss Eglantine Price (Angela Lansbury) written by Richard M. and Robert B. Sherman for the film fantasy *Bedknobs and Broomsticks* (1971). The charlatan magician Professor Brown (David Tomlinson) sings the peppy, march-tempo number to Miss Price, proclaiming her wondrous talents and trying to get her to go into show business with him. Miss Price responds in song, saying her magic is for more important things, such as the war effort in 1940.

"Elaborate Lives" is the featured love song in the Broadway musical *Aida* (2000) written by Elton John (music) and Tim Rice (lyric). The Egyptian captain Radames (Adam Pascal) and the Nubian princess Aida (Heather Headley) find the world complicated with ambition and pretense but believe that their love is simple and pure and they can avoid the elaborate snares in life. The two lovers reprise the ballad near the end of the musical when they are sentenced to die by being entombed together. Headley made a solo recording of the ballad before the musical opened on Broadway, and there was a later duet version by Vanessa A. Jones and Sean McDermott.

"The Elegant Captain Hook" is the rousing tribute to the villain in the animated fantasy movie *Peter Pan* (1953). Sammy Fain (music) and Sammy Cahn (lyric) wrote the jolly number about the talents of Captain Hook, and it is sung by the pirates on board their ship as they celebrate the capture of Wendy, Michael, John, and the Lost Boys. The silly hornpipe dance that follows nearly convinces the boys to sign up and become pirates until Wendy reminds them that Peter is sure to rescue them all. Lee Wilkof and Gregory Jbara made a playful duet recording of the song.

"The Elephant March" is a brassy and catchy instrumental piece written by George Bruns for the movie short *Goliath II* (1960). Throughout the tale, about a puny little elephant named Goliath II who tries to prove to his father, Goliath, that he can be brave, the elephant herd goes on the march and is accompanied by this memorable musical piece in which trombones and tubas make the sounds for the moving elephants. The music was popular with marching bands for many years.

"The Emperor's New School Theme Song" is the rocking march number by Michael Tavera that opens each episode of the 2006 animated television series inspired by the film *The Emperor's New Groove* (2000). A chorus sings the pastiche college fight song while Kuzco, the self-centered emperor with attitude, is seen bouncing around the school campus trying to keep all the focus on himself.

"Empty Heart" is the sensitive "I am" song for the lonely toymaker Geppetto (Drew Carey), who longs to have a son to teach his craft and to love. Stephen Schwartz wrote the delicate number for the television musical *Geppetto* (2000), which looked at the Pinocchio tale from the toymaker's point of view.

"Enchantment Passing Through" is an affecting duet written by Elton John (music) and Tim Rice (lyric) for the Broadway musical *Aida* (2000). The Egyptian captain Radames (Adam Pascal) confesses to the slave girl Aida (Heather Headley), whom he hardly knows, that he is not looking forward to giving up exploring and waging war to marry the pharaoh's daughter. Aida argues that he can change his fate, whereas she is a slave and cannot. The poignant duet links the two very different people and paves the way for their love story. At the end of the musical, Radames and Aida reprise the song as they are entombed together to die. Dru Hill recorded the song before *Aida* opened on Broadway.

"Encyclopedia" is the catchy number sung by Jiminy Cricket (voice of Cliff Edwards) on the original *Mickey Mouse Club* television show (1955) when he introduces a section of the program that is informative. The spirited number claims that the best way to solve your curiosity about anything in the world is to open the encyclopedia. In the animated sequence, Jiminy opens pages in various volumes of the encyclopedia, and the tuneful song even rhythmically spells out the difficult word; a generation of kids knew how to spell "encyclopedia" because of this simple ditty.

"End of the Line" is the pop ballad by John Van Tongeren and Oz Scott that laments the end of a relationship, featured in the television film *The Cheetah Girls* (2003). When the four teens Galleria (Raven-Symoné), Chanel (Adrienne Bailon), Aqua (Kiely Williams), and Dorinda (Sabrina Bryan) realize that their girl singing group is breaking up, each is seen separately in sorrow as Christi Mac sings the tearful song on the soundtrack.

"Endless Night" is the mystifying plea for direction sung by the adult lion Simba (Jason Raize) in the 1997 Broadway version of *The Lion King*. Hans Zimmer, Lebo M, Jay Rifkin (music), and Julie Taymor (lyric) wrote the song, in which Simba prays to his deceased father for help in deciding what he should do: remain hidden from the world's problems or return to the devastated Pride Lands and help the other lions. He is accompanied by a chorus, who remind him that even the longest night is followed by sunrise.

"Enemy Within" is the revealing character song for the newly appointed King Saul (Martin Vidnovic) in the Broadway pageant-concert *King David* (1997). The character-driven number bemoans the troubles of a monarch and his worst enemy: his internal doubts and conflicts. Alan Menken composed the regal melody and Tim Rice wrote the incisive lyric.

"Enjoy It" is the song of optimism written by Richard M. and Robert B. Sherman for the adventure film *In Search of the Castaways* (1962). The search party has survived a flash flood by taking refuge in a tree, and the next morning Professor Jacques Paganel (Maurice Chevalier) and Mary Grant (Hayley Mills) look on the bright side of life and sing the cheerful ditty as they prepare a breakfast made from leaves, eggs, fish, and other natural ingredients.

"Entry into Jerusalem" is the exotic choral number from the Broadway concert *King David* (1997) that captures the grandeur and pageantry of the

biblical tale. As the Ark of the Covenant is brought into the city of Jerusalem, the crowd sings this Middle Eastern–flavored number. Alan Menken
wrote the vibrant music and Tim Rice penned the lyric, which is inspired
by Psalm 24. The song is also listed as "The Ark Brought into Jerusalem."

"Ever Ever After" is the unlikely rock song that concludes the modern
fairy tale movie *Enchanted* (2007). Alan Menken (music) and Stephen
Schwartz (lyric) wrote the pop number about everyone believing that fairy-
tale endings are possible, and it is sung on the soundtrack by Carrie Underwood at the end of the film in which each of the characters is seen enjoying
just such a happy ending. The number was recorded by Jordan Pruitt.

"Every Little Piece" is the dandy list song by Joel Hirschhorn and Al Kasha sung by the two villains in the movie musical *Pete's Dragon* (1977). The
charlatan salesman Dr. Terminus (Jim Dale) and his sidekick, Hoagy (Red
Buttons), have discovered the dragon Elliott and plot to capture him and
sell his body parts as miracle cures. The two crooks sing of each anatomical
part and the remedy it will bring, the list growing faster and more furious
as the song progresses.

"Every Story Is a Love Story" is the pop-rock song that opens the
Broadway musical *Aida* (2000) and transports the audience to the days of
ancient Egypt. In the Egyptian wing of a modern museum, the statue of
the princess Amneris (Sherie Rene Scott) comes to life and sings of the
many kinds of love stories over the centuries. When she begins to tell a
story of two lovers in the land of pharaohs, the museum disappears and the
story begins. Elton John (music) and Tim Rice (lyric) wrote the haunting
number, which is reprised at the end of the musical when the scene shifts
back to the museum.

"Everybody Has a Laughing Place" is the bouncy comic number written by Allie Wrubel (music) and Ray Gilbert (lyric) for the innovative musical film *Song of the South* (1946), which successfully mixed animation and
live action. During one of the animated Uncle Remus tales, Brer Rabbit
(voice of Johnny Lee), captured by Brer Fox and Brer Bear and about to be
cooked, happily sings about his secret laughing place. The ploy works; Rabbit's captors let him free to show them the special place, only to discover a
beehive that attacks the two and indeed provides Brer Rabbit with plenty
to laugh about. Burl Ives's recording of the song was a popular children's
record.

"Everyday" is the pop love song about losing your direction and needing to find yourself in order to find your way back to the one you love, as heard in the television movie *High School Musical 2* (2007). Jamie Houston wrote the ballad, which is sung by estranged teenage sweethearts Troy (Zac Efron) and Gabriella (Vanessa Anne Hudgens) when they are reunited on stage during the summer talent show.

"Everyday Super Hero" is the driving rock song about saving the world one day at a time, written by Matthew Gerrard, Steve Harwell, and Robbie Nevil for the film *The Pacifier* (2005). Songwriter Harwell sings the deprecating tongue-in-cheek song, which looks upon superpowers as just an everyday thing, over the final credits of the movie. A popular recording of the rock number was made by Harwell's band, Smash Mouth.

"Everything Has a Useness" is the peppy song of cockeyed logic written by Mack David, Jerry Livingston, and Al Hoffman in 1948 for the animated movie *Alice in Wonderland* (1951), but it was not used. Even the seemingly most useless of things have a purpose, the song argues, even if that usefulness is nonsensical to the normal brain. The list song is very much in the style of author Lewis Carroll's wry satire in the book, but perhaps it was too

Although it runs only seventy-five minutes, *Alice in Wonderland* (1951) has more songs than any other Disney animated film. Many of them are short, yet manage to be memorable, such as "The Unbirthday Song" sung by the March Hare (voice of Jerry Colonna), Alice (Kathryn Beaumont), and the Mad Hatter (Ed Wynn). (Walt Disney/Photofest)

literate for a children's movie. The number was later altered and sung by Jimmie Dodd on the television show *The Mickey Mouse Club*.

"Everything Is Food" is the silly list song written by Harry Nilsson for the odd movie musical *Popeye* (1980). When the itinerant sailor Popeye (Robin Williams) arrives in the town of Sweethaven looking for his long-lost Pappy, he goes into a local restaurant where the patrons and the staff sing about the importance food has in their lives. Among the patrons is the always-broke Wimpy (Paul Dooley), who punctuates the song with his attempts to get a hamburger on credit.

"Everything Is Honey" is the humorous character song sung by Winnie the Pooh (voice of Jim Cummings) in the 2011 animated film *Winnie the Pooh*. When the stuffed bear is searching for his missing friend Christopher Robin, he tries to focus on the task at hand, but his grumbling stomach won't let him hear anything but the word "honey." Soon, Pooh is transported into his fantasy world where everything is made of the sticky sweet treat; there he sings about his relationship with his favorite food. The catchy number, by Robert Lopez and Kristen Anderson-Lopez, is reprised at the end of the film when Pooh wins a giant pot of honey.

"Everything Is Not What It Seems" is the lite-rock theme song written by John Adair and Steve Hampton for the television series *Wizards of Waverly Place* (2007), about a family of wizards-in-training living in modern Manhattan. Selena Gomez, who plays the daughter, Alex, in the series, sings the pop song about illusions and dreams on the soundtrack during the opening credits.

"Everything Is Right" is the merry march number written by Michael Abbott and Sarah Weeks for the happy ending of the video *Pooh's Grand Adventure: The Search for Christopher Robin* (1997). After Winnie the Pooh (voice of Jim Cummings) and his friends are reunited with Christopher Robin (Frankie J. Galasso), everyone sings this happy number about how nothing can be amiss now that they are all together again.

"Everything That I Am" is a penetrating trio number of self-discovery written by Phil Collins for the 2006 Broadway version of *Tarzan*. The adult Tarzan (Josh Strickland) encounters a vision of himself as a child (Daniel Manche or Alex Rutherford) who is wondering what kind of creature he is.

The ape Kala (Merle Dandridge) has revealed to the adult Tarzan who he really is and how she found him, and he is torn between his feelings for his ape family and his newfound human existence. He comes to the conclusion that he is indeed a man and must pattern his future after that fact. Collins made an effective solo recording of the ballad.

"Ev'rybody Wants to Be a Cat" is the contagious jazz number by Floyd Huddleston and Al Rinker about how everyone wishes they had the new hot jazz sound, written for the animated film *The Aristocats* (1970). Parisian alley cat Thomas O'Malley (voice of Phil Harris) and Scat Cat (Scatman Crothers) and his band perform the swinging number while the sophisticated lady cat Duchess (Eva Gabor) sings a slower and cooler section of the song. The jumping sequence climaxes as the Paris townhouse where the jam session is taking place collapses from all the jubilant music. Jazz Networks gave the number a contemporary rendition in a 1992 recording, Steve Tyrell recorded it in 2006, and Andrew Samonsky recorded it with backup vocals by Meredith Inglesby, Andy Karl, Tyler Maynard, and Keewa Nurullah. A bluegrass rendition of the song was recorded by Mike Toppins, Glen Duncan, Billy Troy, Jim Brown, James Freeze, and David Chase.

F

"Fa La La La Fallen in Love" is the doo-wop-flavored number written by Walter Edgar Kennon for the animated video sequel *The Hunchback of Notre Dame II* (2002). Laverne (singing voice of Mary Jay Clough), Victor (Charles Kimbrough), and Hugo (Jason Alexander), the gargoyles who perch atop the cathedral, are thrilled to see their friend Quasimodo in love and sing this catchy song of celebration, which is soon picked up by the citizens of Paris and is heard across the city.

"Fabulous" is the satiric list song that itemizes the priorities of the self-centered, spoiled teenager Sharpay (Ashley Tisdale) in the television sequel *High School Musical 2* (2007). Sitting by the pool at her family's country club, Sharpay sings of the shallow things that mean the most to her, and she is joined by her clueless brother Ryan, (Lucas Grabeel), and her two toadies. The number soon grows into an elaborate production number in and around the swimming pool. David Lawrence and Faye Greenberg wrote the wry and revealing character song.

"Family" is the easygoing soft-shoe number about mutual appreciation and camaraderie written by Randy Newman for *James and the Giant Peach* (1996), the movie fantasy that mixed live-action and stop-motion animation. The Grasshopper (voice of Simon Callow) plays his violin and sings the song to the orphaned James (Paul Terry) as they float through the sky on the giant peach. They are joined in song by his friends the Earthworm (David Thewlis), Spider (Susan Sarandon), Glow Worm (Miriam Margolyes), Lady Bug (Jane Leeves), and Centipede (Richard Dreyfuss), assuring James that they consider him one of the family.

"Fantasmic" is the surging theme song for the park attraction Fantasmic!, which premiered in Disneyland in 1992. Fantasmic! is a water-and-light show with projections and live actors portraying Mickey Mouse and characters from various Disney animated films. The theme song is heard at the beginning of the show and is reprised in the grand finale in which dozens of characters glide by on illuminated boats. Bruce Healey composed the sparkling instrumental piece, which mixes a symphonic orchestra with some rock-and-roll sounds.

"Farewell" is the reflective ballad that adds a touch of authenticity to the adventure movie *Davy Crockett, King of the Wild Frontier* (1955). The pioneer Davy Crockett penned a poem the night before the attack on the Alamo, looking back with thanks on the many blessings he had enjoyed throughout his life and urging Americans to fight for their beliefs even as he saw certain defeat facing him the next day. George Bruns set the poem to music and it is sung by Crockett (Fess Parker) in a pensive moment in the film.

"Fat Cat Stomp" is the energetic swing number written by Michael and Patty Silversher for an episode of the animated television series *Chip 'n Dale Rescue Rangers* (1989). In order to distract the villains, the chipmunk sleuths Chip and Dale disguise themselves as chorus girls in a casino floor show and sing this vibrant musical salute to the mobster Fat Cat, who owns the place. Soon everyone in the club joins in, including Fat Cat himself, who proclaims he has nine lives to burn on the dance floor.

"Father and Son" is the comic list song written by Kevin Quinn and Randy Petersen for the video sequel *Aladdin and the King of Thieves* (1995). The Genie (voice of Robin Williams) welcomes Cassim (Merwin Foard), the long-lost father of Aladdin (Brad Kane), to the palace and lists all the things they can do as father and son as they make up for lost time. Aladdin and Cassim join in, adding comments on the Genie's suggestions and making for a bouncy trio.

"Fathoms Below" is the rousing sea chantey that is used in the opening of the animated movie musical *The Little Mermaid* (1989). The sailors aboard Prince Eric's ship sing the brief Alan Menken (music) and Howard Ashman (lyric) song about King Triton, who rules the sea. The number was expanded for the 2008 Broadway version of *The Little Mermaid*, and Glenn Slater wrote additional lyrics, which were sung by the sailors and Eric (Sean Palmer).

"Fee Fi Fo Fum" is the bouncy character song for Willie the Giant (voice of Billy Gilbert) in the "Mickey and the Beanstalk" section of the animated anthology movie *Fun and Fancy Free* (1947). Paul J. Smith and Arthur Quenzer wrote the catchy ditty, in which Willie boasts that he can turn himself into anything if he uses the magic words of the title.

"Feed the Birds" is the haunting lullaby-ballad by Richard M. and Robert B. Sherman sung by the title character in the film musical *Mary Poppins* (1964). The nanny Mary (Julie Andrews) puts her two charges to bed and sings to them of the old Bird Woman, who sits on the steps of St. Paul's Cathedral and sells bird seed at tuppence a bag. As Mary sings, the scene dissolves to a dreamy view of St. Paul's and the old woman (veteran actress Jane Darwell in her last screen appearance) is surrounded by loving pigeons. Laura Michelle Kelly portrayed Mary in the 2004 London stage version of *Mary Poppins* and sang the number about the Bird Woman, played by Julia Sutton, who also joined in singing it. In the 2006 Broadway production the number was sung by Ashley Brown as Mary and Cass Morgan as the Bird Woman. Louis Prima and Gia Maione made a duet recording of the ballad. Other records were made by Hubert Nuss, Liz Callaway, and Barbara Hendricks and the Abbey Road Ensemble. Legend has it that "Feed the Birds" was Walt Disney's personal favorite of all the songs written for his company.

"Feel Like a Million" is the jazzy specialty number sung by Eartha Kitt in the animated made-for-video sequel *The Emperor's New Groove 2: Kronk's New Groove* (2005). The sinister Yzma (voice of Kitt) urges the naive chef Kronk to help her sell her fake youth potion so that both of them can become rich, conjuring up a Las Vegas–like production number in which they are showered with gold coins. Jeanine Tesori wrote the slinky song, which fits Kitt's purring delivery well. The number is also reprised by Kitt at a slower tempo during the end credits of the video.

"Feels Like Home" is the country-western-flavored love song written by Matthew Gerrard and Robbie Nevil for the animated video sequel *Brother*

Bear 2 (2006). Kenai, a Native American who has been transformed into a bear, brings his human sweetheart Nika to the waterfall where they once forged their love, and the two realize that their old feelings are still there. The tender lyric is about discovering an old friend and picking up where you left off. Melissa Etheridge and Josh Kelly sing the ballad on the soundtrack during the scene and the song is heard again during the closing credits of the video.

"Femininity" is the outdated but still entertaining song from the film *Summer Magic* (1963) that teaches a girl to be demure and feminine and not talk or laugh too much if she wants to win a man. Richard M. and Robert B. Sherman wrote the number, sung by Maine cousins Nancy (Hayley Mills) and Julia (Deborah Walley) to the shy Lallie Joy Popham (Wendy Turner) before going to a barn dance.

"Ferdinand the Bull" is the Spanish-flavored title song written by Albert Hay Malotte (music) and Larry Morey (lyric) for the 1938 film short, but only the music survived the final cut of the Oscar-winning movie. The narrative song relates the story of the peaceful bull Ferdinand, who would rather smell flowers than fight other bulls or matadors. When the short film was rewritten and nonsinging narration by Don Wilson was added, the song was not necessary, and only the music was used on the soundtrack. The playful number was published and showed up on children's records, and Michael Feinstein made a zesty recording of the song in 1992.

"Fidelity Fiduciary Bank" is the wry anthem-like tribute to the British banking system written by Richard M. and Robert B. Sherman for the movie musical *Mary Poppins* (1964). Aged bank chairman Mr. Dawes Sr. (Dick Van Dyke), Mr. Banks (David Tomlinson), and some stuffy bankers sing the pious number to young Michael Banks (Matthew Garber), urging him to deposit his tuppence in their bank and invest in the great British Empire. Instead of inspiring the youth, the men only succeed in frightening him with their greedy and antiquated views.

"Find Yourself" is the gentle song of reflection written by Brad Paisley for the computer-animated movie *Cars* (2006). Paisley sings the folk-like number, about having to be in a strange and new place in order to discover who you truly are, on the soundtrack at the end of the film. The song, sometimes listed as "When You Find Yourself," was recorded by Drew Seeley in 2007.

"Fire" is the explosive techno-rock song from the made-for-TV movie *Camp Rock 2: The Final Jam* (2010) that is performed by the campers at the rival Camp Star for the teens from Camp Rock at a bonfire in their honor. Dapo Torimiro and Lyrica Anderson created the intense number about igniting the fire in a performer's soul. The piece is led by Luke Williams (Matthew "Mdot" Finley) with assistance from the chorus.

"First" is the driving rock song written by Kara DioGuardi and John Shanks for the movie sequel *Herbie: Fully Loaded* (2005). The lyric is the boast of a jealous girl who is determined to become the first in the eyes of a certain guy. Lindsay Lohan, who starred in the film, sings the heavy metal number over the opening credits. The song is reprised at the beginning of the final credits as well. Lohan made a music video of the number.

"First Sign of Spring" is the pop ballad by Michelle Lewis and Daniel Petty that was used for a montage in the animated video sequel *Bambi II* (2006). With the coming of spring, the young Bambi is taught by his father how to be brave and act like a prince of the forest. On the soundtrack, songwriter Lewis sings the upbeat number about new beginnings, not only in nature but also for the father-son relationship.

"Flitterin'" is a sparkling ragtime number written by Richard M. and Robert B. Sherman for the period film *Summer Magic* (1963). When a player piano is delivered to the Carey home in Boston, siblings Nancy (Hayley Mills) and Gilly (Eddie Hodges) play one of the rolls, an energetic song about moving on in life and taking what comes with a positive attitude. The two sing the words that appear on the piano roll, and soon other family members and the two servants join them in dancing to the exuberant music.

"Fly to Your Heart" is the pop ballad written by Michelle Tumes for the animated video *Tinker Bell* (2008), a prequel of sorts to *Peter Pan* (1953). Selena Gomez sings the lightly pulsating number, about finding your own hidden talents and securing happiness by pursuing them, over the closing credits of the video.

"Follow Me, Boys!" is the rousing title song about team spirit and cooperation written by Richard M. and Robert B. Sherman for the 1966 film about a former jazz musician who starts a Boy Scout troop in a troubled midwestern town. Lem Siddons (Fred MacMurray) and his scouts sing the robust march song about working together, and for a time the Boy Scouts of America considered making the optimistic number their official anthem.

"Follow Your Heart" is the musical realization that being true to yourself means being yourself. It was written by Alan Zachary and Michael Weiner for the animated video sequel *Cinderella II: Dreams Come True* (2002). The newlywed Cinderella (voice of Jennifer Hale) is taught how to walk, sit, dress, and behave like a princess by the court events planner Prudence, but the lessons are a disaster until Cinderella embraces the idea that she should just act like herself. While the lessons unfold, this encouraging song is sung on the soundtrack by Brooke Allison.

"Following the Leader" is the contagious march that Oliver Wallace, Ted Sears, and Winston Hibler wrote for the animated film *Peter Pan* (1953). Londoners John (voice of Tommy Luske) and Michael (Paul Collins) lead the Lost Boys on an expedition to explore the island of Never Land, the group singing and whistling merrily as they bounce along. The tuneful sing-along number is also known as "Tee Dum–Tee Dee" and "March of the Lost Boys."

"For a Moment" is the melodic duet written by Michael and Patty Silversher for mother and daughter in the made-for-video animated sequel *The Little Mermaid II: Return to the Sea* (2000). The human girl Melody (voice of Tara Charendoff) is turned into a mermaid, and she celebrates her ability to join the creatures of the sea as she sings this expansive ballad. At the same time, her mother, Ariel (Jodi Benson), is worried about her and sings of her concerns, the two voices harmonizing together effectively.

"For Now, For Always" is the entrancing love song used throughout the movie *The Parent Trap* (1961). Richard M. and Robert B. Sherman wrote the flowing number about a new love that is bound to last forever, and it is first heard in the film when Maggie (Maureen O'Hara) sings part of it to her daughter Susan (Hayley Mills) as they stroll through a Boston park, recalling that it was the song played at the Italian restaurant on her first date with Susan's father. An instrumental version of the ballad is played on a record when the twin sisters set up a romantic environment for their separated parents, hoping to re-create their first date. Finally, a studio chorus sings it at the end of the movie when the parents remarry. Rebecca Luker made a notable recording of the song in 2003.

"For the First Time" is a piercing ballad of discovering love written by Phil Collins for the 2006 Broadway version of *Tarzan*. Jane Porter (Jenn Gambatese) realizes that the wild man Tarzan (Josh Strickland) makes her feel as no one else has, and she confesses to herself that she loves him. Tarzan reprises the song, experiencing the same feelings and wondering if she could ever love such a man as himself.

"The Forest of No Return" is an adaptation of a song from the 1903 Victor Herbert operetta *Babes in Toyland* which George Bruns (music) and Mel Leven (lyric) wrote for the 1961 screen version of the operetta. When Little Bo Peep (Ann Jillian) loses her sheep and looks for them in a haunted forest, a chorus of trees and children sing this creepy song of warning that uses musical instruments to imitate the sound of people walking on tiptoe.

"Forever and Ever" is the cheerful song of friendship written by Michael Abbott and Sarah Weeks for the made-for-video film *Pooh's Grand Adventure: The Search for Christopher Robin* (1997). Winnie the Pooh (voice of Jim Cummings) and Christopher Robin (Frankie J. Galasso) sing the spirited and sincere number, promising to remain friends forever and be as happy as they are now.

"Forget about Love" is the seriocomic love song written by Patty and Michael Silversher for the made-for-video animated film *The Return of Jafar* (1994). The sarcastic parrot Iago (voice of Gilbert Gottfried) tries to comfort the heartbroken Princess Jasmine (singing voice of Liz Callaway) when she realizes Aladdin (singing voice of Brad Kane) is keeping secrets from her. While Iago urges her to forget about her feelings for Aladdin, the princess sings of the good times she recalls. When Aladdin joins the scene, the song becomes a touching love duet punctuated by Iago's snide commentary.

"Fortune Favors the Brave" is the rock song of victory written by Elton John (music) and Tim Rice (lyric) for the Broadway musical *Aida* (2000). Radames (Adam Pascal), captain of the Egyptian army, and his soldiers sing the triumphant song as they return from conquering their longtime rivals the Nubians. The Egyptians sing that they are victorious because the fates have decreed it so, and Radames sees his future assured.

"Fortuosity" is the silly song of philosophy by Richard M. and Robert B. Sherman that optimistically believes that good luck will always turn up.

Newly arrived Irish butler John Lawless (Tommy Steele) sings the antic number in the film *The Happiest Millionaire* (1967) as he walks the streets of Philadelphia on his way to a job interview. Later in the period musical, he reprises the song as he chases down the pet alligators of his eccentric employer. Jason Graae recorded the number in 2003 as part of a medley of Sherman and Sherman nonsense songs.

"Friend Like Me" is the show-stopping character song from the animated movie *Aladdin* (1992) in which the exuberant Genie (voice of Robin Williams), just released from the lamp after hundreds of years, sings to Aladdin about the magical powers he possesses and how his friendship will take the youth to the top. While the Oscar-nominated song has its charm, it was overshadowed by Williams's vocal pyrotechnics and the Disney animators' Hirschfeld-like artwork in bringing the Genie to life. The song, sometimes listed as "You Ain't Never Had a Friend Like Me," was one of the few numbers Alan Menken (music) and Howard Ashman (lyric) completed years earlier, before they dropped the project. The delightful number was later interpolated into the mostly Menken–Tim Rice score. With a revised lyric by Kevin Rafferty, the Las Vegas–like number was used at the Disney World and Disneyland attraction the Enchanted Tiki Room when it was reworked in 1998. A bluegrass rendition of the original song was recorded by Mike Toppins, Glen Duncan, Billy Troy, Jim Brown, James Freeze, and David Chase.

"A Friendly Face" is the sweet character song Richard Rich wrote for the animated film short *The Small One* (1978). On the night before a young Boy (voice of Sean Marshall) must go into the city and sell his pet donkey Small One, he sings about the kindly man who might buy the undersized animal and care for him. The innocence of the Boy and his song is touching, and the delicate number is very effective.

"Friends for Life" is the swinging song of mutual devotion written by Michael and Patty Silversher for an episode of the animated television series *TaleSpin* (1990). The ape King Louis (Jim Cummings) from *The Jungle Book* (1967) makes a guest appearance at a flight stop in the jungle and sings this slaphappy number with the pilot Baloo the Bear (Ed Gilbert) in which they merrily insult each other but maintain that they are the closest of pals.

"Friends for Life" is the folk ballad about two pals who are alike in spirit written by Marcus Hummon for the animated video sequel *The Fox and the*

Hound 2 (2006). The country-flavored number is sung on the soundtrack by the group One Flew South while the young canine Copper and fox Tod frolic together in a pasture.

"Friends on the Other Side" is the sinister character song for Dr. Facilier (voice of Keith David) that Randy Newman wrote for the jazz-flavored animated film *The Princess and the Frog* (2009). Hoping to make a deal with the penniless Prince Naveen and his valet Lawrence, Facilier reads the tarot cards, guesses their dire circumstances, and offers to give them all they want—for a price. A chorus of demons and spirits from "the other side" back up Facilier in the song as dazzling visuals seem to hypnotize Naveen, Lawrence, and even the audience.

"Fun and Fancy Free" is the swinging title song from the 1947 animated anthology film, a scintillating number that happily suggests that one be happy-go-lucky and enjoy life. George Weiss and Bennie Benjamin wrote the vivacious number, which is sung by a chorus over the opening credits and is reprised by Jiminy Cricket (voice of Cliff Edwards) and the chorus at the end of the movie. Gene Krupa and his Orchestra (vocal by Buddy Hughes) had a popular recording of the song, as did the Dinning Sisters.

"Fun with Music Day" is the zesty theme song by Tom Adair (music) and Sidney Miller (lyric) used for Mondays on the television series *The Mickey Mouse Club* (1955). Jimmie Dodd and the Mouseketeers sing the number about music being a language that all people can understand and prepare the viewers for a program of songs both from home and from foreign lands.

"The Future Has Arrived" is the high-tech-sounding song by Danny Elfman that is heard in the animated movie *Meet the Robinsons* (2007). Over the closing credits of the film, the group All-American Rejects sings the number about letting go of the past and embracing what lies ahead. The song parallels the story of orphan Lewis, who gives up his search for his birth mother and happily adopts the wacky Robinsons as his family.

G

"The Galaxy Is Ours" is the rocking love song of the future, written by Donny Markowitz and Stu Krieger for the made-for-television space sequel *Zenon: The Zequel* (2001). The intergalactic rock star Proto Zoa (Phillip Rhys) and his band, the Cosmic Blush, sing the driving song in concert at the end of the movie, proclaiming that love has made his sweetheart and him the owners of the galaxy. Proto Zoa reprises the number on a television screen in the second television sequel, *Zenon: Z3* (2004).

"Gaston" is the vigorous character song by Alan Menken (music) and Howard Ashman (lyric) about the broad-shouldered, thickheaded villain Gaston in the animated film *Beauty and the Beast* (1991). Gaston (voice of Richard White) has been turned down by Belle, so his sidekick Lefou (Jesse Corti) and the patrons at Gaston's tavern cheer him up with this boneheaded tribute to the man of brawn. The number is reprised later in the movie by Gaston and Lefou, with different lyrics, as they plan to use Belle's father's insanity as a way to win Belle's hand in marriage. The fast-paced waltz was sung by Burke Moses, Kenny Raskin, and the ensemble in the 1994 Broadway version of the tale.

"Genovia Anthem" is the national song of the fictional kingdom of Genovia in the film sequel *The Princess Diaries 2: Royal Engagement* (2004). Bill Larkin (music) and Joel McCrary (lyric) wrote the bold number, full of pomp, which is sung by members of the court when Mia Thermopolis (Anne Hathaway) is crowned.

"Get on the Bus" is the cheery lite-rock song sung by the three Doodlebops—Rooney (Chad McNamara), Deedee (Lisa Lennox), and Moe (Jonathan Wexler)—in the television series *The Doodlebops* (2005). Carl Lenox wrote the sunny number, and the three colorfully costumed pop singers perform it on their magical bus, which opens up into a stage. The bus driver Bob (John Catucci) joins the threesome in inviting the viewers to board the bus that can go anywhere.

"Get'cha Head in the Game" is a cross between a patter song and rap number from the television production *High School Musical* (2006), in which the tempo of the song is set by the bouncing of basketballs and the screeching of sneakers in the school gym. Albuquerque teenager Troy Bolton (Zac Efron) and his fellow basketball players sing and dance the propulsive number, written by Ray Cham, Greg Cham, and Andrew Seeley, about concentrating on your goals as they dribble and slam dunk basket-balls, staged with ingenuity and verve by director-choreographer Kenny Ortega. The number is one of the highlights of the very popular television musical, and the song was recorded by the rhythm-and-blues group B5.

"Girl in the Band" is the eager pop-rock song written by Charlie Midnight and Chico Bennett for *The Lizzie McGuire Movie* (2003), the feature film sequel to the popular television series. When Jo Maguire (Hallie Todd, singing voice of Haylie Duff) is not feeling good about herself, she imagines she is a singer in a rock band and performs this song showing the world what she's got to offer.

"Girl Power" is the lite-rock testament to female empowerment sung by four teenage singers in the television movie *The Cheetah Girls* (2003). Although they are of different races, Galleria (Raven-Symoné), Chanel (Adrienne Bailon), Aqua (Kiely Williams), and Dorinda (Sabrina Bryan) are bound together like a family. They sing this number at an audition, holding their heads high because they have each other. The song, written by Ray Cham and Rawanna M. Barnes, was turned into a popular music video featuring the four Cheetah Girls.

"A Girl Worth Fighting For" is the delightfully ironic comic number writ-ten by Matthew Wilder (music) and David Zippel (lyric) for the animated

film *Mulan* (1998). As they march through the mountains of China, a band of
new recruits (voices of Harvey Fierstein, James Hong, Jerry Tondo, Wilder,
and the chorus) sing of the type of girl they desire, from a ravishing beauty to
a good cook. When the girl Mulan (singing voice of Lea Salonga), disguised
as a male soldier, suggests a bright woman who thinks for herself, the others dismiss the idea as unattractive. The song, with a revised lyric by Alexa
Junge, is also heard in the video sequel *Mulan II* (2005).

"Girls Are Like Boys" is the confused musical lesson Owl (voice of Andre
Stojka) sings in the animated television special *Winnie the Pooh: A Valentine for You* (1999). When Winnie the Pooh finds out that Christopher
Robin is making a valentine for a girl named Winifred, Owl has to explain
to the bear what a girl is, singing that they are just like boys, yet different
in every way. Michael and Patty Silversher wrote the waltzing number that
manages to confuse Pooh more than clarify matters.

"Girls of San Francisco" is the wry musical tribute to the pretty gals
from the California city who are always nice to gentlemen, as long as the
men take out their wallets and spend money on the girls. Richard M. and
Robert B. Sherman wrote the pastiche saloon number for the period film
The Adventures of Bullwhip Griffin (1967), and it was sung by Bostonian
Arabella Flagg (Suzanne Pleshette), who goes out West and gets a job as a
singer in the Lucky Nugget Saloon.

"Give a Little Whistle" is the tuneful song of caution about letting one's
conscience act as a guide in life, written by Leigh Harline (music) and Ned
Washington (lyric) for the animated movie fairy tale *Pinocchio* (1940). The
snappy number is sung by Jiminy Cricket (voice of Cliff Edwards) and
Pinocchio (Dickie Jones) as they dance about Geppetto's toy shop and celebrate Jiminy's being made Pinocchio's conscience by the Blue Fairy. Edwards recorded the number, which, as the title suggests, involves a certain
amount of whistling. The song was heard on children's records for years,
and Barbara Cook made a distinctive recording in 1988.

"The Gnome-Mobile" is the jaunty title song that Richard M. and Robert
B. Sherman wrote for the 1967 film fantasy about gnomes in the redwood
forests of California. The young gnome Jasper (Tom Lowell) tells the lumber tycoon D. J. Mulrooney (Walter Brennan) and his two grandchildren
(Matthew Garber and Karen Dotrice) that he cannot find a mate because
the lumber business has driven so many of the gnomes from the forest.

Mulrooney decides to help, christens his Rolls-Royce Phantom II the "gnome-mobile," and gets the grumpy old gnome Knobby (also Brennan) to join them. The group sets off to find the gnomes, singing this sprightly song about the car that will take them on an adventure.

"Go the Distance" is the stirring "I am" song of the teenage Hercules (voice of Roger Bart) as he laments his awkward super-strength and sets off to find his true identity in the animated film *Hercules* (1997). Alan Menken composed the penetrating music, David Zippel provided the eager lyric, and Michael Bolton sang the Oscar-nominated song over the final credits. Bolton's recording was very popular, and in 2000 Earl Rose made a pleasing jazz version of the song. There was also a notable recording by Lucas Grabeel in 2007.

"God Help the Outcasts" is the simple hymn the gypsy girl Esmeralda (singing voice of Heidi Mollenhauer) and others in the cathedral sing in the animated movie *The Hunchback of Notre Dame* (1996). Alan Menken composed the unadorned music and Stephen Schwartz wrote the fervent lyric, which asks for a blessing on all of life's rejected ones. Bette Midler sings the song over the closing credits of the film. Kerry Butler made a notable recording in 2008, linked with "It's a Small World."

"The Gods Love Nubia" is the rousing first act finale of the Broadway musical *Aida* (2000) written by Elton John (music) and Tim Rice (lyric). When the Nubian princess Aida (Heather Headley) learns that the Egyptians have conquered her land and captured her father, she stirs up the Nubians to revolt with this stirring gospel-like number. Kelly Price recorded the song before the musical opened on Broadway.

"The Golden Touch" is the piquant title song written by Frank Churchill for the 1935 Silly Symphony film short based on the mythological tale of King Midas. The narrative ballad tells of King Midas (voice of Billy Bletcher), who craves riches and is granted the gift of the golden touch by a magical elf called Goldie. When everything Midas touches turns to gold, he is thrilled until he realizes he cannot eat food without it becoming hardened gold before it reaches his mouth. The short movie is practically sung through and resembles a mini-operetta.

"Goliath of Gath" is the powerful musical scene from the Broadway pageant-concert *King David* (1997). The title character (Marcus Lovett) confronts the giant Goliath (Bille Nolte) in an explosive musical fight to the death. The soldiers of the Philistine army look on as young David eradicates this massive bully to the strains of Alan Menken's aggressive melody. Soon the song evolves into exclamations by an awestruck chorus. Tim Rice wrote the lyrics, which are full of exposition, character development, and raw emotion.

"Gonna Take You There" is the joyous hillbilly number that Randy Newman wrote about traveling through the bayou with the help of all the critters, heard in the animated movie *The Princess and the Frog* (2009). The big-hearted firefly Ray (voice of Jim Cummings) sings the number with a thick Cajun accent to Prince Naveen and Tiana, two humans turned into frogs, and his crooning is backed by a jubilant jug band.

"Good Company" is the simple but memorable childlike lullaby written by Rob Minkoff and Ron Rocha for the animated film *Oliver & Company* (1988). The wealthy Manhattan girl Jenny (singing voice of Myhanh Tran) sings the song about being together forever with her new pet kitten, Oliver, the human playing the piano and the cat exploring the instrument. The music continues under a montage of the twosome playing together in Central Park, and then Jenny sings it again to Oliver as they go to bed.

"Good Doggie, No Bone!" is the bluesy country-western number written by Marcus Hummon for the made-for-video animated sequel *The Fox and the Hound 2* (2006). The canine singer Dixie (voice of Reba McEntire), joined by backup singers, laments the fleeting nature of fame and how no one remembers you when you're not on top. The song is accompanied by howls that are both silly and touching.

"Good Life" is the carefree rock song written by Boots Ottestaad for the made-for-TV movie *Stuck in the Suburbs* (2004). During a montage in which the teenager Brittany Aarons (Danielle Panabaker) writes lyrics for the pop star Jordan Cahill (Taran Killam), Jesse McCartney is heard singing on the soundtrack this musical suggestion to enjoy your life before it slips away from you.

"Good Life" is the pop ballad about finding happiness in your own hometown written by Jeannie Lurie and Brandon Christy for the television movie *The Muppets' Wizard of Oz* (2005). Dorothy (Ashanti) sings the lite-rock number on a television broadcast from the Emerald City and then reprises it with the Muppets as they tour the country with their show.

"Good News" is the catchy exposition song that ends the part-live-action, part-stop-motion movie *James and the Giant Peach* (1996). Randy Newman wrote the number and sings it over a montage of newspaper headlines showing the fame that awaits James and his animal friends after they travel over the Atlantic Ocean to New York City on a giant floating peach. The narrative song recaps the plot of the film just viewed and concludes with the happy ending covered by the press.

"Good Night Valais" is the delicate lullaby written by G. Haenni and Tom Adair for the movie *Third Man on the Mountain* (1959), set in the Swiss Alps. During a village festival, the town chorus of Kurtal sings the sleepy number about putting a city to bed for the night. The lyric uses the poetic metaphor of the sky becoming a jeweled cape wrapped around the earth, and the dreamy melody is delicate, lulling the listener into a restful slumber.

 "Goodbye May Seem Forever" is the farewell song that Richard Rich (music) and Jeffrey C. Patch (lyric) wrote for the animated film *The Fox and the Hound* (1981). As the Widow Tweed (voice of Jeanette Nolan) drives through the countryside, taking her pet fox Tod to the game reserve where he will be safe, she talk-sings her thoughts about parting with her beloved animal friend. A chorus picks up the song and sings it on the soundtrack as the two part ways in the forest.

"Goodbye So Soon" is the light and breezy farewell song that is used for a sinister purpose in the animated movie *The Great Mouse Detective* (1986). Henry Mancini (music), Larry Grossman, and Ellen Fitzhugh (lyric) wrote the mocking number and it is sung by the villain Ratigan (voice of Vincent Price) on a phonograph record. In an elaborate device to kill the detective Basil and his assistant, Dr. Dawson, Ratigan has attached a string to the arm of the phonograph, and as the record plays, the string pulls a mechanism that sets off a deadly set of weapons aimed at the two victims. The ending of the song is not heard because Basil outwits Ratigan and stops the device. A studio chorus reprises the number over the end credits of the film.

"Goodbye Song" is the up-tempo lullaby by Tyler Bunch that closes each episode of the children's television series *Bear in the Big Blue House*

(1997). At the end of the show, the oversized Muppet Bear (voice of Noel MacNeal) asks the moon, Luna (Lynne Thigpen), to sing a farewell song, and the two of them sing goodbye to viewers and promise to return again.

"Goof Troop" is the rocking title number from the 1992 animated television series, a number that celebrates the father-son team of Goofy and Max, who have adventures together, often to the embarrassment of the son. Robert Irving, Randy Petersen, and Kevin Quinn wrote the very 1950s-like song, filled with backup "bop bop bee bop" vocals, and it is sung by a male chorus over the opening credits.

"The Gospel Truth" is the vivacious opening song by Alan Menken (music) and David Zippel (lyric) for the animated film *Hercules* (1997). The mock-gospel number is sung by the Muses (voices of Lilias White, La Chanze, Tawatha Agee, Roz Ryan, Cheryl Freeman, and Vanessa Thomas) as they begin the adventure story, giving expositional information about the baby Hercules and setting the comic, anachronistic tone for the film.

"Gotta Find You" is the lonely torch song about a young man who is looking for something special and unique, written by Adam Watts and Andy Dodd for the television musical *Camp Rock* (2008). Pop singer Shane Gray (Joe Jonas) of the music group Connect 3 is sent to be a counselor at Camp Rock to improve his bad-boy image. In this number, he tries to revamp his writing style to sound more like the music he wants to sing.

"Gotta Fly" is the bubbly closing song for the television series *Dumbo's Circus* (1985), which uses "puppetronics" to present a new adventure at the circus each week. Phillip Baron wrote the tuneful number, which is not about Dumbo's ability to fly but rather explains to the audience that the show is over and the characters have to leave. A chorus sings the circus-like song while all the puppets pack up their things in the wagons and depart for another town.

"Gotta Go My Own Way" is the pop duet for two sweethearts parting written by Andy Dodd and Adam Watts for the television movie *High School Musical 2* (2007). When teenager Gabriella (Vanessa Anne Hudgens) realizes that her boyfriend Troy (Zac Efron) has changed since he has been spending time with his manipulating benefactress Sharpay Evans (Ashley Tisdale), she decides she can no longer be his girlfriend and sings this heartfelt pop ballad as she tells Troy they must break up. He pleads with her in song to not leave him, but Gabriella insists on going her own way.

"The Grandest Easter of Them All" is the sprightly holiday number that Randy Rogel (music and lyric) and Grant Geissman (lyric) wrote for the animated video *Winnie the Pooh: Springtime with Roo* (2004). Rabbit (voice of Ken Sansom) has just about ruined Easter with all his rules about how to celebrate it, but he comes to his senses and sings this bubbly song as he quickly prepares eggs and decorations for his friends.

"Great Spirits" is the rocking narrative ballad by Phil Collins that opens the animated movie *Brother Bear* (2003) about a Native American who is turned into a bear. As three Inuit siblings set out in their kayaks and are seen living in harmony with nature, Tina Turner sings the propulsive folk song about three brothers who will be changed by the great spirits of nature, making all creatures brothers. Collins also recorded the number.

Walt Disney hired top songwriters for even his theme park attractions, seeing a "ride" as another theatrical production. Buddy Baker and Xavier Attencio wrote the sly song "Grim Grinning Ghosts" for the Haunted Mansion (pictured here) and it was sung by the deep-voiced Thurl Ravenscroft, an actor heard in several Disney theme park attractions. (Walt Disney/Photofest)

"Grim Grinning Ghosts" is the merry song of haunting written by Buddy Baker (music) and Xavier Attencio (lyric) for the theme park attraction the Haunted Mansion, which opened at Disneyland in 1969 and was later recreated in the other parks. The silly, spooky song, recorded by Thurl Ravenscroft and a male chorus of ghosts, is heard throughout the ride, punctuated by howls, moans, and other ghostly noises. Although the song warns about the hundreds of spirits that haunt the mansion, the number is upbeat and comedic, managing—like the attraction itself—to be both scary and funny at the same time. The song was also used in the film *The Haunted Mansion* (2003). A recording of the number was made by the band Barenaked Ladies.

"Grimpons" is the flavorful French ditty written by Richard M. and Robert B. Sherman for the adventure movie *In Search of the Castaways* (1962). As the search party travels through the Andes Mountains, Professor Jacques Paganel (Maurice Chevalier) sings the catchy number about facing adversity without fear. Mary Grant (Hayley Mills) and the young aristocrat John Glenarvan (Michael Anderson Jr.) soon join the French professor in singing the song.

"Guest Star Day" is the happy theme song used for Tuesdays on the television series *The Mickey Mouse Club* (1955). Adult host Jimmie Dodd wrote the ditty and sang it with the Mouseketeers, announcing that Tuesday is the day the club receives a visit from a special guest, so everyone prepares by sweeping (and dancing) with brooms and literally rolling out a red carpet for the guest star. Sometimes Jimmie and the kids wore formal wear for the number: white tie and tails for the boys and long evening gowns for the girls. The song is sometimes listed as "Today Is Tuesday."

"Gummi Bears Theme" is the scintillating march song written by Michael and Patty Silversher for the 1985 television series *Disney's Adventures of the Gummi Bears*. The theme song, sung over the opening credits of each show, praises the magical bear residents of Gummi Glen, who use their powers of bravery and caring to protect the citizens from evil. The song was originally sung by a harmonizing chorus, but later in the series' run the theme was given a more throbbing, forceful rendition.

"Gummiberry Juice" is the playful musical recipe that figured in several episodes in the animated television series *Disney's Adventures of the Gummi Bears* (1985). Michael and Patty Silversher wrote the pop song, which has a touch of medieval accompaniment, listing the ingredients needed to make the special potion that allows one to bounce like a kangaroo. The simple number is sung by a children's chorus over sequences in which the Gummi Bears make and drink the beloved gummiberry concoction.

"A Guy Like You" is the comic vaudeville-style number by Alan Menken (music) and Stephen Schwartz (lyric) that seems a bit out of place in the dark animated film *The Hunchback of Notre Dame* (1996) but is delightful in its own way. Three cathedral gargoyles (singing voices of Jason Alexander, Mary Stout, and Charles Kimbrough) try to cheer up hunchbacked Quasimodo (Tom Hulce) by pointing out his unique features and the unusual appeal he must have for the ladies.

H

"Hail the Princess Aurora" is the regal opening number from the animated movie *Sleeping Beauty* (1959) in which the Disney Studio Chorus sings the welcoming song on the soundtrack as royalty, gentry, and peasants arrive at the castle to honor the newborn princess. George Bruns wrote the music, based on the final movement of Tchaikovsky's *The Sleeping Beauty* ballet, and Tom Adair wrote the majestic lyric.

"Hakuna Matata" is the dandy Oscar-nominated song of easygoing philosophy written by Elton John (music) and Tim Rice (lyric) for the animated film *The Lion King* (1994), introducing the African phrase to popular Western culture. Meerkat Timon (voice of Nathan Lane) and warthog Pumbaa (Ernie Sabella) try to cheer up the guilt-ridden lion cub Simba (Jason Weaver) with this snappy number, the title being a Swahili phrase meaning "no worries." Young Simba joins in the song, and in a montage showing the passage of time, grown-up Simba (voice of Matthew Broderick) joins them as well. In the 1997 Broadway version of *The Lion King*, the waggish number was sung by Max Casella, Tom Alan Robbins, Scott Irby-Ranniar, and Jason Raize as the first-act finale. "Hakuna Matata" is the theme song for the television series *The Lion King's Timon and Pumbaa* (1995) and is used throughout the made-for-video sequel *The Lion King 1½* (2004), becoming a sing-along number at one point. A noteworthy recording of the song was made by Jimmy Cliff and Lebo M, and the number was included in the chorale recording *Rhythm of the Pridelands*. The group Baha Men recorded the song in 2002.

"Half of Me" is the romantic ballad about love being the union of two different halves, heard over the opening credits of the film *The Last Flight of Noah's Ark* (1980). Maurice Jarre wrote the flowing number, and it is sung by Alexandra Brown, the lyric foreshadowing the relationship in the movie between a surly pilot and a missionary.

"Handy Manny Theme Song" is the Spanish-flavored number by Fernando Rivas that introduces the title character of the 2006 animated television series about a Latino handyman. During the opening sequence, in which Manny is seen with his magic tools as he makes repairs, a male chorus sings the easygoing rumba song with a lyric that is simply a rhythmic repetition of his name.

"Hang in There, Baby" is the catchy pop anthem to tenacity that serves as the theme song for the 2010 Disney Channel sitcom *Good Luck Charlie*. The program follows the Duncan family, who has just welcomed their fourth child into the family. Each episode features the oldest sibling, Teddy (Bridgit Mendler), creating an instructional video for her baby sister, offering her advice on how to survive in the household. The theme song, performed by Mendler, reassures the toddler that she just needs to hang in there no matter how crazy things get. Jeanne Lurie, Chen Neeman, and Aris Archontis provided the music and lyrics.

"The Happiest Girl Alive" is the gushing "I am" song for Nebraska farm girl Alice Bower (Lesley Ann Warren) in the movie musical *The One and Only, Genuine, Original Family Band* (1968). Contemplating a future married to Joe Carder, a newspaperman she has been corresponding with but has never met, Alice sings the Richard M. and Robert B. Sherman number as she cavorts in a pasture with some horses.

"The Happiest Home in These Hills" is the raucous song sung by the backwoods redneck Gogan family in the part-animated, part-live-action movie *Pete's Dragon* (1977). Lena Gogan (Shelley Winters) and her crude family (Jeff Conaway, Gary Morgan, and Charles Tyner) search the woods for the runaway youth Pete, promising baked goods, campouts, and other fun things if he will return to them. Yet under their breath the family revels in the torturous things they plan to inflict on the boy once they get their hands on him. Al Kasha and Joel Hirschhorn wrote the humorous yet devious number, which bounces back and forth between playful and menacing images.

"Happy, Happy Birthday" is the alternate birthday song written by Michael and Patty Silversher to be used in Disney celebrations, avoiding the copyright restrictions of the familiar "Happy Birthday" standard. This number is more pop and danceable than the old favorite and lends itself to various kinds of uses. The number debuted on the 1983 Disney album *Mickey Mouse Splashdance* and the next year was used in the television special *Donald Duck's 50th Birthday*. Since then, the birthday song has been used in the theme parks' parades to celebrate special occasions.

"Happy Pooh Year" is the brief and sunny march written by Michael and Patty Silversher for the seasonal video *Winnie the Pooh: A Very Merry Pooh Year* (2002). Winnie the Pooh (voice of Jim Cummings) sings the cheerful little ditty as he trudges through the snow with his "hunny" pot to attend a New Year's Eve party with his friends in the Hundred Acre Wood.

"Happy Working Song" is the hilarious spoof of "Whistle While You Work" written by Alan Menken (music) and Stephen Schwartz (lyric) for the modern fairy tale movie *Enchanted* (2007). The naive Giselle (Amy Adams) from the cartoon kingdom of Andalasia finds herself in a ritzy but messy Manhattan apartment, so she sings out to her animal friends, and soon rats, pigeons, and cockroaches come and help her make the place clean as a whistle. The idiotically cheerful music is complimented by wry lyrics about scrubbing toilets and using vermin for cleanliness. The clever song was nominated for an Oscar, one of three from the movie given that distinction.

"Hasta La Vista" is the driving hip-hop number performed by teenage camper Baron (Jordan Francis) for the "Final Jam" night in the television movie musical *Camp Rock* (2008). Toby Gad, Pam Sheyne, and Kovasciar Myvette wrote the insistent music and repetitive lyric about it being time to go home.

"Hawaiian Roller Coaster Ride" is the catchy pseudo-Polynesian song by Alan Silvestri and Mark Keali'i Ho'omalu that is used effectively in the animated movie *Lilo and Stitch* (2002). When the Hawaiian girl Lilo spends a day at the beach with her sister Nani and Nani's boyfriend, David, she brings along the alien Stitch. Songwriter Keali'i Ho'omalu and the Kamehameha Children's Chorus sing the traditional yet poppy number during a montage of the characters' beach adventures. The song is reprised during the opening credits of the video sequel *Lilo and Stitch 2: Stitch Has a Glitch* (2005), and an upbeat, more contemporary version of the song was recorded by the group Jump 5, who are heard singing it over the closing credits of the video.

"He Needs Me" is the sweet and awkward ballad written by Harry Nilsson for the surreal film *Popeye* (1980). The gangly Olive Oyl (Shelley Duvall) sings the pathetically charming song on the streets of Sweethaven when she finds out that Popeye loves her. As her awkward voice happily climbs the musical scale, all the neighbors slam their windows shut, and Olive goes into an odd, disarming dance solo that is like a cartoon come alive.

"The Headless Horseman" is a dandy narrative ballad about the mysterious phantom who haunts Sleepy Hollow in the animated film *The Adventures of Ichabod and Mr. Toad* (1949). Gene de Paul and Don Raye wrote the evocative number, which is sung by Bing Crosby and the Rhythmaires on the soundtrack while the brawny Brom Bones tells the story to the fearful schoolmaster Ichabod Crane in order to scare him out of town.

"The Healing of a Heart" is the pop ballad about forgiveness and coming through adversity written by Marcus Hummon for the animated video sequel *Bambi II* (2006). Anthony Callea sings the smooth number over the final credits of the video, the lyric commenting on the difficult relationship between the young Bambi and his father.

"Heart & Soul" is the honky-tonk-flavored number performed by pop-stars-turned-camp-counselors Shane (Joe Jonas), Nate (Nick Jonas), and Jason (Kevin Jonas) Gray in the 2010 made-for-TV film *Camp Rock 2: The Final Jam*. The three brothers, in prepping the camp for its final showcase, perform this upbeat number about putting your heart and soul into whatever you do. The toe-tapping number was written by Tim James, Antonina Armato, Steve Rushton, and Aaron Dudley.

"Heaven's Light/Hellfire" is the contrasting song combination by Alan Menken (music) and Stephen Schwartz (lyric) from the animated film *The Hunchback of Notre Dame* (1996). When the lonely hunchback Quasimodo (voice of Tom Hulce) receives a friendly smile from the gypsy girl Esmeralda, his heart is filled with the kind of glow he has seen in others who are in love. This airy ballad is then overtaken by the prayer of the sinister judge Frollo (Tony Jay), who lusts after Esmeralda and wants her destroyed if he cannot have her. "Hellfire," with its Latin chanting by priests in the background, the lyric's many references to Frollo's burning desire, and the sensual graphics as Frollo sees the voluptuous Esmeralda in the fire of his imagination, is perhaps the most erotic scene to be found in any Disney animated film.

"Heffalumps and Woozles" is the musical nightmare experienced by Winnie the Pooh in the Oscar-winning movie short *Winnie the Pooh and the Blustery Day* (1968). Richard M. and Robert B. Sherman wrote the slightly menacing number about fantastic creatures (somewhat resembling elephants and weasels) that haunt Pooh's dreams when he is asleep. The Mellomen sing the eerie song on the soundtrack, and it is not unlike the "Pink Elephants on Parade" sequence in *Dumbo* (1941), though less frightening and surreal. The song's nightmarish creatures later inspired the animated feature film *Pooh's Heffalump Movie* (2005) and the made-for-video film *Pooh's Heffalump Halloween Movie* (2005).

"Heigh-Ho (It's Off to Work We Go)" is the unforgettable marching song the seven little miners sing and whistle as they go to and come home from work in the animated fairy tale movie *Snow White and the Seven Dwarfs* (1937). Frank Churchill (music) and Larry Morey (lyric) wrote the familiar ditty, which has been used as a work song in many situations over the years, such as in the 1938 film comedy *Having Wonderful Time*. The simple, repetitive number has been recorded by such diverse artists as Louis Armstrong, Mary Martin, and Horace Heidt and his Musical Knights, and a bluegrass rendition was recorded by Mike Toppins, Glen Duncan, Billy Troy, Jim Brown, James Freeze, and David Chase. Sometimes listed as "The Dwarfs' Marching Song," it remains one of the most recognized pieces of music in American popular culture.

"Help Me Plant My Corn" is the catchy, repetitive little ditty written by Leigh Harline for the Silly Symphony film short *The Wise Little Hen* (1934) which is mostly remembered for introducing the character of Donald Duck. Mother Hen (voice of Florence Gill) sings to Donald and other animals, asking for help in planting the corn, but everyone complains of a stomachache and begs off. When the corn is harvested and the lazy animals want to share in eating the corn, Mother Hen gives them a bottle of castor oil for their upset stomachs.

"Her Voice" is the heartfelt ballad written by Alan Menken (music) and Glenn Slater (lyric) for the 2008 Broadway version of *The Little Mermaid*. Prince Eric (Sean Palmer) is haunted by the voice of the unseen beauty who rescued him, and he prays for her to come and set him free. The lyric is simple and direct, yet the music has a lush and regal flavor that is appropriate for a prince in a fairy tale.

"Here Beside Me" is the gentle love song about the compromises people make when they are in love, written by Joel McNeely (music) and Kate Light (lyric) for the animated video sequel *Mulan II* (2005). Hayley Westenra sings the romantic number on the soundtrack over the closing credits, the lyrics commenting on the compromises the sweethearts Mulan and Shang have made in the preceding story.

"Here I Am" is the soothing theme song for the television series *Nurses* (1991), a spin-off of the popular sitcom *Empty Nest* (1988). George Tipton wrote the gentle music, set to the pulse of a heart monitor, and John Bettis penned the lyric paying tribute to the dedication and compassion of nurses, the subject of the series.

"Here I Am" is the driving rock number by John Adair and Steve Hampton that serves as the theme song for the television series *The Suite Life of Zack and Cody* (2005), a situation comedy about twin boys who live in a Boston hotel suite and wreak havoc on the staff and guests. The insistent song, sung on the soundtrack by Loren Ellis and the Drew Davis Band, invites viewers to come on down to the "suite life," where everyone can have the place to themselves.

"Here I Am" is the demanding character song teenage camper Peggy (Jasmine Richards) sings at the "Final Jam" music competition that concludes the summer in the made-for-television movie musical *Camp Rock* (2008). Peggy, who until now has been the backup singer to camp diva Tess, steps out of the shadows and demands to be heard in this potent cry to be noticed. Jamie Houston wrote the frustrated rock melody and the forceful lyric.

"Here in Higglytown" is the lite-rock theme song for the animated television series *Higglytown Heroes* (2004) about a town populated by round and rolling citizens, in which firemen, Coast Guard workers, and others are celebrated as heroes. John Flansburgh, John Linnell, and Dan Miller wrote the happy number, which is sung on the soundtrack by They Might Be Giants, who also made a music video of the song that teaches that you too can be a hero.

"Here on Land and Sea" is the festive calypso number written by Michael and Patty Silversher for the ending of the made-for-video animated sequel *The Little Mermaid II: Return to the Sea* (2000). After Ariel's daughter, Melody, has been rescued from the sea witch Morgana, the crab Sebastian (voice of Samuel E. Wright) leads the humans and the sea creatures in this song of celebration, promising happiness now that the two worlds are at peace with each other.

"Here We Go, Another Plan" is the comic character song for the frustrated pirate Mr. Smee (voice of Jeff Bennett) in the animated movie sequel *Return to Never Land* (2002). Randy Rogel wrote the sea chantey–like number, which Smee sings to himself after Captain Hook (Corey Burton) announces a new plan to capture Peter Pan. Smee reflects on Hook's failures in the past and sees another bungle in this new plot.

"Here's the Happy Ending" is the finale number written by Jay Blackton (music) and Joe Cook (lyric) for the 1979 Radio City Music Hall stage version of *Snow White and the Seven Dwarfs*. Snow White (Mary Jo Salerno) and Prince Charming (Richard Bowne) led the company in the joyous song that celebrates the defeat of the witch and the awakening of Snow White to be reunited with the prince. The production was taped and broadcast on pay TV in 1980 and on the Disney Channel in 1987 as *Snow White Live*.

"He's a Tramp" is the cool and sexy tribute to an unfaithful lover written by Peggy Lee and Sonny Burke for the animated film *Lady and the Tramp* (1955). When the well-bred cocker spaniel Lady is put in the dog pound, the worldly-wise canine Peg (voice of Peggy Lee) sings to her about the freewheeling mutt Tramp, whom she loves even though he is a bounder. The group Jazz Networks made a notable recording of the song in 1996, as did the Beu Sisters in 2004. There was a pleasing duet version in 2005 by Ashley Brown and Kaitlin Hopkins, and the next year it was recorded by Steve Tyrell.

"He's Gonna Make It" is the zippy song about unlikely success that is heard over the opening credits of the movie comedy *The Barefoot Executive* (1971), about a mail clerk who uses monkeys to determine which television shows will be successful. Robert F. Brunner wrote the pop music, Bruce Belland penned the lyric about working your way to the top, and it is sung by a studio chorus on the soundtrack.

"He's Large" is the awkward song of admiration sung by the insecure Olive Oyl (Shelley Duvall) in the surreal movie musical *Popeye* (1980). When asked by her girlfriends what she sees in her bullying fiancé Bluto, his size is the only attribute she can come up with. Harry Nilsson wrote the enharmonic number, which perfectly matches the fragile nature of Olive Oyl.

"Hey, Jessie" is the theme song for the 2011 Disney Channel series *Jessie*, about an eighteen-year-old Texas country girl who leaves home and finds a job as a nanny in New York City. There she takes care of the four Ross children whose wealthy parents are constantly traveling. The song, a lively pop number, is sung by series star and Disney Channel favorite Debbie Ryan. With music and lyrics by Toby Gad and Lindy Robbins, the ditty is told from Jessie's point of view and relates how she keeps hearing her name being called by the kids she is taking care of.

"Hi-Diddle-Dee-Dee (An Actor's Life for Me)" is the tuneful ode to the lure of show business, written for the animated film *Pinocchio* (1940) by Leigh Harline (music) and Ned Washington (lyric). The sly fox J. Worthington Foulfellow (voice of Walter Catlett) sings of the glory of the stage to the wooden puppet Pinocchio (Dickie Jones) as he leads him to enslavement with Stromboli's marionette troupe. The merry, carefree song is in contrast to the sinister situation, although out of context it is a cheerful celebration of the acting profession.

"High School Musical" is the energetic number the seniors of East Side High School sing at graduation in the film sequel *High School Musical 3: Senior Year* (2008). Matthew Gerrard and Robbie Nevil wrote the upbeat number, which the graduates sing and then dance to, the whole musical sequence serving as a curtain call for the three-part musical series.

"High Times, Hard Times" is the rousing nineteenth-century pastiche number written by Alan Menken (music) and Jack Feldman (lyric) for the period musical film *Newsies* (1992). Vaudeville star Medda Larkson (Ann-Margret) lends her theatre to the striking newsboys so they can have a rally. She joins the boys in singing this upbeat number that looks at life's good times and bad.

"Higitus Figitus" is the clever song of magic written by Richard M. and Robert B. Sherman for the animated movie *The Sword in the Stone* (1963). The wizard Merlin (voice of Karl Swenson) sings the playful incantation of English and fake Latin phrases as he makes all the objects in his cottage shrink in size and disappear into his carpetbag. The number is the first of several Sherman brothers songs to use a made-up nonsense title. Jason Graae recorded the number as part of a medley of nonsense songs in 2003.

"Hip-Hip-Pooh-Ray!" is the joyous song of celebration written by Richard M. and Robert B. Sherman for the ending of the Oscar-winning movie short *Winnie the Pooh and the Blustery Day* (1968). After Winnie the Pooh (accidentally) rescues Piglet from a flood in the Hundred Acre Wood, all of Pooh's friends celebrate while a studio chorus sings the happy number on the soundtrack.

"Hoedown Throwdown" is the boot-stomping, country-western dance number performed by Miley Stewart/Hannah Montana (Miley Cyrus) at a fundraising hoedown in *Hannah Montana: The Movie* (2009). Offered the open microphone, Miley takes the stage and soon she has the whole room moving to the ditty, which is basically a list song of all the moves you have to do to participate. The invigorating number, written by Adam Anders and Nikki Anders, is reprised over the closing credits.

"Hoist the Colours" is the haunting song that calls forth the "brethren court" of pirates in the movie sequel *Pirates of the Caribbean: At World's End* (2007). Hans Zimmer and Gore Verbinski wrote the hypnotic music and Ted Elliott and Terry Rossio penned the foreboding lyric, which demands that the pirates answer the call and convene. The song is first heard in the opening sequence when pirates are being hanged in large clusters for their treachery. A young cabin boy (Brendyn Bell) starts the singing, and soon all of the condemned join in. The chilling song is reprised by Elizabeth Swann (Kiera Knightley) in Singapore as she prepares to meet the pirate Barbossa (Geoffrey Rush) to discuss going to the world's end to bring back pirate Jack Sparrow (Johnny Depp) from Davy Jones's locker.

"Home" is the poignant ballad written by Alan Menken (music) and Tim Rice (lyric) for the 1994 Broadway version of *Beauty and the Beast*. Having agreed to become the Beast's prisoner in order to free her sickly father, Belle (Susan Egan) recalls her happy home and wonders if she will ever get to return to it. Later in the show, Mrs. Potts (Beth Fowler) reprises the song and encourages Belle to think of the Beast's castle as her new home.

"Home Is" is the warm ballad in the pop mode that Ariel (voice of Jodi Benson) sings about her underwater domain in an episode of the animated television series *The Little Mermaid* (1992). In the up-tempo song, Ariel expresses her love for her world, a place of warmth and wonders where various sea creatures and plant life abound.

"Home Is Where the Heart Is" is the up-tempo lullaby written by Michael and Patty Silversher for an episode of the animated television series *TaleSpin* (1990). The bear Becky Cunningham (voice of Sally Struthers) sings this affectionate ballad, promising always to hold a place in her heart that is like home, to her young daughter Molly as she puts her to bed.

"Home on the Range" is the western-flavored title song for the 2004 animated movie, a number used as a leitmotif throughout the film to accentuate the desert setting and satirically comment on the clichés of the Wild West. Alan Menken (music) and Glenn Slater (lyric) wrote the pastiche number, complete with "yeehaws" punctuating the song, and it is sung by Tim Blevins, Gregory Jbara, William Perry, Wilbur Pauley, and Peter Samuel on the soundtrack each time the bovine characters in the story move on to their next adventure. The number is sometimes listed as "You Ain't Home on the Range."

"Honor to Us All" is the tuneful character song from the animated film *Mulan* (1998) that establishes the traditions of China and introduces the title character. Two Chinese women (voices of Beth Fowler and Marni Nixon) sing the Oriental-flavored number as they prepare the maiden Mulan (singing voice of Lea Salonga) for presentation at the matchmaker's, hoping to get her a good husband and maintain the family heritage. Mulan reprises the song as a prayer to her ancestors, hoping she will not disappoint them. Matthew Wilder (music) and David Zippel (lyric) wrote the revealing number that has a trace of an Asian sound to it.

"Hooray Hooray!" is the joyful little ditty Winnie the Pooh (voice of Jim Cummings) sings on Thanksgiving Day as he looks forward to giving thanks and eating honey in the made-for-video film *Winnie the Pooh: Seasons of Giving* (1999). Michael and Patty Silversher wrote the tuneful number, which is as simple as it is innocent.

"The Horribly Hazardous Heffalumps" is the facile song by Carly Simon (music) and Brian Hohlfeld (lyric) that describes the mysterious creatures in the animated film *Pooh's Heffalump Movie* (2005). The silly list song, in which the Heffalumps are described with contradictory characteristics, is sung by Winnie the Pooh (voice of Jim Cummings), Rabbit (Ken Sansom), Tigger (also Cummings), Eeyore (Peter Cullen), Piglet (John Fiedler), and Roo (Nikita Hopkins) as they plan an expedition to hunt the strange, unseen Heffalumps. The song is reprised later in the film as the group sets out on the hunt.

"Hound Dude" is the country-western spoof of "Hound Dog" that was used in a satirical way in the animated video sequel *The Fox and the Hound 2* (2006). Will Robinson wrote the wry number and it is sung by the show-biz hound Cash (singing voice of Joshua Gracin) to the pup Copper, filling his head with visions of fame that will come from becoming a singing star.

"How Are the Mighty Fallen" is the stirring tribute to a deceased king, written by Alan Menken (music) and Tim Rice (lyric) for the concert-pageant *King David* (1997) and presented by the Disney company on Broadway. When his mentor and predecessor King Saul dies, the young King David (Marcus Lovett) sings this swelling number that pays honor to the deceased and then turns into an anthem about the plans David has for the future of Jerusalem.

"How Do You Do?" is the farcical musical greeting that Robert MacGimsey wrote for the folklore film *Song of the South* (1946), which successfully mixes live action and animation. In one of the animated Uncle Remus tales in the film, Brer Rabbit (voice of Johnny Lee) sings the resplendent number with various animals as he travels the road leading to an encounter with the lifeless tar baby.

"How D'Ye Do and Shake Hands" is a silly song of introduction that composer Oliver Wallace set to words by Lewis Carroll for the animated movie *Alice in Wonderland* (1951). When Alice (voice of Kathryn Beaumont) meets the roly-poly twins Tweedle-Dum and Tweedle-Dee (both voiced by J. Pat O'Malley), they try to teach her their offbeat idea of manners with this incongruous number.

"How I Know You" is a brief musical conversation from the Broadway musical *Aida* (2000) written by Elton John (music) and Tim Rice (lyric).

The Nubian slave Mereb (Damian Perkins) recognizes the Egyptian princess Amneris's new handmaiden, Aida (Heather Headley), as the daughter of the Nubian king, but Aida encourages him to remain silent and let her pass as just another Nubian captive. Later in the musical, Mereb reprises the song when he realizes he doesn't understand Aida's desire to return to the Egyptian captain Radames (Adam Pascal). James Taylor made a recording of the number before *Aida* opened on Broadway.

"How to Be a Tigger" is the amusing song of instruction written by Richard M. and Robert B. Sherman for the animated film *The Tigger Movie* (2000), the brothers' first Disney assignment since 1971. Winnie the Pooh (voice of Jim Cummings) and his friends decide to dress up like Tiggers and pass themselves off as family members. As they sing about the ways to be like Tigger, they paint stripes on themselves and practice bouncing on springs. Finally the young Roo (Nikita Hopkins) suggests that the best way to be like their friend is to act happy, as he always does.

"Human Again" is the sparkling production number from *Beauty and the Beast* in which all the enchanted objects in the Beast's castle savor the expectation of the spell being broken. Alan Menken (music) and Howard Ashman (lyric) wrote the French-flavored song for the original score of the 1991 film version, but after animation the song was cut from the final print to shorten the movie. The number was finally used in the 1994 Broadway version of *Beauty and the Beast*, where it was sung by Lumière (Gary Beach), Madame de la Grande Bouche (Eleanor Glockner), Cogsworth (Heath Lamberts), Mrs. Potts (Beth Fowler), Chip (Brian Press), Babette (Stacey Logan), and the ensemble. When the film was re-released in 2002 in IMAX theatres, the scene and the song were restored, and both were included in the DVD release later that year.

"Human Stuff" is the delightful character song for the seagull Scuttle (Eddie Korbich) written by Alan Menken (music) and Glenn Slater (lyric) for the 2008 Broadway version of *The Little Mermaid*. The enthusiastic but lame-brained gull identifies the objects Ariel has collected from the human world, misnaming them and using fractured English phrases to describe their purposes to Ariel (Sierra Boggess). Other gulls try to correct Scuttle, but end up joining in on the comic number.

"Humphrey Hop" is the merry dance number from the Disney animated short *In the Bag* (1956). Park ranger J. Audubon Woodlore (voice of Bill

Thompson) tries to get Humphrey (James MacDonald) and the other bears in the park to clean up all the litter left by campers by introducing them to a silly dance in which they bump hips as they pick up trash and put it in bags. George Bruns (music) and Daws Butler (lyric) wrote the amusing number whose lyric contains the instructions for doing the dance. The number is a spoof of the Bunny Hop and is similar to the Hokey Pokey.

"Humuhumunukunukuapua'a" is the mock Hawaiian song written by David Lawrence and Faye Greenberg for the television sequel *High School Musical 2* (2007), but it was cut before broadcast to trim the film's running time. At a summer talent show, the teenage diva Sharpay Evans (Ashley Tisdale) and her fey brother Ryan (Lucas Grabeel), complete with leis and hula skirts, sing and act out the story of the Pineapple Princess Tiki, who is searching for her prince but has been turned into a large, scaly fish. The silly ditty oozes Hawaiian clichés and the music is reminiscent of Don Ho's island song hits. The number was reinstated in the DVD extended version of the film.

"Hunny, No Not for Me" is the somber lament of Winnie the Pooh (voice of Jim Cummings) in the holiday video *Winnie the Pooh: A Very Merry Pooh Year* (2002). Patty and Michael Silversher wrote the sad little song in which Pooh, who has promised Rabbit he would give up his obsession with honey, sings as he fights the urge to indulge in the contents of his "hunny" pot.

"Hunted Partridge on the Hill" is the complex expository number by Alan Menken (music) and Tim Rice (lyric) from the Biblical concert-pageant *King David* (1997), which was presented on Broadway to open the restored New Amsterdam Theatre. When King Saul (Martin Vidnovic) becomes paranoid about the possibility that David (Marcus Lovett) will murder him and steal his throne, followers of both camps sing this song of plot twists, intrigue, and fear. Soon, David's beloved Michal (Judy Kuhn) becomes a pawn to hurt David when Saul gives her to another man.

"A Huntin' Man" is the brief hillbilly number the gun-crazy Amos Slade (voice of Jack Albertson) sings in the animated movie *The Fox and the Hound* (1981). Jim Stafford wrote the folk number about the joys of hunting, which is sung by Amos as he drives home after a long winter of hunting in the forest.

I

"I Am Not Afraid" is the soft song of self-encouragement Piglet (voice of John Fiedler) sings in the television special *Boo to You Too! Winnie the Pooh* (1996). Michael and Patty Silversher wrote the touching little ditty in which Piglet tries to convince himself to be brave so he can go out trick-or-treating with his friends, but even his own shadow frightens him and he seems no more confident at the end of the song than at the beginning. The sequence and the song were first seen in an episode of the television series *The New Adventures of Winnie the Pooh* (1988) and years later the same sequence was repeated in the made-for-video film *Pooh's Heffalump Halloween Movie* (2005).

"I Am So Alone" is the heartfelt "I am" song written by William Finn for the heroine in the animated made-for-video film *The Adventures of Tom Thumb and Thumbelina* (2002). Having spent her whole life a prisoner of an evil circus proprietor, the diminutive Thumbelina (voice of Jennifer Love Hewitt) longs to meet other tiny people like herself and sings this pop ballad about escaping and finding them. Hewitt reprises the number as "I Was All Alone" over the closing credits of the video, a commentary on her finding a romantic soul mate in Tom Thumb.

"I Am What I Am" is the peppy character song by Harry Nilsson for the cartoonish live-action movie *Popeye* (1980). After an argument with his girl-friend Olive Oyl about how to properly raise the orphaned infant Swee'pea,

Even in the most action-packed live-action Disney adventure movie, there is often time for a song and dance, as with *Swiss Family Robinson* (1960). The film was filled with Disney mainstays, such as James MacArthur (far left), Tommy Kirk, Janet Munro, and Dorothy McGuire (seated at the organ). Although it was the only major Disney role for John Mills (far right), his daughter Hayley Mills appeared in many studio movies in the years following. (Walt Disney/Photofest)

the rough-mannered sailor Popeye (Robin Williams) comes to the conclusion that he is what he is and cannot change his ways, so he resolves to leave town with the baby. Like the character, the song is gruff and feisty.

"I Asked My Love a Favor" is the quaint folk song written by Paul J. Smith (music) and Lawrence Edgar Watkin (lyric) for the movie *The Light in the Forest* (1958). Kidnapped and raised by Native Americans, True Son (James MacArthur) is returned to civilization, and as the adult Johnny Butler, he tries to fit into the ways of white society. At his first dance, Johnny hears the musicians play and sing this amusing list song in which a beau asks his girl for various favors, such as a dance and a kiss, before offering her a wedding ring. The music accurately pastiches an early American folk tune and the lyric is humorous in a quaint way.

"I Didn't Know I Could Feel This Way" is the pop love song Melissa Manchester and Norman Gimbel wrote for the animated video sequel

Lady and the Tramp II: Scamp's Adventure (2001). When the young canine Scamp (voice of Scott Wolf) falls into puppy love with the female pup Angel (Alyssa Milano), they romp about the town and through the park playing with fireflies and even stopping at Tony's restaurant for some spaghetti and meatballs. The two canines' thoughts are sung on the soundtrack by Roger Bart and Susan Egan.

"I Don't Dance" is the clever song about dancing that uses baseball imagery in the television movie *High School Musical 2* (2007). When the effeminate drama geek Ryan (Lucas Grabeel) tries to convince macho athlete Chad (Corbin Bleu) that the jock can learn to dance for a country club talent show, Chad insists that he doesn't dance. To prove to him that anyone can learn to do something outside of his or her comfort zone, Ryan takes up baseball, and Chad agrees to give dancing a try. The resulting pop duet is smooth and seething with machismo, reflecting Chad's need to be perceived as a man in spite of the request that he dance. Matthew Gerrard and Robbie Nevil wrote the sly duet that comments on stereotypes as it uses baseball terms to describe dance steps.

"I Found a New Friend" is the sprightly song about recognizing a fellow spirit, written by Frank De Vol for the film sequel *Herbie Goes Bananas* (1980). After a series of adventures in Mexico, the VW Herbie and his new owner, Pete Stanchek (Stephen W. Burns), realize they have become close friends, and their thoughts are conveyed in this Latin-flavored number, complete with Spanish expressions, which is sung by a children's chorus over the final credits of the movie.

"I, Ivan Frank" is the tango-flavored "I am" song for the crackpot scientist–villain in the animated film *Teacher's Pet* (2004), inspired by the popular television series. Kevin Quinn, Cheri Steinkellner, and Randy Petersen wrote the satirical number in which the wacko Dr. Frank (voice of Kelsey Grammer) sings that he is a man ahead of his time, greater than Dr. Frankenstein, and that someday the world (and even his own mother) will appreciate his genius for turning animals into humans.

"I Just Can't Wait to Be King" is the ambitious "I am" song for the young lion cub Simba (singing voice of Jason Weaver) in the animated movie *The Lion King* (1994). The future king sings enthusiastically of his plans while he frolics across the savanna with young Nala (Laura Williams) and tries to lose the watchful hornbill Zazu (Rowan Atkinson), who punctuates the song with wry comments about the young prince's faults. Soon various birds and other creatures join in, the scene turning into a mock Las Vegas revue number. Elton John wrote the rhythmic music, Tim Rice penned the busy lyric, and Mark Mancina provided the African arrangement that made the number bounce with joy. John recorded the song, which in the 1997 Broadway version of *The Lion King* was sung by Scott Irby-Ranniar, Kujuana Shuford, Geoff Hoyle, and the ensemble. The number is also briefly heard in the made-for-video sequel *The Lion King 1½* (2004). Andrew Samonsky recorded the number with a quartet comprised of Meredith Inglesby, Andy Karl, Tyler Maynard, and Keewa Nurullah; Aaron Carter recorded it in 2002.

"I Know the Truth" is the bitter song of realization for the princess Amneris (Sherie Rene Scott) in the Broadway musical *Aida* (2000) written by Elton John (music) and Tim Rice (lyric). When the Egyptian princess realizes that her fiancé, Radames, is in love with the Nubian slave Aida, she confronts the truth with acceptance and misery. Elton John recorded the song with Janet Jackson before *Aida* opened on Broadway, and a later version was recorded by Michael Crawford.

"I Love to Laugh" is the buoyant song about the power of laughter written by Richard M. and Robert B. Sherman for the film musical *Mary Poppins* (1964). Nanny Mary Poppins (Julie Andrews) and chimney sweep Bert (Dick Van Dyke) come to the aid of Bert's daffy Uncle Albert (Ed Wynn) whose laughing fits make him weightless. The three sing the song with Mary's two young charges (Karen Dotrice and Matthew Garber) as they all have a tea party while floating in the air. Uncle Albert and the song were cut from the 2004 stage version of *Mary Poppins*.

"I Need to Know" is the touching lament of the boy Tarzan (Alex Rutherford or Daniel Manche) from the 2006 Broadway version of *Tarzan*. Spurned by the ape leader Kerchak, the young human gazes at himself in a pool of water, wondering who he is and whether there are any others out there who are like him. Phil Collins wrote the affecting, prayer-like song which is based on the number "Leaving Home," which he wrote and sang on the soundtrack of the made-for-video sequel *Tarzan II* (2005).

"I Put a Spell on You" is the darkly comic song by Jay Hawkins that the three witches in the movie *Hocus Pocus* (1993) sing in order to put a dancing curse on Halloween partygoers. Although they were burned as witches in Salem in 1693, Winifred Sanderson (Bette Midler) and her sisters Sarah (Sarah Jessica Parker) and Mary (Kathy Najimy) come back to life three hundred years later and need a special potion, which includes the life force of children, in order to stay alive. In their efforts to lure the children to their house, the three sisters go to a Halloween dance for the parents and use this song to put a spell on the adults, forcing them to dance to death. Winifred leads the spooky and intense song, full of incantations and Latin phrases, and her sisters sing backup.

"I Remain" is the Middle Eastern–flavored song that serves as both a love theme and tribute to the lead character's determination in the 2010 action-adventure film *The Prince of Persia: The Sands of Time*, which was based on the popular video game. The fugitives Prince Dastan (Jake Gyllenhaal) and Princess Tamina (Gemma Arterton) overcome an evil villain who has a special dagger that can be used to reverse time, and in the process the two fall in love. The song "I Remain," by Alanis Morissette and Mike Elizondo and performed by Morissette, is the musical expression of Daston's and Tamina's experience overcoming insurmountable obstacles and falling in love.

"I Remember" is the flowing ballad written by Jeanine Tesori for the animated made-for-video prequel *The Little Mermaid: Ariel's Beginning* (2008). In an underwater kingdom where music is forbidden, the mermaid princess Ariel (voice of Jodi Benson) hears some notes from a lullaby her deceased mother once sang to her and suddenly recalls in song the music and love that once filled her family.

"I Saw a Dragon" is the high-kicking, high-energy production number written by Joel Hirschhorn and Al Kasha for the partially animated movie *Pete's Dragon* (1977). After the drunken lighthouse keeper Lampie (Mickey Rooney) encounters the friendly dragon Elliott, he rushes into the local pub and informs the townspeople, who do not believe him but mock him by joining in the song which is part music hall number, part sea chantey. With Onna White's vigorous choreography, the rousing number is almost a cartoon in itself.

"I See the Light" is the Oscar-nominated ballad about finally seeing the truth about another person, written by Alan Menken (music) and Glenn Slater (lyric) for the animated movie *Tangled* (2010). Rapunzel (voice of Mandy Moore) and Flynn Rider (Zachary Levi) sing the love song to each other while sitting in a small boat as they watch floating lanterns fill the sky. During the entrancing duet, Rapunzel discovers that all of her dreams about the outside world are realized by falling in love with Flynn while the on-the-run thief finds out that he need run no longer now that he has found a girl who accepts him as he is. Slater's lyric is simple and tender while Menken's music is graceful and disarming.

"I See Spots" is the jaunty ditty by Randy Rogel that songwriter Roger Radcliffe (voice of Tim Bentinck) makes up on the spot in the made-for-video animated sequel *101 Dalmatians II: Patch's London Adventure* (2003). While his wife, Anita (Jodi Benson), is packing and singing "Dalmatian Plantation," Roger composes and sings this playful song about being surrounded by spotted dalmatians, the two songs blending together contrapuntally.

"I Still Believe" is the pop-rock ballad about the possibility of true love written by Matthew Gerrard and Bridget Benenate for the animated video sequel *Cinderella III: A Twist in Time* (2007). Hayden Panettiere sings the romantic number on the soundtrack during the closing credits of the musical.

"I Thought I Lost You" is the driving pop song written by Miley Cyrus and John Travolta that is heard over the closing credits of the animated film *Bolt* (2008). Cyrus and Travolta, who voice the two major characters in the film, sing the number about the joyous relief of finding one who was thought lost forever, the lyric paralleling the plot of the movie.

"I 2 I" is the pounding rock song by Patrick DeRemer and Roy Freeland that is sung by the rock star Powerline (voice of Tevin Campbell) in concert near the end of the animated film *A Goofy Movie* (1995). The rhythmic number about a love that took a long time to be discovered is reprised by Campbell and Rosie Gaines on the soundtrack over the closing credits of the movie.

"I Wanna Be a Boy" is the satirical "I am" song written by Brian Woodbury and Peter Lurye for the brainy dog Spot (voice of Nathan Lane) in the animated movie *Teacher's Pet* (2004), based on the 2000 television series. As Spot disguises himself as a boy and heads for school, he sings about his dream of becoming a real boy someday, just like Pinocchio did. The fast and funny number is picked up by various children also going to school, the tots proclaiming that Spot wants to be human.

"I Wan'na Be Like You" is one of the most swinging and contagious of all Disney songs, a jazzy number by Richard M. and Robert B. Sherman that is a highlight of the animated movie *The Jungle Book* (1967). The orangutan King Louis of the Apes (voice of Louis Prima) sings the enthusiastic number about how he wishes he were human to the kidnapped man-cub Mowgli, and then he and the other apes break into a wild and farcical dance. The bear Baloo (Phil Harris) tries to rescue Mowgli by performing the song disguised as an ape, but he gets so carried away singing and dancing that his plot is discovered. A fun duet recording of the number was made by Brian Sutherland and Andrew Samonsky, and a bluegrass rendition was recorded by Mike Toppins, Glen Duncan, Billy Troy, Jim Brown, James Freeze, and David Chase in 1998. A recording by the group Smash Mouth was heard on the soundtrack of the video sequel *The Jungle Book 2* (2003), and the Jonas Brothers recorded the number in 2007.

"I Wanna Scare Myself" is the silly and lighthearted song Michael and Patty Silversher wrote for Tigger (voice of Jim Cummings) to sing in the television special *Boo to You Too! Winnie the Pooh* (1996). As Tigger prepares to go trick-or-treating, he sings the rapid number while putting on various masks and disguises and trying to frighten himself. The sequence and the song were first seen in an episode of the television series *The New Adventures of Winnie the Pooh* (1988) and years later the same sequence would be repeated in the made-for-video film *Pooh's Heffalump Halloween Movie* (2005).

"I Want It All" is the egotistical extravaganza about wanting and expecting to be rich and famous, sung by the self-centered drama diva Sharpay (Ashley Tisdale) and her performing sidekick brother Ryan (Lucas Grabeel) in the movie sequel *High School Musical 3: Senior Year* (2008). The number, written by Matthew Gerrard and Robbie Nevil, starts off with the rich brat Sharpay imagining her future full of fame and wealth and envisioning herself the toast of Broadway and Hollywood. Ryan wonders how he fits into her plans and is soon sucked into the fantasy, which explodes into a lavish production number staged by Kenny Ortega. Ryan and the chorus reprise the song during the school's spring musical.

"I Want the Good Times Back" is the deliciously devious "I am" song for the sea witch Ursula (Sherie Rene Scott) written by Alan Menken (music) and Glenn Slater (lyric) for the 2008 Broadway version of *The Little Mermaid*. The vain and self-centered Ursula laments the loss of the good old days when she and her evil powers ruled the sea, and she vows to her henchmen Flotsam (Tyler Maynard) and Jetsam (Derrick Baskin) to be revenged on King Triton. During the song the sea witch comes up with the idea of using Triton's daughter, Ariel, as a way to get to the father. Later in the show the trio reprises the song as they plan to foil the romance blooming between Ariel and Prince Eric.

"I Will Go Sailing No More" is the bluesy song of disillusionment written by Randy Newman for *Toy Story* (1995), the first fully computer-generated feature film. Newman sings the number, about finding out who you really are and giving up on your dreams, on the soundtrack as the spaceman Buzz Lightyear sees himself on a television commercial and realizes he is just a toy. During the song Buzz even attempts to fly but finds he cannot, convinced that he is not a real spaceman. Pleasing recordings of the ballad were made by Michael Crawford in 2001 and Brian Sutherland in 2005.

"I Will Sing" is the gospel-like number by Jeanine Tesori that concludes the animated made-for-video prequel *The Little Mermaid: Ariel's Beginning* (2008). When King Triton announces that once again music will be allowed in his kingdom, the mermaids and sea creatures celebrate and Jeanette Bayardelle sings this rousing testament to music, vowing to sing for the rest of her life, on the soundtrack.

"I Wish I Could Be Santa Claus" is the wishful ballad that the Great Gonzo (voice of Dave Goelz) and Fozzie Bear (Eric Jacobson) sing in the television special *A Muppets Christmas: Letters to Santa* (2008). Paul Williams wrote the gliding melody and the gentle lyric about wanting to be Santa for just one day so one can give away gifts and love.

"I Wonder" is the wistful character song that George Bruns (music), Winston Hibler, and Ted Sears (lyric) wrote for the animated movie *Sleeping Beauty* (1959). Princess Aurora (voice of Mary Costa) does not know of her royal lineage and grows up in a forest cottage under the name Briar Rose. She sings this song of forlorn contemplation as she watches some singing lovebirds and wonders why she has no one to share a love song with. Her singing is accompanied by some happy chirping birds yet there is a sad tone to the song. In 1987 Yma Sumac made an unusual recording of the number, creating her own bird sounds.

"I Won't Say I'm in Love" is the contradictory love song the calculating Meg (voice of Susan Egan) sings, with the gospel-singing Muses backing her up, in the animated movie *Hercules* (1997). Alan Menken composed the compelling music and David Zippel wrote the lyric, in which Meg denies her true feelings yet admits that she is quite taken with the brawny but naive hero Hercules. The song has the feel and style of a 1960s "girl group" number, complete with backup singers doing the expected "oohs" and "ahs." Andrew Samonsky recorded the number with backup vocals by Meredith Inglesby, Andy Karl, Tyler Maynard, and Keewa Nurullah, and the catchy song was recorded by the Cheetah Girls in 2005.

"I Would Like to Be a Bird" is the lighthearted song of yearning written by Frank Churchill and Bert Lewis for the Silly Symphony movie short *The Flying Mouse* (1934). As a little mouse looks up at the birds of the air and dreams of having the power to fly, a chorus sings this inspiring song on the soundtrack, a musical plea for the impossible.

"Ichabod" is the charming exposition song that Bing Crosby and the Rhythmaires sing on the soundtrack of the animated film *The Adventures of Ichabod and Mr. Toad* (1949). Gene de Paul and Don Raye wrote the pleasant character song that introduces the character of Ichabod Crane, the schoolmaster of Sleepy Hollow, who is awkward and feeble when in the company of men but a favorite of the ladies.

"I'd Like to Be You for a Day" is the bouncy pop song that Al Kasha and Joel Hirschhorn wrote for the film comedy *Freaky Friday* (1976). Barbara Harris and Jodie Foster, who play mother and daughter in the movie, are heard singing the simple, repetitive ditty over the opening credits as cartoon cutouts of mother and daughter are seen switching everyday jobs, as will happen in the plot. The number was briefly heard in the 2003 remake of the movie.

"I'd Stick with You" is the charming duet about friendship written by Walter Edgar Kennon for the animated video sequel *The Hunchback of Notre Dame II* (2002). When the young child Zephyr (voice of Haley Joel Osment) gets separated from his parents in the Paris throng, the hunchback Quasimodo (Tom Hulce) finds him and assures the boy that he will always take care of him. In the duet, Zephyr lists various scenarios of crisis, and Quasimodo happily replies that he will not leave the youth no matter what the circumstances. The musical scene is observed by the circus worker Madellaine, who sees the misshapen hunchback in a tender and more affectionate light.

"If I Can't Love Her" is the soul-searching ballad for the Beast (Terrence Mann) in the Broadway version of *Beauty and the Beast* (1994). The tormented prince-turned-beast fights off despair and considers his ability to fall in love with Belle (Susan Egan) in this stirring first-act finale song. The Beast reprises the song later in the show, after he has allowed Belle to return home and wonders if he will ever see her again. The number was written for the stage version by Alan Menken (music) and Tim Rice (lyric) and has a resounding, operatic tone that is far heavier than anything found in the animated film version. Among the handful of recordings of the song are those by James Graeme with the National Symphony Orchestra and by Ron Raines.

"If I Didn't Have You" is the Oscar-winning song about friendship written by Randy Newman for the computer-animated film *Monsters, Inc.* (2001). A jazz instrumental version of the song is heard over the opening credits of the movie, and a slower, soft-shoe rendition is sung on the soundtrack by Billy Crystal and John Goodman during the final credits. The lyric for the old-time vaudeville number states that without a friend, one is nothing. Crystal and Goodman retain the vaudeville style by ad-libbing comments between the lines, and, though they are not seen, the two are heard engaging in a dance. A recording of the number was made by Mitchell Musso.

"If I Never Knew You" is the romantic duet written by Alan Menken (music) and Stephen Schwartz (lyric) for the animated film *Pocahontas* (1995). Captured by the Native American tribe and tied up in a hut, Captain John Smith (voice of Mel Gibson) is visited by his beloved Pocahontas (singing voice of Judy Kuhn), and the two sing about how grateful each is for having known the other, no matter what the consequences of their love. Michael Crawford recorded the ballad in 2001, and touching duet versions of the song were made by Kaitlin Hopkins and Brian Sutherland, and by Shanice and Jon Secada. There was also a recording by the Cheetah Girls in 2006. The number is sometimes listed as "Love Theme from *Pocahontas*."

"If I Wasn't So Small" is the slightly swinging lament of the diminutive Piglet (voice of John Fiedler) written by Carly Simon for the animated film *Piglet's Big Movie* (2003). After Piglet has been excluded from his friends' latest adventure because he is too small, the little fellow wanders sadly through the Hundred Acre Wood while composer Simon is heard singing the piquant song about wanting to be needed. The number is also listed as "The Piglet Song."

"If It Says So" is the waltzing musical tribute to the power of the written word sung by Rabbit (voice of Ken Sansom) in the made-for-video movie *Pooh's Grand Adventure: The Search for Christopher Robin* (1997). Michael Abbott and Sarah Weeks wrote the incongruous number about trusting the map rather than your own eyes or ears when on an expedition, and Rabbit sings the funny, illogical song to Winnie the Pooh and his friends, who are searching for Christopher Robin.

"If Only" is a revealing quartet written by Alan Menken (music) and Glenn Slater (lyric) for the 2008 Broadway version of *The Little Mermaid*. Human but mute, Ariel (Sierra Boggess) laments that Prince Eric (Sean Palmer) cannot know how she feels about him, while Eric sings to himself about his ambiguous feelings for the silent girl. Then the crab Sebastian (Tituss Burgess) expresses his hopes that Ariel will find happiness, and King Triton (Norm Lewis) mourns the loss of his daughter and expresses his regrets for driving her away. The four independent voices end up blending together as their different hopes complement each other. The song is reprised near the end of the show when King Triton grants Ariel's wish to return to the human world and gives his blessing to her and Eric.

"I'll Always Be Irish" is the ardent tribute to Ireland written by Richard M. and Robert B. Sherman for the movie musical *The Happiest Millionaire* (1967). The Irish immigrant John Lawless (Tommy Steele) has been hired as the new butler in the household of the eccentric Biddle family of Philadelphia, and he proclaims in song that although he hopes to become an American citizen someday, he will always remain Irish as well. He sings the number to his employer, Anthony J. Drexel Biddle (Fred MacMurray), and his daughter, Cordelia (Lesley Ann Warren), then the two join him in the song and in an Irish jig, which brings out the Irish housekeeper Mrs. Worth (Hermione Baddeley), who also joins them in the dance.

"I'll Make a Man Out of You" is the rhythmic military song written by Matthew Wilder (music) and David Zippel (lyric) for the animated movie *Mulan* (1998). The Chinese warrior Shang (singing voice of Donny Osmond) must turn a group of misfit soldiers, including the girl Mulan disguised as a young man, into a tough fighting force. He sings this forceful number to them, and then his voice continues on the soundtrack during a montage showing the raw recruits becoming tougher and more successful as fighters. Action star Jackie Chan recorded the song in Chinese for a music video featuring himself doing his fight movements in time to the music.

"I'll Try" is the revealing character song written by Jonatha Brooke for the animated film sequel *Return to Never Land* (2002). Instructed by her mother, Wendy, to entertain her little brother, Daniel, with stories about Peter Pan, the frustrated Jane (voice of Harriet Kate Owen) begrudgingly agrees, even though she does not believe in the boy hero. Jane's thoughts are sung by songwriter Brooke on the soundtrack, torn between her mature self and the child her mother wants her to be. The melodic number is reprised over the closing credits of the movie. Jesse McCartney made a recording of the song in 2006, and Kerry Butler made a delightful version in 2008.

"I'm a Happy-Go-Lucky Fellow" is a chirping number by Leigh Harline (music) and Ned Washington (lyric) that Jiminy Cricket (voice of Cliff Edwards) sings on a floating leaf and then in a library to introduce the first part of the animated film anthology *Fun and Fancy Free* (1947). The optimistic song about not worrying about life was originally written and recorded by Edwards for the earlier movie *Pinocchio* (1940), but was cut from the final print.

"I'm a Reluctant Dragon" is the gentle "I am" song by Charles Wolcott (music), T. Hee, and Erdman Penner (lyric) for the docile title character in the animated film *The Reluctant Dragon* (1941). While having a picnic and pouring tea for himself, the meek Dragon (voice of Barnett Parker) sings this sprightly ditty about the virtues of peace and harmony and how he is not a killing kind of dragon but one who reads and writes poetry.

"I'm Blue for You, Boo-Boo-Boo-Boo-Boo" is the slapstick pastiche of a Bing Crosby crooning number from the 1930s that Richard M. and Robert B. Sherman wrote for the mini-musical *A Symposium on Popular Songs*, which was shown on the television program *Walt Disney's Wonderful World of Color* in 1962. Professor Ludwig von Drake (voice of Paul Frees) conducts the symposium in his mansion and introduces the mellow number, which is sung by a paper cutout animated singer (voice of Skip Farrell) who is a caricature of Crosby. As he sings the teary torch song into a dancing microphone, the sounds of swooning females are heard. Al Sherman, the songwriter father of the Sherman brothers, actually wrote some songs for Crosby in the 1930s, so the satiric number is also a tribute by the brothers to their father.

"I'm Gone" is the Caribbean-flavored song of freedom from care written by Michael and Patty Silversher for an episode of the animated television series *TaleSpin* (1990). Baloo the Bear (Ed Gilbert) from the film *The*

Jungle Book (1967) appears as a freewheeling pilot and sings this moderate calypso number about how he leaves his troubles on the ground and takes to the air when his spirits need a boost.

"I'm Gonna Love You" is the pop ballad about the ways love allows you to see things differently, heard in the animated video sequel *The Hunchback of Notre Dame II* (2002). Jennifer Love Hewitt, who provided the voice of Madellaine, Quasimodo's love interest in the movie, wrote the song with Chris Canute, and she sings it over the closing credits. The number is also listed as "Madellaine's Love Song."

"I'm in the Middle of a Muddle" is the buoyant and sprightly musical number written for the ever-cleaning title character in the 1950 animated movie *Cinderella*, but it was not used in the final print of the film. The song was intended to be a character number for Cinderella, singing of her mounting tasks and wishing that her arms would become brooms and her feet mops. The song was composed by Tin Pan Alley composers Mack David, Al Hoffman, and Jerry Livingston and recorded by them as a demo. This cut of the song was featured on the 2005 re-release of the CD of the *Cinderella* soundtrack.

"I'm Late" is the furious ditty by Sammy Fain (music) and Bob Hilliard (lyric) that is heard in quick snatches throughout the animated film *Alice in Wonderland* (1951). The White Rabbit (voice of Bill Thompson) sings the number as he rushes down the rabbit hole near the beginning of the movie, and he reprises it as he reappears in various places in Wonderland. It was recorded by Barbara Hendricks and the Abbey Road Ensemble, and Barbara Cook, Michael Feinstein, and Mary Martin each recorded a playful version of the song.

"I'm Lonely, My Darlin'" is the cowboy torch song written by George Bruns (music) and Fess Parker (lyric) for the adventure film *Westward Ho, the Wagons!* (1956). John Grayson (Parker), the doctor traveling with a wagon train on the Oregon Trail, plays the guitar and serenades the pretty Laura Thompson (Kathleen Crowley) with this western lament of a cowboy who pines for the girl who left him to run off with another. Laura joins him in the final refrain of the song, turning the sad song into a romantic one.

"I'm Looking Out for Me" is the sarcastic song of freedom from the made-for-video animated film *The Return of Jafar* (1994). Randy Petersen and Kevin Quinn wrote the raucous number in which the sidekick parrot Iago (voice of Gilbert Gottfried) declares his independence from the evil wizard Jafar and vows to no longer serve his former master or his sinister schemes.

"I'm Mean" is the rockabilly character song for the villainous Bluto (Paul L. Smith) in the cartoonish live-action movie *Popeye* (1980). Harry Nilsson wrote the fiery number, which Bluto sings as he destroys all the furniture when Olive Oyl doesn't show up for their engagement party.

"I'm Moving On" is the fast and satirical song that Randy Petersen, Cheri Steinkellner, and Kevin Quinn wrote for the animated movie *Teacher's Pet* (2004). The Broadway-style number about dealing with change is sung by the dog-turned-human Scott (voice of Nathan Lane); his boy master, Leonard (Shaun Fleming); Leonard's mother, Mary Lou (Debra Jo Rupp); the mad scientist Ivan Frank (Kelsey Grammer); and other characters as the screen splits into several squares showing what each person is feeling. The song is a droll spoof of the kind of concerted numbers that end the first act of serious Broadway musicals such as *Les Misérables*.

"I'm No Fool" is the tuneful ditty that Jiminy Cricket (voice of Cliff Edwards) sang before a series of animated shorts on the television program *The Mickey Mouse Club*. Jimmie Dodd wrote the simple, memorable tune about being careful while playing in the neighborhood. The series covered such subjects as keeping away from heavy traffic, strangers, electric wires, and dangerous places. Before each segment Jiminy sang "I'm No Fool" and proclaimed that he was going to live to a ripe old age because he was careful.

"I'm Odd" is the song of self-proclaimed insanity written by Sammy Fain (music) and Bob Hilliard (lyric) for the animated film *Alice in Wonderland* (1951), but it was cut from the final print. The Cheshire Cat (voice of Sterling Holloway) proudly admits that he has lost his reason in the risible song. The number was cut, along with "Beware the Jabberwock," when the whole sequence based on Lewis Carroll's poem "Jabberwocky" was eliminated from the movie.

"I'm Professor Ludwig Von Drake" is the daffy "I am" song by Richard M. and Robert B. Sherman that describes Donald Duck's eccentric, brilliant, but silly Uncle Ludwig. The not-very-modest character song was sung by the Professor (voice of Paul Frees) in a 1961 episode of the television program *Walt Disney's Wonderful World of Color* as he explained his superior mind but ended up being blown to pieces by his own twenty-one-gun salute. The music has a catchy German oompah-pah flavor, and the risible lyric details how he is an expert on everything from science to art. There is an amusing patter section in the middle of the number, which is in the Gilbert-and-Sullivan style, where Ludwig rhymes several of the fields of study in which he excels.

"I'm Still Here" is the rock song John Rzeznik wrote for the animated adventure movie *Treasure Planet* (2002), an updated version of Robert Louis Stevenson's *Treasure Island*. As he slaves away aboard the flying galleon *RLS Legacy*, Jim Hawkins recalls his unhappy childhood and the day his father walked out on him and his mother. Songwriter Rzeznik sings the harsh song on the soundtrack as Jim's memories are interwoven with scenes of his present situation, in which the cyborg cook John Silver teaches him various tasks aboard ship. Rzeznik made an effective music video of the song, which is sometimes listed as "Jim's Theme."

"I'm Wishing" is the echoing "I am" song for the title heroine in the animated fairy tale movie *Snow White and the Seven Dwarfs* (1937) that was scored by Frank Churchill (music) and Larry Morey (lyric). Snow White (voice of Adriana Caselotti) sings into a wishing well the winsome number about her hopes of a true love, and her own voice echoes back to her. At the end of the song Prince Charming (voice of Harry Stockwell) appears behind her and, his face reflected in the water, sings the last notes of the song for her. Mary Martin recorded the ballad, and a pleasing duet version was made by Ashley Brown and Kaitlin Hopkins.

"In a World of My Own" is the restless "I am" song the Victorian girl Alice (voice of Kathryn Beaumont) sings at the beginning of the animated film fantasy *Alice in Wonderland* (1951). Sammy Fain (music) and Bob Hilliard (lyric) wrote the dreamy number, in which Alice expresses her boredom with her studies and everyday life and wishes for a place full of wonders. The song replaced a quieter number titled "Beyond the Laughing Sky."

"In Harmony" is the mellifluous number about living together in peace from an episode of the animated television series *The Little Mermaid* (1992). The mermaid Ariel (voice of Jodi Benson) sings the slightly bossa nova–style number to the various sea creatures who have been quarreling, suggesting they should be friends and live in harmony together, as in a song.

"In Me Jaunting Car" is the whimsical charm song written by Richard M. and Robert B. Sherman for the movie fantasy *The Gnome-Mobile* (1967). Lumber tycoon D. J. Mulrooney (Walter Brennan) and his two grandchildren, Rodney (Matthew Garber) and Elizabeth (Karen Dotrice), take his Rolls-Royce Phantom II, a custom-made car, on a trip to Seattle for business. In the vehicle, they sing this propulsive and agreeable song that pays homage to the car's one-of-a-kind beauty and speed.

"In My Blue Backyard" is the gentle calypso number Ariel (voice of Jodi Benson) sings about her underwater kingdom in an episode of the animated television series *The Little Mermaid* (1992). The rhythmic song is about the glories of living among the sea creatures and the beautiful gardens under the sea. Ariel's singing was backed up by a harmonizing female chorus on the soundtrack.

"In the Darkness" is the eerie theme song for the television series *So Weird* (2001), about a teenager with visions into the paranormal. Annmarie Montade (music) and Jon Cooksey (lyric) wrote the echoing rock number, which Mackenzie Phillips sings on the soundtrack over the opening credits. The lyric, about being lost in a dark web of confusion on the other side of paradise, reflects the mental state of the teen heroine of the series.

"In the Name of the Hundred Acre Wood" is the tuneful march song by Carly Simon that is used throughout the animated film *Pooh's Heffalump Movie* (2005). During an expedition to hunt the mysterious Heffalumps, Winnie the Pooh (voice of Jim Cummings) and his friends sing a brief portion of the number every time they think they are cornering one of the strange creatures. During the end credits of the movie, songwriter Simon sings the complete song with a children's chorus, asking what does one do when something new comes across one's path. The spirited number is also listed as "What Do You Do?"

"Instant Muscle" is the recurring musical theme by Robert F. Brunner that runs throughout the film *The Strongest Man in the World* (1975) as a kind of pop leitmotif. A chorus sings the song about physical power, the music moving from jazz to an Asian flavor and back again, throughout the silly comedy about a breakfast cereal that imparts superhuman strength.

"Introducing Me" is the charming and funny character song sung by camp counselor Nate (Nick Jonas) to Dana Turner (Chloe Bridges), the daughter of the camp director of the rival Camp Star, in the TV-movie *Camp Rock 2: The Final Jam* (2010). When Dana accuses Nate of playing his feelings too close to the vest, he writes her this song about all the weird and goofy things that go through his head. The quirky list of his likes and dislikes helps her to see him for who he really is: an insecure guy with a heart of gold. The gentle song was written by James Houston Scoggin.

"Israel and Saul" is the intense opening number for the pageant-like musical *King David* (1997), which the Disney company presented on Broadway in its newly restored New Amsterdam Theatre. Saul (Martin Vidnovic) has just been made king of Israel, and the people sing this song of celebration while commentary and criticism of the new appointee are made by Joab (Stephen Bogardus) and Samuel (Peter Samuel). Alan Menken wrote the mysterious-sounding music and Tim Rice provided the insightful lyrics.

"It Feels Like Christmas" is the felicitous holiday carol written by Paul Williams for the movie *The Muppet Christmas Carol* (1992). The giant-like Ghost of Christmas Present (voice of Jerry Nelson) sings the glowing song as he takes Ebenezer Scrooge (Michael Caine) through the streets of London, where everyone, from workers to families to carolers, sings about finding Christmas where you find love.

"It Will Be Me" is the reflective and moving ballad about feeling the presence of those who are gone, written for the animated video sequel *Brother Bear 2* (2006) by Matthew Gerrard and Robbie Nevil. After the Native American Kenai has been transformed into a bear, he can no longer communicate with his human sweetheart Nika, yet both still feel the presence of the other. Melissa Etheridge sings the engaging song on the soundtrack, the lyrics about always being there for someone applying to Kenai and Nika, but also to Nika and her deceased mother and to the bear cub Koda and his dead parents. The number is reprised over the closing credits of the video.

"It Won't Be Long 'Til Christmas" is a quiet charm song written by Richard M. and Robert B. Sherman for the film musical *The Happiest Millionaire* (1967), but it was cut after the long movie did poorly at the box office and was re-released in a shorter version. The number is not a Christmas song but a wistful realization that children grow up and you must let them go, hoping they will come home at Christmas to visit. The married couple Anthony Biddle (Fred MacMurray) and his wife, Cordelia (Greer Garson), sing the quiet, heartfelt lament after their daughter has married and their large Philadelphia house seems so quiet. The song was restored when the movie was aired on television in 1984 and in the subsequent video/DVD versions.

"It's a Dog" is the rapping theme song written by James Houston for the television movie *Life Is Ruff* (2005). Kyle Massey, who plays Calvin Wheeler, a teenager who enters a mutt in a prestigious dog show, sings about the carefree canine life on the soundtrack. He also made a music video of the song.

"It's a Small World (After All)" is the insistent and catchy ditty by Richard M. and Robert B. Sherman that is one of the most familiar songs ever written for a nontheatrical attraction. The optimistic number, about the children of the world finding peace and harmony together, was written for the Pepsi-Cola attraction at the 1964–1965 World's Fair in New York City. Disneyland designers created the ride, all proceeds of which went to UNICEF, where hundreds of dolls of children in colorful costumes from around the globe sang the simple song as visitors rode in boats through idealized depictions of the seven continents. The ride was so popular, it was reassembled at Disneyland after the fair closed and has remained a favorite at all Disney theme parks ever since. Appropriately, most recordings of the song have been made by children's choirs in many different languages. Because the song plays throughout the ride, the verse-less music never fully resolves itself at the end of the refrain, allowing the tune to repeat itself indefinitely. The insistency of the song has long been the source of jokes about the unrelenting number, and when the hornbill Zazu (voice of Rowan Atkinson) starts to sing it in the film *The Lion King* (1994), the evil lion Scar (Jeremy Irons) goes into a rage. Recent recordings include those by Baha Men in 2004, a rap version by Fan 3 in 2005, and a unique rendition by Kerry Butler in 2008.

"It's All about Heart" is the up-tempo list song that Paul Williams wrote for the television special *A Muppets Christmas: Letters to Santa* (2008). Kermit the Frog (voice of Steve Whitmire), the Great Gonzo (Dave Goelz), Fozzie Bear (Eric Jacobson), and friends sing about the reasons for doing favorite things at Christmastime as they start off to the North Pole to see Santa.

"It's Gonna Be Great" is the peppy song with a springy melody sung by Tigger (voice of Jim Cummings) to Eeyore (Bud Luckey) as he tries to teach the gloomy donkey to be more like a "Tigger" in the animated movie *Winnie the Pooh* (2011). As they go in search of the monster called the "Backson," who has kidnapped their friend Christopher Robin, the frenetic tiger enthusiastically tries to show Eeyore how much better things will be with two Tiggers in the forest. The humorous number has music and lyrics by Robert Lopez and Kristen Anderson-Lopez.

"It's Not Easy" is the affecting character duet written by Joel Hirschhorn and Al Kasha for the part-live-action, part-animated movie *Pete's Dragon* (1977). The young orphan Pete (Sean Marshall) and the lighthouse keeper's daughter, Nora (Helen Reddy), each find a sympathetic friend in the other, and they sing this number about finding a soul mate who understands them. By the end of the song, the two are trusting friends.

"It's Not Easy Bein' Me" is a bizarre duet about being unpleasant that Harry Nilsson wrote for the cartoonish live-action film *Popeye* (1980). Popeye's father, the irascible Poopdeck Pappy (Ray Walston), sings about how hard it is to change when you've been grumpy all your life, and he is joined in these sentiments by the bully Bluto (Paul L. Smith), the two singing together about their unfortunate plight.

"It's On" is the pulsating rock number by Toby Gad, Lyrica Anderson, and Kovasciar Myvette, introduced in the 2010 made-for-TV film *Camp Rock 2: The Final Jam*. When the campers from Camp Rock decide to take on their rivals at Camp Star, they offer a challenge to their competitors with this song, letting them know they are up against some healthy competition. The angst-infused number is performed by the choruses from both camps.

"It's Our House Now" is the manic but fun song by Kevin Quinn and Randy Petersen sung by various Disney villains in the made-for-video Halloween special *Mickey's House of Villains* (2001). When Mickey and his friends gather at the House of Mouse to watch spooky film shorts, they are invaded by Hades, Maleficent, Ursula, Jafar, and other villains, who take Mickey and his pals hostage then sing this vivacious number about taking over the House of Mouse.

"It's Over" is the pop farewell ballad written by David Lawrence and Faye Greenberg for the television sequel *The Cheetah Girls 2* (2006). The American singing group, consisting of Galleria (Raven-Symoné), Chanel (Adrienne Bailon), Aqua (Kiely Williams), and Dorinda (Sabrina Bryan), have a falling out while they are in Barcelona, and it looks like the foursome is breaking up. While each of the girls is seen separately, they take turns singing this song of regret.

"It's Tough to Be a Bird" is the wry title song by Mel Leven for the 1969 tongue-in-cheek animated documentary short that looks at the history of man's feathered friends over the ages. The big-beaked M. C. Bird (voice of Richard Bakalyan) introduces the "mockumentary" with this jazzy song that complains about how humans hunt, shoot, trap, and stuff birds, taking their eggs and feathers without so much as a thank-you.

"It's Tough to Be a Bug" is the old-time vaudeville-like title song for the 3-D film shown since 1998 inside the Tree of Life attraction at Walt Disney World's Animal Kingdom. The slaphappy number is sung by the bugs, reminding the audiences of the great services insects perform, from making honey to getting rid of dung. The movie (and the song) was added to Disneyland's California Adventure in 2001.

"It's Whatcha Do with Whatcha Got" is the spirited song by Gene de Paul (music) and Don Raye (lyric) that was featured in an animated sequence in the live-action film *So Dear to My Heart* (1948). To encourage the young Jeremiah Kincaid not to give up on his dream of bringing his black ram to the county fair, the Wise Old Owl (voice of Ken Carson) in Jeremiah's scrapbook comes to life and encourages the boy to be resourceful and keep on trying. The owl is joined by a trio of singing birds and then other animated animals who chime in singing the tuneful song.

"It's What's Inside That Counts" is the lyrical pop song by Randy Rogel about realizing one's inner value, used as commentary in the animated video sequel *Cinderella II: Dreams Come True* (2002). Cinderella's stepsister Anastasia is smitten with a baker and fusses over makeup, clothes, and jewelry to catch his eye. While Cinderella tries to teach Anastasia to be more like her true self, Brooke Allison sings this hopeful ballad on the soundtrack.

"I've Got a Dream" is the raucous sing-along number that Hook Hand (voice of Brad Garrett), Big Nose (Jeffrey Tambor), and the other Pub Thugs sing in the animated movie *Tangled* (2010). The large and ugly Thugs sing about the softer, hidden side of their personalities as they express the desire to be a concert pianist, an interior decorator, and a mime, the yearning to find a true love, and so on. Rapunzel (Mandy Moore) joins in with the Thugs and sings about how she wants to see the mysterious floating lights. Alan Menken wrote the catchy honky-tonk piano music and Glenn Slater penned the clownish lyric.

"I've Got My Eyes on You" is the song of determination sung by Princess Jasmine (singing voice of Lea Salonga) in the animated video *Disney Princess Enchanted Tales: Follow Your Dreams* (2007). Amy Powers and Russ DeSalvo wrote the driving ballad about keeping your eye on the prize you want and not giving up. Jasmine sings the song to a wild white horse, saying she will capture and tame him. By the end of the song, she has indeed done that, and the two ride off into the sunset.

"I've Got No Strings" is the carefree song of freedom that the puppet Pinocchio (voice of Dickie Jones) sings and dances to as he performs at Stromboli's marionette theatre in the animated movie *Pinocchio* (1940). The simple ditty by Leigh Harline (music) and Ned Washington (lyric) includes an amusing section in which puppets from different nations sing and dance with Pinocchio in a mock *Folies Bergère* routine. Gene Krupa and His Orchestra (vocal by Irene Daye) recorded the song in the 1940s, Barbra Streisand made a recording of the song in the 1960s, and the Gipsy Kings recorded it in 1995. It is the only song from the original *Pinocchio* to be reprised in the television musical *Geppetto* (2000).

J

"Jack's Lament" is the eerie but romantic "I am" song for Jack Skellington, the Pumpkin King, in the stop-motion film *The Nightmare Before Christmas* (1993). Danny Elfman, who wrote the haunting song, did the singing vocals for Jack as he strolls through a cemetery and admits to himself that he finds the thrill of Halloween is gone and he hopes for more out of life than the usual sounds of screams.

"Jake and the Pirates Main Title Theme," which also goes by the title "Yo Ho, Let's Go," is the rousing ditty by Kevin Hendrickson and Loren Hoskins that opens the Disney Junior cartoon series *Jake and the Never Land Pirates* (2011). The show, about a band of young pirates who fight the comically evil Captain Hook of Never Land, opens with this tuneful melody that introduces all of the characters while illustrating their swashbuckling adventures. The number is performed by an uncredited singer in a stereotypical, gruff pirate voice.

"John Colter" is the cowboy ballad written by George Bruns (music) and Tom W. Blackburn (lyric) for the adventure movie *Westward Ho, the Wagons!* (1956), about pioneers traveling the Oregon Trail. To entertain the members of a wagon train at night, Dr. John Grayson (Fess Parker) plays his guitar and sings this narrative ballad about the brave mountain man John Colter, who was captured by Indians while trapping in the wilderness, but escaped and ran three miles to safety. The song, which is sometimes listed as "The Ballad of John Colter," is both a tall tale and a sincere tribute to the legendary trapper.

"Johnny and the Sprites" is the tuneful title song for the 2005 television series about a musician who moves into a secluded house in the woods where he is the only one able to see invisible sprites. Stephen Schwartz wrote the pleasing number, in which Johnny (John Tartaglia) sings about how he is not the same Johnny since he came to this house and urges viewers to sing with him and they too will see the sprites.

"Johnny Fedora and Alice Blue Bonnet" is the delightful narrative song by Allie Wrubel (music) and Ray Gilbert (lyric) that tells one of the stories in the animated anthology movie *Make Mine Music* (1946). The harmonizing Andrews Sisters sing the facile ballad on the soundtrack as the tale is told from a hat's point of view. Johnny and Alice sit side by side in a hat shop window and fall in love, but are separated when they are bought by two different patrons. As Johnny is worn all over town, he struggles and strains to find Alice but is unsuccessful and is eventually discarded. He is rescued by an iceman, who puts the hat on one of his horses—and Johnny is thrilled to find Alice sitting on the head of the companion horse. The number is slightly swinging throughout, but at the end the Andrews Sisters break into a vivacious boogie-woogie for the last stanza. Edith Piaf recorded a French version of the song, and years later Michael Feinstein recorded it as well.

"Johnny Shiloh" is the marching title song written by Richard M. and Robert B. Sherman for the 1963 Civil War television drama. The Disney Studio Chorus sings the catchy ballad over the opening credits, chronicling the tale of the eleven-year-old Union Army recruit John Clem, who managed to shoot and kill a Confederate officer at the Battle of Shiloh and earned the nickname "Johnny Shiloh" for his heroics. The drama was a two-part episode on the *Disneyland* television program.

"Johnny Tremain" is the title ballad about a Revolutionary War patriot in the 1957 history-adventure film. George Bruns (music) and Tom W. Blackburn (lyric) wrote the narrative folk song about young Johnny, who participates in the Boston Tea Party and fights at the Battle of Lexington, but the song was cut in production and only the music was used in the background of some scenes.

"Joie de Vivre" is the tuneful testament to enjoying the little things in life, used throughout the film comedy *Monkeys, Go Home!* (1967), set in a small town in France. Richard M. and Robert B. Sherman wrote the incessantly chipper ditty, which was first sung in French by the local clergyman Father Sylvain (Maurice Chevalier in his last screen role) and the children of the village. Later, at the Festival of St. Prioust, Sylvain sings the song in English in honor of his new American friend Hank (Dean Jones), convincing him to stop worrying about making money and to enjoy life.

"JoJo's Circus Theme Song" is the lite-rock song by Stuart Kollmorgen that welcomes children to the stop-motion animated television series *JoJo's Circus* (2003) on Playhouse Disney. A chorus of children sings the happy number on the soundtrack, promising fun to follow as the clown JoJo and his friends arrive in town with the circus. The series and the opening song are reminiscent of the children's show *Dumbo's Circus* (1985), which entertained kids two decades earlier.

"Jolly Holiday" is the resplendent song by Richard M. and Robert B. Sherman from the movie musical *Mary Poppins* (1964) that provides one of filmdom's finest sequences of live action mixed with animation. British nanny Mary (Julie Andrews) and her two charges (Karen Dotrice and Matthew Garber) join sidewalk artist Bert (Dick Van Dyke) as they jump into one of his chalk drawings and experience a fun-filled holiday in animation. At an outdoor café staffed by penguin waiters, Bert sings that a day outing with Mary is like a holiday, and she returns the compliment in song and dance. After doing an ingenious dance with the penguins, Bert joins Mary and the children on a merry-go-round where the horses break loose and dash across the countryside, Mary's horse coming in first place in a race. The song is happy and carefree, with the flavor of an old vaudeville soft-shoe routine. In the 2004 London stage version of *Mary Poppins*, the number was performed in a fantasy park in which Bert (Gavin Lee), Mary (Laura Michelle Kelly), and the children were joined by a group of dancing statues come to life. In the 2006 Broadway production, Lee reprised his Bert and sang the song with Ashley Brown (as Mary). Louis Prima and Gia Maione made a notable duet recording of the song.

"Jolly Rovers" is the hand-clapping, knee-slapping sing-along song written by Stan Jones (music) and Lawrence Edgar Watkin (lyric) for *Ten Who Dared* (1960), the adventure film about the men who first navigated and mapped the Colorado River. As the men camp and rest on the shore of the river one day, they sing this merry but incongruously maudlin ditty about ten roving boys, each one meeting with a comedic and gruesome death.

"The Journey (Who Will Rescue Me?)" is a moving ballad by Ayn Robbins and Carol Connors that is heard in the opening sequence and credits of the animated movie *The Rescuers* (1977). The kidnapped orphan Penny drops a bottle with a plea for help inside and in a series of stills behind the credits we see the bottle travel from the swamps of Louisiana to New York Harbor, while Shelby Flint sings on the soundtrack the affecting song asking to be rescued.

"Jump in the Line" is the vivacious calypso number Jeanine Tesori wrote for the animated made-for-video prequel *The Little Mermaid: Ariel's Beginning* (2008). Although music is not allowed in the kingdom of King Triton, the crab Sebastian (voice of Samuel E. Wright) and other sea creatures secretly meet at the underground Catfish Club to play music and sing this lively number that asks listeners to shake to the music and involves some scat singing as well. The song is later reprised by Sebastian, Flounder (Parker Goris), Ariel (Jodi Benson), and some other fugitives from the kingdom after they escape from prison.

"Jungle Rhythm" is the swinging number about the call of the wild written by Lorraine Feather and Paul Grabowsky for the video sequel *The Jungle Book 2* (2003). The young boy Mowgli (voice of Haley Joel Osment) explains to the other children in the "man village" that there is a rhythm that drives all the creatures in the wild. Urging them to feel that rhythm, Mowgli sings the effervescent number and breaks into a rhythmic dance, and soon the kids are joining him in both song and dance.

"Junkyard Society Rag" is the freewheeling list song about free living written by Melissa Manchester and Norman Gimbel for the animated video sequel *Lady and the Tramp II: Scamp's Adventure* (2001). When the puppy Scamp runs away from home and finds himself in a junkyard filled with stray dogs, he is told about life without propriety by the canines Sparky (voice of Mickey Rooney), Angel (Melissa Manchester), Ruby (Cathy Moriarty), Buster (Jess Harnell), Mooch (Bill Fagerbakke), and Francois (Bronson Pinchot). The stimulating number is in the form of a lively rag, appropriate for the early-twentieth-century setting of the tale.

"Just a Little Love" is the heartfelt ballad from an episode of the animated television series *The Little Mermaid* (1992). Ariel (voice of Jodi Benson) befriends a lost baby killer whale and sings this warm number about offering him a little love and making him part of her family. The two sea creatures then swim a pas de deux together, the young mammal making strange whale sounds as he joins her in the song.

"Just Around the Riverbend" is the exhilarating "I am" song for the Native American heroine in the animated movie *Pocahontas* (1995). The tribal princess Pocahontas (singing voice of Judy Kuhn) contemplates the future, wondering if she should marry the noble but cold tribesman Kocoum. Alan Menken composed the stirring music and Stephen Schwartz penned the expert lyric filled with nature imagery and a rich imagination. Christiane Noll and Ashley Brown each made a heartfelt recording of the ballad.

"Just Because It's Magic" is the insightful song about the difficulty of parenting written by Stephen Schwartz for the live-action television musical *Geppetto* (2000). After Pinocchio keeps getting into trouble, the toymaker Geppetto (Drew Carey) asks the Blue Fairy (Julia Louis-Dreyfus) to use her magic to make him a better son. The fairy explains that magic cannot make for a strong relationship between parent and child. The thoughtful duet is reprised throughout the musical; every time Geppetto becomes frustrated with Pinocchio, the Blue Fairy appears to remind him that parenting is something learned, not a magic trick.

"Just One Mistake" is the dandy song of ambition sung by the villainess Marina Del Ray (voice of Sally Field) in the animated made-for-video prequel *The Little Mermaid: Ariel's Beginning* (2008). The conniving mermaid Marina wants the job of attaché to King Triton, so she waits for the day when the current aide, Sebastian the Crab, makes an error that will put him out of favor. Jeanine Tesori wrote the rhythmic number, which Marina reprises when she finds out that Sebastian, against the law forbidding music, sings and plays with a band in the underground Catfish Club.

"Just Say Auf Wiedersehen" is the wistful farewell song written by Richard M. and Robert B. Sherman for the World War II–era movie *The Miracle of the White Stallions* (1963). Austrian soldiers at a Vienna riding school are called away to war by the Germans, and at a farewell party Rider Otto (Eddie Albert) sings this pensive goodbye song with a heavy heart.

"Just the Goin'" is the gentle country-western number by John Hiatt that is used effectively in the movie *The Country Bears* (2002), inspired by the Disney World attraction. The young bear Beary Barrington (voice of Haley

Disney's contribution to the war effort in the 1940s ranged from animated documentary films to movie shorts created to boost morale, none more popular than *Der Fuehrer's Face* (1943), originally titled *Donald in Nutzi Land*. The song "Der Fuehrer's Face," which Oliver Wallace wrote for the short, became so popular before the release date that the cartoon was retitled. In Donald Duck's nightmare, he is forced to salute the dictators Tojo, Hitler, and Mussolini day and night. (Walt Disney/Photofest)

Joel Osment) has been adopted by a human family but decides to run away to find himself, and hopefully his real bear family. Hiatt sings on the soundtrack about making such an important decision, while Beary packs up and sets out on his journey.

"Just Wanna Be with You" is the gentle, affecting love song by Andy Dodd and Adam Watts that is used for two different couples in the movie sequel *High School Musical 3: Senior Year* (2008). Sent by his overeager sister Sharpay to get a good song from student composer Kelsi (Olesya Rulin) for her to sing in the spring musical, Ryan Evans (Lucas Grabeel) joins Kelsi at the piano and the two sing her latest creation together, a tender number that pleads for companionship. The song is then reprised by teen performers Troy Bolton (Zac Efron) and Gabriella (Vanessa Anne Hudgens), performing in rehearsal the song Sharpay so coveted. Finally, an upbeat version of the song is sung by the cast of the spring musical.

"Kanine Krunchies Commercial" is the droll musical spoof of television advertisements written by Mel Leven for the animated film *One Hundred and One Dalmatians* (1961). While the dalmatians Pongo and Perdita watch television with their fifteen puppies in their London home, the canine adventure program is interrupted by a commercial selling Kanine Krunchies dog treats, sung by animated dogs with chipmunk-like voices. The commercial and the song are reprised in the made-for-video animated sequel *101 Dalmatians II: Patch's London Adventure* (2003), when the ninety-nine dalmatian puppies watch television together.

"Kansas" is the pop ballad by Jeannie Lurie and Brandon Christy that serves as the "I am" song for Dorothy (Ashanti) in the television movie *The Muppets' Wizard of Oz* (2005). During the opening credits of the film, Dorothy works in her Aunt Em's diner and sings about her wish to leave her Kansas home and become a singing star. The whole sequence was later turned into a music video for Ashanti. The number is sometimes listed as "I Gotta Get Outa Kansas."

"Katrina" is the adoring ballad about the lovely Katrina Van Tassel of Sleepy Hollow, who is wooed by the silly schoolteacher Ichabod Crane even though she loves the more manly Brom Bones in the animated movie *The Adventures of Ichabod and Mr. Toad* (1949). Bing Crosby and the Rhythmaires sing the expositional number by Gene de Paul and Don Raye on the soundtrack as the romantic triangle is revealed on screen. Crosby's recorded version was very popular, and there were also discs by Lawrence Welk, Kay Kyser, and Tex Beneke.

"Keys to the Kingdom" is the ardent song of determination sung by Princess Aurora (singing voice of Cassidy Ladden) in the animated video *Disney Princess Enchanted Tales: Follow Your Dreams* (2007). Left in charge of the palace for two days while her parents are away, the eager Aurora sings proudly about having the keys to the entire kingdom, and she will use the opportunity to show everyone what a princess can be. Amy Powers and Russ DeSalvo wrote the flowing number, flavored with some regal and medieval touches, and Aurora sings it as she races through the castle and the gardens, the servants and staff joining in on the song.

"Kick Buttowski," by Andy Sturmer and James Childs, is the adventure-inciting theme song that opens the 2010 animated Disney cartoon series of the same name. Performed by Sturmer, the song is just a repetition of the title character's name played during images of him suiting up for adventure. The show's premise is a simple one: a kid with a big imagination wants to become the world's greatest daredevil, and each episode is a glimpse into how he finds thrills in the boring suburbia of his everyday life.

"Kick It into Gear" is the vivacious country-western number John Hiatt wrote for the film *The Country Bears* (2002), based on the Disney World attraction. A waitress (Jennifer Paige) at a restaurant hopes to become a country singer, and when the famous band Country Bears comes into the place, she breaks into a rousing rendition of one of the group's hits. Soon everyone in the restaurant is singing, dancing, and banging out the rhythm on pots and pans and with their silverware.

"Kickin' It with You" is the raucous pop theme song performed by Victoria Rocks during the opening for the Disney XD sitcom *Kickin' It* (2011). The show follows a group of misfit teenage boys who are members of a down-on-its-luck karate dojo as they band together and look out for each other. The song, by Ali Dee Theodore, Jordan Yaeger, Julian Michael Davis, and Jason Gleed, is all about how karate is great, but not as great as having someone to spend time with.

"Kidnap the Sandy Claws" is a gleeful but oddball trio written by Danny Elfman for the stop-motion movie *The Nightmare Before Christmas* (1993). The three ghoulish trick-or-treaters Lock (voice of Paul Reubens), Shock

(Catherine O'Hara), and Barrel (Elfman) sing the darkly comic list song about the different ways they can kidnap Santa Claus, and then they revel in the methods in which they can torture him. Although the number is in three-part harmony, there is something enharmonic about the resulting sounds coming from the three little monsters.

"King of New York" is the jubilant song about the power of the press Alan Menken (music) and Jack Feldman (lyric) wrote for the period film *Newsies* (1992). When the newsboys who carry the New York newspaper the *World* go on strike, their story and a picture of them is put on the front page of the rival paper the *Sun*. The "newsie" Racetrack Higgins (Max Casella) and reporter Bryan Denton (Bill Pullman) lead the boys in celebrating their newfound fame by singing this energetic number, in which they claim to be the king of the city.

"King of the River" is the boastful song by George Bruns (music) and Tom W. Blackburn (lyric) that is used in an exciting race scene in the adventure film *Davy Crockett and the River Pirates* (1956). The rowdy number is sung by an omniscient off-camera chorus to introduce the loud and boisterous Mike Fink (Jeff York) as Davy Crockett (Fess Parker) and George Russel (Buddy Ebsen) are about to meet this hero of the rivers. Soon they engage him in a keel boat race, and, as both parties navigate the waters, Fink leads a chorus of this ditty in counterpoint to Russel leading the Crockett team in a reprise of "The Ballad of Davy Crockett."

"Kiss the Girl" is the calypso-flavored love song sung by the crab Sebastian (voice of Samuel E. Wright) in the animated film *The Little Mermaid* (1989) with other marine animals as they urge Prince Eric to kiss Ariel and make her a human forever. The Oscar-nominated song was written by Alan Menken (music) and Howard Ashman (lyric) and was sung in the 2008 Broadway version of *The Little Mermaid* by Tituss Burgess and the ensemble. The group Soul II Soul recorded the song with Kolfi in 1995, and there were also recordings made by Jazz Networks, Steve Tyrell, Ashley Tisdale, Colbie Caillat, No Secrets, and Vitamin C.

L

"La La Lu" is the warm and entrancing lullaby written by Sonny Burke and Peggy Lee for the animated movie *Lady and the Tramp* (1955). The new mother Darling (singing voice of Peggy Lee) sings the quiet number to the newborn in her arms as the canine Lady comes into the bedroom and sees the infant for the first time. Jane Sherberg made a graceful recording of the lullaby.

"Lack of Education" is the brief song of instruction the wise old owl Big Mama (voice of Pearl Bailey) sings in the animated film *The Fox and the Hound* (1981). Jim Stafford wrote the hillbilly-flavored number, which Big Mama sings to the young fox Tod to make him understand that his best friend, the hound dog Copper, has been trained to hunt foxes.

"Ladies in the Sky" is the pleasing cowboy ballad written by George Bruns for the television series *The Saga of Andy Burnett* (1957), which was shown on the weekly program *Disneyland*. The flowing number is not about women, but is rather a love song to the giant mountains out West that fill the sky. Pioneer Andy Burnett (Jerome Courtland) sings how he misses those mountains and will remain faithful to them, dreaming of the day he will return to the "ladies" in the sky.

"Lambert, the Sheepish Lion" is the playful title song by Eddie Pola and George Wyle that is used throughout the 1952 animated film short about a lion raised by sheep. A studio chorus sings the bouncy number about how a stork (voice of Sterling Holloway, who did the vocals for the same stork in the earlier film *Dumbo*) delivers the baby lion Lambert to a ewe. The song is reprised by the baby lambs and the stork as they make fun of Lambert, who does not fit in with the rest of the flock. The number is heard again at the end of the film after Lambert saves his mother from a hungry wolf and everyone rejoices.

"Lavender Blue (Dilly Dilly)" is the simple but unforgettable ditty Larry Morey and Eliot Daniel fashioned from a seventeenth-century English folk song to be used in the nostalgic movie *So Dear to My Heart* (1948). The blacksmith Uncle Hiram (Burl Ives, in his film debut) plays the guitar and sings the childlike song of affection to Granny Kincaid (Beulah Bondi), Jeremiah (Bobby Driscoll), and Tildy (Luana Patten) in the farmhouse one evening after supper. The Oscar-nominated song was recorded by Ives (with Captain Stubby and the Buccaneers) and by Dinah Shore, and each had a hit with it. Records were also made by Sammy Kaye (vocal by the Three Kaydets), Jack Smith, Sammy Turner, Mary Martin, Ashley Brown, and Barbara Cook. Vera Lynn sang the number in the film *A Safe Place* (1971).

"Laws of Motion" is the disco-flavored rock song written by Brock Walsh for the innovative but short-lived television musical series *Hull High* (1990). High school students in science class studying the universe break into a production number, singing about moving together as a force of nature. The vibrant number was choreographed by Kenny Ortega, who later found greater fame staging similar numbers in *High School Musical* (2006) and its sequels.

"Lazy Countryside" is the dreamy lullaby by Bobby Worth that is used in the "Bongo" sequence in the animated anthology film *Fun and Fancy Free* (1947). On the soundtrack, Dinah Shore and a female chorus sing the smooth and lulling number about relaxing and enjoying nature while the performing bear Bongo, who has escaped from the circus, enjoys his freedom in the wilderness and frolics with small animals and lounges in the tall, soft grass.

"Le Festin" is the lyrical and memorable French ditty about celebrating life by appreciating food, written for the animated film *Ratatouille* (2007). During a montage that shows the young chef Linguini becoming famous and Gusteau's Restaurant making a comeback, the chanteuse Camille sings the sidewalk café–style song in French on the soundtrack. Michael Giacchino wrote the music and an English lyric, which was translated into French by Boualem Lamhene.

"Le Jour D'Amour" is the festive dance song by Randy Petersen and Kevin Quinn that opens the animated video sequel *The Hunchback of Notre Dame II* (2002). While Paris is celebrating the Festival of Love and the citizens, led by the harlequinesque Clopin (voice of Paul Kandel), sing of the romantic holiday, the hunchback Quasimodo (Tom Hulce) watches the proceedings from the bell tower and longs for a romance of his own. His singing of the medieval-flavored number receives musical commentary by the resident gargoyles Victor (Charles Kimbrough), Hugo (Jason Alexander), and Laverne (Jane Withers).

"Leaving Home (Find My Way)" is the sad lament Phil Collins wrote for the animated video sequel *Tarzan II* (2005). The boy Tarzan, feeling that he does not fit in with the gorilla tribe, sets off on his own to try to discover where he is wanted. Collins sings the heartfelt number on the soundtrack and later adapted it into the song "I Need to Know" for the 2006 Broadway version of *Tarzan*.

"The Legend of Lobo" is the western-flavored title song written by Richard M. and Robert B. Sherman for the 1962 movie about a brave wolf named Lobo. The narrative ballad, which tells the story of the king of the hunters, is sung over the opening credits of the movie by Rex Allen and the Sons of the Pioneers. The number is reprised throughout the film as Allen narrates and comments on the different adventures of Lobo.

"The Legend of the Sword in the Stone" is the narrative ballad that is sung over the prologue of the animated movie *The Sword in the Stone* (1963). Richard M. and Robert B. Sherman wrote the troubadour-like number, which explains how a magical sword appeared in a stone one day, the inscription stating that whoever could pull the sword out of the stone would be the rightful king of England.

"Les Poissons" is the French-flavored character song for the chef Louis (voice of René Auberjonois) that Alan Menken (music) and Howard Ashman (lyric) wrote for the animated movie musical *The Little Mermaid* (1989). As he prepares Prince Eric's dinner, the sadistic Louis slices, chops, and boils different sea creatures as he sings about how delicious fish is. The crab Sebastian watches the scene in horror and barely escapes with his life. The music is similar to a can-can number in tone, yet the frivolity is a bit too gruesome for some tastes. In the 2008 Broadway version of *The Little Mermaid*, it was sung by Louis (John Treacy Egan) and fellow chefs, the song turning into a production number with added lyrics by Glenn Slater. A playful recording of the number was made by Brian Sutherland, with backup vocals by Meredith Inglesby, Andy Karl, Tyler Maynard, and Keewa Nurullah.

"Lesson Number One" is the clever musical lesson Jeanine Tesori (music) and Alexa Junge (lyric) wrote for the animated video sequel *Mulan II* (2005). Mulan (singing voice of Lea Salonga) has become a role model for the village girls, who like to watch her train as a warrior, and they implore her to teach them her skills. So she instructs them in the two most important aspects of being a warrior: balance and flexibility. The song is split into two parts: the sharper, more syncopated melody of "balance" and the meditative, hypnotic melody of "flexibility." Soon, Mulan has two groups of girls, each trying to master one of the two aspects. The two groups sing the song's halves in a clever and humorous counterpoint. The song itself is a foreshadowing of the problems Mulan will soon face in her own life, realizing how different she and her fiancé Shang are.

"Lester's Possum Park" is the hillbilly spoof written by Randy Petersen and Kevin Quinn for the animated film *A Goofy Movie* (1995). While on a family road trip, Goofy and his son, Max, stay overnight at a dumpy campsite called Lester's Possum Pond, where the nighttime entertainment is a concert by ragtag mechanical creatures who sing about the glories of the park even as they break down and fall apart. The fun number can be seen as a satire of Disney entertainment attractions such as the Country Bear Jamboree and the Hoop-Dee-Doo show. Songwriter Quinn provides the lead vocals on the soundtrack for the silly country song.

"Let Her Alone" is the mournful yet urgent song written by Terry Gilkyson for the nature adventure film *Run, Cougar, Run* (1972). When the mother cougar Seeta sees her mate killed by a hunter, she guides her kitten to safety and must now work alone to protect the two of them in the wilderness. The duo Ian and Sylvia sing the musical plea over the opening credits, urging man to let the wild beasts of nature live free.

"Let It Ride" is the gently rolling country-western song by John Hiatt about taking new chances every day in order to find yourself. The reflective number was sung by Hiatt on the soundtrack during the opening credits of the movie *The Country Bears* (2002), inspired by the Disney World attraction. The song echoes the plight of the film's main character, Beary Barrington (voice of Haley Joel Osment), who is searching for his bear family.

"Let Me Be Good to You" is the vampy, seductive number Melissa Manchester wrote for the animated movie adventure *The Great Mouse Detective* (1986). In a tough Victorian saloon in London, a sexy mouse songstress (voice of Manchester) calms an unruly crowd with this provocative music-hall number promising to treat listeners with attention and affection. She is soon joined by a few comely mouse chorines, who sing and dance with her, much to the enjoyment of the rowdy male mouse audience.

"Let the Rain Pour Down" is the pastiche "Negro" work song written by Foster Carling and Ken Darby for the part-live-action, part-animated movie *Song of the South* (1946). As the African American plantation workers set off in the morning for the cotton fields, they sing this infectious number about the problems of the weevil and the cotton, praying that it will rain and they can all go back to bed. The Hall Johnson Choir provides the rich, harmonic singing on the soundtrack.

"Let's Get Crazy" is the insistent, pop-rock number that Hannah/Miley (Miley Cyrus) performs onstage at her best friend Lily's birthday party at a beachside carnival in *Hannah Montana: The Movie* (2009). Written by Colleen Fitzpatrick, Michal Kotch, David Derby, Michael Smith, Stefanie Ridel, Miriam Nervo, and Olivia Nervo, the song is a high-energy pledge to let one's hair down and have a good time.

"Let's Get Together" is the very 1960s-sounding pop song written by Richard M. and Robert B. Sherman for the film comedy *The Parent Trap* (1961). The up-tempo and happily naive number about joining forces parallels the plot of the movie, in which two separated twins are reunited and an estranged married couple is brought back together. The song is first heard at a dance at summer camp, where Annette Funicello is heard singing it on a record. Later in the film the twins Sharon and Susan (both played by Hayley Mills) sing it to entertain their parents, one accompanying herself on the piano, and the other on the guitar. The silly bubblegum number was popular for a time thanks to recordings by Mills and Funicello. Kristen Bell and Ryan Driscoll made a snappy duet recording of the song in 2003, and two years later Ashley Brown recorded the number with backup vocals by Meredith Inglesby, Andy Karl, Tyler Maynard, and Keewa Nurullah. There was also a recording by the Go-Gos in 2007.

"Let's Go Fly a Kite" is the waltzing song of joy written by Richard M. and Robert B. Sherman for the end of the film *Mary Poppins* (1964). Edwardian father Mr. Banks (David Tomlinson) realizes it is time to enjoy life and his own family and sings the joyous number with his wife (Glynis Johns) and children (Karen Dotrice and Matthew Garber) as they are joined by other Londoners in the park, singing and flying kites. In the 2004 London stage version of *Mary Poppins*, the number was sung by David Haig, Linzi Hateley, and the company. Daniel Jenkins and Rebecca Luker led the cast in singing it in the 2006 Broadway production. Burl Ives made a memorable recording of the song, as did Louis Prima and Gia Maione in a duet version.

"Let's Have a Drink on It" is the frantic drinking song with a player piano–like flavor written by Richard M. and Robert B. Sherman for the movie musical *The Happiest Millionaire* (1967). The disillusioned Angie Duke (John Davidson) breaks off his wedding engagement and goes to an Irish bar in Philadelphia where the butler John Lawless (Tommy Steele) gets him drunk. The two sing together and are later joined by the male patrons in the bar, who partake in a vigorous dance as well. The number is reprised at the end of the film when the millionaire Anthony J. Drexel Biddle (Fred MacMurray) is made a captain in the Marine Corps and all his cronies join him in celebrating the occasion.

"Let's Put It Over with Grover" is the tuneful campaign song for candidate Grover Cleveland prepared by the Nebraska Bower family for the 1888 Democratic Convention in the period movie musical *The One and Only, Genuine, Original Family Band* (1968). Richard M. and Robert B. Sherman wrote the brash number, sung by avid Democrat Grandpa Bower (Walter Brennan), his Nebraska family (Buddy Ebsen, Lesley Ann Warren, and Janet Blair), and the grandchildren as they audition for a representative from the convention. Grandpa reprises the number with the children on the street when the family moves to Dakota, and it is heard a third time the night of the election, when it is used in competition with the Republican campaign song "Oh, Benjamin Harrison."

"Let's Sing a Gay Little Spring Song" is the chipper number by Frank Churchill (music) and Larry Morey (lyric) that welcomes spring in the animated movie *Bambi* (1942). A female chorus sings the radiant song on the soundtrack while animals frolic and birds whistle and chirp, all in time with the music, and annoy Friend Owl, who is trying to sleep. In the animated video sequel *Bambi II* (2006), the song is reprised by a nervous groundhog (voice of Brian Pimental) who wakes up and doesn't see his shadow, joined in singing by the other forest animals.

"Let's Talk about Me" is the arrogant, comic-rap number, by Ali Dee Theodore and Bret McKenzie, sung by the sinister Tex Richman (Chris Cooper) in the 2011 film *The Muppets*. Tex celebrates his plan to gain control of the Muppet Studios and the Muppet name, and rubs it in with this comic ditty that is essentially a list song about how terrific he is. The number drives home to Kermit and his friends how they have failed to beat Tex at his sinister game.

"The Liberty Tree" is the patriotic anthem George Bruns (music) and Tom W. Blackburn (lyric) wrote for the Revolutionary War film *Johnny Tremain* (1957). After throwing the British tea into the Boston harbor, the Sons of Liberty sing this cry for freedom as they carry lanterns through the city and then hang them on a huge tree, calling it the Liberty Tree and comparing its strength and endurance to that of their cause.

"Life Goes On" is the easygoing rhythm-and-blues theme song for the television series *Empty Nest* (1988). George Aliceson Tipton and John Bettis wrote the number about sharing the everyday ups and downs of life and it was sung over the opening credits by Billy Vera and the Beaters.

"The Life I Lead" is the song of smug satisfaction that the Edwardian banker Mr. Banks (David Tomlinson) sings throughout the film *Mary Poppins* (1964). While his wife (Glynis Johns) tries to tell him that their two children have run away again, the pompous Mr. Banks is too busy complimenting himself on his well-ordered, civilized life to hear her. He reprises the number later when dictating what kind of nanny they need to find, and he sings it again, under the title "A British Bank," when he praises the solidity of the English banking system to Mary Poppins (Julie Andrews). Near the end of the film, Mr. Banks sings part of the song again, with less pompous lyrics, to the chimney sweep Bert (Dick Van Dyke) after he realizes that his financial status is a disaster and the life he loves will be destroyed.

The Disney studio's experiments with mixing live action and animation culminated in the very popular *Mary Poppins* (1964). Before the use of computers, the artists and cinematographers worked together tirelessly to create such delightful scenes as "Jolly Holiday" in which Bert (Dick Van Dyke) and some penguin waiters entertain Mary (Julie Andrews). (Walt Disney/Photofest)

Richard M. and Robert B. Sherman wrote the march-like number, which has a military flavor to it. David Haig played Mr. Banks in the 2004 London stage version of *Mary Poppins* and sang only a brief section of the song with Bert (Gavin Lee). On Broadway two years later it was sung by Daniel Jenkins as Mr. Banks, with Lee reprising his role as Bert.

"Life with Derek Theme Song" is the bouncy lite-rock number by Gary Koftinoff and Ron Proulx that is heard in the opening of the 2005 television series about the changes that occur when a mother with two daughters marries a man with two sons. The song takes the point of view of the teenager Casey MacDonald (Ashley Leggat), who sings about how simple life was before her stepbrother Derek came into her life.

"Life's a Happy Song" is the overtly perky production number that comes early in the 2011 film *The Muppets*. With music and lyrics by Bret McKenzie, the piece is purposely a sugary celebration of all the joy and sunshine to be found in the world. The number, which begins small and grows to involve the entire town, is sung by Gary (Jason Segal), his Muppet brother Walter (voice of Peter Linz), and Gary's fiancée Mary (Amy Adams) as they prepare for their big trip from small-town America to Hollywood, where Walter hopes to visit the Muppet Studios. They dance through their town as the neighbors join in, including a cameo from actor Mickey Rooney. The song is reprised at the end of the movie by Gary, Mary, and Walter (with all the Muppets) after they have made a huge television comeback with their popular variety show.

"The Light in the Forest" is the title ballad for the 1958 film about a white youth kidnapped and raised by Native Americans who must learn how to adjust to adult life in white society. Paul J. Smith wrote the sweeping melody and Gil George (pseudonym for Hazel George) penned the knowing lyric, which is a poetic assessment of a boy who is trapped between two worlds. A studio chorus sings the evocative ballad over the opening credits of the movie.

"Light Magic Theme" is the electronic-rock song, flavored with a Scottish folk sound, featured in the 1997 parade at Disneyland that was termed a "streetacular" by the Disney imagineers but ended up being one of the most costly failures in the history of the park. As four eighty-foot-long floating stages moved through Fantasyland carrying hundreds of pixies and Disney characters lit by fiber optics, the theme song invited audiences to take a journey through the darkness to a magical light that makes dreams come true. While the show impressed many patrons, most spectators preferred the Main Street Electrical Parade, which Light Magic replaced. The new presentation was retired after only three months and was never seen again.

"Like Father, Like Son" is the pulsating rock song from the Broadway musical *Aida* (2000) in which the Egyptian prime minister Zoser (John Hickok) and his son, Radames (Adam Pascal), argue over the son's giving up a brilliant career in politics because of his love for the Nubian slave Aida (Heather Headley). The ministers of the court join in the song and urge Radames to see reason and be more like his father. Elton John composed the harsh music and Tim Rice wrote the ironic lyric. Lenny Kravitz recorded the song before the musical opened on Broadway.

"Like No Man I've Ever Seen" is a revealing duet written by Phil Collins for the 2006 Broadway version of *Tarzan*. Jane Porter (Jenn Gambatese) tries to explain to her father (Timothy Jerome) about the wild man she has been encountering in the jungle and how he is so different from all others. Professor Porter asks a series of questions and then concludes that his daughter has lost her heart to Tarzan.

"Like Other Girls" is the wistful song of longing written by Jeanine Tesori (music) and Alexa Junge (lyric) for the animated video sequel *Mulan II* (2005). Three princesses (singing voices of Beth Blankenship, Mandy Gonzalez, and Judy Kuhn), traveling to be wed to husbands chosen for them by the emperor, have fallen in love with the three misfit but lovable warriors who are guarding them. The trio of girls sing this spirited lament, wishing they were like other women and not bound by duty. A pop version of the number is sung by Atomic Kitten over the final credits of the video.

"Listen with Our Hearts" is the flowing ballad about speaking your mind but listening to others with empathy, sung by the heroine in the animated video *Belle's Magical World* (1998). Belle (voice of Paige O'Hara) and the Beast (Robby Benson) have each been too stubborn to really hear what the other has been trying to say. By the end of the video, Belle realizes their mistakes and sings this understanding number, written by Michael and Patty Silversher.

"Listen with Your Heart" is the hypnotic song of wonder by Alan Menken (music) and Stephen Schwartz (lyric) that is used effectively throughout the animated movie *Pocahontas* (1995). The restless Pocahontas asks the aged tree Grandmother Willow (voice of Linda Hunt) what path should she take in life, and the old ancestor sings about the voices of the past that are within you, and that if you listen to them, they will guide you. The song is heard later, when Pocahontas first meets Captain John Smith, and Grandmother Willow reprises the number even later when Pocahontas introduces her to Smith.

"The Litterbug" is the jazzy, up-tempo title song by Mel Leven for the 1961 movie short, the last Donald Duck cartoon made. During the opening credits which showed live-action footage of litter along the highways and all across America, a studio chorus sings the peppy number, which cries "shame on you" to all those who destroy the beauty of the city and countryside. The number is reprised at the end of the short film as Donald (voice of Clarence Nash) drives past a "Keep America Beautiful" sign.

"Little April Shower" is the plucky little ditty that takes its rhythm from nature in the animated movie *Bambi* (1942). Frank Churchill (music) and Larry Morey (lyric) wrote the sprightly number, which uses the pattern of raindrops falling: starting off hesitantly, then increasing in speed as the rain pours, only to dwindle to a plunking rhythm by the end. A chorus sings on the soundtrack about the rain as small animals are seen running for shelter in the spring shower, all seen through the eyes of the young fawn Bambi as he experiences his first rainfall. A bluegrass rendition of the song was recorded by Mike Toppins, Glen Duncan, Billy Troy, Jim Brown, James Freeze, and David Chase.

"A Little Black Rain Cloud" is the childlike ditty by Richard M. and Robert B. Sherman that sounds like a nursery rhyme song, with its simple melody and unimposing lyric. Winnie the Pooh (voice of Sterling Holloway) rolls in the mud and attaches himself to a helium balloon in order to disguise himself as a rain cloud in the film short *Winnie the Pooh and the Honey Tree* (1966). The purpose of the ruse is to get close to the honeycomb high up in a tree, but the bees are not fooled and the amusing plot fails. The number is sometimes listed as "I'm Just a Little Black Rain Cloud."

"Little Einsteins Theme" is the simple title song written by Billy Straus for the 2005 animated television series about four brainy tots. Harrison Chad, Jesse Goldberg, Emma Straus, and Philip Trencher provide the singing voices for the foursome, who take off in their rocket ship and invite the viewers to join them as they travel the world looking for new adventures. The program was based on a series of *Baby Einstein* videos, which introduce children to classical music.

"Little Mr. Roo" is a lilting lullaby the mother kangaroo Kanga (voice of Kath Soucie) sings to her child Roo (Nikita Hopkins) in the animated film *Pooh's Heffalump Movie* (2005). Carly Simon wrote the tender number urging Roo not to grow up too fast so he'll have plenty of time for dreams, and Simon sings it on the soundtrack while Kanga puts Roo to bed. Later in the movie Roo reprises the soothing song to the frightened young elephant Lumpy, who cannot find his mother.

"Little Patch of Heaven" is the toe-tapping country-western song by Alan Menken (music) and Glenn Slater (lyric) that opens the animated film *Home on the Range* (2004). k. d. lang sings the catchy number on the soundtrack as viewers are introduced to the various animals who live on the farm called Patch of Heaven. The song is reprised at the end of the movie when all the animals celebrate their having saved the farm from being repossessed for back taxes.

"A Little Thought" is the musical lesson in kindness that Belle (voice of Paige O'Hara) sings in the animated video feature *Belle's Magical World* (1998). Michael and Patty Silversher wrote the gentle but spirited song, which Belle sings to the enchanted objects about little acts of caring and understanding that add up to something not so little.

"Little Toot" is the swinging narrative ballad the Andrews Sisters sing on the soundtrack of the animated anthology film *Melody Time* (1948). Allie Wrubel wrote the musical fable about the young tugboat Little Toot, who is always getting into mischief in the New York Harbor because he'd rather have fun than work. But all is forgiven when the little tug saves a floundering ocean liner at sea and he gets a hero's welcome back at the harbor.

"Little Wonders" is the moving pop song about life's simple joys written by Rob Thomas for the animated movie *Meet the Robinsons* (2007). At the end of the film, when the orphan Lewis finds happiness in the home of the eccentric, madcap Robinson family, songwriter Thomas sings this sweet, reflective number on the soundtrack, celebrating life's tiny miracles of love.

"Little Wooden Head" is the toe-tapping dance number written by Leigh Harline (music) and Ned Washington (lyric) for the animated movie *Pinocchio* (1940). After the toymaker Geppetto (voice of Christian Rub) completes his new marionette, which he names Pinocchio, he works the strings and has the puppet dance around the shop with him, the both of them doing some fancy footwork while Geppetto sings about the wooden-headed puppet.

"Live Alone and Like It" is the breezy song of independence written by Stephen Sondheim for the film *Dick Tracy* (1990), but little survived the editing and Mel Tormé is heard singing only a portion of the number on the soundtrack. The upbeat song proclaims that life without commitment to others is the only way to go, though the subtext of the number hints at dissatisfaction. John Barrowman sang the song in the Broadway revue *Putting It Together* (1999), and it was also recorded by Mandy Patinkin. James

Naughton sang the number for the benefit *Sondheim at Carnegie Hall*, and his recording is much admired.

"Live to Party" is the upbeat pop theme song that opens the 2009 Disney Channel sitcom *JONAS* and was retained for its revamping as *JONAS L.A.* The show was a fictional account of the Jonas Brothers, the famous boy band, and it followed them as they dealt with their teenage problems and with balancing school with their recording and concert obligations. The song "Live to Party" is a celebration of all the fun there is to be had in life. During the show's original inception, the number was performed by the Jonas Brothers as they sang with school and the recording studio as backgrounds. When the show made its transition to Los Angeles, the song was used again, this time showing the boy band in various Hollywood locales. The piece was written and performed by Nick, Joe, and Kevin Jonas.

"Livin' One Day at a Time" is the optimistic number about taking each day as a gift, heard at the beginning of the movie *Charley and the Angel* (1973). Shane Tatum and Ed Scott wrote the pastiche big-band swing number, and it is sung on the soundtrack by a female chorus. Since Charley (Fred MacMurray) is visited by the angel Roy (Harry Morgan), who tells him that his time is up, the song effectively conveys the theme of the movie.

"Lizzie McGuire Theme Song" is the pop song by Sam Winans that opens each episode of the live-action television series *Lizzie McGuire* (2001), about an adolescent whose alter ego is an animated version of herself. Hallie Todd sings the lite-rock number about dealing with life and figuring things out along the way.

"The Long, Long Day" is the powerful finale of the biblical concert-pageant *King David* (1997). The aging David (Marcus Lovett) sings this soaring musical number, in which he looks death in the eye and thinks back on his life, reviewing his efforts on behalf of what the Lord wanted. Alan Menken composed the lofty music and Tim Rice penned the lyrics of undaunted courage and faith.

"Look at Me" is the romantic song about first love Frank De Vol wrote for the movie sequel *Herbie Goes Bananas* (1980). The new owner of the VW "love bug" Herbie, Pete Stanchek (Stephen W. Burns), meets the nerdy Melissa (Elyssa Davalos) on a vacation cruise to Mexico, and the two fall in love while dancing during a shipboard costume party. An uncredited singer sings the quiet number, about saying yes to new love, as the two dance together.

"Look Out for Mr. Stork" is the waggish number written by Frank Churchill (music) and Ned Washington (lyric) for the animated movie *Dumbo* (1941). As the stork (voice of Sterling Holloway) flies over the countryside with a bundle hanging from his beak, the chorus sings on the soundtrack about the surprise the stork often brings. The sequence ends with the stork landing on the roof of the elephant car in the moving circus train and delivering the bundle to Dumbo's mother. A decade later Holloway would voice the same stork in the film short *Lambert, the Sheepish Lion* (1952) and deliver a baby lion to a ewe.

"Look Through My Eyes" is the pop-rock ballad Phil Collins wrote for the animated movie *Brother Bear* (2003) about an Inuk hunter who is changed into a bear and is forced to see the world from a different point of view. Collins sings the pulsating number on the soundtrack and made a music video of the song. It was also recorded by the group Everlife in 2006.

"Looking for Romance" is the dreamy love song written by Frank Churchill (music) and Larry Morey (lyric) for the bucolic animated film *Bambi* (1942). Donald Novis and a chorus sing the romantic number on the soundtrack while the adult deer Bambi and Faline frolic across a meadow and fall in love. The ballad is also listed as "I Bring You a Song," the title under which Mary Martin recorded it.

"The Lord Is Good to Me" is the cheerful hymn Johnny Appleseed (voice of Dennis Day) sings in one sequence in the animated movie anthology *Melody Time* (1948). Kim Gannon and Walter Kent wrote the upbeat number, in which Johnny expresses his happiness caring for his apple trees and harvesting the fruit each season.

"Los Angeles" is the pop-folk number about traveling along without a care in the world, heard in the movie comedy *Superdad* (1973). Shane Tatum wrote the freewheeling song, which is sung by a gang of teenagers as they ride in a friend's ambulance from the beach into the city of the title.

"Love" is the romantic ballad by George Bruns (music) and Floyd Huddleston (lyric) from the animated adventure film *Robin Hood* (1973). The Oscar-nominated song is sung on the soundtrack by Nancy Adams during a montage showing the fox Robin Hood falling in love with the vixen Maid Marian, the two of them walking through the forest at night surrounded by fireflies. The number is briefly reprised later in the film at the wedding of Robin and Marian. While the lyric is in the courtly love vein, the music has a driving pop flavor.

"Love Is a Song" is the Oscar-nominated ballad that opens and closes the animated movie *Bambi* (1942). Frank Churchill (music) and Larry Morey (lyric) wrote the flowing number about love being like music, since it never ends. It is sung by Donald Novis and a chorus on the soundtrack during the opening credits and during the pastoral establishing shots of the film. The chorus reprises the song when Faline's twin fawns are born and Bambi becomes the new Great Prince of the Forest. The music from the number is used on the soundtrack for some scenes in the animated video sequel *Bambi II* (2006).

"Love Led Us Here" is the heartfelt love duet by Barry Mann and Cynthia Weil that was used for a comic love scene in the movie *Muppet Treasure Island* (1996). Captain Smollett, played by Kermit the Frog (voice of Steve Whitmire), and his long-lost sweetheart Benjamina Gunn, played by Miss Piggy (Frank Oz), have been captured by pirates and tied up, hanging upside down together over a cliff. As the rope holding them up slowly burns away, the two sing this cheerful duet about how all their past troubles have brought them together again. During the end credits the ballad is sung as a serious duet on the soundtrack by John Berry and Helen Darling.

"Love Power" is the pulsating reggae number written by and performed by Ziggy Marley and the Melody Makers at the end of the movie *Muppet Treasure Island* (1996). As the lifeboat carrying Long John Silver (Tim Curry) and the treasure slowly sinks into the Caribbean, the lively number about letting love lift you up is heard, the fish and rat tourists swimming in time to the music.

"Love Will Find a Way" is the romantic ballad written by Tom Snow (music) and Jack Feldman (lyric) for the video sequel *The Lion King 2: Simba's Pride* (1998). The lion Kovu (singing voice of Gene Miller) is falsely convicted of a crime and is driven away from the Pride Lands. He leaves behind his true love Kiara (Liz Callaway), and, though separated, they each sing this song, believing love will bring them together again.

"Ma Belle Evangeline" is the effervescent Cajun ballad that the big-hearted firefly Ray (voice of Jim Cummings) sings in the animated movie *The Princess and the Frog* (2009). Randy Newman wrote the tender love song and Ray sings it to a star in the sky, which he is convinced is a fellow firefly named Evangeline whom he loves. The French-flavored music and the heartfelt lyric afford the prolific voice actor Cummings one of the most memorable moments in his long and busy career.

"Mad Madame Mim" is the gleeful "I am" song for the cheerful villainess in the animated film *The Sword in the Stone* (1963). Richard M. and Robert B. Sherman wrote the bouncy number in which the mischievous wizard Madame Mim (voice of Martha Wentworth) introduces herself to the boy Wart, who has been turned into a sparrow, by gloating in song over her evil powers. To display her talents, she changes herself into a sexy beauty and a grotesque ogre during the raucous number.

"The Madness of King Scar" is an extended character song for the dissatisfied lion monarch written by Elton John (music) and Tim Rice (lyric) for the 1997 Broadway version of *The Lion King*. Although he is king, the villainous Scar (John Vickery) is not content. Both the lions and the hyenas dislike him, a drought has devastated the Pride Lands, and he is paranoid about being compared unfavorably to the previous king, his brother

Mufasa. During the course of the song, Scar decides what he needs is an heir and he makes overtures to the lioness Nala (Heather Headley), who vehemently refuses him. The stream-of-consciousness number alternates between buffoonish comedy and cold-blooded evil. The title is a wry reference to the then-recent film *The Madness of King George* (1994).

"Main Street Electrical Parade" is the memorable synthesizer composition for one of the most popular of all Disney attractions. Based on the playful piece "Baroque Hoedown," the music for the 1972 Disneyland parade uses a synthesizer to not only play the rapid, catchy melody that runs up and down the scale furiously but to create synthesized sounds that punctuate the music. The parade, which featured thousands of small, twinkling lights on floats and characters, was so well received that it ran for twenty-four years in California and was re-created at all of the other Disney theme parks, although it was sometimes called "Disney's Electrical Parade" if it did not use Main Street.

"Maison des Lunes" is the silly but creepy song about an insane asylum written by Alan Menken (music) and Tim Rice (lyric) for the 1994 Broadway version of *Beauty and the Beast*. Monsieur D'Arque (Gordon Stanley), the owner of the title asylum, sings the number with the thwarted bully Gaston (Burke Moses) and his sidekick Lefou (Kenny Raskin), plotting to incarcerate the cockeyed inventor Maurice in order to force Belle to marry Gaston. The number feels much like a Halloween song as it makes listeners both laugh and shudder.

"Make a Wish" is the lite-rock song Matthew Gerrard and Robbie Nevil wrote for the made-for-TV movie *Stuck in the Suburbs* (2004). While the teen heartthrob Jordan Cahill (Taran Killam) performs in a music video about making dreams come true, a group of suburban teenage girls watch him on television and break into a dance all over the living-room furniture.

"Make Mine Music" is the waltzing title number for the 1946 animated anthology movie that illustrated various kinds of music. During the opening credits of the film, a studio chorus sings on the soundtrack the breezy song by Ken Darby and Eliot Daniel about the power of song, claiming that music is what is needed to bring joy to life.

"Making Christmas" is a grinding and demonic song of joy sung by the citizens of Halloween Town in the stop-motion movie *The Nightmare Before*

Christmas (1993). Danny Elfman wrote the unusual number in which the music attempts to be happy but comes out painfully morose because of its minor chords and odd tempo. The villagers are following the instructions of Jack Skellington to create yuletide perfection, but they keep applying their instinctual gore to all the presents and preparations.

"A Man Has Dreams" is the brief but affecting song of regret sung by Mr. Banks (David Tomlinson) in the movie musical *Mary Poppins* (1964). Richard M. and Robert B. Sherman wrote the quiet lament, in which Mr. Banks confesses to the chimney sweep Bert (Dick Van Dyke) that he is financially ruined and that his guidelines for happiness may have been wrong. David Haig played Mr. Banks in the 2005 London stage version of *Mary Poppins* and sang the number to Gavin Lee as Bert. On Broadway two years later, Daniel Jenkins played Mr. Banks and sang it with Lee reprising his role as Bert.

"Man or Muppet" is the power ballad and character song sung by Gary (Jason Segal) in the 2011 movie *The Muppets*. When Gary's fiancée Mary leaves him because he had not shown that she takes priority over his Muppet brother Walter, she writes him a note telling him it is time to decide if he is "a man or a Muppet." Gary wanders the town contemplating that very question and, while looking in a store window, sees a Muppet version of himself (also voiced by Segal). Soon, the song becomes a duet for the man and the Muppet. In Hollywood, Gary's Muppet brother Walter (voice of Peter Linz) is having his own doubts about his place as the newbie in the Muppet World. He joins in, turning the number into a trio and, while looking into a mirror, sees the human version of himself (played by Jim Parsons), and the song then becomes a quartet. "Man or Muppet," with music and lyrics by Bret McKenzie, is a moving and humorous look at self-doubt and how believing in yourself is what makes you a man.

"March of the Cards" is a regal piece of instrumental music by Sammy Fain that is used to introduce the Queen of Hearts (voice of Verna Felton) in the animated film fantasy *Alice in Wonderland* (1951). The Queen's army, in the form of a pack of playing cards, enters the garden as this musical piece full of pomp and blaring brass instruments is played, followed by the Queen of Hearts and her feeble husband, the King. The musical piece has enjoyed popularity with marching bands, particularly in the Disney theme parks.

"Marley and Marley" is the daffy yet haunting song for Scrooge's dead business partners in the film *The Muppet Christmas Carol* (1992). Paul Williams wrote the sinister number that the crotchety old Muppets Statler (voice of Dave Goelz) and Waldorf (Jerry Nelson) sing as the two ghosts of Scrooge's deceased business partners, Marley and Marley. The oppressive number about the evils of money is accompanied by the clinking of the heavy chains that the two wear as they float through the air.

"The Martins and the Coys" is the hillbilly narrative ballad by Al Cameron and Ted Weems that makes up one of the sequences in the animated movie anthology *Make Mine Music* (1946). The King's Men sing the banjo-strumming number on the soundtrack while the tale of two feuding families in the Appalachian backwoods unfolds. The Martins and the Coys have been feuding so long that only one member of each brood is left alive: the beautiful Grace Martin and the dashing Henry Coy. When they wed, it seems the feud is over, but marital discontent brings on a new rivalry, much to the delight of all the deceased Martins and Coys watching from the clouds above. One section of the sequence is a lively square dance song at the Martin-Coy wedding. The whole piece is a satire on the famous Hatfields and Mc-Coys feud, with tongue-in-cheek lyrics and a lighthearted tone. Because of all the violence and the politically incorrect gunplay, the tale is upsetting to some modern audiences, and the whole sequence was cut when *Make Mine Music* was released on DVD in 2000.

"Matecumbe" is the calypso-like number that has a tribal beat even as it borders on lite rock, written by Shane Tatum and Richard McKinley for the adventure film *Treasure of Matecumbe* (1976). A male studio chorus sings about the shadows calling, urging listeners to journey to a place where there is promise of new life, and it is heard on the soundtrack during the opening credits of the movie.

"May the Best Man Win" is the narrative ballad by Joel Hirschhorn and Al Kasha that tells the premise of the film *Hot Lead and Cold Feet* (1978). Michael Dees sings the western-flavored song over the opening credits, explaining how two brothers, one a cowboy and the other a missionary, decide to run a race to determine who inherits their late father's fortune.

"Me" is the boastful, egocentric marriage proposal that is one of the comic highlights of the Broadway version of *Beauty and the Beast* (1994). The swaggering Gaston (Burke Moses) sings the clownish number, painting a vivid picture of what married life with him will be like, while the less-than-impressed Belle (Susan Egan) makes sly comments that go over his thick head. Alan Menken (music) and Tim Rice (lyric) wrote the prankish song.

"Me Party" is the character duet of female empowerment sung by Mary (Amy Adams) and Miss Piggy (voice of Eric Jacobson) in the 2011 film *The Muppets*. With music and lyrics by Bret McKenzie and Paul Roeman, the song is sung by the two female leads who are tired of being overlooked by the men in their lives. The lively, up-tempo number is performed by the duo with gusto as they decide to take control of their destinies and become responsible for their own happiness.

"The Medfield Fight Song" is the spirited rah-rah song Richard M. and Robert B. Sherman wrote for the film *The Absent-Minded Professor* (1961), the first of many songs the songwriting brothers wrote for Disney feature films. A studio chorus sings the vigorous number over the opening credits, and it is heard later in the film during the climactic basketball game between the fictitious Medfield and Rutland Colleges.

"Meet the World" is the peppy, optimistic song written by Robert B. and Richard M. Sherman for an attraction at Tokyo Disneyland in 1983. The Meet the World exhibit was a carousel-type theatre where the center stage rotated rather than the audience rotating around it, as in the Carousel of Progress. It told the story of Japan, and between each scene the song was sung in Japanese. The melody starts out with a mystical air, but soon develops into a perky number on the line of "It's a Small World." The lyric is about the origins of Japan, born out of a "great Mother Sea," and how the island nation has reached out to the world with love. Although the song and the attraction followed history, it was thought best to make no mention of World War II.

"Melody Time" is the breezy title number George Weiss and Bennie Benjamin wrote for the 1948 animated movie anthology. Buddy Clark and a female chorus sing the lilting song on the soundtrack over the opening credits for the film, merrily urging you to join in and sing when life has got you down.

"The Merchants' Song" is a slapstick song about greed written by producer-director Don Bluth for the animated film short *The Small One*

(1978). While the young Boy (voice of Sean Marshall) sings the tender ballad "Small One" and tries to sell his undersized donkey in the town, a trio of merchants interrupts to sing this harmonizing number about doing deals, making money, and taking it to the bank. The musical sequence also includes various businessmen turning down the sale of the animal and mocking the scrawny creature.

"Merlin Jones" is the peppy song of admiration sung by Annette Funicello over the opening credits of the movie comedy *The Misadventures of Merlin Jones* (1964). Richard M. and Robert B. Sherman wrote the vibrant dance number, the kind of song likely to be heard at a 1960s sock hop, about a girl in love with the college science whiz who intrigues her because he is always working on peculiar things. Funicello sings with a backup chorus and some interjections by Merlin Jones (Tommy Kirk), and her recording of the pop song was very popular.

"Merrily on Our Way" is the frantic and funny song that lists all the destinations you can experience, especially if you are heading nowhere in particular, in the animated film *The Adventures of Ichabod and Mr. Toad* (1949). Frank Churchill, Oliver Wolcott (music), Larry Morey, and Ray Gilbert (lyric) wrote the farcical number, which is sung as a vivacious duet by Mr. Toad (voice of Eric Blore) and his horse, Cyril Proudbottom (J. Pat O'Malley), as they ride wildly across the English countryside, destroying nature and man-made structures along the way. The number is sometimes listed as "The Merrily Song" or "Nowhere in Particular."

"Mexico" is the Latin-flavored ballad about the land of romance south of the border written by Charles Wolcott (music) and Ray Gilbert (lyric) for the animated travelogue *The Three Caballeros* (1944). Carlos Ramirez sings the gliding song on the soundtrack while Donald Duck, Joe Carioca, and Panchito fly over live-action footage of Mexico on a magic serape.

"Miami, You've Got Style" is the peppy song of appreciation from an episode of the television series *The Golden Girls* (1985) that later became a cult favorite and the unofficial theme song for the city of Miami, Florida. Senior citizens Dorothy Zbornak (Beatrice Arthur) and Rose Nylund (Betty White) enter a songwriting contest to find an anthem for their city. The two come up with this snappy list song that counts off all the fun things there are to do in Miami. Dorothy and Rose sing the number for their housemates Blanche Devereaux (Rue McClanahan) and Sophia Petrillo (Estelle Getty), and at the end of the episode all four gather around the piano and reprise the song.

"The Mickey Mouse Club Alma Mater" is the gentle farewell song sung by the Mouseketeers at the end of each episode of the popular television show *The Mickey Mouse Club* (1955). Jimmie Dodd, the adult host of the show, wrote the pastiche of a school alma mater, complete with a fervent tone, a promise to always remember the club, and a vow to remain friends with each other forever. The most remembered part of the song is the final spelling of Mickey's name, broken up with good wishes for viewers from the cast.

"The Mickey Mouse Club March" is the popular theme song for the original television series *The Mickey Mouse Club* (1955) and was one of the most recognized of all songs by children in the 1950s. Adult cast member Jimmie Dodd wrote the rousing march, which celebrated Mickey and his club, spelling out his name and cheering happily despite the attempts by Donald Duck to work his name into the song. The march is sung by a male chorus and some children singers on the soundtrack over the animated opening credits of the series, always ending with Donald striking a gong and getting some kind of explosive reaction. As the series changed over the years, the song stayed pretty much the same, even as the animation altered. The number, which is sometimes listed as "The Mickey Mouse Club Theme," was also used on *The New Mickey Mouse Club* in the 1970s and again in the 1990s, though the song was given a lite-rock interpretation.

"Mickey, She's Got a Crush on You" is the pop love song by Michael and Patty Silversher that looks at the famous mouse through the adoring eyes of Minnie Mouse. Gail Loptata introduced the bubblegum song on the 1983 Disney album *Mickey Mouse Splashdance* and the recording was popular with the preteen crowd.

"Mickey's the Mouse for Me" is the adoring number that Minnie Mouse sings about her sweetheart in a show at Mickey's Toontown Fair, a section of the Walt Disney World Magic Kingdom that was featured from 1996 to 2011. The music has a moderate country-western flavor and the lyric explains how Minnie fell for Mickey the first time she set eyes on him. Just as in the "Mickey Mouse Club Alma Mater," the song spells out Mickey's name and finds words that rhyme with certain letters.

"Midnight Madness" is the breezy title song written by David and Julius Wechter for the 1980 film about a college all-nighter. The disco-flavored list song is sung by Donna Fein over the opening credits while two college bimbos on roller skates deliver invitations to a scavenger hunt that pits stereotypical groups against each other for a night of madcap fun.

"The Mighty Ducks Theme" is the heavy-metal song by Patrick DeRemer for the animated television series *The Mighty Ducks* (1996) about half-duck, half-human hockey players who are also superheroes. The pounding theme song tells viewers to clear the way, because the fearless band of crime fighters is coming through.

"Mine, Mine, Mine" is the merry song of greed sung by the sinister Governor Ratcliffe (voice of David Ogden Stiers) in the animated film *Pocahontas* (1995). Alan Menken (music) and Stephen Schwartz (lyric) wrote the sprightly number in which Ratcliffe urges his men to dig up the Virginia countryside to find the gold that will make them famous and rich. The song has a pseudo-Renaissance period flavor, complete with "hey nonny" and a jig-like rhythm. As Ratcliffe sings, he has visions of grandeur, including his presentation at the court and the king's bestowing a title on him. In contrast, Captain John Smith (Mel Gibson) sees Virginia as a land of adventure

Disney Theatrical Productions' first Broadway effort was *Beauty and the Beast* (1994), a colorful stage musical that was dismissed by the critics but thrilled audiences for thirteen years. Susan Egan (center) was the first of several actresses to play Belle before going on to other Disney projects, most memorably as the voice of Megara in *Hercules* on screen and television. (Joan Marcus/Photofest)

and sings how the New World is his to make his life complete. The song's title refers to both possessions and to digging up the land for gold.

"Minnie's Yoo-Hoo" has the distinction of being the first Disney song to be published, and it became popular long before it was sung in some Disney film shorts. Walt Disney himself provided some of the lyric for the Carl W. Stalling ditty, which praises Minnie and imitates various farm animals who sing her praises as well. The number was written for the first Mickey Mouse Clubs, actual clubs sponsored by local movie theatres that started in 1929, which kids joined in different locations. The song was the official theme song for the clubs and, using the sheet music, it was sung by kids across the country. Mickey sang the playful number in the film short *Mickey's Follies* (1929), complete with the lyrics shown to encourage a sing-along, and the next year the clip from the movie was distributed to the clubs. Over the years the song was a favorite on Disney records, and in the 1970s it was played, in a slightly speeded-up version, at the end of the television series *The Mouse Factory* (1972). A quartet recording of the happy number was made by Meredith Inglesby, Andy Karl, Tyler Maynard, and Keewa Nurullah, and Kerry Butler made a playful version in 2008.

"The Mob Song (Kill the Beast)" is the frightening call to arms Gaston (voice of Richard White) sings to rouse the townspeople in the animated film *Beauty and the Beast* (1991). Alan Menken (music) and Howard Ashman (lyric) wrote the vigorous number, which is used by the jealous Gaston to encourage the local citizens to attack the enchanted castle and kill the frightful beast before he comes to destroy their children. Burke Moses led the ensemble in singing the song in the 1994 Broadway version of *Beauty and the Beast*.

"Mon Amour Perdu" is the French love song by Robert B. and Richard M. Sherman that provides a touching moment in the film *Big Red* (1962), set in French Canada. One evening while the youth René Dumont (Gilles Payant) plays the harmonica in the kitchen of groundskeeper Émile Fornet (Émile Genest) and his wife Therese (Janette Bertrand), the couple sing this haunting little ditty about lost love. The French lyric foreshadows the young René's feelings when he temporarily loses his favorite Irish setter, Big Red. The Shermans originally wrote the melody for a number called "West Wind" for the movie *Mary Poppins* (1964) which they were scoring at the same time but the song was discarded and used in *Big Red* instead. The number is sometimes listed as "The *Big Red* Theme."

"Monkey in Your Tank" is the harmonizing quartet that satirizes 1950s singing guy groups, written for an episode of the animated television series *TaleSpin* (1990) but never used. Chuck Tately and Michael and Patty Silversher wrote the spoof of the Four Seasons and similar male groups, complete with high falsetto howls and rhythmic scat singing. The ridiculous lyric advertises the gas station run by the monkey Louie, promising great service and a monkey in your fuel tank. The risible song was published and recorded and showed up on Disney records.

"The Monkey's Uncle" is the memorable nonsense title song Richard M. and Robert B. Sherman wrote for the 1965 film comedy, a sequel to the popular *The Misadventures of Merlin Jones* (1964). Annette Funicello, who was popular in the 1960s for her "Beach Party" films, was the ideal choice to sing the silly number with the Beach Boys over the opening credits. The song is about a girl who is in love with a guy who is the uncle of a chimpanzee, and in the film Funicello plays a college coed who is in love with science student genius Merlin Jones (Tommy Kirk), who is indeed the guardian of a monkey. Funicello's recording was very popular, and in 2006 a new version was recorded by Devo 2.0.

"The Moon-Spinners Song" is one of the most evocative of all Disney title songs, as haunting, mysterious, and exotic as the film's suspenseful premise of a jewel theft on the island of Crete. Terry Gilkyson wrote the Greek-flavored folk song for *The Moon-Spinners* (1964), and a studio chorus sings the ethnic number over the opening credits, the lyric asking the moon-spinners to make the moon bright tonight so that one's love can see it clearly, and for it to shine on the water, which covers a treasure.

"More" is a snazzy pastiche number, written by Stephen Sondheim for the cartoonish live-action film *Dick Tracy* (1990), in which the hedonistic lyric cries out for excess in love, money, and fame. The jazzy song is first heard at a rehearsal where club owner/gangster Big Boy Caprice (Al Pacino) is running the chorus girls through their paces, demonstrating himself how the number ought to be performed. Later in the movie, the nightclub star Breathless Mahoney (Madonna) and the girls sing the song onstage as part of a New Year's Eve celebration. The number, like most of those in the film, is undercut with scenes in other locales and is barely intact in the final cut. Later, Madonna and Jennifer Simard each recorded the complete song, and it proved to be a masterful 1930s pastiche.

"The More I Look Inside" is the delicate ballad written by Carly Simon for the animated film *Piglet's Big Movie* (2003). When Piglet has gone from the Hundred Acre Wood, all his friends miss him and realize that he means much more to them than they had thought. Songwriter Simon sings the heartfelt number on the soundtrack while Piglet's friends draw pictures of the little pig and recall how much fun he was.

"The More It Snows (Tiddely-Pom)" is the happy and carefree song Piglet (voice of John Fiedler) and Winnie the Pooh (Jim Cummings) sing in the animated film *Piglet's Big Movie* (2003). Carly Simon wrote the bouncy number, the lyrics taken from A. A. Milne's volume *The House at Pooh Corner*.

"More Than a Dream" is the heartfelt torch song written by Alan Zachary and Michael Weiner for the animated video sequel *Cinderella III: A Twist in Time* (2007). When the Evil Stepmother gets hold of the Fairy Godmother's magic wand and uses it to erase the prince's memory, she arranges for the prince to wed her daughter Anastasia. Cinderella (singing voice of Tami Tappan Damiano) sings this sorrowful lament, sure that the prince would remember her and the night they first met at the ball if only she could get into the castle and see him. Later in the story when she is banished from the kingdom, another of her stepmother's schemes, Cinderella reprises the number aboard a ship taking her away.

"More Than Me" is the heartfelt rock-folk song featured in the television movie *Stuck in the Suburbs* (2004). Niv Davidovitch, Peter Rafaelson, and Jeffrey Vincent wrote the number about how a loved one has helped someone become much more than he thought he could be. The pop star Jordan Cahill (Taran Killam) sings the song at a rally to save a historic old house, and at the end of the movie it is performed as a music video on television.

"Moreover and Me" is the easygoing folk ballad that serves as the theme song for the film *The Biscuit Eater* (1972). Shane Tatum wrote the country number about the friendship between a boy and his dog and he also sings it, with harmonica accompaniment, over the opening credits of the movie while Lonnie McNeil (Johnny Whitaker) and his dog are seen playing together.

"The Morning Report" is a delightful character song for the pompous hornbill Zazu (Geoff Hoyle) written by Elton John (music) and Tim Rice (lyric) for the 1997 Broadway version of *The Lion King*. As secretary to King Mufasa (Samuel E. Wright), Zazu sings the silly list song, which chronicles what all the different animal species are up to that day, the description full of puns and snide comments. All the time Zazu sings, the lion cub Simba (Scott Irby-Ranniar) practices sneaking up on Zazu, and then pounces on him at the end of the report.

"A Most Befuddling Thing" is a philosophical number about the power of love written by Richard M. and Robert B. Sherman for their first animated Disney film, *The Sword in the Stone* (1963). When the wizard Merlin (voice of Karl Swenson) turns his pupil Wart into a squirrel to learn about life, a female squirrel is attracted to the boy and will not leave him alone. Merlin sings the intellectual song about the puzzling nature of love, which, he concludes, is stronger than gravity itself.

"Mother Knows Best" is the wry, creepy song of affection that Mother Gothel (voice of Donna Murphy) sings twice in the animated feature *Tangled* (2010). When Rapunzel asks to leave her tower, Gothel warns her about the dangers of the outside world and how she knows best what is good for her teenage "daughter." Later in the film, when Rapunzel is attracted to the bandit Flynn Rider, Gothel reprises the number, scoffing at the girl and telling her Flynn is only after her diamond tiara. Alan Menken's music is soothing and flowing, then becomes harsh as it builds. Glenn Slater's elaborate lyric is often funny and sarcastic, but the subtext is quietly threatening. Murphy's performance, which ranges from silly baby talk to ice-cold sneering, is one of the reasons the song works so effectively.

"Mother's Intuition" is a well-meaning song of assistance that provides a humorous sequence in the animated film *Piglet's Big Movie* (2003). Carly Simon wrote the risible number about trusting to a mother's understanding, and she sang it on the soundtrack over a sequence in which the mother kangaroo Kanga forces the unwilling Piglet to take a bath in a tub of sudsy water.

"The Motion Waltz" is the simple pop ballad about the dizzying feeling of being in love written by Rufus Wainwright for the animated movie *Meet the Robinsons* (2007). Songwriter Wainwright sings the waltz number on the soundtrack over the closing credits of the film, reveling in the "emotional commotion" you experience while dancing with the one you love. The song is sometimes listed as "Emotional Commotion."

"**Mouseketeer Roll Call**" is the peppy list song that introduces the young club members on the popular television show *The Mickey Mouse Club* (1955). After a vigorous tap dance set to swing music, the Mouseketeers sing this rousing number, reminiscent of a school fight song, in which they proclaim their pride in the club and in the mouse ears they wear. The song then moves into a roll call in which each member, child and adult, shouts his or her name. On certain days of the week, the roll call was added to the theme song for the day instead of the usual "Mouseketeer Roll Call" number.

"**Mousercise**" is the disco-flavored aerobics song for kids written by Dennis Melonas and Beverly Bremers for Disney Records in 1982. The number was popular enough that a television exercise program was created in 1983, titled *Mousercise* after the song. A studio chorus sings the up-tempo, rhythmic number on the soundtrack at the opening of each show, inviting everyone to join and exercise with hosts Kelly Plasscharet and Mickey Mouse, and soon human kids and Disney characters are doing aerobics together.

"**My Best Christmas Yet**," the finale number for the television special *A Muppets Christmas: Letters to Santa* (2008), is a gently rocking song that lists all the different things that make Christmas special. The Paul Williams number is sung by Kermit the Frog (voice of Steve Whitmire) and the entire cloth and human cast on Christmas morning in New York City.

"**My Date with the President's Daughter**" is the silly Beach Boys–like song by Chris Hajian that serves as the title number for the 1998 television movie. The 1960s-flavored pop song is sung by a male singing group much like the Beach Boys, who croon about an unforgettable outing with the U.S. president's teenage daughter.

"**My Favorite Dream**" is the lilting ballad the magical Singing Harp (voice of Anita Gordon) sings in the "Mickey and the Beanstalk" section of the animated anthology movie *Fun and Fancy Free* (1947). William Walsh and Ray Noble wrote the soothing foxtrot number, and the harp sings it to put Willie the Giant to sleep so that Mickey, Goofy, and Donald Duck can escape from the castle.

"**My Funny Friend and Me**" is the Oscar-nominated song written by David Hartley (music and lyric) and Sting (lyric) for the animated movie *The Emperor's New Groove* (2000). Sting sings the pop-rock ballad on the soundtrack during the end credits of the film, telling about a friend who stayed when others would have walked away. The song parallels the relationship between the peasant Pacha (voice of John Goodman) and Emperor Kuzco (David Spade) in the movie. Sting's recording enjoyed some popularity, and he also recorded the number in Spanish.

"My Heart Was an Island" is the melodic and dreamy ballad written by Terry Gilkyson for the adventure film *Swiss Family Robinson* (1960), but it was used very briefly in the final print. The shipwrecked mother (Dorothy McGuire) of the Robinson family recalls an island she once dreamed of, singing to herself as she arranges the curtains in the bedroom of her tree house and adjusting to her new home.

"My Hero Is You" is the soft-rock ballad by Jamie Houston from the made-for-television movie *Tiger Cruise* (2004), about civilians aboard an aircraft carrier when it is called into combat mode after September 11, 2001. Hayden Panettiere, who plays the teenager Maddie on board the ship, sings the gentle ballad on the soundtrack, declaring that when the world goes crazy there is someone you can depend on. Panetierre also made a music video of the song.

"My Lovey-Dovey Baby" is the coquettish pastiche of a nineteenth-century vaudeville number from the period movie musical *Newsies* (1992). Alan Menken (music) and Jack Feldman (lyric) wrote the alluring music hall number, which is sung by Medda Larkson (Ann-Margret), known as the "Swedish Meadowlark," in her vaudeville theatre in 1899 New York City.

"My Lullaby" is one of the most evil and dark songs ever written for a Disney production, a diabolical number by Joss Whedon and Scott Warrender for the video sequel *The Lion King 2: Simba's Pride* (1998). The sinister lioness Zira (voice of Suzanne Pleshette) plans to avenge the death of her husband Scar and plots in song with her two children Vitani (Crysta Macalush) and Nuka (Andy Dick) how they will kill the lion king Simba and put her youngest son, Kovu, on the throne. The odd combination of motherly love and bloodthirsty determination makes the "lullaby" powerfully creepy.

"My Name Is James" is the quiet, heartfelt "I am" song for the orphaned hero of the live-action/stop-motion animation movie *James and the Giant Peach* (1996). Forced to work for his two nasty aunts, James (Paul Terry) has no friends, but when he sees a spider on the windowsill, he tries to befriend the insect by singing this gentle number about how he must go inside his own head to have friends and find happy moments. Randy Newman wrote the intimate music and the introspective lyric.

"My Own Home" is an alluring little ditty the Indian girl Shanti (voice of Darleen Carr) sings to herself in the animated film *The Jungle Book* (1967). Richard M. and Robert B. Sherman wrote the soothing number, which attracts the attention of the man-cub Mowgli (Bruce Reitherman). When he spots Shanti going back to the man-village, Mowgli starts to understand the appeal of humans.

"My Science Project" is the rocking title song for the 1985 movie about two high school seniors who get involved in a time-traveling science project. Bob Held, Michael Colina, and Bill Heller wrote the throbbing number about how Einstein started it all and science is here to stay. The song is sung over the final credits of the film by the Tubes.

"My Strongest Suit" is the jumping and jiving number about fashion written by Elton John (music) and Tim Rice (lyric) for the Broadway musical *Aida* (2000). The princess Amneris (Sherie Rene Scott) claims that she is what she wears and that outrageous clothes are all that matter to her. The ladies of the court provide the backup singing for the satiric number, which eventually turns into a bizarre fashion show of quasi-Egyptian duds. The rhythmic song is atypical of the score, being the only lighthearted number in the musical. In a somber reprise later in the show, Amneris confesses to her slave Aida (Heather Headley) that her obsession for clothes is a mask to hide her own unhappiness, and the Nubian handmaiden urges the princess to find what is really her strongest suit. The Spice Girls recorded the song before *Aida* opened on Broadway, and in 2008 it was recorded by Kaycee Stroh.

"My, What a Happy Day" is the bouncy song of joy that opens the "Mickey and the Beanstalk" sequence in the animated anthology movie *Fun and Fancy Free* (1947). The golden Singing Harp (voice of Anita Gordon) sings the catchy number by Ray Noble and William Walsh from her room in the castle, as the animal residents of Happy Valley join her in celebrating another perfect day. The song is reprised at the end of the tale when the harp, stolen away by the giant, is returned to the valley.

N

"The Name Game" is a jolly, childlike ditty Carly Simon (music and lyric) and Brian Hohlfeld (lyric) wrote for the animated film *Pooh's Heffalump Movie* (2005). When the young elephant Lumpy (voice of Kyle Stanger) makes friends with the young kangaroo Roo (Nikita Hopkins), he teaches Roo a song in which you come up with all kinds of words that rhyme with your name. Later in the film Roo and Lumpy reprise the simple but catchy number as they play in the Hundred Acre Wood.

"Never Again" is the haunting song of farewell written by Alan Menken (music) and Tim Rice (lyric) for the biblical concert piece *King David*, which was presented on Broadway in 1997. Having been hurt by the young King David (Marcus Lovett), the maiden Michal (Judy Kuhn) sings this stinging number about how she will never be in a position to be let down by him again.

"Never Give Up" is the ardent ballad sung by the mermaid Ariel (voice of Jodi Benson) and the crab Sebastian (Samuel E. Wright) in an episode of the animated television series *The Little Mermaid* (1992). In the spirited number, Ariel urges Sebastian to persevere and not give up on himself. He eventually agrees with her and joins her in singing about personal perseverance to make your dreams come true.

"Never Knew I Needed" is the rhythmic pop song heard during the final credits of the animated movie *The Princess and the Frog* (2009). Ne-Yo (alias Shaffer Smith) wrote and sings the number about a special someone who at first didn't seem needed but ended up being what one was looking for all along.

"Never Smile at a Crocodile" is the humorous ditty by Frank Churchill (music) and Jack Lawrence (lyric) that was written for the animated movie *Peter Pan* (1953), but the lyrics were cut from the final print and only the music was used as a leitmotif for the crocodile throughout the film. Yet the song still managed to become popular. The plodding, silly song cautions listeners that it is not possible to become friendly with a crocodile, so the only thing to do when you meet one is to rudely walk away. The number has long been a favorite on children's records, and other recordings have been made by Henry Calvin, Gracie Lou, Joe Reisman and His Orchestra, the Paulette Sisters, and Mitch Miller and his Singers.

"The Night Before Christmas" is the melodious title song from the 1933 Silly Symphony film short, which is loosely adapted from Clement Moore's poem "A Visit from Saint Nicholas." While the children spy on Santa on Christmas Eve, Donald Novis sings the omniscient song on the soundtrack, revealing the thoughts of the kids and Santa himself. Leigh Harline wrote the comforting music and the gentle lyric, which is a variation on the first few stanzas of Moore's poem.

"A Night to Remember" is the enthusiastic and sly number sung by high-schoolers as they anticipate the night of the senior prom in the film sequel *High School Musical 3: Senior Year* (2008). While the girls sing breezily about manicures, hair appointments, and massages, the less confident boys marvel and grouse over the oddities of corsages and tuxedos. The clever number then segues into a rehearsal for the spring musical, where the song is part of the show reenacting their senior year. Matthew Gerrard and Robbie Nevil wrote the witty and knowing number.

"No Matter What" is the warmhearted song of affection Maurice (Tom Bosley) sings to his daughter Belle (Susan Egan) in the 1994 Broadway version of *Beauty and the Beast*. Alan Menken (music) and Tim Rice (lyric) wrote the flowing ballad, in which father vows to daughter that she is special to him even if the townspeople think her odd. Belle responds by singing that she feels the same way about Maurice, even though he is branded a crackpot inventor.

"No Other Way" is the somber song of decision written by Phil Collins for the 2006 Broadway version of *Tarzan*. The gorilla Kerchak (Shuler Hensley) coldly and gravely tells his mate Kala (Merle Dandridge) that the young human Tarzan is not of their kind and must be banished from the ape tribe. Kala protests throughout the song, but Kerchak argues that he has no other choice, so Kala decides to move away with the boy.

"No Way Out" is the sorrowful song of regret Phil Collins wrote for the animated movie *Brother Bear* (2003), about an Inuk hunter who is turned into a bear. After the once-human Kenai (voice of Joaquin Phoenix) confesses to the bear cub Koda (Jeremy Suarez) that, when he was a human, he killed the young cub's mother, Collins sings this tender yet disturbing folk song about how regret puts one in a dark place from which there is no escape. The number is also listed as "Theme from *Brother Bear*."

"Nobody Else but You" is the rolling song of affection between father and son in the animated film *A Goofy Movie* (1995). After a family road trip fraught with mishaps, Max (singing voice of Aaron Lohr) and his father, Goofy (Bill Farmer), find themselves floating down a river on top of their submerged car, and they admit to each other in song that, despite their faults, each would be lost without the other. Tom Snow (music) and Jack Feldman (lyric) wrote the tender and sincere number.

"Nobody's Problems for Me" is the wistful character song written by Richard M. and Robert B. Sherman for the film fantasy *Bedknobs and Broomsticks* (1971), but it was cut from the final print to shorten the length of the movie. After the friendly witch Miss Eglantine Price (Angela Lansbury) bids goodbye to her friend Professor Emelius Brown (David Tomlinson), she regrets losing him, but tells herself in song that she is happiest on her own and doesn't want the worry of caring for someone else too much. The brief but potent number was restored in the 1996 reconstruction of the film.

"Not in Nottingham" is the country-blues ballad Roger Miller wrote and sang in the animated adventure film *Robin Hood* (1973). When the vengeful Prince John again raises the taxes, the people of Nottingham are destitute, and many are thrown into debtors' prison—including the rooster troubadour Alan-a-Dale (voice of Roger Miller), who sings the folk-like lament about every place having more ups than downs, except Nottingham.

"Not Me" is a revealing character song Elton John (music) and Tim Rice (lyric) wrote for the Broadway musical *Aida* (2000). The Egyptian captain Radames (Adam Pascal) surprises himself, sparing the Nubians because he is in love with the Nubian slave Aida (Heather Headley). He asks himself who would ever have guessed he was capable of such an action, and the answer from Radames, Aida, the princess Amneris (Sherie Rene Scott), and the servant Mereb (Damian Perkins) is "not me." The group Boyz II Men recorded the song before the musical opened on Broadway.

"Nothing in the World (Quite Like a Friend)" is the merry list song the Genie (voice of Dan Castellaneta) sings in the made-for-video animated sequel *The Return of Jafar* (1994). Dale Gonyea and Michael Silversher wrote the Las Vegas–like production number in which the Genie, having returned from a trip around the world, lists all the places he's been but concludes that none of them compare to true friendship. Aladdin (Brad Kane) and Jasmine (singing voice of Liz Callaway) join the Genie in the vivacious song, which is reminiscent of "A Friend Like Me" from the original *Aladdin* (1992).

"Now or Never" is the syncopated pop song written by Matthew Gerrard and Robbie Nevil for the film sequel *High School Musical 3: Senior Year* (2008). With only a few moments left on the clock during the season's final basketball game, team captain Troy Bolton (Zac Efron) leads his teammates in singing this intense number, hoping for one last victory in their high school basketball careers. Troy's girlfriend, Gabriella (Vanessa Anne Hudgens), offers musical and emotional support from the bleachers.

"Oh, Benjamin Harrison" is the boastful campaign song for the Republican candidate in the period film musical *The One and Only, Genuine, Original Family Band* (1968). Richard M. and Robert B. Sherman wrote the rousing number, which was sung by a group of Dakota Republicans on election night 1888 as a response to the Democrats' campaign song for Grover Cleveland, titled "Let's Put It Over with Grover."

"Oh Fleecy Cloud" is the musical ode to nature written by Charles Wolcott (music), T. Hee, and Erdman Penner (lyric) for the animated film *The Reluctant Dragon* (1941). When the doddering knight Sir Giles (voice of Claude Allister) comes upon the Dragon and learns that the passive creature likes to write poetry, the knight shares one of his own odes with him, talk-singing this bucolic poem with great rapture.

"Oh Sing, Sweet Nightingale" is the operatic aria by Al Hoffman, Mack David, and Jerry Livingston that is used in contrasting ways in the animated movie *Cinderella* (1950). The Ugly Stepsisters (voices of Rhoda Williams and Lucille Bliss) practice vocalizing and playing the flute in the music room, destroying the music and shattering the ears. At the same time, Cinderella (Ilene Woods) is downstairs scrubbing the floor and singing the same aria, her lovely voice lifting up like the soap bubbles rising from her bucket. This was the first time the Disney artists used the technique of overdubbing (a relatively new sound process), so Woods could essentially sing with herself in harmony. As she washes the floor and the bubbles rise out of the scrub bucket, each bubble reflects Cinderella, and the Cinderella images sing the harmony while the actual Cinderella performs the melody. The number, sometimes listed as "Sing, Sweet Nightingale," was recorded as a duet by David Sanborn and David Benoit in 1995.

"Oh, What a Merry Christmas Day" is the warm carol written by Irwin Kostal (music) and Frederick Searles (lyric) for the animated film short *Mickey's Christmas Carol* (1983). Complete with bells and chimes, a Dickensian chorus sings the graceful number, listing the simple joys of Christmas Day, over the opening credits. The song is reprised at the end of the movie as well. An up-tempo version of the carol has been used for parades and other holiday activities at the Disney theme parks.

"Ol' Dan Patch" is the quaint folk song sung by the rural blacksmith Hiram Douglas (Burl Ives) at different points in the movie *So Dear to My Heart* (1948). After the rural residents in a small Indiana town see the famous race horse Dan Patch stop for exercise while traveling by train across the country, the local blacksmith sings about the celebrated horse to the youngsters Jeremiah (Bobby Driscoll) and Tildy (Luana Patten) as they ride in his wagon. At other times in the movie, Hiram reprises the song with different lyrics, commenting on the latest development in the story. The music is based on a traditional folk tune and the uncredited lyric is simple but playful, with a wry sense of humor.

"Old Father William" is a delightful musical ditty, based on a poem by Lewis Carroll, that is used in the animated film fantasy *Alice in Wonderland* (1951). Composer Oliver Wallace adapted the poem into a silly duet for the rotund twins Tweedle-Dum and Tweedle-Dee (both voiced by J. Pat O'Malley), about the aged Father William, who insists on turning somersaults and eating inedible food. Alice (Kathryn Beaumont) uses their self-absorbed performance to escape from the nutty pair.

"The Old Home Guard" is the military march song performed by a troop of aging veterans in the film fantasy *Bedknobs and Broomsticks* (1971). Richard M. and Robert B. Sherman wrote the number about the people of England defending their island from invaders, and it is sung by a squad of World War I veterans as they march into town near the beginning of the film. The same soldiers reprise the song at the end of the movie when they accompany the newly enlisted Professor Brown (David Tomlinson) to the train station.

"The Old Mill" is the dramatic instrumental piece Leigh Harline wrote for the animated 1937 Silly Symphony movie short of the same title. An old Dutch-style windmill is the dilapidated home of wild birds, mice, and bats. A storm approaches and the animals must fight the damage the wind and rain bring, and the mill itself looks like it will fall apart until the weather subsides. The classically inspired score augments the action by building with intensity, congruous with the storm, and the piece ends with a denouement that brings nature and music back to the peaceful and calm. The Oscar-winning film is also memorable for being the first to use the multiplane camera, allowing for more realistic movement as the camera slowly zooms in on an object.

"Old Yeller" is the rustic yet bold title song written by Oliver Wallace (music) and Gil George (lyric) for the 1957 movie about a mongrel who befriends and rescues the Coates family in 1860s Texas. Jerome Courtland sings the musical tribute to the heroic yellow dog on the soundtrack during the opening credits. Gil George was the pseudonym for Hazel George, a nurse at the Disney studio.

"On My Way" is the rhythmic folk-rock number Phil Collins wrote for the animated movie *Brother Bear* (2003). Collins sings the throbbing song, about going off to new places with new friends, during a montage when the human-turned-bear Kenai befriends the rambunctious bear cub Koda. The number is sometimes listed as "Send Me on My Way."

"On the Front Porch" is a pleasing folk song sung with warmth and style by Burl Ives in the film *Summer Magic* (1963). One evening after a summer afternoon picnic, the Carey family and some of their guests gather on the porch, and postmaster Osh Popham (Ives) sings about how pleasant it is to sit on the porch with a loved one. He accompanies himself on the guitar and the Careys' son, Gilly (Eddie Hodges), joins him on his guitar. Richard M. and Robert B. Sherman wrote the simple, homespun number.

"On the Open Road" is the contagious traveling song that is used for a fun production number in the animated film *A Goofy Movie* (1995). On a less-than-successful family road trip, Goofy (voice of Bill Farmer) drives along and sings about the glories of travel while his teenage son Max (singing

While not as well known as other Disney musical films, *Summer Magic* (1963) boasts a superior score by the Sherman brothers, evocative production values, and some charming performances. Before the fatherless Carey family is evicted from their Boston townhouse, they gather around the piano to enjoy the new ragtime sound with the song "Flitterin'." Pictured, left to right, are Dorothy McGuire, Eddie Hodges, Jimmy Mathers, and Hayley Mills. (Walt Disney/Photofest)

voice of Aaron Lohr) sings about all the negative aspects of being stuck on the road with his father. Soon drivers and passengers in other cars—from country singers to nuns to convicts—join in, and eventually everyone is dancing on car roofs and singing the happy song. Even hitchhikers Mickey Mouse and Donald Duck make a singing cameo appearance. Tom Snow wrote the country-flavored music and Jack Feldman penned the light-hearted lyric.

"On Top of the World" is the lite-rock song by Matthew Gerrard and Robbie Nevil that is heard on the soundtrack over the opening credits of the television movie *Stuck in the Suburbs* (2004). Taran Killam, who plays the rock star Jordan Cahill, sings the throbbing number, which claims that anyone can become a star in his or her own eyes.

"Once and For All" is the determined song for justice by Alan Menken (music) and Jack Feldman (lyric) that the newsboys sing in the period musical film *Newsies* (1992). In order to print flyers announcing their strike against newspaper mogul Joseph Pulitzer, "newsie" Jack Kelly (Christian Bale) and some of his pals break into the basement of Pulitzer's printing building with the reporter Bryan Denton (Bill Pullman). Fellow newsboy David Jacobs (David Moscow) and his sister Sarah (Ele Keats) join them in singing this high-energy number about stopping the exploitation of the newsboys.

"Once in a Lifetime" is the rocking opening number for the short-lived television series *Hull High* (1990), in which the students at a southern California high school break out in song to express themselves. Stanley Clarke (music) and Lawrence Edwards (lyric) wrote the rap-like song about grabbing opportunities, which is sung by various students on the bus, in the halls, and on the athletic fields as school begins. The production number (and the series) is very similar to the later *High School Musical* television movies.

"Once Upon a Dream" is the waltzing love ballad the Princess Aurora (voice of Mary Costa) sings to herself as she dances through the forest with her animal friends in the animated movie *Sleeping Beauty* (1959). The princess is soon discovered by Prince Philip (Bill Shirley), who joins her in song, and the two dance beside a stream, their bodies reflected in the water. Sammy Fain (music) and Jack Lawrence (lyric) wrote the song, which was adapted from a theme in Tchaikovsky's *The Sleeping Beauty* ballet. Barbra Streisand sang the ballad in concert and recorded it, as did Steve Tyrell, and a pleasing duet recording was made by Kaitlin Hopkins and Brian Sutherland.

"Once Upon a Time in New York City" is the sparkling opening number by Barry Mann (music) and Howard Ashman (lyric) from the animated movie update of *Oliver Twist*, titled *Oliver & Company* (1988). Over the opening credits, Huey Lewis sings the number about the tough city that is home to a thousand stories and dreams and how one should overcome shyness and get out and experience the metropolis. Lewis's recording enjoyed some popularity.

"Once Upon a Wintertime" is a bucolic song by Bobby Worth (music) and Ray Gilbert (lyric) that was used effectively in the animated film anthology *Melody Time* (1948). Frances Langford and a studio chorus sing the flowing number about the joys of winter on the soundtrack while a courting couple rides a two-horse open sleigh through the countryside to go ice skating on a pond. After a dramatic episode in which the two lovers quarrel and are saved from drowning in the freezing water by some helpful animals, the song is reprised as we see a Victorian picture frame of the happily married couple years later. The background art for the sequence has a stylized Currier and Ives look to it, and the song itself is lush and romantic, but at a cheerful pace that matches the prancing horses.

"The One and Only, Genuine, Original Family Band" is the boastful title song by Richard M. and Robert B. Sherman for the 1968 movie musical, set during the 1888 presidential election. Nebraska family patriarch Grandpa Bower (Walter Brennan) sings the proud march number with family members (Buddy Ebsen, Lesley Ann Warren, Janet Blair) and the Bower grandchildren as they all rehearse for the Democratic Convention, singing, marching, and playing musical instruments.

"One by One" is the intoxicating African chant number written by Lebo M for the 1997 Broadway version of *The Lion King*. At the beginning of the second act, the ensemble sings the chorale piece, which uses African and English phrases, urging the lions to persevere and be true to themselves even as it celebrates Africa and the African races. The stirring song was included in the chorale recording *Rhythm of the Pridelands* and was also featured in the 2004 film short *One by One*, about children in South Africa who fly homemade kites as a sign of freedom.

"101 Dalmatians" is the 1950s-like rock-and-roll song by Patrick DeRemer that serves as the theme song for the animated television program *101 Dalmatians: The Series* (1997). A guy group sings the pop number on the soundtrack during the opening credits, celebrating all the fun you can have with so many puppies and so many spots.

"One Jump" is the frantic "I am" song for the title "street rat" in the animated film *Aladdin* (1992). Alan Menken (music) and Howard Ashman (lyric) wrote the light-footed number, which Aladdin (voice of Brad Kane) sings as he dodges angry merchants and runs away from the sultan's guards through the streets of Agrabah. Later, in a quieter moment in the movie, Aladdin reprises the song, revealing his hopes of bettering his lot someday. Debbie Shapiro Gravitte made a noteworthy recording of the song in 1994.

"One Last Hope" is the comic character song for the satyr Philoctetes (voice of Danny DeVito) written by Alan Menken (music) and David Zippel (lyric) for the animated film *Hercules* (1997). Although the hero-trainer "Phil" has prepared many strong and brave men in the past, none of them has become a superhero. He sings to Hercules that the attempt to train him to become a hero will be his last.

"One Moment" is the emotionally charged song about friendship written by Brahm Wenger for the movie sequel *Air Bud: Golden Receiver* (1998). During the closing credits of the film, Melinda Myers sings the heartfelt ballad about having someone at your side you can depend on, echoing the thoughts of the young football player Josh and his canine teammate, Buddy.

"One More Sleep Till Christmas" is the yearning list song Paul Williams wrote for the film *The Muppet Christmas Carol* (1992). After Scrooge leaves his office, Bob Cratchit, played by Kermit the Frog (voice of Steve Whitmire), and a band of bookkeeping rats close up shop and sing the happy number that lists all the things to look forward to on Christmas Day. A bit later in the film, Bob Cratchit and his young son Tiny Tim (Jerry Nelson) reprise a scat version of the song, titled "Christmas Scat," as Bob carries his son through the streets of London.

"One of a Kind" is the jazzy number about being a unique individual from the made-for-video animated sequel *101 Dalmatians II: Patch's London Adventure* (2003). Noko, Trevor Gray, Richard Gibb, Howard Gray, and Mel Leven wrote the raspy song, which was sung by Apollo 440 over the closing credits of the video.

"One of Us" is the uncomfortable song of mob psychology written by Tom Snow (music) and Jack Feldman (lyric) for the video sequel *The Lion King 2: Simba's Pride* (1998). The lion Kovu is banished from the Pride Lands for a crime he did not commit, and while he slinks away in shame, the animals chant this violent and accusatory song as Kovu passes through the crowd.

The music is very syncopated as the animals pound the earth with their hooves and feet, driving the innocent lion into exile.

"One Song" is the operatic "I am" song for Prince Charming in the animated fairy tale film *Snow White and the Seven Dwarfs* (1937). Frank Churchill (music) and Larry Morey (lyric) wrote the number in which the prince (voice of Harry Stockwell) sings that he has only one song in his heart and he is saving it for someone special. He sings it to the shy Snow White, whom he has just met at the wishing well, and, true to his word, the prince sings no other song in the movie. A studio chorus sings the ballad on the soundtrack over the opening credits, and at the end of the film it is reprised by the prince and a chorus. Mary Martin, Debbie Shapiro Gravitte, En Vogue, and Kaitlin Hopkins each made recordings of the song.

"One Step Closer" is a charming dance number written for the 2008 Broadway version of *The Little Mermaid*. Prince Eric (Sean Palmer) teaches the mute Ariel (Sierra Boggess) how to dance, explaining that movement can speak as clearly as words. Alan Menken composed the flowing music and Glenn Slater wrote the lighthearted but sincere lyric.

"1–2–Cha-Cha-Cha" is the spicy Cuban number William Finn wrote for the animated made-for-video musical *The Adventures of Tom Thumb and Thumbelina* (2002). The tiny Tom Thumb (singing voice of Brad Kane) and Thumbelina (Jennifer Love Hewitt) have escaped, with a band of Latino mice, from the clutches of a little boy who has held them all captive in a glass jar. The whole group celebrates with this cha-cha number that affords the diminutive hero and heroine an opportunity to dance and fall in love.

"Only Solutions" is the driving rock song written and performed by the 1980s band Journey for the groundbreaking computerized film *Tron* (1982). The pulsating number is heard in the background during an early scene that takes place in a video arcade. The melody and lyrics are intense reflections on the stamina and skill required to win a video game. This foreshadows the story that follows, about some characters trapped inside an arcade computer game who must fight their way out.

"Oo-De-Lally" is the enjoyable pseudo-medieval folk ballad written by Roger Miller for the animated movie *Robin Hood* (1973). The rooster Alan-a-Dale (voice of Miller) acts as the film's narrator and lazily plays the lute and sings and whistles the ditty, providing exposition at the top of the film and introducing Robin Hood and some of the other characters. The number is briefly reprised by a chorus on the soundtrack at the end of the movie. A bluegrass rendition of the song was recorded by Mike Toppins, Glen Duncan, Billy Troy, Jim Brown, James Freeze, and David Chase in 1998.

"Oogie Boogie's Song" is a jazzy blues number sung by the grotesque villain of the stop-motion film *The Nightmare Before Christmas* (1993). Danny Elfman wrote the fast-paced song of glee in which the deep-voiced Oogie Boogie (voice of Ken Page) sings and dances because he has captured Santa Claus and revels in the thought of torturing the merry fellow.

"An Ordinary Miracle" is the heartfelt character song written by Walter Edgar Kennon for the animated video sequel *The Hunchback of Notre Dame II* (2002). Sitting atop the bell tower of Notre Dame Cathedral, the hunchback Quasimodo (voice of Tom Hulce) wonders if there is someone who will love him in spite of his physical deformities and social anxiety. The number is reminiscent of the song "Out There" from the original *Hunchback* film, with a building melodic intensity. The sad, introspective lyric longs for something Quasimodo perceives as unattainable and nothing short of a miracle.

"Our Thanksgiving Day" is the festive song written by Patty and Michael Silversher for the made-for-video film *Winnie the Pooh: Seasons of Giving* (1999) about Thanksgiving and Christmas in the Hundred Acre Wood. Although their Thanksgiving dinner has turned out strangely, with the menu consisting of acorns, honey, and lemonade, Pooh (voice of Jim Cummings) and the other friends of Christopher Robin (Brady Bluhm) celebrate the holiday with this song, which rates sharing with friends above any kind of dinner.

"Our Time Is Here" is the celebratory number performed near the end of the television movie *Camp Rock* (2008). Teenager Mitchie Torres (Demi Lovato) visits her friend Caitlyn's (Allison Stoner) garage recording studio, where she records this song with all the female friends she made at camp. Tim James and Antonina Armato wrote the brisk music and the optimistic lyric, which celebrates tomorrow and what is still to come for these talented teens.

"Our Town" is the Oscar-nominated folk song written by Randy Newman for the computer-animated movie *Cars* (2006). During a flashback in which it is shown how the new interstate highway bypassed several rural towns, James Taylor sings the easygoing but poignant ballad about the days back when one grew up, stayed, and grew old in one's hometown.

"Out of Thin Air" is a revealing character song David Friedman wrote for the video sequel *Aladdin and the King of Thieves* (1995). In the affecting duet, Aladdin (voice of Brad Kane) wants to ask the oracle about his long-lost father, but fears who he might be. The princess Jasmine (Liz Callaway) encourages him, knowing that the father must be like the son and arguing that Aladdin did not come out of thin air.

"Out of This World" is the pop-rock ballad written by Matthew Gerrard and Lisa Benenate for the television movie *Zenon: Z3* (2004), the third film about the title teenage girl living in the twenty-first century. The intergalactic rock star Proto Zoa (Phillip Rhys) and his band, the Cosmic Blush, sing about the way a loved one's smile can send you into space. Rhys made a music video of the lite-rock number.

"Out There" is the stirring "I am" song for the deformed Quasimodo (voice of Tom Hulce) in the animated film *The Hunchback of Notre Dame* (1996). Alan Menken (music) and Stephen Schwartz (lyric) wrote the expansive ballad, which the lonely hunchback sings as he climbs the towers of Notre Dame and looks down upon the ordinary people on the street, wishing he could be like them. Jason Danieley recorded the song, and Andrew Samonsky made an effective version with Kaitlin Hopkins and Brian Sutherland in 2005.

"Over It" is the breezy rock song by Adam Watts and Andy Dodd that encourages one to let go of the past and move on, as heard in the television movie *Stuck in the Suburbs* (2004). Anneliese van der Pol sings the carefree number on the soundtrack during the closing credits of the film.

"The Oz-Kan Hop" is the swinging charm song written by Buddy Baker (music) and Tom Adair (lyric) for the proposed film *The Rainbow Road to Oz*, and although the movie was never made, the song was performed by the Mouseketeers on the television show *Disneyland* in 1957. The Cowardly Lion has been put under a spell that makes him vain and cruel, so Dorothy (Darlene Gillespie) leads the cast in this silly song and dance that incorporates footwork in the Kansas and Ozian styles.

P

"Painting the Roses Red" is a gleeful rhythmic number with a disturbing subtext written by Sammy Fain (music) and Bob Hilliard (lyric) for the animated film fantasy *Alice in Wonderland* (1951). A pack of cards (voices of the Mellomen) sing the cheerful-sounding march as they paint all the white roses in the garden of the Queen of Hearts red, yet the lyric makes it clear that they will have their heads cut off if the Queen encounters even one white rose.

"The Parent Trap" is the jazzy title song Richard M. and Robert B. Sherman wrote for the 1961 movie about twin teenagers who use tricks to trap their estranged parents into getting back together. Annette Funicello and Tommy Sands sing the pop number over the clever stop-motion animated credits of the film, the lyric promising to straighten out the mess the parents have made of their marriage.

"Part of Your World" is the lyrical "I am" song for the title character in the animated film *The Little Mermaid* (1989). The mermaid princess Ariel (voice of Jodi Benson) looks through her collection of objects from the human world and sings of her desire to join them on land and live as they do. Later in the film, Ariel reprises the song as she looks upon the unconscious Eric after she has rescued him and placed him on the beach. The song, written by Alan Menken (music) and Howard Ashman (lyric), is somewhat similar in sentiment and melody to "Somewhere That's Green," written by Menken and Ashman for the Off-Broadway musical *Little Shop of Horrors* (1982), in which a city girl yearns for a life in the suburbs. Ann Marie Boskovich sings the number over the closing credits of the animated video sequel *The Little Mermaid II: Return to the Sea* (2000) and Sierra Boggess sang it in the 2008 Broadway version of *The Little Mermaid*. Recordings of the song include those by Skye Sweetnam, Debbie Shapiro Gravitte, Jessica Simpson, Ashley Brown, Miley Cyrus, and Barbara Hendricks and the Abbey Road Ensemble.

"The Party's Just Begun" is the throbbing rock song by Matthew Gerrard and Robbie Nevil that the teenage singing stars Galleria (Raven-Symoné), Chanel (Adrienne Bailon), Aqua (Kiely Williams), and Dorinda (Sabrina Bryan) sing in concert in the television sequel *The Cheetah Girls 2* (2006). The ardent number announces that the fun is just beginning and asks the audience to make noise and join in the party.

"Passamaquoddy" is the dandy soft-shoe number that the charlatan Dr. Terminus (Jim Dale) sings to impress the citizens of the Maine town of Passamaquoddy with his miracle cures in the part-animated movie *Pete's Dragon* (1977). Joel Hirschhorn and Al Kasha wrote the hat-and-cane number, in which the crook Terminus keeps mispronouncing the name of the town.

"The Past Is Another Land" is the touching "I am" song for the Nubian princess Aida (Heather Headley) in the Broadway musical *Aida* (2000). Her country defeated by the Egyptians and herself taken as a slave, the strong-willed Aida recalls her happy past and faces the grim reality of the future. Elton John (music) and Tim Rice (lyric) wrote the engaging pop ballad.

"Pastures Green" is the smooth and lazy ballad that Rod McKuen wrote for the movie *Scandalous John* (1971), about a crusty old rancher who defends the open spaces of the West from industrialists. McKuen sings the western-flavored tribute to the beauty of nature on the soundtrack.

"The Patchwork Girl" is the bouncy list song that introduces a major character in the planned movie *The Rainbow Road to Oz*, based on stories from the L. Frank Baum books. Although the movie was only partially scored and was never made, three of the songs were performed by the Mouseketeers on an episode of the television program *Disneyland* in 1957. The Patchwork

Girl (Doreen Tracey, with singing by Gloria Wood) meets the Scarecrow (Bobby Burgess), and together they sing about all the different kinds of fabrics that are incorporated in her costume. The optimistic character number was written by Buddy Baker (music) and Tom Adair (lyric).

"Paul Bunyan" is the sing-along title song that George Bruns (music) and Tom Adair (lyric) wrote for the Oscar-nominated 1958 film short about the legendary folk hero. The narrative ballad relates the tall tale of the lumberjack Bunyan (voice of Thurl Ravenscroft), his cohort Babe the Blue Ox, and their amazing accomplishments because of their towering height and incredible strength. The Mellomen sing the folk-like number on the soundtrack, with Bunyan joining in for sections. The vivid refrain inspires the listener to join in, as in a traditional folk song.

"PB&J Otter Theme" is the calypso-like theme song for the animated television series *PB&J Otter* (1998) about three playful river otters. Fred Newman and Dan Sawyer wrote the spirited number, the lyric consisting mostly of fun sounds like "day-o," and it is sung on the soundtrack by a children's chorus over the opening credits.

"Peace on Earth" is the warm Christmas carol written by Sonny Burke and Peggy Lee for the animated movie *Lady and the Tramp* (1955). A studio chorus sings the traditional-sounding carol on the soundtrack at the beginning of the film, when a small New England town is seen on a snowy Christmas Eve and the camera moves in on the home of Darling and Jim Dear. The chorus reprises the carol at the end of the film, when it is Christmas once again and Lady and Tramp have a basketful of puppies.

"Peacock Princess" is the determined song of self-esteem written by Amy Powers and Russ DeSalvo for the animated video *Disney Princess Enchanted Tales: Follow Your Dreams* (2007). No one at the palace takes Princess Jasmine (singing voice of Lea Salonga) seriously, and as she tries on a ridiculous feather gown that makes her look like an overgrown peacock, she sings this driving ballad about being more than a "peacock princess" and how she will show them all what she is really capable of. The wisecracking parrot Iago (Gilbert Gottfried) joins her in the ardent number.

"Pecos Bill" is the western-flavored narrative ballad by Eliot Daniel (music) and Johnny Lange (lyric) that provides the tale for the final sequence in the animated anthology movie *Melody Time* (1948). In a live-action introduction, Roy Rogers and the Sons of the Pioneers sing to two children (Bobby Driscoll and Luana Patten) about why coyotes howl, and then the animated tall tale of Pecos Bill is told. As a boy he is raised in the desert by coyotes. After he loses his sweetheart, Slue-Foot Sue, he returns to his animal friends and in his misery bays at the moon.

"The Penguin Is a Very Funny Creature" is the barbershop quartet number Leigh Harline wrote for the animated Silly Symphony movie short *Peculiar Penguins* (1934). Fifty million arctic birds live on Penguin Island, and their strangely humanlike behavior is the subject of this harmonizing song, sung by the Disney Studio Singers on the soundtrack.

"A Perfect Day" is the optimistic song about happy endings that concludes the animated made-for-video film *The Adventures of Tom Thumb and Thumbelina* (2002). The tiny hero Tom Thumb and his sweetheart, Thumbelina, finally arrive at a village of diminutive citizens and are reunited with their families. William Finn wrote the frolicsome number, which is sung on the soundtrack by Bob Poynton as the little lovers wed and take off for their honeymoon at the end of the video.

"Perfect Isn't Easy" is the decadent "I am" song for the pampered poodle Georgette (voice of Bette Midler) in the animated film version of *Oliver Twist*, titled *Oliver & Company* (1988). Barry Manilow, Bruce Sussman, and Jack Feldman wrote the amusing character song in which the wealthy Manhattan pet laments the trials of being perfect, her indifferent yawns turning into canine screeches of pleasure.

"The Perfect Nanny" is the simple and childlike advertisement for a nanny that the two young Banks children write and sing in the movie musical *Mary Poppins* (1964). Having been saddled with mean and ugly nannies, Jane (Karen Dotrice) and Michael Banks (Matthew Garber) write a newspaper ad asking for a kind, pretty, and understanding nanny who likes to play games and will love them as if they were her own children. The sweet, sincere ditty, by Richard M. and Robert B. Sherman, was sung in the 2004 London stage version of *Mary Poppins* by Charlotte Spencer and Harry Stott, and in the 2006 Broadway production by Katherine Doherty or Katheryn Faughnan and Matthew Gumley or Henry Hodges.

"Perfect World" is the Las Vegas–like production number sung by the Elvis look-alike lounge singer Theme Song Guy (voice of Tom Jones) in the satiric animated movie *The Emperor's New Groove* (2000). David Hartley (music and lyric) and Sting (lyric) wrote the pulsating song about the pampered life that Emperor Kuzco (David Spade) leads, and the number turns into a floor show in which the emperor joins in the singing and dancing. Theme Song Guy reprises the song briefly when the emperor returns to the palace near the end of the film.

"Perfectly Perfect" is the lighthearted exposition song by Alan Zachary and Michael Weiner that is used at the beginning of the animated video sequel *Cinderella III: A Twist in Time* (2007) to allow the audience to catch up on what has happened to the major characters since the wedding of Cinderella and the prince. On their first wedding anniversary, Cinderella (singing voice of Tami Tappan Damiano) and the prince (Christopher Daniel Barnes) celebrate in song as they frolic about the castle. At the Tremaine château, the Stepmother (Susan Blakeslee) and the stepsisters Anastasia (Lesli Margherita) and Drizella (Russi Taylor) complain in song about how a life of housework is not suited to them. Then, in the forest, the Fairy Godmother (also Taylor) sings the number as she prepares for an anniversary party for the couple with the help of the mice Jaq (Rob Paulsen) and Gus (Corey Burton).

"The Phony King of England" is the hillbilly ballad mocking the evil Prince John in the animated movie *Robin Hood* (1973). Johnny Mercer wrote the rustic song, which is sung by Little John (voice of Phil Harris) and other followers of Robin Hood as they celebrate their outwitting the upstart King John once again. The number turns into a merry hoedown dance, and then the song is heard circulating throughout Nottingham, much to the displeasure of the "phony" king.

"Pictures in My Head" is a song of yearning for the old days, sung by Kermit the Frog (voice of Steve Whitmire) as he walks down a long corridor adorned with pictures of his old friends in the 2011 film *The Muppets*. As he reminisces about times gone by, the pictures come to life and Kermit recalls each Muppet's individual talents, wishing they could all, once again, create the magic they used to generate as a team. The sentimental number features music and lyrics by Jeannie Lurie, Aris Archontis, and Chen Neeman.

"The Pied Piper" is the operetta-like title song for the 1933 Silly Symphony animated film short based on the tale of the Pied Piper of Hamelin.

Leigh Harline wrote the flowing theme song, sung by a chorus on the soundtrack, which relates how the Pied Piper rids the townspeople of rats. When the mayor refuses to pay, the piper uses the same magic to enchant all the children and lead them away as well. All the characters in the film sing their lines in operatic style; the music is a variation of the theme song and the lyrics a paraphrase of the famous Robert Browning poem.

"Pink Elephants on Parade" is the very unusual march song by Oliver Wallace, Ned Washington, and Frank Churchill that is used in a famous dream sequence in the animated movie *Dumbo* (1941). When some alcohol is accidentally dumped into the water trough and the young elephant Dumbo drinks it, he has bizarre visions of pink elephants as they pass in parade, defying physics by changing shape and color. A studio chorus sings the hypnotic march on the soundtrack as the visuals go berserk, creating one of the most surreal scenes in Disney film animation. The sequence is animated in the style of artist Salvador Dali, and the pounding song becomes menacing as the images pile up on the screen. Barbara Cook made a farcical recording of the odd but engrossing song.

"The Pink of Perfection" is the sarcastic number about a girl who thinks she is perfect, sung by Maine resident Nancy Carey (Hayley Mills) and her brother Gilly (Eddie Hodges) in the film *Summer Magic* (1963). Richard M. and Robert B. Sherman wrote the risible number, and the Carey siblings sing it when they learn that their snobby cousin Julia is coming to live with them.

"The Pioneer Song" is the rousing choral number sung by optimistic settlers in the "Johnny Appleseed" section of the animated anthology movie *Melody Time* (1948). Kim Gannon and Walter Kent wrote the rugged song about getting in a wagon and joining the pioneers in striking out for new land in the West. Johnny (voice of Dennis Day) hears the song but realizes he is too scrawny and weak to be a pioneer.

"Pioneer's Prayer" is the solemn hymn by Paul J. Smith that is used during a somber moment in the adventure movie *Westward Ho, the Wagons!* (1956). After a youth from their party is kidnapped by the Pawnee tribe, the members of the wagon train on the Oregon Trail sing this prayer asking God to shine His light down on the prairie and give them strength to face all adversity. Smith originally composed the melody for the film documentary *The Vanishing Prairie* (1954) and it was heard as part of his soundtrack score. He added the reverent lyric for the pioneer feature movie.

"The Pirate Song" is the friendly song of comradeship that Frank Churchill (music) and Ray Kelly (lyric) wrote for the animated movie *Peter Pan* (1953), but it was replaced by "The Elegant Captain Hook." The pirates sing the number to the captured Lost Boys, hoping to get them to join the buccaneer crew by pointing out all the pluses (no bedtime, no work, no washing) of being a pirate.

"A Pirate's Life (for Me)" is the rugged sea chantey Oliver Wallace (music) and Erdman Penner (lyric) wrote for the animated fantasy film *Peter Pan* (1953). While the pirates wait on board ship for Captain Hook to come up with a plan to capture Peter Pan, they sing this brief but catchy number about the joys of a buccaneer life. The pirate Mr. Smee (voice of Bill Thompson) reprises the ditty when he shaves Captain Hook a bit later in the movie. The song is not to be confused with "Yo Ho (A Pirate's Life for Me)," written for the theme park attraction Pirates of the Caribbean.

"Pirates of the Caribbean Main Theme" is the high-intensity musical composition written by Hans Zimmer for the film *Pirates of the Caribbean: The Curse of the Black Pearl* (2003), and the memorable piece is reprised in the two movie sequels. The theme is an accurate musical interpretation of the type of swashbuckling adventure the films portray, and its melody evokes images of racing ships on the water, exotic locales, and an urgency of epic proportions.

"Places in the Heart" is the touching song of friendship written by Michael and Patty Silversher for the animated television special *Winnie the Pooh: A Valentine for You* (1999). When Winnie the Pooh (voice of Jim Cummings) learns that Christopher Robin (Brady Bluhm) has sent a valentine to a girl, the boy assures the bear that there is still plenty of room in his heart for old friends as well as new ones. Pooh's friends echo the sentiment and sing the affectionate song together.

"Play My Music" is the pop list song about what happens when some rockers listen to their music, written by Kara DioGuardi and Greg Wells for the television musical *Camp Rock* (2008). Pop musician and camp counselor Shane Gray (Joe Jonas) decides to share a new song with the campers at

Camp Rock, and he invites his music group Connect 3 (the Jonas Brothers) to perform with him.

"Pleasure Island" is the happy carnival-like song with a dark subtext that Stephen Schwartz wrote for the live-action television musical *Geppetto* (2000). The Ringleader (Usher Raymond) and the other devilish carnies on Pleasure Island sing a song of welcome to Pinocchio and the other boys who have just arrived, promising them plenty of fun at the amusement park. Yet the music and the lyrics have a sinister quality as well, foreshadowing the fact that all the boys will be turned into donkeys.

"A Pooh Bear Takes Care of His Tummy" is the jolly "I am" song that introduces the title character in the 2011 animated film *Winnie the Pooh*. Pooh Bear (voice of Jim Cummings), facing a new day, wakes up to a grumbling stomach and goes off to find some breakfast while he sings this pleasant ditty. The simple and catchy song is by Robert Lopez and Kristen Anderson-Lopez.

"The Pooh Will Soon Be Free" is the wryly comic song sung by various A. A. Milne characters in the first Disney Winnie the Pooh film short, *Winnie the Pooh and the Honey Tree* (1966). After eating too much honey in the home of Rabbit, Pooh gets stuck in the entrance, and his friends have to push and tug on the bear to set him free. An earlier version of the number, titled "Mind Over Matter," urged Winnie to think thin in order to get unstuck, but the song evolved into the more farcical one involving a lot of heave ho. Richard M. and Robert B. Sherman wrote the number, which is sometimes listed as "The Heave Ho Song."

"Pooh's Lullabee" is the brief waltzing lullaby written by Richard M. and Robert B. Sherman for the animated film *The Tigger Movie* (2000). Anxious to get at the honey stored inside the trunk of a tree, Winnie the Pooh (voice of Jim Cummings) sings this soothing number to make the bees sleepy, and he even puts them to bed in their honeycomb beds with the song.

"Poor Jack" is the reflective character song for the Pumpkin King, Jack Skellington (singing voice of Danny Elfman), in the stop-motion film *The Nightmare Before Christmas* (1993). After his sleigh is blasted out of the sky, Jack falls, landing in the arms of an angel monument in a graveyard, and sings this regretful lament about the mistakes he has made in trying to take over Christmas. Elfman wrote the song, during which Jack comes to the conclusion that scaring people is what he is best at and that he will focus his energies on next Halloween.

"Poor Unfortunate Souls" is the dandy character song for the villainous squid Ursula (voice of Pat Carroll) that Alan Menken (music) and Howard Ashman (lyric) wrote for the animated movie *The Little Mermaid* (1989). Ursula sings to the young mermaid Ariel (Jodi Benson) about those seeking her help and how she always manages to oblige them—for a price. The sea witch agrees to make Ariel human, but the price is her lovely voice. The number turns into an enthralling chant, filled with classical Latin invocations, as Ursula transforms the mermaid into a girl. Debbie Shapiro Gravitte made a colorful recording of the song in 1994; Kaitlin Hopkins recorded it with a quartet made up of Meredith Inglesby, Andy Karl, Tyler Maynard, and Keewa Nurullah; Emily Skinner and Alice Ripley made a duet version; and it was recorded and made into a music video by the Jonas Brothers. The number was sung by Sherie Rene Scott in the 2008 Broadway version of *The Little Mermaid*.

"Portobello Road" is the musical tribute to the famous London street market written by Richard M. and Robert B. Sherman for the movie fantasy *Bedknobs and Broomsticks* (1971). Professor Emelius Brown (David Tomlinson), the friendly witch Miss Eglantine Price (Angela Lansbury), and her three young evacuees (Ian Weighill, Cindy O'Callaghan, and Roy Snart) go to the Portobello market to find a rare book of spells, and the professor sings about the fabled street where treasures, both true and false, can be found. Various vendors join in the song and soon it turns into a lengthy and elaborate production number, with dancing customers and sections of swing, calypso, and folk dancing.

"Positoovity" is the optimistic nonsense song that opens the second act of the 2008 Broadway version of *The Little Mermaid*. The seagull Scuttle (Eddie Korbich) leads the other gulls in having a positive attitude in life, the lame-brained bird making up words and destroying other words in the process. Alan Menken composed the jaunty music and Glenn Slater wrote the glittering lyric, which is in the tradition of such Disney songs as "Fortuosity" and "Supercalifragilisticexpialidocious."

"Practically Perfect" is the straightforward "I am" song written by George Stiles and Anthony Drewe for the stage version of *Mary Poppins*, which opened in London in 2004. The newly arrived nanny Mary Poppins

(Laura Michelle Kelly) explains to her two young charges that she is just about perfect in character, appearance, and abilities. Like the character of the mysterious nanny, the number comes across as honest and not conceited. The song title also has a double meaning, because Mary is indeed practical, even when she uses her magic. Ashley Brown played Mary and sang the song in the 2006 Broadway production.

"Pretty Irish Girl" is the pastiche of an Irish ballad used throughout the film *Darby O'Gill and the Little People* (1959) for the blossoming romance between the old caretaker's daughter Katie O'Gill (Janet Munro) and the new caretaker Michael McBride (Sean Connery). The sprightly love song about a beloved lassie is sung by Michael and then later reprised by Katie, the two of them singing it together at the end of the film. Oliver Wallace (music) and Lawrence E. Watkin (lyric) wrote the simple and authentic-sounding Irish number.

"Prince Ali" is the silly and tuneful production number in the animated film *Aladdin* (1992) in which the "street rat" Aladdin, disguised as a prince, arrives in Agrabah with a massive singing and dancing entourage. The Genie (voice of Robin Williams) leads the song and the parade (which spoofs the Macy's Thanksgiving Day Parade), becoming different characters while spouting the ridiculous praises of the young prince. Later in the movie, the evil wizard Jafar (Jonathan Freeman) reprises the number with an altered lyric, gloating over his revenge on Aladdin. Alan Menken (music) and Howard Ashman (lyric) wrote the daffy song, which is both musically and lyrically busy and gleeful. Kaitlin Hopkins recorded the number with backup vocals by Meredith Inglesby, Andy Karl, Tyler Maynard, and Keewa Nurullah.

"A Professional Pirate" is the dandy sea chantey sung by Long John Silver (Tim Curry) and his henchmen in the movie spoof *Muppet Treasure Island* (1996). Barry Mann and Cynthia Weil wrote the Gilbert-and-Sullivan-like number, which the one-legged Silver sings to the cabin boy Jim Hawkins (Kevin Bishop), trying to get him to join his pirate gang. The pirates claim they could have been lawyers, politicians, and other legitimate professionals, but they are convinced that being a pirate is best of all.

"Psalm 8" is the gentle ballad about understanding faith through God's mercy, heard in the Broadway concert *King David* (1997). Tim Rice adapted the biblical psalm into a lyric, Alan Menken composed the placid melody, and it was sung by the young David (Marcus Lovett).

"Puppy Love Is Here to Stay" is a farcical satire on the pop music of the late 1950s that was included in the sarcastic animated mockumentary *A Symposium on Popular Songs* first shown as a 1962 segment on the television program *Walt Disney's Wonderful World of Color*. A Frankie Valli–like tenor (voice of Billy Storm) sings in his falsetto voice about young love as teenagers are seen drinking sodas at a malt shop and dancing to the jukebox. The number by Richard M. and Robert B. Sherman is extremely facetious about young love lasting forever and ever.

"Radish So Red" is the musical ditty that spoofs the poetic ode form, written by Charles Wolcott (music), T. Hee, and Erdman Penner (lyric) for the animated movie *The Reluctant Dragon* (1941). When the flaky knight Sir Giles (voice of Claude Allister) learns that his opponent, the docile Dragon, likes to write poetry, the amateur poet shares one of his own creations, talk-singing this musical tribute to the red root vegetable.

"The Rain, Rain, Rain Came Down, Down, Down" is the insistent staccato song by Richard M. and Robert B. Sherman that has a plinking sound that imitates the sound of raindrops falling. A studio chorus sings the rhythmic number on the soundtrack of the Oscar-winning film short *Winnie the Pooh and the Blustery Day* (1968) as Pooh and his friends brave a rainstorm and a flood in the Hundred Acre Wood.

"The Rainbow Road to Oz" is the repetitive but catchy title song Buddy Baker (music) and Tom Adair (lyric) wrote for a proposed Disney film based on the stories by L. Frank Baum. Walt Disney gave viewers a preview of the movie in 1957, when three musical numbers were performed by the Mouseketeers on an episode of the weekly television show *Disneyland*. Princess Ozma (Annette Funicello) leads the cast in showing Dorothy (Darlene Gillespie), the Scarecrow (Bobby Burgess), and the Patchwork Girl (Doreen Tracey) which road will take them to the city of Oz.

"Reach" is the driving pop song written by Matthew Gerrard and Kara DioGuardi for the movie *Ice Princess* (2005), about a girl's quest to become a champion figure skater. Caleigh Peters is heard on the soundtrack singing the pulsating number about reaching out to someone when you are falling, no matter how impossible help may seem.

"Ready" is the reflective pop ballad about being ready for a new challenge, written by Mick Jones, Kara DioGuardi, Lukas McGuire Burton, Jamie Alexander Hartman, and Sacha Skarbek for the film *Confessions of a Teenage Drama Queen* (2004). The pop singer Cherie sings the song over the opening credits while New Yorker Lola moves with her family from Manhattan to a New Jersey suburb, not happy about the change but willing to meet the adventure head-on.

"Real Gone" is the pounding rock song written by Sheryl Crow and John Shanks for the computer-animated movie *Cars* (2006). Crow sings the urgent song on the soundtrack, the lyric about getting out of town, hitting the road, and finding a better place. Her recording was popular, and the number was also recorded by Billy Ray Cyrus.

"Reflection" is the knowing "I am" song the young Chinese girl Mulan (singing voice of Lea Salonga) sings in the animated movie adventure *Mulan* (1998) as she wonders if anyone will ever understand what she is really like inside. Matthew Wilder (music) and David Zippel (lyric) wrote the slightly pop ballad, which Mulan sings as she prays to her ancestors, her face reflected dozens of times on the shiny stone tablets in the family shrine. Recordings of the song were made by Michael Crawford, Ashley Brown, Keke Palmer, Everlife, and Christina Aguilera.

"The Replacements Theme Song" is the folk-rock number that introduces each episode of the 2006 animated television series about two orphans who adopt replacement parents who turn out to be secret agents. Jason Frederick and Darian Sahanaja wrote the pop ballad that tells about the wily pair of kids and how they picked out their foster parents.

"Rescue Aid Society" is the musical pledge of allegiance written by Carol Connors and Ayn Robbins for the animated film *The Rescuers* (1977). The mice Bernard (voice of Bob Newhart), Bianca (Eva Gabor), and other members of the all-mouse Rescue Aid Society from across the globe sing their anthem, vowing to help those in distress, when they gather at their international headquarters inside the United Nations building in New York City.

"Rhyme-Around" is the rousing charm song that is featured in a rustic scene of jubilation in the film *Those Calloways* (1965). At a party in rural Vermont to celebrate the completion of the Calloway cabin by the townsfolk, Lydia Calloway (Vera Miles) suggests that they play a musical game called "Rhyme-Around" in which each player has to make up a musical rhyme about someone else in the room. Soon all the neighbors are playing and singing, each creating a verse. The final rhyme is performed by the crusty Alf Simes (Walter Brennan), who uses it as a comical way to get Cam Calloway's son Bucky (Brandon De Wilde) and his romantic interest, Bridie Mellott (Linda Evans), to go outside and admit their love for each other. Richard M. and Robert B. Sherman wrote the contagious square dance music and the fun lyric, which serves as a witty commentary on the locals.

"Right Here, Right Now" is the pop love song about making the most of the time given to you, written by Jamie Houston for the movie sequel *High School Musical 3: Senior Year* (2008). High school senior Troy Bolton (Zac Efron) and his girlfriend, Gabriella (Vanessa Anne Hudgens), meet in his tree house after the final basketball game of the season and sing this bittersweet duet, knowing that time is running out and soon they will no longer be high school students.

"Right Where I Belong" is the pop ballad about finding yourself and the place where you are happiest, heard in the video sequel *The Jungle Book 2* (2003). Lorraine Feather and Joel McNeely wrote the soaring ballad, the lyric commenting on the young hero in the story, and it is sung by Windy Wagner on the soundtrack over the final credits of the video.

"Rolie Polie Olie" is the tuneful title song for the 1998 animated children's television series that takes place in a world where everything is round. The calliope-like number is sung by a studio chorus over the opening credits, singing the praises of the six-year-old Olie, who is small, round, and a swell kid.

"Roll Along" is the mournful, pensive ballad with an old-time Southern flavor that is heard in the adventure movie *Ten Who Dared* (1960). Two of the men on an expedition down the Colorado River, the southerner George Bradley (Ben Johnson) and the Yankee Walter Powell (James Drury), settle their differences when George saves Walter's life, and the two later harmonize together with this tender song. Stan Jones wrote the graceful music and Lawrence Edgar Watkin penned the melancholy lyric about the lonely life of an explorer and how it compares to the ambling journey of a lonely river.

"Roses and Rainbows" is the confident song of liberation written by Marvin Hamlisch (music) and Carole Bayer Sager (lyric) for the movie *The Devil and Max Devlin* (1981). Would-be star Stella Summers (Julie Budd) has overcome her lack of confidence, no longer needs the devil's assistant, Max (Elliott Gould), to promote her career, and sings this eager song about taking both the good and the bad in life and understanding it is okay to be alone sometimes. Budd also made a record of the song.

"The Rough, Tough, Burly Sailor Song" is the slightly satirical sea chantey written by Michael and Patty Silversher for an episode of the animated television series *Disney's Adventures of the Gummi Bears* (1985). While some citizens of Gummi Glen build a ship and prepare to make it seaworthy, they sing this happy number and profess to be rugged sailors who eat gummiberry pies and burly barley stew, but admit they don't know where they are sailing to.

"Round My Family Tree" is the farcical song Richard M. and Robert B. Sherman wrote for the animated film *The Tigger Movie* (2000). As Tigger (voice of Jim Cummings) sings about the glorious ancestors of the Tigger family, his imagination sees them playing important roles throughout history. His reverie climaxes in a spectacular Las Vegas–like show with Tiggers of all kinds performing.

"Rumbly in My Tumbly" is the simple song about Winnie the Pooh's continual craving for honey, his favorite food. Richard M. and Robert B. Sherman wrote the lighthearted ditty for *Winnie the Pooh and the Honey Tree* (1966), the first of many film shorts based on A. A. Milne's characters.

"The Rutabaga Rag" is a silly pastiche of a ragtime number that Richard M. and Robert B. Sherman wrote for a 1962 segment, *A Symposium of Popular Songs*, on the television program *Walt Disney's Wonderful World of Color*. Professor Ludwig von Drake (voice of Paul Frees) holds the symposium in his mansion where, to demonstrate turn-of-the-century rags, stop-action animated fruits and vegetables on a kitchen table sing this song. The music is a lively piano rag, and the ridiculous lyric includes rhyming all kinds of food names.

"The Saga of Andy Burnett" is the strumming title song George Bruns wrote for the 1957 television series, which was featured on the weekly program *Disneyland*. Fess Parker introduced the folk song on the first episode, playing the guitar and singing about the restless Andy Burnett, who was always on the move and had many adventures out West. The number was then heard on the soundtrack at the beginning of the subsequent episodes. Parker did not play Andy; the pioneer was portrayed by Jerome Courtland. But Walt Disney hoped the *Davy Crockett* star would help the Andy Burnett series find similar popularity. Neither the title song nor the show enjoyed the success of Parker's series, but it was still fairly popular and is fondly remembered by many.

"The Saga of Windwagon Smith" is the extended cowboy operetta written by George Bruns (music) and C. August Nichols (lyrics) for the 1961 film short of the same title. The entire movie is written in rhymed verse, and at several points in the story the characters break into song, ranging from western ballads to sea chanteys to Gilbert-and-Sullivan-like musical scenes. The tall tale about Captain Smith, who attempts to sail the Santa Fe Trail in a wind-powered Conestoga wagon, is narrated by Rex Allen, who also provides the singing voice for Smith, and the Sons of the Pioneers provide the choral singing in the funny, lyrical piece.

"Sail with Me" is the oddball love song for Popeye (Robin Williams) and Olive Oyl (Shelley Duvall) in the cartoonish live-action movie *Popeye* (1980). Harry Nilsson wrote the awkward but affectionate duet, in which the two sweethearts profess their love and see their future together at sea.

"Sailing for Adventure" is the rousing sea chantey written by Barry Mann and Cynthia Weil for the musical film *Muppet Treasure Island* (1996). Long John Silver (Tim Curry), Jim Hawkins (Kevin Bishop), and the sailors and passengers (both cloth and human) on the *Hispaniola* sing the Gilbert-and-Sullivan-like chorus number as they set sail from England to find treasure in the Caribbean.

"Sally's Song" is an odd but affecting torch song for the Frankenstein-like creature Sally (voice of Catherine O'Hara) in the stop-motion movie *The Nightmare Before Christmas* (1993). Danny Elfman wrote the sad lament in which Sally admits her love for the dashing Pumpkin King Jack Skellington, but she knows he will never pay any attention to her. The maudlin music box–like melody has a tender yet creepy quality to it.

"Saludos Amigos" is the festive title number by Charles Wolcott (music) and Ned Washington (lyric) for the 1942 part-live-action, part-animated travelogue about South America. The Oscar-nominated song was sung on the soundtrack during the opening credits by a male chorus welcoming Americans to the colorful world of their neighbors to the south. Although the subject of the film is South America, the title song is more swinging than Latin.

"Samuel Anoints David" is the intense operatic number from the Broadway concert *King David* (1997), which the Disney Company presented to premiere its newly restored New Amsterdam Theatre. Samuel (Peter Samuel), Joab (Stephen Bogardus), and Jesse (Michael Goz) sing the song as King Saul anoints the young David (Marcus Lovett), then the young man meekly shares his ideas in a delicate character song. Alan Menken composed the contrasting melodies and Tim Rice penned the innocent, idealistic lyric.

"Santa's Workshop" is the sprightly title song by Frank Churchill for the 1932 Silly Symphony film short. As the elves in the North Pole finish making the toys, ready the reindeer, check over the "naughty" and "nice" lists with their employer, and prepare the sleigh, they sing this lively song, which climaxes with Santa's departure on his Christmas Eve voyage.

"Santa Fe" is the eager "I am" song for the orphaned newsboy Jack Kelly (Christian Bale) in the period movie musical *Newsies* (1992). Alan Menken (music) and Jack Feldman (lyric) wrote the number about longing to escape 1899 Manhattan and head out West. Jack sings it as he wanders the streets late at night, breaking into a rousing cowboy dance step as he imagines a new life for himself in the great outdoors. The song is reprised, with altered lyrics, later in the film when Jack is torn between taking a bribe and selling out his friends or continuing as leader of a major newsboy strike. Debbie Shapiro Gravitte made a lovely recording of the song of yearning.

"Sarah's Theme" is the haunting and hypnotic song by James Horner (music) and Brock Walsh (lyric) that is used so effectively in the movie *Hocus Pocus* (1993). In order to stay alive past Halloween, three witches must make a potion that includes the life force of children. The witch Sarah Sanderson (Sarah Jessica Parker) flies through the night sky singing this eerie number in order to lure children to the Sanderson house. The song is also listed as "Come Little Children."

"Satisfaction Guaranteed" is the wild tarantella number with a sinister subtext written by Stephen Schwartz for the live-action television musical *Geppetto* (2000). While searching for his lost son, Pinocchio, the toymaker Geppetto (Drew Carey) comes to the town of Idyllia, where the crazy inventor Professor Buonragazzo (René Auberjonois) has a machine that turns out perfect children. As the townspeople sing and dance in the square, praising the Professor's flawless singing moppets, Geppetto is alarmed to see the creatures lacking any personality, and prefers his own mischievous Pinocchio.

"Saul Has Slain His Thousands" is the kinetic song of celebration and decision written by Alan Menken (music) and Tim Rice (lyric) for the concert-pageant *King David*, which was presented on Broadway in 1997. The chorus of Hebrews realizes that Saul (Martin Vidnovic) is no longer a great king, and in this stirring number they turn to David (Marcus Lovett) as their new hope.

"Savage Sam and Me" is the rambling folk song by Terry Gilkyson that introduces the canine hero of the adventure movie *Savage Sam* (1963), a sequel to the popular film *Old Yeller* (1957). A male chorus sings the narrative ballad about the brave and mischievous dog Savage Sam during the opening credits, while the canine is seen chasing a fox and sniffing out other critters. The number, sometimes listed as "The Land of the Old Countree," is reprised at the very end of the film.

"Savages" is a potent chorus number by Alan Menken (music) and Stephen Schwartz (lyric) that is featured with great effect in the animated film *Pocahontas* (1995). Governor Ratcliffe (voice of David Odgen Stiers) and the other European settlers sing about the heathen Native Americans in Virginia, considering them less than human and hoping to drive them away from the colony. The song is reprised by the natives, who, seeing the settlers destroy the natural resources, look on the Europeans as invading savages. Soon the two choruses are united in a warlike chant of destruction.

"Say It with a Slap" is the energetic hillbilly number written by Buddy Kaye and Eliot Daniel for the "Bongo" sequence in the animated film anthology *Fun and Fancy Free* (1947). The circus bear Bongo escapes to the wilderness, where he meets other bears and falls in love with Lulu Belle, who gives him a slap. Bongo doesn't understand that this is a sign of affection among bears until this merry song is sung by Dinah Shore on the soundtrack. The bears join in singing it then break into a lively square dance, slapping each other with abandon.

"Scales and Arpeggios" is the inventive music lesson written by Robert B. and Richard M. Sherman for the animated movie *The Aristocats* (1970). The feline Duchess (voice of Eva Gabor) and her three kittens practice their piano playing in their wealthy Paris home by jumping back and forth on the keyboard, singing about how important it is to master the two piano techniques of the song title.

"Scarecrow" is the rousing folk ballad by Terry Gilkyson that serves as the theme song for the television movie *The Scarecrow of Romney Marsh* (1964) on the *Disneyland* program. A male soloist sings the marching number—all about the eighteenth-century English vicar who disguises himself as a scarecrow and helps the oppressed people with his Robin Hood–like night activities—on the soundtrack during the credits. The song is punctuated by a squealing laugh, the trademark of the mysterious scarecrow hero.

"Scream" is the intense soliloquy about the pressures of being a high school senior facing the future, written by Jamie Houston for the film sequel *High*

School Musical 3: Senior Year (2008). Troy Bolton (Zac Efron) is feeling pressure from every direction. His father wants him to go to his alma mater and play basketball, while his drama teacher wants him to accept a theatre scholarship from Juilliard. Yet Troy wants to go to Stanford University to be near his girlfriend, Gabriella. All these forces come together in an explosive, angry song sung by Troy as he dances through his school, the hallways turning into spinning fun-house rooms and the gymnasium raining legions of basketballs.

"Scrooge" is the pulsating descriptive song that Paul Williams wrote to introduce the miserly main character in *The Muppet Christmas Carol* (1992). As Ebenezer Scrooge (Michael Caine) strides purposefully through the streets of London, various cloth and human citizens and animals sing about the cold-hearted character, and even some vegetables join in to sing about his sourness.

"Seasons of Giving" is the warmhearted number by Richard M. and Robert B. Sherman that is used in the made-for-video film *Winnie the Pooh: Seasons of Giving* (1999). During an opening sequence showing a montage of the different seasons in the Hundred Acre Wood, a female chorus sings the flowing song about each season bringing a reason for happiness. The song is reprised in a section of the video in which autumn arrives and Christopher Robin is seen playing with his friends. The number is heard again in a winter sequence, and then an instrumental version plays over the final credits.

"The Second Star to the Right" is the expansive ballad by Sammy Fain (music) and Bob Hilliard (lyric) that serves as the theme song for the animated movie *Peter Pan* (1953). A studio chorus is heard singing the song over the opening credits of the film, pointing out the star that one must follow to pursue one's dreams. The number is reprised near the end of the movie when the pirate ship magically floats up into the sky to return Wendy and her brothers to London. The song is a rewritten version of an earlier number titled "Beyond the Laughing Sky," which Fain and Hilliard had written for the film *Alice in Wonderland* (1951); the melody was retained and a new lyric was written by Sammy Cahn for *Peter Pan*. Doris Day recorded "The Second Star to the Right" with Paul Weston's Orchestra, and years later Crista Moore, Jesse McCartney, and Brian Sutherland each made effective recordings of the dreamy ballad. There was a memorable jazz version made in 2000 by Earl Rose, a hip-hop version by T-Squad in 2007, and a lovely rendition by Kerry Butler in 2008.

"See the Funny Little Bunnies" is the peppy Easter song Frank Churchill and Leigh Harline wrote for the Silly Symphony film short *Funny Little Bunnies* (1934). At the end of the rainbow, the Easter bunnies gather to prepare painted eggs and are helped by birds and other animals as they make plaid, striped, polka-dotted, and other designs on the eggs. A studio chorus sings the merry theme song on the soundtrack while all the activity is going on.

"Seize the Day" is the hymnlike march sung by David Jacobs (David Moscow) and the other newsboys when they go on strike and dance in the streets of 1899 New York City in the film *Newsies* (1992). Alan Menken (music) and Jack Feldman (lyric) wrote the stirring number that has a compelling Irish-jig flavor to it. Debbie Shapiro Gravitte recorded the song in 1994.

"Seven Moons of Beta-Lyrae" is the bizarre love song written in an alien language for *The Moon Pilot* (1962), the first Disney feature dealing with space. The French-accented space creature Lyrae (Dany Saval) helps the American astronaut Captain Richmond Talbot (Tom Tryon) in his country's first attempt to orbit the moon, and she sings this perky little ditty in the language of her homeland, the star Beta-Lyrae. Richard M. and Robert B. Sherman wrote the nonsense lyric to accompany their melodious music. As the film ends, Talbot joins Lyrae in singing the number, which is sometimes listed as "The Moon Pilot Song."

"Shadowland" is the hauntingly beautiful ballad written by Hans Zimmer (music), Lebo M (music and lyric), and Mark Mancina (lyric) for the 1997 Broadway version of *The Lion King*. When drought plagues the Pride Lands, the lionesses weep and chant about the home of their ancestors. The lioness Nala (Heather Headley) decides she must journey to another place and look for a better land for the pride. The number uses music from Zimmer's soundtrack score for the 1994 film and the lyric uses both English and African phrases to give the song a beguiling tribal flavor. Michael Crawford recorded an effective medley of *The Lion King* songs that included "Shadowland."

"The Shaggy D.A." is the up-tempo title song that Shane Tatum and Richard McKinley wrote for the 1976 movie sequel to the popular *The Shaggy Dog* (1959). Wilby Daniels (Dean Jones) sings the patter song over the opening credits, taking the point of view of a political candidate who is going to bring a clean image and change to the office of the district attorney. Soon a chorus chimes in and sings his praises, and the music segues into a parade march, complete with brass instruments and drums.

"Sheer Perfection" is the soaring love song Alan Menken (music) and Tim Rice (lyric) wrote for the Broadway concert-pageant *King David* (1997). The maiden Michal (Judy Kuhn) decides to give herself to David (Marcus Lovett) because she chose him before his celebrity and heroics. He reciprocates because she is the only person who understands what is in his heart. During the duet, Joab (Stephen Bogardus) and King Saul (Martin Vidnovic) make comments about the lovers as Saul's fear of David's usurpation of the crown begins to bud.

"She's in Love" is the pop pastiche song written by Alan Menken (music) and Glenn Slater (lyric) for the 2008 Broadway version of *The Little Mermaid*. Ariel's mermaid sisters try to determine the reason for her strange behavior and come to the conclusion that it is love, a fact that shocks and disturbs Ariel's friend Flounder (Trevor Braun). The number takes the

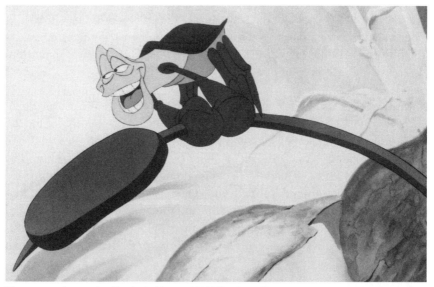

The extremely popular *The Little Mermaid* (1989) ushered in a new golden age for Disney animated musical films and began a series of hit songs composed by Alan Menken, who worked with Howard Ashman, Tim Rice, Stephen Schwartz, and other notable lyricists. Sebastian the Crab (voice of Samuel E. Wright) uses a cattail as a microphone to sing "Kiss the Girl" in order to evoke the proper romantic atmosphere for Ariel and Prince Eric. (Walt Disney/Photofest)

form of a girl-group song from the 1960s, complete with harmonized backup singing and interjected "shoop-shoop" throughout.

"Shiver My Timbers" is the pseudo–sea chantey Barry Mann and Cynthia Weil wrote for the film *Muppet Treasure Island* (1996). During the opening credits of the movie, a gang of pirates (both cloth and human) sing the fervent march number as they drag treasure chests through an island jungle and then bury them inside a cave. Joining in on the song are singing animals, trees, and even skulls.

"Shoulder to Shoulder" is the snappy march song about friendship written by Carly Simon for the animated film *Pooh's Heffalump Movie* (2005). While the young kangaroo Roo and the young elephant Lumpy play in the Hundred Acre Wood and become fast friends, songwriter Simon sings the spirited number on the soundtrack, the lyric proudly proclaiming that friends stand side by side and never let the other get lost. Simon reprises the song over the end credits of the film, joined by a children's choir named the Heffalump Chorus.

"The Siamese Cat Song" is the brief but memorable little ditty Sonny Burke and Peggy Lee wrote for the animated film *Lady and the Tramp* (1955). A pair of mischievous Siamese felines, Si and Am (both voiced by Lee), sing in harmony as they check out their new home and merrily start to destroy it, as the abashed cocker spaniel Lady tries to stop them. Bobby McFerrin made a delightful double-track recording of the song in 1995, the group Jazz Networks did its own version the next year, Hilary and Haylie Duff made a duet version in 2004, and a quartet rendition was recorded by Meredith Inglesby, Andy Karl, Tyler Maynard, and Keewa Nurullah. Most recently there was a recording by the group B5 in 2007.

"Since I Gave My Heart Away" is the simple and affecting song written by Stephen Schwartz for the live-action television musical *Geppetto* (2000). The toymaker Geppetto (Drew Carey) gives everything he owns to the villainous puppeteer Stromboli (Brent Spiner) in order to get his son Pinocchio (Seth Adkins) back, singing that nothing else has mattered since he gave his heart to Pinocchio. The Blue Fairy (Julia Louis-Dreyfus) turns Pinocchio into a real boy, making him useless to Stromboli, and she joins the townspeople in singing about the love between parent and child. The melodic ballad is reprised by Sonya Isaacs over the end credits of the TV movie.

"Sing a New Song" is the calypso-flavored song from an episode of the animated television series *The Little Mermaid* (1992). When an ugly, oversized purple sea monster complains that he is a misfit and everyone is afraid of him, the mermaid Ariel (voice of Jodi Benson) befriends him and suggests that he change his song to a happier one and take on a new point of view about life.

"Sing Ho for the Life of a Bear" is the merry march number written by Carly Simon for the animated film *Piglet's Big Movie* (2003). Simon sings it on the soundtrack and is joined by Winnie the Pooh (voice of Jim Cummings), Tigger (also Cummings), Kanga (Kath Soucie), Roo (Nikita Hopkins), Eeyore (Peter Cullen), and Piglet (John Fiedler) as they set off on an "expotition" for high adventure. The number is also listed as "Expotition March."

"Sister Suffragette" is the pastiche march song of protest that Mrs. Banks (Glynis Johns) sings in the movie musical *Mary Poppins* (1964). Returning from a women's rights meeting, the activist wife and mother Mrs. Banks sings the sprightly number urging votes for women. The cook Mrs. Brill (Reta Shaw) and the housekeeper Ellen (Hermione Baddeley) join her in singing the rousing number, and all the while, the nanny Katie Nana (Elsa Lanchester) tries to tell Mrs. Banks that she is quitting. Richard M. and Robert B. Sherman wrote the song, which is among the handful not used in the 2004 London and 2006 Broadway versions of *Mary Poppins*, because the character of Mrs. Banks was changed from a suffragette to an ex-actress.

"The Skumps" is the comic duet that pastiches a medieval drinking song, written by George Bruns (music), Erdman Penner, and Tom Adair (lyric) for the animated film *Sleeping Beauty* (1959). King Stefan (voice of Taylor Holmes) and King Hubert (Bill Thompson) celebrate the impending nuptials of their betrothed offspring by toasting each other with the silly title phrase, getting drunker as they repeat it over and over.

"Sleeping Beauty Song" is the dreamy lullaby-like number by George Bruns (music) and Tom Adair (lyric) that the chorus sings on the soundtrack as each of the three Good Fairies presents a magical gift to the infant Princess Aurora in the animated movie *Sleeping Beauty* (1959). Flora (voice of Verna Felton) grants the baby the gift of beauty and Fauna (Barbara Jo

Allen) gives her the gift of song before the wicked fairy Maleficent (Eleanor Audley) appears and puts a curse on the Princess. So the friendly fairy Merryweather (Barbara Luddy) makes her gift the power of love's first kiss to break the spell.

"Slow but Sure" is the plucky little ditty Frank Churchill (music) and Larry Morey (lyric) wrote for the Silly Symphony movie short *The Tortoise and the Hare* (1935), but only the music was retained in the final print. The song is a tuneful tribute to those who take their time and are rewarded by their "slow but steady" efforts, and the melody is used as a leitmotif for the tortoise throughout the short film.

"Slowly He Sank into the Sea" is one of the handful of new songs George Bruns (music) and Mel Leven (lyric) wrote for the 1961 screen version of Victor Herbert's 1903 operetta favorite *Babes in Toyland*. The sinister henchman Gonzorgo (Henry Calvin) relates what happened to the youth Tom Piper (Tommy Sands) when he and his silent assistant, Roderigo (Gene Sheldon), kidnapped the boy from the arms of Mary Quite Contrary (Annette Funicello) and tossed him into the sea. While the deep-voiced Gonzorgo sings the narrative ballad, Roderigo pantomimes the tale in a Harpo Marx manner.

"Small but Mighty" is the satirical march song written by Kevin Quinn and Randy Petersen for the animated movie *Teacher's Pet* (2004), based on the 2000 television series. The wisecracking parrot Pretty Boy (voice of Jerry Stiller) convinces the scared cat Mr. Jolly (David Ogden Stiers) that they should set out to save their fellow pet, the dog Spot, by singing this patriotic spoof about size not making any difference when you are strong of heart. Pretty Boy is joined by a chorus of ants and cockroaches who crawl out of the woodwork in the kitchen and march in formation to the song.

"Small One" is the lullaby-like ballad used throughout the animated film short *The Small One* (1978) and is easily remembered because of its gentle but haunting melody. Producer-director Don Bluth wrote the number, which is first sung over the opening credits, urging a small one to do his best and he will be rewarded. Forced to sell his undersized donkey Small One, the Boy (voice of Sean Marshall) later sings the song as he tries to interest merchants in buying the aging animal. His melodic pleading is interrupted by various businessmen singing the crass "The Merchants Song."

The ballad is again reprised by a chorus on the soundtrack at the end of the film as Small One carries Mary to Bethlehem.

"Smart Guy Theme Song" is the lighthearted rap number by Paul Buckley and Jonathan Wolff that introduces the young hero of the television series *Smart Guy* (1997) about a ten-year-old kid with a sky-high IQ. A kids' chorus sings the rocking number on the soundtrack during the opening of the program and marvels at the cool and intelligent youngster T. J. Henderson (Tahj Mowry) who is even a hit with the girls. During the run of the show, the theme song was changed to a less kid-friendly number, with adults singing a cool rhythm-and-blues tribute to the smart guy and a rap section that is very fast and menacing.

"Sniffly Sniff" is the brief and tuneful song Winnie the Pooh (voice of Jim Cummings) sings in the animated video *Winnie the Pooh: Springtime with Roo* (2004). During spring cleaning, the bear Pooh inhales so much dust that he feels a giant sneeze coming on. He sings this amusing song by John Kavanaugh (music) and Tom Rogers (lyric) as he gets ready for the big sneeze.

"Snow Snows" is the short and playful song about wintertime written by Michael and Patty Silversher for the seasonal video *Winnie the Pooh: A Very Merry Pooh Year* (2002). The bear Pooh (voice of Jim Cummings) sings the happy little ditty as he and the young kangaroo Roo frolic in the snow in the Hundred Acre Wood.

"So Close" is the Oscar-nominated pop ballad used in the film *Enchanted* (2007) as a contrast to the fairy-tale songs sung by the animated characters. Alan Menken (music) and Stephen Schwartz (lyric) wrote the contemporary-sounding song about being physically close to someone but still trying to get close to one's heart, and it was sung by a soloist (Jon McLaughlin) at the Kings and Queens Ball while couples danced, particularly the fairy-tale princess Giselle (Amy Adams) and the lawyer Robert (Patrick Dempsey) as they realize they love each other.

"So Dear to My Heart" is the lilting title song by Irving Taylor and Ticker Freeman for the 1948 film about life in rural Indiana in 1903. The ballad about remembering the past is sung on the soundtrack by John Beal and a studio chorus over the opening credits, and then again during an animated sequence showing rural scenes of the four seasons of the year, each new scene revealed by the turning of the pages of a scrapbook. The song is reprised by the chorus during the final moments of the film.

"So Long" is the sunny song about friendship that plays during the closing credits of the 2011 animated film *Winnie the Pooh*. Set to images of the stuffed animals posed around Christopher Robin's nursery, Zooey Deschanel sings the ditty on the soundtrack about how nice it is to make new friends. Deschanel also wrote the heartwarming music and lyrics.

"So This Is Love" is the soft and reticent love song for Cinderella (voice of Ilene Woods) and the Prince (Mike Douglas) when they first meet and start dancing in the animated movie *Cinderella* (1950). Mack David, Jerry Livingston, and Al Hoffman wrote the number, which begins as a lush waltz as the two dance, then becomes more tentative as the two lovers remove themselves from the ballroom and have a quiet moment together while singing the romantic lyric. The song replaced an earlier number, titled "Dancing on a Cloud," in which the two lovers literally danced up into the heavens. Ashley Brown made a warm recording with backup vocals by Meredith Inglesby, Andy Karl, Tyler Maynard, and Keewa Nurullah, and the song was also recorded by the Cheetah Girls.

"So to Be One of Us" is the lively list song the group They Might Be Giants wrote for the animated film sequel *Return to Never Land* (2002). When Wendy's daughter, Jane, is kidnapped by Captain Hook and taken to Never Land, she attempts to become like the Lost Boys. But the boys (voices of Jonnie Hall, D. J. Harper, Nils Montan, Wally Wingert, Lauren Wood, and Bobbi Page) find Jane too girlish, too clean, and too well behaved, and give her instructions in song on how to be more like them.

"Some Day My Prince Will Come" is the plaintive song of yearning Snow White (voice of Adriana Caselotti) sings to the dwarfs and some curious animal friends as she dreams of Prince Charming in the animated movie *Snow White and the Seven Dwarfs* (1937). Frank Churchill composed the flowing, operetta-like music and Larry Morey wrote the simple but poignant lyric. Among those who have recorded the song are Lena Horne, Mary Martin, Barbara Cook, Kaitlin Hopkins, Ashley Tisdale, Barbara Hendricks and the Abbey Road Ensemble, the Cheetah Girls, Anastacia, En Vogue, and Barbra Streisand. The number has been a particular favorite of jazz artists, with recordings by Dave Brubeck, the Manhattan Jazz Quintet, the Chet Baker Trio, Wynton Kelly, Great Jazz Trio, Jazz Networks, Earl Rose, and Miles Davis.

"Somebody Rubbed Out My Robin" is the comic character song for the sexy bird Jenny Wren (voice of Martha Wentworth) that Frank Churchill wrote for the Silly Symphony movie short *Who Killed Cock Robin?* (1935). After Jenny has witnessed the murder of her love, Cock Robin, she melodramatically sings, in a funny caricature of Mae West, of her grief and her demand for justice.

"Someday" is the soft rhythm-and-blues number by Alan Menken (music) and Stephen Schwartz (lyric) that dreams of a day when everyone can live and let live. The group All-4-One sang the enticing song over the end credits of the animated film *The Hunchback of Notre Dame* (1996). Earl Rose made a distinctive jazz recording of the song in 2000.

"Someone Like Me" is the sincere pop ballad about the hope that your beloved will finally discover that she loves you, heard during the final credits of the animated film *Doug's 1st Movie* (1999). William Squier and Jeffrey Lodin wrote the affecting number, and it is sung on the soundtrack by Michael Africk.

"Someone Like Me Lullabee" is the lazy folk song Richard M. and Robert B. Sherman wrote for the animated film *The Tigger Movie* (2000), the brothers' first Disney project in twenty-nine years. Sad because none of his friends has time to bounce with him, Tigger (voice of Jim Cummings) sings this country-flavored lament about being lonely for someone who is more like him. Various woodland creatures serve as backup singers for the number, which also has the tone of a lullaby.

"Someone's Waiting for You" is the Oscar-nominated song of assurance written by Sammy Fain (music), Carol Connors, and Ayn Robbins (lyric) for the animated film *The Rescuers* (1977). While the kidnapped orphan Penny puts her teddy bear to bed and then stands on the deck of a dilapidated riverboat and dreams of being rescued, Shelby Flint sings the tender lullaby on the soundtrack, encouraging her to be brave and be patient. Barbara Cook made a memorable recording of the ballad in 1988.

"Something Better" is the hopeful ballad that Barry Mann and Cynthia Weil wrote for the farcical adventure film *Muppet Treasure Island* (1996). Orphan Jim Hawkins (Kevin Bishop) sings the heartfelt "I am" song with Muppets Rizzo the Rat (voice of Steve Whitmire) and Gonzo (Dave Goelz) as they clean up the tavern and imagine a life of adventure at sea rather than drudgery on land.

"Something Good Is Bound to Happen" is the pastiche hymn written by Al Kasha and Joel Hirschhorn for the period film *Hot Lead and Cold Feet* (1978). Missionary Eli Bloodshy (Jim Dale) sings the rousing number on the streets of 1880s Philadelphia in his efforts to convert the misguided citizens. Eli and the company reprise the peppy number at the happy ending of the film.

"Something That I Want" is the pulsating lite-rock number that is heard over the closing credits of the animated movie *Tangled* (2010). Grace Potter wrote and performed the number about needing someone to tell you what you really want in the world. Although stylistically the song does not fit with the fairy tale movie, its lyric parallels the plight of the long-lost princess Rapunzel and the thief Flynn Rider in the story.

"Something There" is the charming character song written by Alan Menken (music) and Howard Ashman (lyric) for the animated film *Beauty and the Beast* (1991). As Belle (voice of Paige O'Hara) starts to see the Beast in a new light and even begins to fall in love with him, she sings this restless and contemplative number, with musical comments from Mrs. Potts (Angela Lansbury), both noticing something there that wasn't there previously. Then the Beast (Robby Benson) sings his own reflections on the situation. Also adding commentary to the number are Lumière (Jerry Orbach) and Cogsworth (David Ogden Stiers). In the 1994 Broadway version of *Beauty and the Beast*, Susan Egan and Beth Fowler, as Belle and Mrs. Potts, sang the number with Lumière (Gary Beach), Cogsworth (Heath Lamberts), and the Beast (Terrence Mann). A pleasing quartet version of the song was made by Meredith Inglesby, Andy Karl, Tyler Maynard, and Keewa Nurullah in 2005.

"Something's Up with Jack" is the driving song of anticipation Danny Elfman wrote for the stop-motion movie *The Nightmare Before Christmas* (1993). While Jack Skellington (singing voice of Elfman) locks himself up in a tower and investigates the various holiday objects he has taken from Christmas Town, the citizens of Halloween Town sing this insistent number as they try to guess what is the matter with their Pumpkin King. The song builds to a frenzy and Jack has an epiphany: to take over the production and execution of Christmas. The number is also listed as "Jack's Obsession."

"Son of Man" is the pulsating rock number about finding your place in the world written by Phil Collins for the animated movie *Tarzan* (1999). Collins sings the driving song on the soundtrack as the young Tarzan grows up into a man and gains strength and wisdom, and Collins reprises the number on the soundtrack of the animated video sequel *Tarzan II* (2005). In the 2006 Broadway version of *Tarzan*, the number was sung by Terk (Chester Gregory II) and the other apes, encouraging Tarzan to fulfill his dreams of becoming an adult man as strong as any ape.

"The Song of Life" is the rhythmic pop song about appreciating life every day that Don Harper and Mark Mancina wrote for the animated video sequel *Tarzan and Jane* (2002). As Tarzan and Jane celebrate their first anniversary, a montage shows how happy they are together, working and playing in the jungle. Mandy Moore sings the joyous number on the soundtrack, and the ape Terk and other animals accompany her by making music on various objects. Moore made a music video of the song, which is sometimes listed as "Sing to the Song of Life."

"Song of the Roustabouts" is a vigorous choral number by Frank Churchill (music) and Ned Washington (lyric) from the animated film *Dumbo* (1941). When the circus train reaches its destination late at night, the muscular roustabouts sing this hearty number as they pull ropes and lift up the huge circus tent even as the rain pours down on them. The brief sequence is an animated masterwork of light, shadows, and movement.

"Song of the South" is the evocative title song by Arthur Johnston (music) and Sam Coslow (lyric) for the part-live-action, part-animated movie *Song of the South* (1946). The Disney Studio Chorus sings the smooth ballad over the opening credits, the lyrics recalling the cottonwoods in blossom and the gentle voices of Dixie.

"Sons of Old Aunt Dinah" is the patriotic Confederate folk song written by Stan Jones (music) and Lawrence Edward Watkin (lyric) for the adventure movie *The Great Locomotive Chase* (1956). As a group of Union spies ride a train behind enemy lines, the Confederate soldiers aboard sing the boastful song about how they beat the Yankees at Shiloh because they come from fighting stock, progeny of the legendary Aunt Dinah.

"Sooner or Later" is the warm song of affection the southern plantation slave Tempy (Hattie McDaniel) sings to Uncle Remus (James Baskett) as

The part-animated, part-live-action movie *Song of the South* (1946) has sometimes been criticized for its "Negro" stereotypes, but the film is filled with authentic-sounding African American music and sterling performances by the black actors. James Baskett's heartwarming portrayal of Uncle Remus is most remembered, but just as radiant is Hattie McDaniel as Aunt Tempy, seen here making a pie and singing "Sooner or Later." (Walt Disney/Photofest)

she feeds him some fresh apple pie in a live-action sequence in the film *Song of the South* (1946). Charles Wolcott (music) and Ray Gilbert (lyric) wrote the pleasant number about the inevitabilities of life. The song was recorded by Sammy Kaye's Orchestra (vocal by Betty Barclay), Les Brown and His Orchestra (vocal by Doris Day), Rosemary Clooney, and Barbara Cook.

"Sooner or Later (I Always Get My Man)" is the Oscar-winning song of seduction written by Stephen Sondheim for the stylized movie *Dick Tracy* (1990). Nightclub vamp Breathless Mahoney (Madonna) sings the sultry number on stage wearing a slinky black dress and warning all men that she always wins. Madonna is heard reprising the song on the soundtrack later in the film, during a montage showing Dick Tracy's raids on illegal operations across town. Rachel York sang the bluesy song Off-Broadway in the revue *Putting It Together* (1993) and the ballad has been recorded by Madonna,

Karen Akers, Bernadette Peters, Karen Ziemba, Susan Egan, and Jane Krakowski.

"SpectroMagic" is the regal song of celebration that was heard at the beginning and end of the popular SpectroMagic Parade, which was featured at the Magic Kingdom at Disney World from 1991 to 1999. The number features blaring trumpets and a chorus singing about a magic found all over the world that is like a million stars. The parade, which used fiber optics effectively, was so popular that it returned in 2001.

"The Spectrum Song" is a wacky and bouncy ditty by Richard M. and Robert B. Sherman that was introduced by the animated character of Professor Ludwig Von Drake (voice of Paul Frees) in the premiere episode of *Walt Disney's Wonderful World of Color*. First airing on NBC on September 24, 1961, the song was part of a cartoon segment titled "An Adventure in Color." The piece featured Von Drake, a thickly accented professor of science, discussing color and assigning each hue to a note on the musical scale. As he jumped up and down on an animated staff, the notes were sung as the names of the colors coincided according to the professor's assignments. This episode also happened to be the debut of the Sherman and Sherman song "The Wonderful World of Color," which set up the introduction of "The Spectrum Song" and its segment beautifully.

"Spin and Marty Theme" is the pastiche camp song used in the serial *The Adventures of Spin and Marty*, which was a regular feature on the television show *The Mickey Mouse Club* (1955). The number is an easygoing folk song about how a tenderfoot comes to the Triple-R knowing nothing about horses and gets saddle sores, but eventually learns that it is the best horse camp of all. The catchy song, filled with repeating versions of "yippee yay hay yipper-o," is usually sung by the boys sitting around the campfire at night or as they ride along together on a trail. The tale of two boys, who are rivals at first at the Triple-R Ranch summer camp then become friends, was so popular that the one-season series was extended into *The Further Adventures of Spin and Marty* (1956) and *The New Adventures of Spin and Marty* (1957). There was even a television movie in 2000 called *The New Adventures of Spin and Marty: Suspect Behavior*. The song was heard in all the different versions.

"The Spirit of Adventure," with music and lyrics by Michael Giacchino, is a jaunty pastiche of a 1920s-style ditty that serves as the theme for the computer-animated Disney/Pixar film *Up* (2009). The story of an unlikely friendship between a crotchety old man and an eager-to-please little boy is summed up in the song's assertion that one's spirit of adventure is heightened by sharing it with someone else. The lively number is performed by Craig Copeland.

"A Spoonful of Sugar" is the contagious march number by Richard M. and Robert B. Sherman that teaches how to make a game out of an unpleasant task. Nanny Mary Poppins (Julie Andrews) sings the tuneful ditty in the film *Mary Poppins* (1964) as she snaps her fingers and magically makes her young charges' room tidy, then adds sugar to their bedtime medicine. At one point in the scene Mary trills away in a duet with a chirping bird that sits on her finger. The march melody is also used throughout the film as a kind of theme song for Mary and her unorthodox ways. In the 2004 London stage version of *Mary Poppins*, Laura Michelle Kelly played the nanny and led others in the household in the song. On Broadway two years later it was sung by Ashley Brown as Mary Poppins. Burl Ives made a notable recording of the march tune.

"The Stage Blight Opera" is the mock opera sequence written by George Kahn and Diana Zaslove for an episode of the animated television series *Chip 'n Dale: Rescue Rangers* (1989). The chipmunk sleuths Chip and Dale want to see an action movie, but by mistake they go into an opera house where a Puccini-like piece is being performed. A huge Wagnerian diva and a dashing cavalier sing of their love for each other separately and then in a duet, the scene ending with a sword fight, which pleases the chipmunks more than the music.

"Stand Out" is the driving rock song Patrick DeRemer and Roy Freeland wrote for the animated film *A Goofy Movie* (1995). The teenager Max impersonates the rock star Powerline (voice of Tevin Campbell) and lip-synchs to the idol's video as he performs on the stage of his high school auditorium during an assembly. The lyric is a cry to be noticed, and Max sings it to get the attention of Roxanne, a pretty student in the audience.

"Stanley Theme Song" is the Latin-flavored number written by Peter Lurye for the animated children's television series *Stanley* (2001). While the imaginative little boy Stanley draws pictures and imagines adventures during the opening credits, the Baha Men sing the rhythmic song about the clever kid who can solve problems and knows what life is all about.

"A Star Is Born" is the rousing gospel-like number by Alan Menken (music) and David Zippel (lyric) that concludes the animated film *Hercules* (1997). When Zeus finally allows his son Hercules to become one of the gods and have his star in the night sky, the Muses—Calliope (voice of Lilias White), Terpsichore (La Chanze), Melpomene (Cheryl Freeman), Clio (Vanessa Thomas), and Thalia (Roz Ryan)—celebrate by singing this joyous number that spoofs a religious revival hymn.

"Start of Something New" is the romantic pop ballad that Matthew Gerrard and Robbie Nevil wrote to establish the love story in the television movie *High School Musical* (2006). At a mountain resort, teenagers Troy Bolton (Zac Efron, with singing assist by Andrew Seeley) and Gabriella Montez (Vanessa Anne Hudgens) do not know each other, but are forced to sing a karaoke number together at a party, and while they sing the duet, their romantic relationship begins.

"Start the Party" is the exhilarating list song written by Matthew Gerrard and Robbie Nevil for the made-for-television musical *Camp Rock* (2008). Teenage camper Baron (Jordan Francis) sings the enthusiastic number over a sequence where camp counselor/pop musician Shane Gray (Joe Jonas) teaches the denizens of Camp Rock how to hip-hop dance.

"Stay Awake" is the reverse-psychology lullaby by Richard M. and Robert B. Sherman that Mary Poppins (Julie Andrews) uses to put her charges to sleep in the movie musical *Mary Poppins* (1964) after an exciting day of fantasy and adventure. Mary sings of lively, stimulating things to do, urging the children to keep their eyes open, but the music is soothing and lulling and soon the two kids are in slumber. Louis Prima and Gia Maione made duet recordings in English and Italian, and years later a recording was made by Karen Taylor-Good.

"Steady as a Beating Drum" is the pseudo–Native American tribal song written by Alan Menken (music) and Stephen Schwartz (lyric) for the animated movie *Pocahontas* (1995). During the opening credits of the film, a chorus sings the rhythmic number on the soundtrack as the native inhabitants of Virginia work in the fields, fish in the rivers, teach the young ones, play, and gather together as a tribe. The song is reprised later in the movie by the tribal leader Powhatan (singing voice of Jim Cummings).

"**A Step in the Right Direction**" is the gleeful song of self-satisfaction written by Richard M. and Robert B. Sherman for the movie fantasy *Bedknobs and Broomsticks* (1971), but it was cut from the final print even though it serves as the "I am" song for the central character of Miss Eglantine Price (Angela Lansbury). When the apprentice witch Miss Price receives her first magic broom in the mail, she feels it is the start of a wonderful career in sorcery and sings the march-tempo song to herself and does a peppy little dance with the broom. When the film was reconstructed in 1996, it was learned that the film footage from the song was lost, but the recording survived and was presented with stills from the scene as an extra on the DVD version.

"**Step in Time**" is the vibrant polka song that provided the most rousing musical number in the film *Mary Poppins* (1964). Chimney sweep Bert (Dick Van Dyke), nanny Mary Poppins (Julie Andrews), and a crew of sooty sweeps sing and dance to the lively song on the rooftops of London. Richard M. and Robert B. Sherman wrote the contagious music and repetitive nonsense lyric in which randomly chosen words or phrases are used as excuses to dance. The memorable choreography by Marc Breaux and DeeDee Wood is equally vivacious and silly.

"**Step Too Far**" is a pop trio for the characters caught in a romantic triangle in the Broadway musical *Aida* (2000), written by Elton John (music) and Tim Rice (lyric). The Egyptian captain Radames (Adam Pascal) is engaged to the princess Amneris (Sherie Rene Scott) but is in love with the Nubian slave Aida (Heather Headley). Amneris questions Radames's love for her, and Aida is torn between her love for Radames and her concern for her fellow Nubian slaves. Each one is worried about what next step to take and wonders if it will be one step too far. Elton John recorded the trio with Headley and Scott before *Aida* opened on Broadway.

"**Step Up**" is the lite-rock number by Matthew Gerrard and Robbie Nevil that four teenage singing sensations sing and dance to in the made-for-television sequel *The Cheetah Girls 2* (2006). Galleria (Raven-Symoné), Chanel (Adrienne Bailon), Aqua (Kiely Williams), and Dorinda (Sabrina Bryan) rehearse in a dance studio, singing, dancing, and doing aerobics as they boast that they are superstars and plan to prove it.

"**Stick to the Status Quo**" is the wry character song about breaking away from stereotypes written by David N. Lawrence and Faye Greenberg for the television movie *High School Musical* (2006). When basketball player Troy Bolton (Zac Efron) and mathematics whiz Gabriella Montez (Vanessa Anne Hudgens) go against type and audition for the school's "Spring Musicale," other students start to break the mold and express their hidden dreams: A nerd wants to be a hip-hop dancer, a basketball player longs to be a baker, a skater dude confesses his affinity for playing the cello, and so on. This is all to the chagrin of the two drama mainstays, the snobbish Sharpay Evans (Ashley Tisdale) and her brother, Ryan (Lucas Grabeel), who feel their territory is being threatened by outsiders. Other students agree and warn all these rebels to stick to the things they know in this piquant and funny song.

"Stick-to-it-ivity" is the bouncy song of resilience written by Larry Morey and Eliot Daniel for an animated sequence in the rustic film *So Dear to My Heart* (1948). When it looks like the Indiana youth Jeremiah Kincaid will never raise enough money to bring his pet ram, Danny, to the county fair, he is encouraged by the Wise Old Owl (voice of Ken Carson) in the boy's scrapbook. The animated bird sings about not giving up and illustrates his point with scenes showing explorer Christopher Columbus and the Scottish freedom fighter Robert the Bruce pursuing their dreams despite the odds against them.

"Stop, Look, and Listen" is the instructional ditty about pedestrian safety that Jiminy Cricket (voice of Cliff Edwards) sang on a 1956 episode of the television program *The Mickey Mouse Club*. George Bruns (music) and Gil George (lyric) wrote the simple, catchy number that cautions children (or anyone) to follow the title's three steps before crossing a street.

"Stories" is the soaring ballad Belle (voice of Paige O'Hara) sings in the made-for-video animated musical *Beauty and the Beast: The Enchanted Christmas* (1997). Rachel Portman (music) and Don Black (lyric) wrote the pleasing song in which Belle imagines how she will read stories to the Beast and allow him to travel to magical places in his imagination. As she sings, her own imagination shows her running through the pages of an illustrated storybook with the Beast.

"Straight to the Heart of Love" is the country-flavored pop song John Hiatt wrote and sang in the satirical movie *The Country Bears* (2002). The popular rock group Country Bears, who broke up over infighting, are reunited in a concert to save Country Bear Hall, the venue where they first got started. The pop star Hiatt sings the song, about finding one's way to true love, with the bears (voices of Diedrich Bader, Brad Garrett, Toby Huss, and Stephen Root) and guest stars E. G. Daily, Don Henley, and Bonnie Raitt.

"Strange Things" is the enthralling blues number about how life changes and old friends grow apart, written by Randy Newman for the computer-animated film *Toy Story* (1995). Newman sings the musical lament on the soundtrack during a montage showing the boy Andy losing interest in his cowboy toy, Woody, and shifting his attention to the spaceman toy Buzz Lightyear. During the song the decor for Andy's room changes from the Wild West to an outer-space environment, paralleling the lyric about something out of the sky changing one's life.

"Strangers Like Me" is the rhythmic rock song by Phil Collins that ex-presses Tarzan's desire to learn how to be like the other humans in the animated movie *Tarzan* (1999). Collins sings the catchy and insistent song on the soundtrack as Tarzan observes lantern slides showing the human world and attempts to learn all he can about it. In the 2006 Broadway version of *Tarzan*, Collins turned the number into a duet for Tarzan (Josh Strickland) and Jane (Jenn Gambatese) in which he pleads with her to teach him about these "strangers." Collins made a music video of the number, and in 2005 there were recordings made by Andrew Samonsky and the group Everlife.

"Streets of Gold" is the throbbing rock song by Tom Snow and Dean Pitchford that explains how New York City can be a hot spot of opportunity for those savvy enough to do more than just survive it. The street-smart canine Rita (voice of Ruth Pointer) and some back-up singing dogs perform the number for the orphan kitten Oliver in the animated film version of *Oliver Twist*, titled *Oliver & Company* (1988).

"Strengthen the Dwelling" is the march-like hymn the eccentric million-aire Anthony J. Drexel Biddle (Fred MacMurray) and his pugilist comrades sing in the film *The Happiest Millionaire* (1967). Richard M. and Robert B. Sherman wrote the pastiche mission song about walking in the spirit of the Lord and protecting the home front should America get involved in World War I.

"The Strummin' Song" is the first of many songs Richard M. and Robert B. Sherman wrote for Walt Disney, this one for the two-part television movie *The Horsemasters* (1961). At a prestigious riding school in England, students from various nations gather for a social occasion and coeds Dinah (Annette Funicello) and Joan (Millicent Martin) lead the group in this simple but sprightly number about the international language of humming along to the strumming of a guitar.

"Strut" is the lite-rock song by Jamie Houston that is sung by four American teens as they explore the city of Barcelona in the television sequel *The Cheetah Girls 2* (2006). While pop singers Galleria (Raven-Symoné), Chanel (Adrienne Bailon), Aqua (Kiely Williams), and Dorinda (Sabrina Bryan) are seen in different locations of the Spanish city, they are heard singing this pounding number on the soundtrack, claiming you must strut like you mean it if you want to get noticed.

"Substitutiary Locomotion" is the bubbly contrapuntal (or double) song written by Richard M. and Robert B. Sherman for the film fantasy *Bedknobs and Broomsticks* (1971). While Professor Emelius Brown (David Tomlinson) and three young evacuees (Ian Weighill, Cindy O'Callaghan, and Roy Snart) chant a spell to make inanimate objects move, the apprentice witch Miss Eglantine Price (Angela Lansbury) sings about the wonders of magical movement. Soon shoes, clothes, and other objects come to life and dance with the humans until the spell runs out of control. Jason Graae recorded the number in 2003 as part of a medley of nonsense songs.

"Summer Magic" is the appreciative title song about the gifts of nature written by Richard M. and Robert B. Sherman for the 1963 period film set in a small Maine town. Boston widow Margaret Carey (Dorothy McGuire, singing dubbed by Marilyn Hooven) sings the warm ballad to her children (Hayley Mills, Eddie Hodges, and Jimmy Mathers) as they sit on the porch of their new home in the country. The lullaby-like number is accompanied by nature footage showing the evening activities of the local animals.

"Summer Sweet" is the evocative ballad by Bobby Russell that captures the lazy days of summer and the hollow ache of change, heard in the period movie *Rascal* (1969). While a montage shows the youth Sterling (Bill Mumy), his dog, Wowser, and a raccoon named Rascal having summer escapades, a harmonic male chorus sings the reflective number on the soundtrack.

"Super Nova Girl" is the supposed-futuristic love song from the television movie *Zenon: Girl of the 21st Century* (1999). Kristian Rex and Sabelle

Breer wrote the throbbing rock song, arranged with eerie electronic instruments of the future, and it is sung by pop star Proto Zoa (Phillip Rhys) and his intergalactic rock band, asking a sweetheart to be his astronomical true love. The song is punctuated throughout with the phrase "zoom zoom zoom" and the number is sometimes listed as "Zoom Zoom Zoom." "Super Nova Girl" is reprised in *Zenon: The Zequel* (2001), and songwriter Rex sings it on the soundtrack of the television movie *Zenon: Z3* (2004).

"Supercalifragilisticexpialidocious" is the most famous of the many Richard M. and Robert B. Sherman songs using an invented word, this one finding fame in the movie *Mary Poppins* (1964). After nanny Mary Poppins (Julie Andrews) wins a horse race in an animated fantasy sequence, she invents the word to express her feelings and sings about it. She is soon joined by the chimney sweep Bert (Dick Van Dyke) and some animated buskers called the Pearlies. The lyric is so nicely patterned rhythmically and the music so catchy that the ridiculous title works and is even easy to remember. Soon after the film opened, kids across America were singing the fun ditty, and the word was even added to some dictionaries. Laura Michelle Kelly led the ensemble in singing the song in the 2004 London stage version of *Mary Poppins*. In 2006, Ashley Brown sang it as Mary in the Broadway stage production. Most recordings of the number have been by children's choruses, although Louis Prima and Gia Maione made duet versions in English and Italian, and years later Jason Graae and Orlando Brown each recorded it.

"Sure as Sun Turns to Moon" is a dramatic musical conversation Phil Collins wrote for the 2006 Broadway version of *Tarzan*. The gorilla leader Kerchak (Shuler Hensley) encounters his estranged mate Kala (Merle Dandridge) and exchanges pleasantries with her, all the while hoping to be reconciled but unable to because of his stubbornness. The song is reprised near the end of the show by the two as Kerchak is dying. The number is unusual in that it is a theatrical character song and not at all like the pop songs for which Collins is famous.

"Swamp Fox Theme" is the simple, repetitive, catchy theme song for the *Swamp Fox* (1959) episodes that were featured on the television program *Disneyland*. Lewis Foster and Buddy Baker wrote the march number, which is sung by the followers of Francis Marion, the American patriot who comes out of the swamp to attack the British during the Revolutionary War. In the first episode of the series, Marion's men proudly chant the number around a campfire, extolling the cleverness of their leader, who wears a foxtail on his hat and eludes the redcoats every time they pursue him into the swamp. The song is reprised over the opening and closing credits of the eight episodes of the show.

"Swee'pea's Lullaby" is the gentle lament of one orphan for another written by Harry Nilsson for the offbeat musical movie *Popeye* (1980). Separated from his adopted baby Swee'pea, the gruff sailor Popeye (Robin Williams) reveals his tender side as he sings this lullaby to himself, recalling how he himself was an orphan and how he and Swee'pea belong together.

"Sweet Child" is the creepy duet for the eels Flotsam (Tyler Maynard) and Jetsam (Derrick Baskin) in the 2008 Broadway version of *The Little Mermaid*. The two henchmen of the sea witch Ursula pretend to sympathize with Ariel's broken heart and slyly suggest that their mistress can solve all her problems. Later in the show the twosome reprise the song as they gloat over Ariel's inability to get Prince Eric to kiss her. Alan Menken composed the eerie music and Glenn Slater wrote the lyric, which consists of short but potent phrases.

"Sweet Surrender" is the affecting, rolling folk song written by John Denver for the film *The Bears and I* (1974) about a Vietnam War vet who returns to nature and raises some bear cubs. Denver sings the bluegrass ballad, about being a free spirit and living without a care, on the soundtrack, and his recording of the song was very popular.

"The Sweetest One of All" is the chipper theme song by Leigh Harline that is used throughout the Silly Symphony movie short *The Cookie Carnival* (1935). In a kingdom made up of baked goods, the Cookie Boy (voice of Pinto Colvig) cheers up a crying female cookie by making her a beautiful dress out of frosting, allowing her to be the hit of the Cookie Carnival Parade and then queen of the land. The sugary ballad later evolves into a vaudeville number in which a series of cookies and cakes dance and entertain the queen.

"Sweethaven" is the lazy folk song by Harry Nilsson that opens the surreal film *Popeye* (1980). The morning after a violent storm, the oddball citizens of the seaside town of Sweethaven sing the number as they go about their daily habits, noting that God must love the town in order for it to keep standing.

T

"Take the Money and Run" is the rapid rhythm-and-blues spoof written by Randy Petersen, Kevin Quinn, and Cheri Steinkellner for the animated film *Teacher's Pet* (2004), based on the 2000 television series. When the dog-turned-human Scott (voice of Nathan Lane) and his boy master Leonard (Shaun Fleming) collect a $500 reward for finding a lost dog, the two go on a spending spree, while Jack Sheldon sings the number on the soundtrack.

"Talent Round-Up Day" is the western theme song by George Bruns (music) and Gil George (lyric) used for Fridays on the television series *The Mickey Mouse Club* (1955). Jimmie Dodd and the Mouseketeers appear in cowboy and cowgirl outfits and sing that Friday is the day for a rodeo of talent. The song has a square dance pattern, and the Mouseketeers either ride artificial horses or do a two-step dance as they get ready to perform in the roundup. The number is sometimes listed as "Round-Up Rodeo." The song was pastiched years later as "Woody's Roundup" in the computer-animated film *Toy Story 2* (1999).

"TaleSpin Theme" is the Caribbean-flavored theme song for the animated television series *TaleSpin* (1990), about the colorful Kit Cloudkicker, who flies his plane through various adventures in the tropics. Michael and Patty Silversher wrote the lively calypso number, filled with tribal sounds,

The medium of television brought the Disney Company a new form of popularity, as with the fondly remembered *Mickey Mouse Club* (1955). Not only was Jimmie Dodd (center) the adult host of the show, he also wrote many songs for the program, including the opening "Mickey Mouse Club March" and the lullaby-like closing number "Mickey Mouse Club Alma Mater." (Walt Disney/Photofest)

about Kit's plane that goes into a tailspin and the many tales he has to spin. The song is sometimes listed as "Spin It!"

"Tall Paul" is the adoring pop ballad by Richard M. and Robert B. Sherman about a girl who is infatuated with a boy who is tall in stature and number one in her heart. The peppy number, very 1960s in temperament and flavor, was written for former Mouseketeer Judy Harriet, and although her 1958 recording got a lot of airplay, it did not sell. Hoping to further Mouseketeer Annette Funicello's singing career, Walt Disney thought the song ideal for her. Funicello's 1959 recording on the Disney label went to number seven on the charts and sold more than seven hundred thousand discs. Kristen Bell made a snappy recording of the pop song in 2003.

"Tapestry of Dreams" is the hypnotic, ritualistic song that was heard during the Tapestry of Nations parade held at Epcot to celebrate the new millennium. Much of the musical piece is rhythmic chanting of sounds and foreign phrases accompanied by drumming, but at times a chorus is heard singing about using one's imagination and envisioning a world where all nations live in harmony. Although the number was used only during the year 2000, millions of spectators at the park heard the engrossing piece and can still recall it vividly.

"Teacher's Pet" is the title ballad by Joe Lubin for the 2000 animated television series about a dog who disguises himself as a boy so he can go to school. Christy Carlson Romano sings the seductive but silly bubblegum kind of song, wanting to be the best in the class in order to win the heart of the teacher. Romano reprises the number over the end credits of the 2004 film version of *Teacher's Pet*, and she made a music video of the song as well.

"Team Sandwich" is the rapping rock song by Brock Walsh that was turned into a clever production number in the short-lived musical television series *Hull High* (1990). In the locker room before a high school football game, the coach and team members sing about how the different levels of operation in a football team are like the layers of a sandwich. The number then bursts into an exciting display of break dancing, warm-up exercises, and leaping over lockers and benches. The sequence was staged by Kenny Ortega, who later performed similar magic in *High School Musical* (2006) and its sequels.

"Teamo Supremo Theme" is the jazzy, rock-flavored theme song for the animated television series *Teamo Supremo* (2004), about three kid superheroes who save the planet in between going to school and doing their homework. Ian Dye wrote the pounding number that introduces the pint-size Captain Crandall, Rope Girl, and Skate Lad each week during the action-packed opening credits.

"Tear It Down" is the driving hip-hop ditty sung by the campers of Camp Star in the 2010 made-for-TV film *Camp Rock 2: The Final Jam* as part of their "sing off" competition with the campers of Camp Rock. The number is led by Luke (Matthew "Mdot" Finley) and Tess Tyler (Meaghan Martin), performers who will do anything to make it to the top. The brazen number was written by Toby Gad, Lyrica Anderson, and Kovasciar Myvette.

"Temper, Temper" is the nightmarish song of caution written by George Stiles and Anthony Drewe for the London stage version of *Mary Poppins* (2004). The toys and dolls in the children's nursery come to life, taking on huge proportions, and haunt the young Jane and Michael Banks because they have lost their temper on occasion. The odd, menacing number takes the form of a trial, with the large objects giving examples of the kids' bad behavior and the court finding them guilty as charged. The number was also used in the 2006 Broadway production of *Mary Poppins*.

"Ten Feet off the Ground" is the jubilant contrapuntal (or double) song of self-satisfaction sung by the Bower family in the film musical *The One and Only, Genuine, Original Family Band* (1968) when they learn they have been selected to entertain at the 1888 Democratic Convention. Richard M. and Robert B. Sherman wrote the zesty number with two distinct melodies about feeling proud about yourself, and it was sung and danced by Buddy Ebsen, Kurt Russell, Janet Blair, Lesley Ann Warren, and the children in the family barn. A memorable aspect of the scene is some fancy footwork by Ebsen that is reminiscent of his dancing in 1930s musicals. Louis Armstrong made a distinctive recording of the song, and decades later Michael Feinstein recorded it with Rosemary Clooney. There was also a duet version recorded by Kate Levering and David Hibbard.

"Texas John Slaughter" is the rustic cowboy ballad Stan Jones wrote for the sixteen television episodes of that name, first aired on the weekly program *Disneyland* in 1958. The easygoing song about the famous Texas Ranger John Slaughter, who wore a white Stetson and carried a pearl-handled gun, is sung by a male trio on the soundtrack at the beginning and end of each episode.

"A Thankful Heart" is the up-tempo Christmas song by Paul Williams that promises gratitude for the holiday season. A reformed Ebenezer Scrooge (Michael Caine) sings the warm song with various human and cloth citizens of London at the end of the movie *The Muppet Christmas Carol* (1992).

"That Darn Cat" is the jazzy title song that Richard M. and Robert B. Sherman wrote for the 1965 film comedy. Bobby Darin sings the smoky narrative ballad on the soundtrack during the opening and the end credits of the movie, relating the adventures of an amorous tomcat who prowls at night looking for adventure and romance. The heavy bass line of the music and the bluesy tone of the song give it a very 1960s beatnik flavor. The song is also heard in the 1997 remake of the film, and Michelle Pawk made a slinky, fun recording of the number in 2003.

"That's All I Need" is the rhythmic "I am" song for the meerkat Timon (voice of Nathan Lane) in the made-for-video sequel *The Lion King 1½* (2004). While he stands guard to protect the meerkat colony from hyenas, the misfit Timon dreams of a place to live where there are no predators and life is more fulfilling. The catchy pop song is also heard over the end credits for the video. Elton John (music) and Tim Rice (lyric) wrote the song as "Warthog Rhapsody" for the original film *The Lion King* (1994), but it was replaced by "Hakuna Matata."

"That's How You Know" is the upbeat calypso number by Alan Menken (music) and Stephen Schwartz (lyric) that was used with panache in the movie *Enchanted* (2007) for one of the biggest and most complex musical numbers in contemporary Disney films. The fairy tale heroine Giselle (Amy Adams) sings to the too-practical lawyer Robert (Patrick Dempsey) as they stroll through Central Park that there are many romantic ways for him to let his fiancée know that he loves her. Soon others in the park pick up on the song and street musicians, senior citizens, break-dancers, brides and bridegrooms, children, and hundreds of others are singing and dancing in celebration. The Oscar-nominated song was recorded by Demi Lovato.

"That's So Raven" is the rock-rap title song written by John Coda for the 2003 television series about a girl who can see into the future. Raven (Raven-Symoné) and her friends Chelsea (Anneliese van der Pol) and Eddie (Orlando Brown) sing the throbbing number, about seeing the future and how it can be scary, over the opening credits. Raven-Symoné also made a music video of the song.

"That's the Life" is the fervent "I am" song for the Spider (voice of Susan Sarandon), Earthworm (David Thewlis), Glow Worm (Miriam Margolyes), Grasshopper (Simon Callow), Lady Bug (Jane Leeves), and Centipede (Richard Dreyfuss) in the part-live-action, part-stop-motion movie *James and the Giant Peach* (1996). When the orphaned James (Paul Terry) goes inside the giant peach, he meets the critters for the first time, and they sing this fun and frenetic song by Randy Newman about each of their hopes and dreams. James suggests they all go to New York City, where these dreams can come true, and they then sing about the wonderful life they will have there.

"That's What Friends Are For" is the harmonizing chorale number, reminiscent of a barbershop quartet piece, that was written by Richard M. and Robert B. Sherman for the animated movie *The Jungle Book* (1967). The Indian youth Mowgli (voice of Bruce Reitherman) comes upon a trio of vultures (J. Pat O'Malley, Chad Stuart, and Lord Tim Hudson) who blend their voices in song and offer to help the young man-cub. Oddly, in the dialogue scenes the three birds sport Liverpool accents, a passing nod to the popularity of the Beatles at the time. The playful number is sometimes listed as "The Vulture Song."

"That's What Makes the World Go Round" is the tuneful song about survival of the fittest written by Richard M. and Robert B. Sherman for their first animated movie, *The Sword in the Stone* (1963). The wizard Merlin (voice of Karl Swenson) turns himself and his pupil Wart (Rickie Sorensen) into fish so that they can swim the castle moat and explore the world underwater. The song is not about love, as the title may suggest, but rather about understanding all the ups and downs and ins and outs of life, particularly when the bigger fish is the predator of the smaller fish. The boy Wart reprises the number later in the film when he is scrubbing out the pots and pans in the castle kitchen.

"That's What Uncle Remus Said" is the pastiche "Negro" folk song written by Johnny Lange, Hy Heath, and Eliot Daniel for the partially animated live-action movie *Song of the South* (1946). A group of African American plantation workers gather around a fire at night and sing about Uncle Remus, recalling such tales as "How the Pig Got a Curly Tail," "How the Camel Got His Hump," and "How the Leopard Got His Spots." The Hall Johnson Choir provides the singing on the soundtrack and the number uses an echoing effect that encourages everyone to join in on the repeats.

"There Are Those" is the sly duet sung by two rival high-society grandes dames in the period movie *The Happiest Millionaire* (1967). The wealthy Philadelphian Mary Drexel (Gladys Cooper) and the snobby New York matron Mrs. Duke (Geraldine Page) meet and immediately do not like each other, singing this wry duet about how some people do not understand the proper way to do things. Richard M. and Robert B. Sherman wrote the comic number, which pits the old regime against the nouveau riche, the music mimicking a minuet and the lyric filled with acid-tongued insults.

"There Is Life" is the bucolic song about nature awaking written by David Friedman for the animated video sequel *Bambi II* (2006). As dawn breaks on a winter morning, the animals come out from under a blanket of snow and begin to play in the forest. Alison Krauss sings this melodic ballad on the soundtrack during the scene, and the number is reprised near the end of the video when it is discovered that Bambi has survived a terrible fall down a rocky slope.

"There's a Great Big Beautiful Tomorrow" is the bouncy, optimistic song written by Richard M. and Robert B. Sherman for the 1964 New York World's Fair exhibit General Electric's Carousel of Progress, an idea of Walt Disney's that was built by his staff. The audience looked at American life at four different times in the twentieth century as they sat in a revolving theatre that moved spectators from one era to another. The peppy song, taken from General Electric's theme for the pavilion, was heard whenever the auditorium revolved, each time looking forward to a new and improved lifestyle for Americans. After the fair closed, the attraction was reassembled at Disneyland in California and was a popular exhibit, as was the catchy song. When the attraction was re-created at Disney World in Florida in 1975, the song was replaced by "The Best Time of Your Life," but the original number was fondly recalled by many, so it was reinstated when the attraction was updated in 1993.

"There's a Party Here in Agrabah" is the rousing song of celebration written by David Friedman for the video sequel *Aladdin and the King of Thieves* (1995). The Genie (voice of Robin Williams) leads Aladdin (Brad Kane), Princess Jasmine (Liz Callaway), the parrot Iago (Gilbert Gottfried), and the people of Agrabah in the exposition number about the impending nuptials between Aladdin and Jasmine, with all the preparations for the festivities. The young lovers later reprise a slower, more reflective version of the song when they share their pre-wedding jitters.

"There's Room for Everyone" is the insistent and repetitive song of acceptance written by Joel Hirschhorn and Al Kasha for the partially animated movie *Pete's Dragon* (1977). The lighthouse keeper's daughter Nora (Helen Reddy), the runaway youth Pete (Sean Marshall), and a chorus of schoolchildren sing the optimistic number that encourages listeners to accept everyone for who they are.

"These Are the Best of Times" is the lite-rock theme song for the television series *Good Morning, Miss Bliss* (1987), about an Indianapolis junior high school history teacher (Hayley Mills) and her students. The appreciative number by Charles Fox (music) and Mark Mueller (lyric) takes the point of view of the young students, who already know that these years are the best and will stand the test of time. After a season, the series was sold to NBC and was retitled *Saved by the Bell*. Only the three principal student characters were retained, and a new theme song was written.

"These Are the Best Times" is the dreamy ballad by Shane Tatum that is used at the beginning and the end of the film comedy *Superdad* (1973). Bobby Goldsboro is heard singing the teary number about appreciating the happy times in one's life over the opening credits, during which teenagers frolic on a California beach in romantic silhouette. A church choir reprises the song at the wedding of Bart (Kurt Russell) and Wendy (Kathleen Cody) at the conclusion of the movie.

"They Live in You" is the fervent and stirring ballad written by Mark Mancina, Jay Rifkin, and Lebo M for the 1997 Broadway version of *The Lion King*. King Mufasa (Samuel E. Wright) sings the number to his young son Simba (Scott Irby-Ranniar) as they gaze up at the stars. The father explains to his son about how all their ancestors are up there looking down on them, finding life in the actions of their descendants. Much later in the show, the conjuring baboon Rafiki (Tsidii Le Loka) sings the song as "He Lives in You" to the grown-up Simba (Jason Raize), showing how the deceased Mufasa can live again through his son. In both versions the song is accompanied by gentle African chanting, which adds to the mystery and effectiveness of the number. Lebo M sings "He Lives in You" on the soundtrack during the opening of the video sequel *The Lion King 2: Simba's Pride* (1998) and Michael Crawford made a notable recording of it as part of a medley of songs from *The Lion King*. The song was included in the chorale recordings *Rhythm of the Pridelands* and *Return to Pride Rock*, and there were also recordings made by Tina Turner and Elijah Kelley.

"Things Are Not What They Appear" is the jolly song of sinister intrigue written by Marty Panzer and Larry Grossman for the made-for-video animated sequel *Pocahontas II: Journey to a New World* (1998). The vengeful

Ratcliffe (voice of David Ogden Stiers) and his henchmen (Craig Copeland, Phil Proctor, and Roger Freeland) plan to expose the refined lady Pocahontas as a savage when she is presented in court to King James, and they sing this dandy song about the dire consequences that will follow.

"This Is Halloween" is the pulsating holiday song written by Danny Elfman for the stop-motion animation film *The Nightmare Before Christmas* (1993). In the opening number of the movie musical, the ghoulish residents of Halloween Town celebrate another successfully ghastly October 31 with this insistent minor-key song that rarely departs from a series of repeated notes. In the video movie *Mickey's House of Villains* (2001), various Disney villains sing the number as they attack a movie theatre on Halloween.

"This Is Me" is the gentle ballad about believing in oneself written by Adam Watts and Andy Dodd for the television movie *Camp Rock* (2008). Mitchie Torres (Demi Lovato), who has confidence issues, is attending a summer camp for teens who want to become rock stars, and this song reflects her reticence to let go and allow her talent to shine. The insightful character song is later reprised in an upbeat pop version at the camp's "Final Jam" night, where Mitchie is joined by instructor Shane Gray (Joe Jonas).

"This Is Our Song" is the heartfelt pop song written by Adam Watts and Andy Dodd for the TV-movie *Camp Rock 2: The Final Jam* (2010). The number, sung by the Camp Rock campers and led by Shane (Joe Jonas) and Mitchie (Demi Lovato), is their entry in the "sing off" competition they are having with rival Camp Star. The gentle pop piece is a reflection on all the wonderful times they have shared together at Camp Rock, and a home video montage of their summer is played while they perform the song. The breezy tune is reprised a few moments later when they lose the "sing off" and then share what they presume will be their final campfire together.

"This New Jerusalem" is the anthem of hope sung by the new king in the Broadway concert-pageant *King David* (1997), written by Alan Menken (music) and Tim Rice (lyric). As the young David (Marcus Lovett) ascends the throne vacated by his mentor, Saul (Martin Vidnovic), he sings this number about making Jerusalem the city of God.

"This Only Happens in the Movies" is the entrancing love song Alan Menken (music) and Glenn Slater (lyric) wrote in 1990 for the film prequel *Who Discovered Roger Rabbit?* but the movie was never made. The heartfelt number compares love in the movies with that in real life and finds true life love the deeper experience. Kerry Butler recorded the lovely song in 2008.

"Thomas O'Malley Cat" is the jazzy "I am" song for the freewheeling alley cat O'Malley (voice of Phil Harris) in the animated movie *The Aristocats* (1970). Terry Gilkyson wrote the breezy number, in which O'Malley introduces himself to the Parisian cat Duchess by singing about his free and happy ways and how the whole world is his backyard.

"Thomasina" is the folk ballad by Terry Gilkyson about the feline heroine of the live-action movie *The Three Lives of Thomasina* (1964). A studio chorus sings the calliope-like song, with a Scottish flavor in the words and music, about the self-reliant and wise cat during the opening credits while Thomasina is seen stalking mice and birds.

"The Three Caballeros" is the hyperactive title song for the 1944 movie musical travelogue that uses animation and live action to explore the exotic side of Latin America. Manuel Esperón wrote the rapid Latin music and Ray Gilbert adapted Ernesto Cortazar's Spanish lyric, in which Donald Duck (voice of Clarence Nash) and his feathered friends Joe Carioca (José Oliveira) and Panchito (Joaquin Garay) introduce themselves and profess their friendship. The animated sequence is filled with visual slapstick and furious comic bits that hilariously illustrate the lyric. The song is also sung by a male chorus over the opening credits of the film and is reprised during the climactic bullfight sequence at the end of the film. Bing Crosby recorded the song with the Andrews Sisters, and the number was performed by Jack Weston, F. Murray Abraham, and Paul B. Price in a gay bathhouse in the film *The Ritz* (1976). In 2007 the song and the characters from the film *The Three Caballeros* were added to the El Rio Del Tiempo ride at the Mexico pavilion at Disney World's Epcot.

"Through Your Eyes" is the reflective ballad by Richard Marx and Dean Pitchford about one's inability to understand another person without seeing the world through the other's eyes. The touching song is sung by Martina McBride over the closing credits of the animated video sequel *Bambi II* (2006), which is about the difficult relationship between Bambi and his father.

"Tico-Tico (No Fubá)" is the contagious Latin number that arrived in the States from Brazil in the early 1940s and found recognition when it was interpolated into the animated film *Saludos Amigos* (1942). Zequinha Abreu composed the festive music, Ervin Drake adapted Aloysio de Oliveira's Portuguese lyric, and José Oliveira sings it on the soundtrack while Donald Duck and Joe Carioca visit the nightlife in Rio de Janeiro. The song is heard in a number of films from the 1940s, including *Thousands Cheer* (1943), where Maxine Barrett and Don Loper dance to it; *Bathing Beauty* (1944), where organist Ethel Smith plays it with Xavier Cugat's Orchestra (the song was long associated with him); as background in *Kansas City Kitty* (1944); and in *Copacabana* (1947), where Carmen Miranda sings it. Popular recordings were made by Smith, Miranda, Charles Wolcott and His Orchestra, and the Andrews Sisters.

"The Tiki Tiki Tiki Room" is the first original song written for Animatronic characters in a Disney theme park attraction. Richard M. and Robert B. Sherman wrote the pseudo-exotic number for the Enchanted Tiki Room attraction at Disneyland in 1963. Four mechanical parrots named Fritz, Michael, Pierre, and José sing the island ditty and are eventually joined by more than two hundred other birds, flowers, and tiki totem poles. The attraction was reproduced at other Disney parks over the years. In 1998 the show was renamed "The Enchanted Tiki Room—Under New Management" and, with Iago from *Aladdin* and Zazu from *The Lion King* as hosts, the attraction used a revised version of the song "A Friend Like Me" from the former movie. A fun quartet version of "The Tiki Tiki Tiki Room" was recorded by Meredith Inglesby, Andy Karl, Tyler Maynard, and Keewa Nurullah; Hilary Duff recorded it in 2002.

"The Time of Your Life" is the bluesy number about living your life well and taking it easy, written by Randy Newman for the computer-animated movie *A Bug's Life* (1998). Newman sings the lazy and carefree number on the soundtrack over the closing credits of the film.

"Tip and Dash" is the merry sea chantey the comic duo Tip the Penguin (voice of Max Casella) and Dash the Walrus (Stephen Furst) sing in the made-for-video animated sequel *The Little Mermaid II: Return to the Sea* (2000). Michael and Patty Silversher wrote the farcical number, and the two sidekicks sing it to Ariel's daughter, Melody (Tara Charendoff), promising to battle the forces of evil under the sea and save the day.

"'Tis Evening" is one of the satirical musical poems Charles Wolcott (music), T. Hee, and Erdman Penner (lyric) wrote for the animated film *The Reluctant Dragon* (1941). When the doddering knight Sir Giles (voice of Claude Allister) and the peace-loving Dragon (Barnett Parker) face off for battle, they instead recite their own poetry to each other. The frustrated Boy (Billy Lee) tries to get the fight going by talk-singing his own poem, an ode to the twilight, but soon it turns into a demand for bloodshed.

"To an Upside Down Cake" is the unintentionally comic ode to dessert that the poetry-writing Dragon (voice of Barnett Parker) sings about one of his favorite foods in the animated movie *The Reluctant Dragon* (1941). Charles Wolcott (music), T. Hee, and Erdman Penner (lyric) wrote the short but catchy ditty that satirizes the classical ode form.

"To Infinity and Beyond" is the musical mantra of the popular toy spaceman Buzz Lightyear, as heard during the closing credits of the made-for-video prequel *Buzz Lightyear of Star Command: The Adventure Begins* (2000). After a spoken lead-in that is an homage to the opening credits of the original *Star Trek* television series, William Shatner and the Star Command Chorus sing the patriotic, Sousa-like march about one's willingness to go to infinity, if not further, in the cause of justice and goodness. Fred LaBour wrote the whimsical song, which echoes the satiric nature of the character of Buzz.

"To the Fairies They Draw Near" is the opening number for the animated video *Tinker Bell* (2008), a prequel of sorts to *Peter Pan* (1953). Loreena McKennitt wrote the folk-like song, filled with the flavor of an old Irish ballad, and sings it on the soundtrack when the new fairy Tinker Bell is born. The lyric explains how the fairies bring about spring, and the number is reprised at the end of the film when Tinker Bell and all the other fairies travel to the mainland to deliver the seeds of spring.

"Today Is Gonna Be a Great Day" is the rapid rock song written and performed by the group Bowling for Soup in the opening sequence of the animated television series *Phineas and Ferb* (2007). The vigorous, satiric number counts the days of summer vacation and lists the cockeyed ways the stepbrothers Phineas and Ferb plan to use them, from fighting a mummy to climbing the Eiffel Tower to locating Frankenstein's brain.

"Together Time" is the merry waltz number that celebrates the mating season in nature, as heard in the movie *Perri* (1957), about a squirrel and a year of life in the forest. With the coming of spring, all the animals in the wooded landscape seem to be pairing off, and a studio chorus sings the cheerful number celebrating the end of winter and the time for two of everything. Paul J. Smith, Gil George, Ralph Wright, and Winston Hibler collaborated on the song, which is reprised at the end of the movie when the squirrel Perri is finally reunited with her mate.

"Together We Can" is the lite-rock song about girl bonding that teenagers Galleria (Raven-Symoné), Chanel (Adrienne Bailon), Aqua (Kiely Williams), and Dorinda (Sabrina Bryan) sing in the television film *The Cheetah Girls* (2003). John Van Tongeren wrote the pop number, in which the four girls boast that they can do anything, including saving the human race, if they do it together. The song was made into a music video featuring the four singers.

"Tomorrow Is Another Day" is the expansive song of optimism Carol Connors and Ayn Robbins wrote for the animated movie *The Rescuers* (1977). As the mice Bernard and Bianca fly on Albatross Airlines from New York City to the Devil's Bayou in Louisiana, Shelby Flint sings the poetic ballad about sharing the joy of a rainbow with someone who means something special to you. Just like the image of two mice soaring into the sunset on the back of the albatross Orville, the song is also very uplifting and lyrical.

"Tonka" is the western-flavored title song for the 1958 movie about a Sioux youth (Sal Mineo) who tames a wild colt he names Tonka Wakan, meaning "The Great One." A studio chorus sings the narrative ballad over the opening credits, praising the proud and courageous horse who took part in the Battle of the Little Big Horn. The number, which has a Native American tribal flavor to it, was written by George Bruns (music) with a lyric by Gil George (pseudonym for Hazel George, who was a studio nurse and a long-time confidante of Walt Disney).

"Too Cool" is the venomous character song sung by camp diva Tess Tyler (Meaghan Martin) in the made-for-television musical *Camp Rock* (2008). Tess performs the pop music number, written by Toby Gad and Pam Sheyne, at a camp bonfire, where she asserts her power and popularity while reminding her competition that she is too cool to be associating with them.

"Too Good to Be True" is the dreamy love song Buddy Kaye and Eliot Daniel wrote for the "Bongo" sequence in the animated anthology movie

Fun and Fancy Free (1947). The circus bear Bongo meets and falls in love with the coquettish bear Lulu Belle in the forest, and in their imagination they float and frolic together through the clouds. On the soundtrack, Dinah Shore and a studio chorus sing the ballad about finding someone who is more like a dream than reality. The number is reprised at the end of the story when Bongo defeats the bully bear Lumpjaw and wins Lulu Belle's love.

"A Toot and a Whistle and a Plunk and a Boom" is the swinging theme song for the animated film short *Toot, Whistle, Plunk and Boom* (1953), which explains the origins of the major ingredients to create music. Sonny Burke and Jack Elliott wrote the jazzy number, which is sung by a studio chorus on the soundtrack at the beginning and the end of the movie, celebrating the four ways to make noises that can be turned into music.

"Top of the World," by Niclas Molinder, Johan Alkenas, Joacim Persson, and Geraldo Sandell, is the bubble-gum pop theme song for the Disney XD situation comedy *Pair of Kings*. When Brady and Boomer, a pair of twin brothers (one Caucasian and one African American), find out that they are the long-lost heirs to the kingdom of Kinkow, the two bumbling teenagers move to the tropical island to become its rulers. "Top of the World," performed by series stars Mitchel Musso and Doc Shaw, is a celebration of Brady and Boomer's newfound positions as royalty.

"Topsy Turvy" is the festive song from the animated movie *The Hunchback of Notre Dame* (1996) that turns ugly for the unfortunate Quasimodo. As the jester Clopin (voice of Paul Kandel) sings about Topsy Turvy Day, in which everything is backward and upside down, the Paris crowd sings and celebrates the riotous holiday. When they hold a contest to see who has the ugliest mask, the hunchback Quasimodo (Tom Hulce) is pushed onto the platform and wins. But when the people realize it is not a mask and that Quasimodo is a deformed creature, they turn on him. Alan Menken composed the vigorous music and Stephen Schwartz wrote the ribald lyric.

"The Torkelsons Theme Song" is the pleasing gospel number Ray Colcord wrote for the 1991 television series about a single mother with five children. The flowing title song, sung by a choir over the opening credits, finds comfort in the sun coming out and each day having the possibility of things being all right. After the first season, the series was re-titled *Almost Home*, but it retained the same theme song.

"Town Meeting" is the sinister and ironic patter song written by Danny Elfman for the stop-motion film *The Nightmare Before Christmas* (1993). The Pumpkin King Jack Skellington (singing voice of Elfman) gathers the citizens of Halloween Town and tries to explain to them the concept of Christmas. They do not comprehend the spirit of the holiday, thinking, for instance, that a stocking ought to have a severed foot in it. The more Jack tries to illustrate the Christmas traditions, the more the villagers inflict their ghoulish Halloween sensibilities on the holiday.

"Toys" is the exuberant and insightful song that illustrates how children and their parents are often uncomfortably alike, written by Stephen Schwartz for the live-action television musical *Geppetto* (2000). In the village toy shop of Geppetto (Drew Carey), obnoxious children and their equally obnoxious parents make demands and fight over purchases, while lonely, childless Geppetto wonders why the wrong people have children. Later in the musical, after Pinocchio has run away, Geppetto and the bungling Magician (Wayne Brady) sing a quieter duet version of the song, reflecting on the delicate nature of the relationship between parents and children.

"Transformation" is the mystical, hymn-like song by Phil Collins that is used effectively in a pivotal moment in the animated movie *Brother Bear* (2003). After the Native American Kenai kills the bear who clawed his brother to death, the Great Spirits turn Kenai into a bear so that he will see nature with a new point of view. While images of different animals are conjured up before Kenai, the Bulgarian Women's Choir sings the ritu-alistic song on the soundtrack, the lyric promising to take one into a new world where all will be made clear. Songwriter Collins also recorded the enthralling number.

"Trashin' the Camp" is the scat-singing delight Phil Collins wrote for the animated movie *Tarzan* (1999), and one of the musical and visual treats of the film. Terk (voice of Rosie O'Donnell) and the other apes discover the camp of the humans deep in the African jungle and joyfully destroy it as they frolic and play with the strange objects they encounter. The rhythmic number cleverly begins with Terk hitting the keys on a typewriter, which sets the beat, and Collins is heard singing the nonsense scat song on the soundtrack as the number builds and the camp is thoroughly trashed. In the 2006 Broadway version of *Tarzan*, the number was performed by Terk (Chester Gregory II) and the apes. A recording of the number and a music video was made by the group 'N Sync.

"The Tree of Life Theme" is the entrancing musical composition by Tish Eastman heard in and around the theme park attraction The Tree of Life, which opened in 1998. The focal point of the Animal Kingdom park in Florida, the giant tree has hundreds of animal figures sculpted into the bark. The theme song consists of echoing voices, hands clapping, African drums, and fluted instruments all combining into a mysterious and exotic piece of music.

"Trick or Treating with Our Friends" is the happy-go-lucky Halloween song written by Michael and Patty Silversher for the made-for-video film *Pooh's Heffalump Halloween Movie* (2005). As they anticipate Halloween, Winnie the Pooh (voice of Jim Cummings), Piglet (John Fiedler), Tigger (also Cummings), and Eeyore (Peter Cullen) sing this merry number about getting candy and searching out Spookables. At the end of the movie, the kangaroos Kanga (Kath Soucie) and Roo (Jimmy Bennett) and the elephant Lumpy (Kyle Stanger) join Pooh and his friends in reprising the song.

"True Love Is an Apricot" is the farcical pastiche of an improvised beatnik song, written by Richard M. and Robert B. Sherman for the space film *The Moon Pilot* (1962). When the American astronaut Captain Richmond Talbot (Tom Tryon) is asked to pick out the foreign spy who tried to conspire with him, he must observe a lineup of women taken off the streets of San Francisco to see if he recognizes the culprit. One of the suspects is a guitar-playing beatnik who strums and sings this risible number about the essence of love, made up on the spot and hilariously pretentious.

"True Love's Kiss" is the satiric love duet written by Alan Menken (music) and Stephen Schwartz (lyric) for the modern fairy tale film *Enchanted* (2007). In the animated section of the movie, the eager Giselle (voice of Amy Adams) sings the soaring song, about a special kiss that promises happy endings, to her animal friends as they decorate a dummy to look like a handsome prince. Later in the animated sequence, after Prince Edward (James Marsden) rescues Giselle from a troll, the two sing the number together as an ultra-romantic duet. After the two characters find themselves in realistic Manhattan, they each sing brief sections of the song, but it seems phony and funny in the real world.

"True to Your Heart" is the pop-rock ballad Matthew Wilder (music) and David Zippel (lyric) wrote for the animated movie *Mulan* (1998). Stevie Wonder and the group 98 Degrees sing the number over the end credits of the film, urging listeners to follow their feelings when they are confused, and they will come out all right. The singer Raven made a recording of the rhythmic song at the time the movie was released, and in 2007 it was recorded by Keke Palmer.

"Trust in Me" is the alliterative lullaby Richard M. and Robert B. Sherman wrote for the animated movie *The Jungle Book* (1967). Kaa the Python (voice of Sterling Holloway) sings the slithering song filled with "sssss" sounds as he tries to hypnotize the man-cub Mowgli.

"Try Again" is the jazzy song of encouragement written by Dean Pitchford and Richard Gibb for the animated video sequel *101 Dalmatians II: Patch's London Adventure* (2003). While the dalmatian puppy Patch tries to prove himself brave and strong to the canine movie star Thunderbolt, Will Young sings this jumping and jiving number on the soundtrack, urging one to not give up. The song is reprised over the closing credits of the video.

"The Turkey Song" is a short and incongruous song Michael and Patty Silversher wrote for the holiday video *Winnie the Pooh: Seasons of Giving* (1999). When the bear Pooh (voice of Jim Cummings) and the fearful Piglet (John Fiedler) are sent into the woods to capture a turkey for Thanksgiving dinner, Pooh explains to Piglet how dangerous and unpredictable turkeys can be in this amusing song, which has a sinister tone and a sense of foreboding that frightens Piglet all the more.

"'Twas Brillig" is a charming nonsense song based on a Lewis Carroll poem and used cleverly throughout the animated film *Alice in Wonderland* (1951). Gene de Paul (music) and Don Raye (lyric) adapted the opening lines of Carroll's "Jabberwocky" into a short signature tune for the Cheshire Cat (voice of Sterling Holloway) to sing every time he appears and disappears in the film. While the melody is jaunty, the nonsensical lyric has an eerie and mystifying air to it.

"Two Silhouettes" is the romantic love song by Charles Wolcott, Ray Gilbert, and Al Sack that was set to a ballet in the animated anthology film *Make Mine Music* (1946). While Dinah Shore sings about two lovers, the silhouettes of live-action dancers Tatiana Riabouchinska and David Lichine are seen in a pastoral setting, the two ballet performers seemingly defying gravity and dancing in the clouds.

"2 Stars" is the musical cry of pain the camp diva Tess Tyler (Meaghan Martin) performs at the "Final Jam" in the made-for-television musical *Camp Rock* (2008). The daughter of a multi-Grammy-winning singer, Tyler hopes to get her mom's attention when she sings this number, pouring out her hope that her mother will see them both as stars, rather than just being caught up in her professional career. Adam Anders and Nikki Hassman wrote the passionate melody and the cathartic lyric.

"Two Worlds" is the pulsating song by Phil Collins that is used in the animated film *Tarzan* (1999) to accentuate the conflicting worlds of humans and animals, insisting that each group has strong family bonds. Collins is heard singing the number at the beginning of the film while the baby Tarzan is shipwrecked off the coast of Africa, his parents are killed by a leopard, and he is taken up by the gorilla Kala, who just lost her infant to the same beast. The number is reprised at the end of the film when Tarzan, Jane, and her father, Professor Porter, bid farewell to the rescue ship and elect to remain in the jungle. Mandy Moore sings the song on the soundtrack for the video sequel *Tarzan and Jane* (2002), and in the 2006 Broadway version of *Tarzan*, Josh Strickland sang the number offstage as the opening events occurred on stage. Collins's recording of the rhythmic song enjoyed some popularity, and it was also recorded by Corbin Bleu.

U

"The Ugly Bug Ball" is the playful narrative ballad the town postmaster Osh Popham (Burl Ives) sings to the young boy Peter Carey (Jimmy Mathers) in the period film *Summer Magic* (1963). Richard M. and Robert B. Sherman wrote the gentle ragtime song about an ugly caterpillar who finds romance at an annual ball for unsightly crawling and flying creatures. The song is accompanied by nature footage of insects and other bugs that seem to keep time to the music. Michael Feinstein made a pleasing recording of the song in 1992.

"The Unbirthday Song" is the silly but contagious song Mack David, Al Hoffman, and Jerry Livingston wrote for the animated movie *Alice in Wonderland* (1951). Alice (voice of Kathryn Beaumont) stumbles upon a bizarre and endless tea party where the Mad Hatter (Ed Wynn) and the March Hare (Jerry Colonna) are celebrating their unbirthday. As the song merrily explains, everyone has only one birthday, but there are 364 unbirthdays to enjoy. Rosemary Clooney recorded the number with the title song from the film, as did Michael Feinstein years later.

"Undeniably Yours" is the smooth ballad pastiching a 1940s Frank Sinatra–type number, written by Brock Walsh for the musical television series *Hull High* (1990). High school student Louis Plumb (Marty Belafsky), sporting a tux and fedora, sings the swinging love song with a big band, crooning about a love that cannot be denied.

"Under the Sea" is the Oscar-winning calypso number by Alan Menken (music) and Howard Ashman (lyric) that is the musical centerpiece of the animated movie *The Little Mermaid* (1989). The crab Sebastian (voice of Samuel E. Wright) tries to explain to the mermaid princess Ariel (Jodi Benson) that life on land is terrible and that she will be much happier staying below the surface where she belongs. The number starts out as a clever list song all about the advantages of life underwater, but soon it erupts into a Ziegfeld Follies–like production number, with various forms of sea life joining in the singing and dancing. Ashman's lyric is particularly artful in its use of the many marine animal names in the rhyming. In the 2008 Broadway version of *The Little Mermaid*, the number was led by Tituss Burgess as Sebastian. There have been several recordings of the song for children: Jazz Networks made a notable disc in 1996, Earl Rose made a jazz version in 2000, the A Teens recorded it in 2002, Raven recorded it in 2005, and there was also a playful recording by Andrew Samonsky with backup vocals by Meredith Inglesby, Andy Karl, Tyler Maynard, and Keewa Nurullah.

"Up, Down, Touch the Ground" is the brief but fondly remembered exercise song Winnie the Pooh (voice of Sterling Holloway) optimistically sings as he does his morning calisthenics. Richard M. and Robert B. Sherman wrote the rhythmic little ditty for *Winnie the Pooh and the Honey Tree* (1966), the first Disney film short based on the A. A. Milne stories.

"Upendi" is the infectious song about a topsy-turvy world written by Randy Petersen and Kevin Quinn for the video sequel *The Lion King 2: Simba's Pride* (1998). The medicine man/baboon Rafiki (voice of Robert Guillaume) sings to the unlikely lion lovers Kiara and Kovu about a place where everything is upside down and the opposite of normal, but a perfect place to fall in love. As Rafiki describes the place, a montage shows the land of Upendi, where hippos swing from trees and rhinos dance a conga line.

V

"Valentine Candy" is the reflective "I am" song tomboy Cordelia Drexel Biddle (Lesley Ann Warren, in her screen debut) sings in the period movie musical *The Happiest Millionaire* (1967). The Philadelphia heiress Cordelia, who likes to box for a hobby, looks at herself in her bedroom mirror and tries to find the woman between the society lady and the little girl with a sweet tooth. Richard M. and Robert B. Sherman wrote the touching and truthful song.

"Very Good Advice" is the somber, revealing song by Mack David, Al Hoffman, and Jerry Livingston for the title character in the animated movie *Alice in Wonderland* (1951). After all her adventures in Wonderland, Alice (voice of Kathryn Beaumont) thinks back on the lessons she has learned and comes to the conclusion that she is better at giving herself advice than she is at following it. Doris Day and the Four Hits made a smooth recording of the ballad, and years later it was recorded by Barbara Hendricks and the Abbey Road Ensemble.

"A Very Important Thing to Do" is a spirited ditty sung by a female chorus on the soundtrack of the 2011 animated film *Winnie the Pooh*. It is performed as the title character posts signs around the Hundred Acre Wood, calling for the help of all his friends in finding him a pot of honey. The jaunty piece, by Robert Lopez and Kristen Anderson-Lopez, has a determined and confident tune, and the lyric expresses the important mission to assuage Pooh's mounting hunger.

"The Virginia Company" is the rousing song of adventure by Alan Menken (music) and Stephen Schwartz (lyric) that is sung by a male chorus on the soundtrack of the animated film *Pocahontas* (1995). While the crew readies their ship in London, Governor Ratcliffe (voice of David Ogden Stiers) and Captain John Smith (Mel Gibson) come aboard, all preparing to sail to the New World and bring back chests of gold. The spirited number is a cross between an English drinking song and a sailors' sea chantey.

"The Void" is the incongruous number by Richard M. and Robert B. Sherman that spoofs the "deep" songs of the beat generation, written for the movie *The Moon Pilot* (1962). When the San Francisco police bring in a bevy of women who hang out on the wharf at night, one of them is drunk and breaks into this pseudo-meaningful song about the emptiness of life. The music sounds improvised, as does the lyric, creating a wicked pastiche of the beatnik songs of the era.

W

"Wait Till He Sees You" is the waltz-tempo song of anticipation written by Larry Grossman and Marty Panzer for the animated video sequel *Pocahontas II: Journey to a New World* (1998). The Englishwoman Mrs. Jenkins (voice of Jean Stapleton) prepares Pocahontas to be presented to King James by dressing her in European clothes and doing up her hair in an English style, singing this cheerful number about how Pocahontas will dazzle the court. The Englishman John Rolfe (Billy Zane) joins in on the number, teaching Pocahontas the dance steps she will need to know at the ball.

"Waiting for This Moment" is the stirring song of wonderment sung by Jane Porter (Jenn Gambatese) in the 2006 Broadway version of *Tarzan*. Phil Collins wrote the number, in which Jane wanders through the jungle, jotting down the Latin names for all the exotic plants she encounters and reveling in the beautiful, primitive world that already feels like home to her. She is so taken with her joy that she does not notice she is being ensnared in the web of a giant spider, and Tarzan has to rescue her.

"Walk Away" is the heartfelt song by Jamie Houston about making a difficult decision that separates one from a loved one, as sung by high school senior Gabriella Montez (Vanessa Anne Hudgens) in the film sequel *High School Musical 3: Senior Year* (2008). Afraid that her boyfriend, Troy (Zac

Efron), is not going to make the best decision about his future because of his devotion to her, Gabriella realizes she must break off their relationship so that he will feel free to do what is best for him.

"The Walrus and the Carpenter" is the clever musical rendition of the Lewis Carroll poem that is one of the highlights of the animated film *Alice in Wonderland* (1951). The rotund twins Tweedle-Dum and Tweedle-Dee tell Alice the story of two con men—a puffed-up, blustering walrus and an off-kilter carpenter—who trick a group of oysters into becoming their meal. Sammy Fain (music) and Bob Hilliard (lyric) adapted the poem into a musical scene that is a tour de force for actor J. Pat O'Malley, who provides the voices for not only the walrus and the carpenter, but for Tweedle-Dum and Tweedle-Dee as well. An amusing quartet recording of the number was made by Meredith Inglesby, Andy Karl, Tyler Maynard, and Keewa Nurullah.

"Warm Spring Night" is the passionate song of love from the biblical concert-pageant *King David*, which was presented on Broadway in 1997. David (Marcus Lovett) falls for the beautiful Bathsheba (Alice Ripley) and sings this song of lust, full of pastoral imagery, describing how his body responds to his carnal feelings and his heated surroundings. Alan Menken composed the potent music and Tim Rice wrote the hot-blooded lyric.

"Watch Your Footwork" is the peppy song about boxing techniques written by Richard M. and Robert B. Sherman for the period musical *The Happiest Millionaire* (1967), the sparkling duet using a Dixieland jazz flavor in its music. The Biddle brothers, Tony (Paul Peterson) and Livingston (Eddie Hodges), warn their sister's suitor, Charlie Taylor (Larry Merrill), about her boxing prowess, singing that she has dynamite up her sleeve. In the course of demonstrating some of her moves, the two brothers knock the fellow out cold.

"The Way It Must Be Done" is the rapid march song Randy Rogel (music and lyric) and Grant Geissman (lyric) wrote for the animated video *Winnie the Pooh: Springtime with Roo* (2004). The over-organized Rabbit (voice of Ken Sansom) instructs his friends in the Hundred Acre Wood on the correct procedure for coloring, drying, and hiding eggs for Easter with this droll number, turning Easter preparations into an efficient and charmless affair. Winnie the Pooh and the others ignore Rabbit's rules and have fun as they sloppily color the eggs and sing about the way they like to do things, which upsets Rabbit very much.

"We Are Here to Change the World" is the rhythmic rock number written and performed by Michael Jackson in the 3-D film *Captain EO* (1986) at the Journey into Imagination attraction at Epcot. Captain EO (Jackson) and his ragtag crew of misfit creatures and robots perform the song about finding a better world to the evil Supreme Leader (Anjelica Huston) in the hopes of softening her cold, cruel heart. The number turns into an energetic dance showcase for Jackson, who later recorded the song for a compilation album. Denise Williams also recorded the song in 1988.

"We Are One" is the song of parental encouragement written by Tom Snow (music), Marty Panzer, and Jack Feldman (lyric) for the video sequel *The Lion King 2: Simba's Pride* (1998). The lion king Simba (singing voice of Cam Clark) sings to his teenage daughter, Kiara, that no matter what differences arise between father and daughter, they will always love and support each other. During the song, a montage is shown of various animal parents spending time with their offspring.

"We Belong Together" is the playful song that accompanies the closing credits of the computer-animated Disney/Pixar film *Toy Story 3* (2010). Written and performed by Randy Newman, the ditty is about friendship and sticking with the people who care about you. While the film's credits roll, the toys from the Sunnyside Daycare Center, who are no longer under the dictatorial rule of Lots-O'-Huggin' Bear, celebrate their freedom to the accompaniment of this amiable tune.

"We Go Together" is the happy hillbilly song by Marcus Hummon that is used effectively during the opening credits of the made-for-video animated sequel *The Fox and the Hound 2* (2006). A pack of singing dogs (voiced by the group Big Little Town) are singing at the Grand Ole Opry about how friends will go anywhere as long as they are together. The singing is broadcast over the radio and is heard in the house of the Widow Tweed, where the young canine Copper and the fox Tod are playing together.

"We Rock" is the jubilant character number performed by the cast of teenagers in the finale of the television musical *Camp Rock* (2008). Kara DioGuardi and Greg Wells wrote the vibrant jam session number, with frenzied music and a poetic lyric about finding one's voice and searching for one's dreams.

"Weasel Rock You" is the hard-rock theme song for the 2009 Disney XD sitcom *I'm in the Band*. When teenager Tripp Campbell gets a chance to show off his musical skills to his favorite rock band, Iron Weasel, the band decides to take him on as their lead guitarist. The band members, who have been living in their van, move into the teenager's family's garage and the comedy grows out of their buffoonery. The ear-assaulting theme is by David Wilde, Karl Cochran, Michael B. Kaplan, Ron Rappaport, and Stacy Wilde and is performed by Chuck Duran.

"The Weekenders Theme" is the rhythm-and-blues number from the animated television series *The Weekenders* (2000) about four teens who search out new adventures each weekend. Roger Neill wrote the carefree number, which is sung by a male soloist over the opening credits, showing the four adolescents at amusement parks and other fun places.

"Welcome (to Our Family)" is the lively gospel-flavored song written by Phil Collins for the animated film *Brother Bear* (2003). When the Native American Kenai is turned into a bear, he is welcomed to the bear colony with this joyous song. Collins, the Blind Boys of Alabama, and Oren Waters sing it on the soundtrack as Kenai learns the ways of the bears, from hunting to playing. In 2004 the song was recorded by the group Jump 5.

"Welcome Home" is the bright and bouncy opening number written by Melissa Manchester and Norman Gimbel for the animated video sequel *Lady and the Tramp II: Scamp's Adventure* (2001). In a small New England town, the citizens prepare for the Independence Day parade and picnic, commenting on all the fun things to do, while the canines Lady (voice of Jodi Benson) and Tramp (Jeff Bennett) join in on the song and list their own favorite pastimes.

"Welcome to My Hole" is the sinister song of welcome written by William Finn for the animated made-for-video *The Adventures of Tom Thumb and Thumbelina* (2002). The tiny princess Thumbelina (voice of Jennifer Love Hewitt) has fallen in love with the equally small Tom Thumb, but she is captured by the evil Mole King (Peter Gallagher), who plans to marry her and make Thumbelina his queen. He sings this creepy character song as he brings her into his dark lair and offers her treasure, unwittingly revealing that this underground monarch is crazy.

"Welcome to the Day" is the magical and invigorating song written by Melissa Etheridge for the opening sequence in the animated video sequel *Brother Bear 2* (2006). Etheridge sings the number on the soundtrack, describing the bond between two brothers and asking the spirits to bless the day, while two bears, Kenai and his little brother, Koda, play together in a river during early morning. The song is reprised in the final moments of the movie when Kenai marries his beloved Nita, an old friend from his human days who has made the transformation to become a bear so that they may be together.

"Welcome to the Forty Thieves" is the vigorous song that the band of thieves sing to Aladdin (voice of Brad Kane) after he has passed a test of bravery and strength in the video sequel *Aladdin and the King of Thieves* (1995). David Friedman wrote the boisterous number in which the thieves (featuring the voices of Scott Barnes, Don Bradford, Merwin Foard, Guy Stroman, Gordon Stanley, Paul Kandel, Peter Samuel, and songwriter Friedman) list the duties and perks of being part of their elite group of outlaws.

"Welcome to the Kingdom" is the spectacular opening number written by Jay Blackton (music) and Joe Cook (lyric) for the 1979 Radio City Music Hall stage version of *Snow White and the Seven Dwarfs*. The citizens of the kingdom sing this introductory song, which tells the audience they are about to enter a magical world of fairy tales. The stage production was taped and broadcast on pay TV in 1980 and on the Disney Channel in 1987 as *Snow White Live*.

"Welcome to Toontown" is the jumping rock song written for the opening of Mickey's Toontown attraction at Disney World in 1993. The happy number, about the joy of being in such a special place, has been used in parades and shows in the colorful re-creation of a cartoon town where Mickey and his friends live. The Fab 5 recorded the number, and their version is used in the parks as well.

"We'll Smoke the Blighter Out" is a silly list song by Oliver Wallace (music), Ted Sears, and Winston Hibler (lyric) for the animated movie fantasy

Alice in Wonderland (1951). After Alice (voice of Kathryn Beaumont) has eaten a piece of cake inside the house of the White Rabbit (Bill Thompson), she grows so large that everyone thinks she's a monster. The Dodo (also voiced by Thompson) sings this merry number listing all the ways they might try to get the monster out of the house.

"We're All in This Together" is the repetitive and catchy song of optimism that Matthew Gerrard and Robbie Nevil wrote for the finale of the television movie *High School Musical* (2006). Although the school's jocks, nerds, skaters, drama geeks, and brainiacs have been at odds with each other over the past weeks, they all unite in singing this plucky, sentimental song about celebrating the differences that make them strong. The number is led by basketball jock Troy Bolton (Zac Efron, with singing assist by Andrew Seeley), math whiz Gabriella Montez (Vanessa Anne Hudgens), drama queen Sharpay Evans (Ashley Tisdale), and her performing brother Ryan (Lucas Grabeel), but soon all the Wildcats are singing and dancing to the hopeful song. The number is reprised by the same characters during the graduation scene in the film sequel *High School Musical 3* (2008).

"We're at the Top of the World" is the Beach Boys–like lite-rock song written by Juliana Theory for the made-for-television movie *Motocrossed* (2001). During film footage in which teen motorcycle riders Andrea Carson (Alana Austin) and Dean Talon (Riley Smith) speed over hills and dales, songwriter Theory sings this 1960s-sounding pop song on the soundtrack, complete with "sha-la-la-la" and a lyric about being the very best in your field.

"We're Huntin' Eggs Today" is the zesty march song John Kavanaugh wrote for the made-for-video movie *Winnie the Pooh: Springtime with Roo* (2004). Tigger (voice of Jim Cummings) leads his friends through the Hundred Acre Wood on Easter as they sing about the big hunt, listing the different kinds of eggs they hope to find.

"We're in Harmony" is the melodic country-western number by Will Robinson that is used throughout the animated video sequel *The Fox and the Hound 2* (2006). A group of singing hounds list the many things that go together in harmony as they perform on the stage of a talent show. Later in the film, the harmonizing song is reprised by the canines Cash (singing voice of Joshua Gracin), Dixie (Reba McEntire), Granny Rose (Vicki Lawrence), Copper (Harrison Fahn), and Floyd (Jim Cummings) as they howl together outside a diner. Chip Davis reprises the number during the end credits of the video.

"Weren't So Bad What Used to Be" is the strumming blues number Mason Daring wrote for the film *Wild Hearts Can't Be Broken* (1991). Eula Lawrence sings the rhythmic blues song about feeling bad about the present and wishing to go back to the past, heard over a montage showing scenes from the Great Depression. The number not only comments on the out-of-work characters in the movie but is also an accurate and evocative pastiche of the music of the period.

"West o' the Wide Missouri" is a pulsating dance number in the movie musical *The One and Only, Genuine, Original Family Band* (1968) that is performed on election night 1888 in a Dakota town anticipating statehood. Richard M. and Robert B. Sherman wrote the square dance song about the land of opportunity west of the Missouri River, and it is sung and danced to by both Democrats and Republicans awaiting the election results. Featured in the production number are John Davidson, Lesley Ann Warren, Buddy Ebsen, Janet Blair, Goldie Hawn, and Steve Harmon.

"Westward Ho, the Wagons!" is the vigorous title song for the 1956 movie about pioneers traveling the Oregon Trail. George Bruns (music) and Tom W. Blackburn (lyric) wrote the western number about going west, where new land is always best. A male chorus sings the spirited song on the soundtrack at the beginning of the film during a montage of a wagon train slowly moving across the prairie.

"A Whale of a Tale" is the silly sea chantey that whaler Ned Land (Kirk Douglas) sings in the adventure film *20,000 Leagues Under the Sea* (1954). Al Hoffman (music) and Norman Gimbel (lyric) wrote the ribald number in which Ned plays the guitar and sings tall tales about all the women he has enjoyed while living the life of a seaman, swearing on his tattoo that they are all true.

"What a Blustery Day" is the innocent list song Winnie the Pooh (voice of Sterling Holloway) sings as he observes the effects of the wind on the Hundred Acre Wood in the Oscar-winning movie short *Winnie the Pooh and the Blustery Day* (1968). Richard M. and Robert B. Sherman wrote the lighthearted song about the natural elements, which Pooh sings as he braves the storm to wish his friends a "Happy Winds-day."

"What a Day in London" is the complex musical number that introduces England to the newly arrived Pocahontas in the made-for-video animated sequel *Pocahontas II: Journey to a New World* (1998). As the citizens of London awake and begin a new day, they sing about their everyday tasks and expectations. People from all different levels of society, from beggars to nobles, are presented in the musical number. Pocahontas (singing voice of Judy Kuhn) takes part in the song, wondering at the marvels of the big city and its strange buildings, various kinds of foods, and diverse types of people. Marty Panzer and Larry Grossman wrote the multilevel number, which has an English Renaissance flavor in its music.

"What Can You Lose?" is the beguiling torch song of sorts written by Stephen Sondheim for the cartoonish live-action movie *Dick Tracy* (1990). Nightclub pianist Eighty-Eight Keys (Mandy Patinkin) and saloon singer Breathless Mahoney (Madonna) briefly sing the ambivalent love song at a rehearsal in the club. The lyric argues that one can never tell the truth about love, but with so much you can win, it's worth the risk. The intriguing number was edited down to just snippets in the movie, but Guy Haines (aka Bruce Kimmel) and Madonna each recorded the full song, and years later Judy Kuhn made a memorable recording.

"What Dreams Are Made Of" is the rhythmic pop love song that was heard twice in *The Lizzie McGuire Movie* (2003), in which the television character Lizzie (Hilary Duff) has romantic adventures in Italy. Matthew Wilder (music) and Dean Pitchford (lyric) wrote the romantic number about finding that special person and the feeling that creates a million dreams. When Lizzie is mistaken for the pop star Isabella, she meets and falls in love with Isabella's boyfriend, Paolo (Yani Gellman), and the two sing the number on a bare concert stage. The song is reprised later in the film by Lizzie and Isabella (also Duff) as a duet before a packed house of fans.

"What Is a Baby?" is the brief but potent song from the animated movie *Lady and the Tramp* (1955) that takes the canine point of view about a new arrival in the house. Sonny Burke and Peggy Lee wrote the number, which is a series of questions going through Lady's mind as she watches people fuss over something in the bedroom and she hears the cries of something new and unusual. Lee provided the singing voice for Lady's thoughts, wondering what could be so special that everyone behaves so oddly.

"What It Takes" is the lively hip-hop number performed by teenage camper Lola (Aaryn Doyle) at the open-mike night in the made-for-television musical *Camp Rock* (2008). Tim James and Antonina Armato wrote the frenetic melody and the sassy lyric about respect being the key thing a girl is looking for from a man.

"What I've Been Looking For" is the pop love song by Andy Dodd and Adam Watts that is given two very different renditions in the television movie *High School Musical* (2006). Drama queen Sharpay Evans (Ashley Tisdale) and her brother Ryan (Lucas Grabeel), who always get the leading roles in the school's "Spring Musicale," perform the heartfelt ballad at auditions with a slick showbiz approach, singing and dancing at a fast tempo and showing off their artificial talents. After auditions, the number is given a softer, slower, and more meaningful rendition by teens Troy Bolton (Zac Efron, with singing assist by Andrew Seeley) and Gabriella Montez (Vanessa Anne Hudgens), who are falling in love with each other.

"What Makes the Red Man Red?" is the politically incorrect song that Sammy Fain (music) and Sammy Cahn (lyric) wrote for the animated fantasy film *Peter Pan* (1953). When the Indians in Never Land celebrate Peter's rescue of Tiger Lily, they sing this pounding number, answering questions such as why they say "ugh" and "how" and why they are so red. The answers are silly (the redness comes from blushing over pretty Indian maidens) and the tribal dance that follows is stylized nonsense. Although the intention is escapist fun, the number proves offensive to some audiences today. A recording of the rhythmic number was made by David Anderson, Anne Lloyd, Mitch Miller, Dan Ocko, and the Sandpipers.

"What Time Is It?" is the hip-hop opening number written by Matthew Gerrard and Robbie Nevil for the television movie sequel *High School Musical 2* (2007). On the last day of high school classes, the students anxiously watch the clock, waiting for the bell to ring as they sing about their anticipation of summer. Once the bell does ring, the teenagers dash into the halls and break into a vivacious celebratory production number that includes various kinds of contemporary dance.

"What's This?" is the fast and excited song of discovery Danny Elfman wrote for the stop-motion film *The Nightmare Before Christmas* (1993). The discontented Pumpkin King Jack Skellington (singing voice of Elfman) lands in Christmas Town and eagerly asks himself the meaning of all the snow, colored lights, making of toys, and warmth of human spirit. The song is reprised toward the end of the film when Santa Claus brings Christmas to Halloween Town and the citizens rejoice in their first experience with falling snow.

"What's Wrong with That?" is the conversational number by Richard M. and Robert B. Sherman that is used throughout the movie *The Happiest Millionaire* (1967) whenever the eccentric millionaire Anthony J. Drexel Biddle (Fred MacMurray) questions the circumstances around him. He first sings it after his finger has been bitten by his pet alligator and he complains that there is no one at home to give him sympathy. His daughter Cordelia (Lesley Ann Warren) reprises it with him, taking pity on him. Later Biddle sings it at a party when he questions whether America is prepared to fight if the nation gets involved in World War I. A group of Marines joins him in the song. Finally, Biddle sings a quieter version of the number to the engaged Cordelia as they ride in a taxi and he questions why a father must lose his daughter to marriage. The song has a vigorous talk-sing quality to it, a style the Shermans thought would suit Rex Harrison, whom they wanted to play the role.

"When I See an Elephant Fly" is the jaunty comic song by Oliver Wallace (music) and Ned Washington (lyric) that Jim Crow (voice of Cliff Edwards) and the other crows (Hall Johnson Choir) sing in the animated movie *Dumbo* (1941) about the impossibility of the baby elephant Dumbo flying up into the tree where he has been found. The song is reprised by the chorus on the soundtrack at the end of the film when Dumbo becomes the star of the circus and rides off into the sunset with his mother. The jazzy number is filled with puns in the lyric and is musically very ambitious. The whole sequence was deemed offensive to African Americans in the 1960s (the crow's name is the only overtly derogatory aspect of the scene), so the movie was not shown very often. Later, more enlightened audiences found it to be the most musically vibrant part of *Dumbo*. Jane Froman made a popular recording of the clever number in the 1940s, and decades later Barbara Cook made a memorable version harmonizing with herself on three tracks. There was also a recording by the group Plain White T's in 2008. The original recording of the song from the film soundtrack is heard in the movie *Operation Dumbo Drop* (1995).

"When I'm Near You" is the slow-dance number heard in the film comedy *Superdad* (1973). Shane Tatum wrote the quiet, romantic love song, and teen couples dance to it at a birthday party, the number heard on the stereo in the home of the McCready family in Los Angeles.

"When I'm with You" is the old-time vaudeville number written by Michael Giacchino, Jeannie Lurie, Steve L. Hayes, and Adam Cohen for the television movie *The Muppets' Wizard of Oz* (2005). Dorothy (Ashanti) sings the soft-shoe number about the importance of friends with the Scarecrow, played by Kermit the Frog (voice of Steve Whitmire); Tin Man, played by Gonzo (Dave Goelz); Lion, played by Fozzie Bear (Eric Jacobson); and Toto, played by Pepe the Prawn (Bill Barretta).

"When in Love" is the contemplative song of love that Alan Menken (music) and Tim Rice (lyric) wrote for the Broadway concert-pageant *King David* (1997). When the beauteous Bathsheba (Alice Ripley) sets eyes on David (Marcus Lovett) and is smitten, she reflects upon her willingness to do anything for him because of her deep love.

"When Love Is Gone" is the heartfelt torch song Paul Williams wrote for the film *The Muppet Christmas Carol* (1992). The pretty Englishwoman Belle (Meredith Braun) sings to the young man Ebenezer Scrooge (Raymond Coulthard) about how his love of money has replaced his love for her and she bids him farewell. At the end of the movie, the old and reformed Scrooge (Michael Caine) sings the number as "When Love Is Found" as he celebrates Christmas with the Cratchit family. Martina McBride sings the song over the closing credits of the film, and her recording received some airplay.

"When She Loved Me" is the heart-tugging torch song not about lovers parting, but about the loss of a friend, used so effectively in the computer-animated movie sequel *Toy Story 2* (1999). In a flashback, the cowgirl doll Jessie (voice of Joan Cusack) recalls when she was the favorite toy of the little girl Emily. But as Emily grew up and her interests changed, she neglected Jessie and eventually left her as a donation to charity. Randy Newman wrote the simple but moving ballad, which is sung on the soundtrack by Sarah McLachlan during the potent sequence. Out of context, the song could be performed as a love song, as with heartfelt recordings by Brian Sutherland, Steve Tyrell, Michael Crawford, Kerry Butler, and Jordan Pruitt.

"When the Buzzards Return to Hinckley Ridge" is the mock opera aria Mel Leven wrote for the sly animated documentary short *It's Tough to Be* *a Bird* (1969) about the history of birds before and after the arrival of man. During live-action film footage of the annual buzzard festival in Hinckley, Ohio, Ruth Buzzi's earsplitting soprano voice is heard on the soundtrack singing this tribute to all the buzzards that descend on the town each spring.

"When the Love Bug Bites" is the menacing yet comic song about the effects of love written by Michael and Patty Silversher for the animated television special *Winnie the Pooh: A Valentine for You* (1999). Winnie the Pooh (voice of Jim Cummings) learns that his friend Christopher Robin is "smitten" by love, and his friends Rabbit (Ken Sansom) and Tigger (Paul Winchell) sing about the medical symptoms of love, none of them pleasant. The clever song is both ominous and playful as their imaginations run away with them.

"When There Was Me and You" is the teenage torch song Jamie Houston wrote for the television movie *High School Musical* (2006). When "brainiac" Gabriella Montez (Vanessa Anne Hudgens) overhears her boyfriend, Troy Bolton (Zac Efron), tell his basketball teammates that auditioning for the school musical is not important to him, she questions if she herself means anything to Troy. She longs for the time when it was just the two of them, before their friends got involved and influenced their relationship.

"When We're Human" is the exuberant Dixieland jazz number by Randy Newman that the trumpet-playing alligator Louis (voice of Michael-Leon Wooley) sings with Prince Naveen (Bruno Campos) and Tiana (Anika Noni Rose) in the animated feature *The Princess and the Frog* (2009). Turned into frogs and lost in a swamp, the prince and Tiana meet Louis, who dreams of being a jazz trumpet player like Louis Armstrong. He sings about what he will do when the sorceress Mama Odie turns him into a human, and the prince joins in by singing about the party life he will return to when he is changed back to his original form. Tiana adds a cautionary observation that humans must work for what they get out of life, but the other two are too busy celebrating to heed her words. The masterful trumpet playing in the number is by Terence Blanchard.

"When Will My Life Begin?" is the rhythmic "I am" song written by Alan Menken (music) and Glenn Slater (lyric) for Rapunzel to sing in the animated feature *Tangled* (2010). The song is performed by Rapunzel (voice of Mandy Moore) three times in the movie. The first time it is an upbeat list song that chronicles all the everyday things Rapunzel does, from painting murals to combing her long long hair, while waiting for the day when she can go out into the world. After Mother Gothel refuses to let Rapunzel leave her tower, the long-lost princess reprises the number with a sadder lyric and context. Once Rapunzel is out of the tower and traveling with Flynn Rider, she again sings "When Will My Life Begin?" as a song of wonderment as she enjoys her first taste of freedom. Menken's music is very flexible as it conveys different moods at different times, and Slater's lyric ranges from clever to heartfelt.

"When You Wish Upon a Star" is one of the most beloved of all movie songs, a dreamy and optimistic number by Leigh Harline (music) and Ned Washington (lyric) that has become the theme song for Walt Disney's entertainment empire. The plaintive ballad, about wishes coming true if you firmly believe in yourself, is first heard (minus the heartfelt verse and release) at the beginning of the movie *Pinocchio* (1940), where Jiminy Cricket (voice of Cliff Edwards) sings it as the camera moves into Geppetto's house and the story begins. Although the music does not have a wide range, it has an expansive feeling as the notes at times seem to reach up to the stars. The ballad immediately became a favorite, won the Oscar for Best Song, and was forever after associated with Disney, being used for everything from the theme song for his weekly television show to ads plugging the various theme parks. Over the years the song has often been recorded by various and diverse artists, including popular discs by Glenn Miller, Kate Smith, Ringo Starr, Johnny Mathis, the Mormon Tabernacle Choir, Barbara Hendricks and the Abbey Road Ensemble, Jack Teagarden, Dick Haymes with the Harry James Orchestra, Louis Armstrong, Linda Ronstadt, Billy Joel, the Drummonds, Mary Martin, the Ken Peplowski Quartet, Jazz Networks, Barbra Streisand, Michael Crawford, 'N Sync, Jimmy Scott, Michael Feinstein, Susan Egan, Steve Tyrell, and Barbara Cook. A violin rendition of the ballad was used in the live-action television musical *Geppetto* (2000), and the Cliff Edwards recording was used in a dream spoof at the beginning of the animated film *Teacher's Pet* (2004).

"Where Do I Go from Here?" is the musical query sung by Pocahontas (singing voice of Judy Kuhn) in the animated video sequel *Pocahontas II: Journey to a New World* (1998). As winter arrives in her homeland and the animals prepare for the change in season, Pocahontas wonders what she should do with her life, being discontented and ready for change herself. The pop ballad was written by Marty Panzer and Larry Grossman.

"Where Is Your Heart At?" is the slightly swinging pastiche song by Rufus Wainwright that echoes the sound of the Rat Pack singers, in particular Frank Sinatra. In the animated movie *Meet the Robinsons* (2007), the orphan Lewis looks into the future and sees his future wife, Franny (voice of Nicole Sullivan), conducting a big band ensemble of frogs. The lead singer is Frankie (Jamie Cullum), who croons the old-style ballad about finding happiness by doing what you feel deep in your heart.

"Where the Dream Takes You" is the pop ballad Diane Warren and James Newton Howard wrote for the animated adventure film *Atlantis: The Lost Empire* (2001). The lite-rock number about following your heart to find your true self is sung by pop singer Mya over the final credits of the movie.

"Wherever the Trail May Lead" is the pleasing country-western song about friendship written by Alan Menken (music) and Glenn Slater (lyric) for the animated movie *Home on the Range* (2004). During the end credits for the film, Tim McGraw sings the warm and optimistic ballad, promising to stick with a friend no matter what.

"Wherever You Are" is the entrancing lullaby-like song by Michael Abbott and Sarah Weeks that Winnie the Pooh (voice of Jim Cummings) sings about his lost friend Christopher Robin in the made-for-video film *Pooh's Grand Adventure: The Search for Christopher Robin* (1997). Believing that Christopher Robin has been imprisoned inside a skull (when he has really just gone to school), Pooh and his friends set off on an expedition to rescue him, but meet with a series of failures. One night Winnie sings to the stars, wishing to be reunited with Christopher Robin and wondering if he is wishing the same thing. As the weary Pooh finishes the tender song, he falls asleep and Rabbit covers him with a blanket. Barry Coffing and Vonda Shepard reprise the lovely number during the end credits of the video.

"Whistle-Stop" is the contagious calliope-like number written by Roger Miller for the animated movie *Robin Hood* (1973). The bouncy music, played during the opening credits of the film, has no lyric but is accompanied by whistling and Miller's vocal imitation of medieval instruments, creating a period yet contemporary sound.

"Whistle While You Work" is the catchy and memorable ditty by Frank Churchill (music) and Larry Morey (lyric) that Snow White (voice of Adriana Caselotti) sings and whistles as she and her animal friends clean up the cottage of the dwarfs in the animated film *Snow White and the Seven Dwarfs* (1937). The simple tune is one of the most recognizable in American pop culture, mainly heard on children's records. Artie Shaw (vocal by Leo Watson) and Louis Armstrong each made a notable recording of the song, and it was later recorded by Mary Martin and Barbara Hendricks with the Abbey Road Ensemble. The number is spoofed in the modern fairy tale movie *Enchanted* (2007) with the "Happy Working Song."

"Who Am I?" is the upbeat, questioning pop ballad for the young boy Tarzan in the animated made-for-video sequel *Tarzan II* (2005). Phil Collins wrote and sings the number on the soundtrack as Tarzan tries to fit in with different animal groups, meeting with comically disastrous results each time. Tiffany Evans sings the number over the end credits of the movie, and she also made a music video of it.

"Who Better Than Me" is the rocking song of friendship written by Phil Collins for the 2006 Broadway version of *Tarzan*. The livewire teenage ape Terk (Chester Gregory II) sings the bouncy number to the younger Tarzan (Daniel Manche or Alex Rutherford) as Terk swings and frolics in the trees, proudly explaining that there is no one more qualified to teach the little human how to survive in the jungle. Terk and the adult Tarzan (Josh Strickland) reprise the number later in the show when they agree to help each other thwart the evil hunter Clayton.

"Who Killed Cock Robin?" is the mock-operatic title song from the 1935 Silly Symphony film short. Frank Churchill wrote the soaring music and adapted a new lyric from an old English folk song about a robin cruelly murdered. The creepy yet silly ballad is sung by a studio chorus over the opening credits of the movie and is reprised at the trial where the burning question is sung by the judge (voice of Billy Bletcher).

"Who Wants to Live Like That?" is the lighthearted song of philosophy written by Foster Carling and Ken Darby for the partially animated live-action movie *Song of the South* (1946). Uncle Remus (James Baskett) sings the sunny number about how worrying does one no good and that it is best to be like Old Brer Possum and play dead when trouble comes. The song takes the form of an Uncle Remus tale, complete with rustic humor and a sly moral.

"Who Will I Be" is the sunny character song performed by teenager Mitchie Torres (Demi Lovato) over the opening credits of the made-for-television musical *Camp Rock* (2008). As she gets ready for school, Mitchie tries on several outfits and hairdos she thinks might fit her personality for the day. The bubblegum pop number was written by Matthew Gerrard and Robbie Nevil.

"Whoever You Are" is the tuneful saloon song Arabella Flagg (Suzanne Pleshette) sings as she welcomes patrons to the Lucky Nugget Saloon during the Gold Rush days in the film *The Adventures of Bullwhip Griffin* (1967). Richard M. and Robert B. Sherman wrote the rousing number, which invites people of all walks of life from all over the globe to come in and enjoy the entertainment.

"A Whole Bunch of World" is the satirical song about the fifty states written by Cheri Steinkellner, Kevin Quinn, and Randy Petersen for the animated movie *Teacher's Pet* (2004). While the boy Leonard, his mother, and his dog, Spot, drive to Florida in an RV, a soundtrack chorus sings this rapid, country-flavored number about the many wonders of America. As every state is mentioned in the song, a series of silly clichés about America is illustrated with fast and furious panache.

"A Whole New World" is the expansive Oscar-winning song by Alan Menken (music) and Tim Rice (lyric) that celebrates the exhilarating feeling of freedom and blossoming love. In the animated film *Aladdin* (1992), Princess Jasmine (singing voice of Lea Salonga) escapes the confines of the palace and sees the world with Aladdin (Brad Kane), the two of them singing the melodic ballad as they travel across the globe on a flying carpet. Peabo Bryson and Regina Belle recorded a duet version of the song that was sung over the film's final credits and was very popular. Andrew Samonsky and Kaitlin Hopkins also recorded the ballad as a duet, Earl Rose made a distinctive jazz recording of the song in 2000, and Jessica Simpson recorded it in 2005.

"The Whoop-de-Dooper Bounce" is the funny and frantic song about Tigger's most complex and spectacular bounce in the animated film *The Tigger Movie* (2000). Richard M. and Robert B. Sherman wrote the vigorous number, which Tigger (voice of Jim Cummings) sings to the young Roo, demonstrating how the wild bounce is achieved.

"Who's Afraid of the Big Bad Wolf?"—perhaps the most famous song to come from a Disney film short—is the seemingly innocent children's song that became internationally known and took on deeper significance during hard times in the Great Depression. Frank Churchill and Ann Ronell collaborated on the simple but tuneful song, sung by the three pigs as they celebrate their victory over the wolf. It was written for the film short *The Three Little Pigs* (1933), and soon everyone was singing it or whistling it on the street. Americans in the 1930s saw the Depression as the "big bad wolf" and the song was a form of defiance against the difficulties of the day. The number was used in at least three subsequent Little Pigs cartoons, including the Silly Symphony shorts *The Big Bad Wolf* (1934), *Three Little Wolves* (1936) and *The Practical Pig* (1939). The song was translated into several foreign languages, becoming popular around the world for the same reasons it caught on in the United States. In Russia it was so successful that it was turned into a popular children's book that claimed the tune was based on an old Russian folk song. Early successful recordings of the ditty were made by Ethel Shutta, Ben Bernie, and Harry Reser, with later discs by such varied artists as Wendy and the Wombats, Barbra Streisand, Jean Sablon (in French), Burl Ives, the Mormon Tabernacle Choir, the group B5, Massimo Farao, and LL Cool J. It can also be heard in the movies *Babes in Toyland* (1934), *Bottoms Up* (1934), and *Ship Cafe* (1935). The song inspired the punning title for Edward Albee's play *Who's Afraid of Virginia Woolf?* (1962).

"Why Not?" is the up-tempo pop song about taking chances written by Charlie Midnight and Matthew Gerrard for *The Lizzie McGuire Movie* (2003), based on the popular television series. Lizzie (Hilary Duff) sings the fervent number about opening your eyes and looking for new aspects of life. Duff's recording of the song was popular and she also made a music video of it.

"Why Should I Worry?" is the driving "I am" song by Dan Hartman and Charlie Midnight for the streetwise canine Dodger (voice of Billy Joel) in the animated movie version of *Oliver Twist*, titled *Oliver & Company* (1988). The confident dog sings the pulsating rock song to the young feline Oliver as he shows him how to survive in New York City using street savvy.

"W-I-L-D" is the jumping doo-wop number written by Lorraine Feather and Paul Grabowsky for the animated video sequel *The Jungle Book 2* (2003). Baloo the Bear (voice of John Goodman) entertains the man-cub Mowgli and a gathering of jungle creatures with this jiving number about the animal-like beat inside of all of us that gives us music. Soon all the animals join in the song and dance, spelling out the world "wild" in the lyric and also spelling out the letters with their bodies like cheerleaders at a football game.

"Will I Ever See Her Again?" is the questioning ballad Jay Blackton (music) and Joe Cook (lyric) wrote for the 1979 Radio City Music Hall stage version of *Snow White and the Seven Dwarfs* in order to develop the character of Prince Charming (Richard Bowne). Failing to find the mysterious girl he met at the wishing well and fell in love with, the prince sings this flowing song of wonder and regret. The stage production was taped and broadcast on pay TV in 1980 and on the Disney Channel in 1987 as *Snow White Live*.

"Will the Sun Ever Shine Again?" is the woeful lament about hard times written by Alan Menken (music) and Glenn Slater (lyric) for the animated movie *Home on the Range* (2004). Faced with bankruptcy and worried that she will lose her farm, the steadfast Pearl puts her animals to bed in the barn, perhaps for the last time, while Bonnie Raitt sings the gentle folk song on the soundtrack. The number manages to be melodic and pleasing even as it is filled with sorrow and worry. Kaitlin Hopkins made a recording of the song in 2005.

"Windsong" is the enthralling African song written by James Horner (music) and Will Jennings (lyric) for the film remake *Mighty Joe Young* (1998). A choir, arranged and directed by Lebo M, sings the haunting tribal song in Swahili, encouraging one to sing and the wind will answer back.

"The Winner Song," by Robert Lopez and Kristen Anderson-Lopez, is the warm exclamation of victory sung in the 2011 animated film *Winnie the Pooh*. When Eeyore (voice of Bud Luckey) loses his tail, the creatures of the Hundred Acre Wood have a contest to see who can come up with the best replacement. Each time someone makes a suggestion, the other characters sing the ditty while the new solution is implemented, only to find that it doesn't work, bringing the song to a halt. The winner of the contest will receive a pot of honey and this makes Pooh (Jim Cummings) especially invested in coming up with an acceptable solution. The song is reprised by Eeyore when he finally decides that a boat anchor is the best choice of items to pin to his derriere, a plan which also ends in disaster. The song is reprised again by all the animals and Christopher Robin when Pooh finds Eeyore's missing tail and the bear is presented with the grand prize.

"Winnie the Pooh" is the narrative ballad that Richard M. and Robert B. Sherman wrote for the opening of *Winnie the Pooh and the Honey Tree* (1966), the first of many animated works featuring the famous bear and other characters created by A. A. Milne. Sung by the Disney Studio Chorus, the song tells about the colorful citizens of the Hundred Acre Wood where the boy Christopher Robin spends his playtime. The song has a warm and comforting quality and the lyric introduces the donkey Eeyore, Kanga and Roo (a mother kangaroo and her joey), Rabbit, Owl, and, of course, the title character. The number was immediately memorable and became the theme song for many subsequent films, both shorts and features, based on the Pooh stories. For example, Carly Simon and Ben Taylor sing it on the soundtrack during the opening credits of the animated film *Piglet's Big Movie* (2003). Also, "Winnie the Pooh," with an altered lyric that includes Tigger the Tiger, is performed by Zooey Deschanel on the soundtrack of the animated film *Winnie the Pooh* (2011).

"The Wishing Song" is the merry, Irish-flavored ditty from the film *Darby O'Gill and the Little People* (1959) that uses silly rhymes and a series of outlandish wishes, all of it bordering on the nonsensical. The number, by Oliver Wallace (music) and Lawrence E. Watkin (lyric), is sung by the Irish scamp Darby (Albert Sharpe) and King Brian (Jimmy O'Dea) of the leprechauns as Darby tries to get the little monarch drunk so he won't notice the coming of dawn, when he loses all his magical powers. The song is also a contest number, the two men trying to out-rhyme each other and enjoying the challenge.

"The Witch Is in the House" is the rocking "I am" song for the Wicked Witch of the West, played by Miss Piggy (voice of Eric Jacobson), in the television movie *The Muppets' Wizard of Oz* (2005). The Witch taunts Dorothy and her friends, singing that she is the only singing star in the land of Oz, and she is backed by Dr. Teeth and his band Electric Mayhem. The rollicking number was written by Steve L. Hayes, Debra Frank, Michael Giacchino, Jeannie Lurie, and Adam Cohen.

"With a Few Good Friends" is the catchy folk-like song written by Carly Simon for the animated film *Piglet's Big Movie* (2003). The rhythmic number, about gathering friends to help build a house in which to entertain everyone, is first heard on the soundtrack sung by Simon with Ben and Sally Taylor. Later in the movie it is reprised by Winnie the Pooh (voice of Jim Cummings), Tigger (also Cummings), Piglet (John Fiedler), Eeyore (Peter

Cullen), and Christopher Robin (Kath Soucie). At the end of the movie, Simon is seen singing the song in live-action footage in between sections of the final credits.

"With a Flair" is the droll song about style written by Richard M. and Robert B. Sherman for the movie fantasy *Bedknobs and Broomsticks* (1971). The charlatan magician Professor Emelius Brown (David Tomlinson) performs his feeble magic tricks for passersby on the street, singing that he may be a fake but he knows how to dazzle audiences with his glittering style.

"With a Smile and a Song" is the buoyant song of optimism for Snow White (voice of Adriana Caselotti) written by Frank Churchill (music) and Larry Morey (lyric) for the animated film *Snow White and the Seven Dwarfs* (1937). After a frightening night in the forest, Snow White awakes and sings the flowing number to her animal friends about her philosophy

The tuneful *Cinderella* (1950) marked an important turning point for Walt Disney and his studio. It was the first full-fledged animated feature after the lean years during and following the war. It was also the first time Disney hired Tin Pan Alley and Broadway songwriters in order to give his scores a more Broadway sound. Pictured is the catchy "The Work Song" by Mack David, Jerry Livingston, and Al Hoffman, which the mice sing as they sew Cinderella's ball gown. (Walt Disney/Photofest)

for happiness. Among the artists to record the cheerful song over the decades are Mary Martin, Doris Day, Barbara Cook, and Barbara Hendricks and the Abbey Road Ensemble.

"Without You" is the heartfelt torch song Andy Russell sings on the soundtrack of the animated movie anthology *Make Mine Music* (1946). The somber German ballad "Bis ans Ende der Welt," by Osvaldo Farrés (music) and Ralph Maria Siegel (lyric), was given a smooth English lyric by Ray Gilbert for the film. The sorrowful lover is never seen in the sequence, but instead a letter and views of nature are illustrated to give the mood of the piece, the raindrops distorting the picture at times, as if tears were obstructing the view. Russell made a recording of the ballad and it found success.

"Without You," by Mike McGarity, Julia Michaels, and Joleen Belle, is the lively techno-pop theme for the Disney Channel series *Austin & Ally* (2011). The sitcom follows two teenagers: one an outgoing guy named Austin (Ross Lynch) who wants to be a singer, and the other a shy, aspiring songwriter named Ally (Laura Marano) who hopes to find success in the professional music business. Soon, the two realize they can go much further as a team, and the theme song (performed by series star Lynch) is testament to their synergy.

"The Wonderful Thing about Tiggers" is the eccentric, boastful song written by Richard M. and Robert B. Sherman for the Oscar-winning film short *Winnie the Pooh and the Blustery Day* (1968). Tigger (voice of Paul Winchell), a toy tiger who likes to bounce, enters the Hundred Acre Wood singing this less-than-humble tribute to himself, celebrating being who he is because he's the only one of his kind. The melody is as full of bounce as the character, and the lyrics are witty, full of nonsensical internal rhyme and joyous exclamations. The number became Tigger's personal theme song, popping up in subsequent Winnie the Pooh shorts, such as *Winnie the Pooh and Tigger Too!* (1974), and in the feature film *The Tigger Movie* (2000), where Tigger (Jim Cummings) reprises the number at the beginning of the movie.

"The Wonderful World of Color" is the soaring theme song for the television series *Walt Disney's Wonderful World of Color*, which premiered on NBC in 1961. Richard M. and Robert B. Sherman wrote the resplendent number, sung by a studio chorus, which welcomes viewers to a television world of color as fireworks explode around the castle at Disneyland. Most viewers watching the new show did not have color TV sets, but even in black and white the graphics were impressive, and audiences could imagine what it must look like in color. Some cultural historians cite this program as a major reason many Americans purchased their first color television sets in the 1960s, which must have pleased the show's sponsor, the television manufacturer RCA.

"Woody's Roundup" is the pastiche cowboy song written by Randy Newman for the movie sequel *Toy Story 2* (1999). When Woody (voice of Tom Hanks) discovers all the memorabilia from his 1950s television show, it includes a period turntable that plays a 78 record with the show's theme song. The group Riders in the Sky sing the western-flavored number, complete with cowboy yodeling, on the soundtrack while Woody and the doll cowgirl Jessie (Joan Cusack) dance on the revolving record. The full song is reprised during the final credits of the movie.

"The Work Song" is the unforgettable charm song from the animated film *Cinderella* (1950), remembered as much for its funny mouse voices as for its catchy melody. Mack David, Jerry Livingston, and Al Hoffman wrote the effervescent number, during which the mice join in with the birds to doctor up an old dress so that Cinderella can wear it to the ball. The chorus of workers is led by the mice Gus and Jaq (both voiced by James MacDonald), but soon all the critters are listing the things that must be done, giving directions, and celebrating the ways in which they can help their friend Cinderella, whom they call "Cinder-elly," as the song is sometimes listed. The little ditty was so popular that it made the top ten on radio's *Your Hit Parade*.

"Work This Out" is the banging and throbbing production number from the television sequel *High School Musical 2* (2007), a rhythmic dance number inspired by the Off-Broadway musical *Stomp*, in which every object becomes a drum. The teenage workers at a ritzy country club find their summer job requires a great deal of kowtowing to the owners' bratty daughter, Sharpay, so, while working in the kitchen, they break out in frustration with this energetic number in which everyone bangs on pots, pans, water goblets, and every surface available as they sing and dance. Randy Petersen and Kevin Quinn wrote the vivacious number about working out your frustration.

"The Workshop Song" is the perky, rhythmic ditty written by George Bruns (music) and Mel Leven (lyric) for the 1961 screen version of *Babes in Toyland*, adapting a song from the original 1903 Victor Herbert operetta.

The Toymaker (Ed Wynn) is joined by Tom Piper (Tommy Sands), Mary Quite Contrary (Annette Funicello), and a workshop full of children in singing the work song, which has a steady beat and emphasizes the importance of time in making all the toys for Christmas.

"The World Above" is the song of wonderment written by Alan Menken (music) and Glenn Slater (lyric) for the 2008 Broadway version of *The Little Mermaid*. The mermaid princess Ariel (Sierra Boggess) swims to the surface and relishes being under a blue sky, feeling that she belongs in this strange other world more than her own. Later in the show the song is reprised by her father, King Triton (Norm Lewis), as he scolds Ariel for her interest in the human world.

"The World Don't Bother Me None" is the driving folk-rock song about the diversity of Americans written by John Mellencamp for the documentary film *America's Heart and Soul* (2004). Mellencamp sings the number, which recognizes the problems still to be solved in the nation but looks at everyday people as encouragement to believe in the future. The song is sung over the opening credits showing a montage of ordinary Americans, the subject of the documentary.

"The World Is Looking Up to You" is the jovial, upbeat character song written by Randy Rogel for the animated video sequel *Cinderella II: Dreams Come True* (2002). Wishing to be more helpful to his friend Cinderella, the mouse Jaq (voice of Rob Paulsen) gets the Fairy Godmother to turn him into a human, and he celebrates the power of his new form while this encouraging song is sung by Brooke Allison on the soundtrack.

"The World Owes Me a Living" is the droll folk-like song about playing today and working tomorrow that Leigh Harline (music) and Larry Morey (lyric) wrote for the Silly Symphony movie short *The Grasshopper and the Ants* (1934). While all the ants are busy preparing for winter, their friend the Grasshopper (voice of Pinto Colvig) fiddles away his time and sings this catchy ditty about a lazy lifestyle. When winter comes, the ants rescue the Grasshopper from starvation and cold and he changes his tune, entertaining his friends by singing the song with a revised lyric that shows he has learned his lesson.

"The World Will Know" is the musical battle cry Alan Menken (music) and Jack Feldman (lyric) wrote for the period film *Newsies* (1992). When the New York newspaper the *World* raises its price for the newsboys who sell it on street corners, the "newsie" Jack Kelly (Christian Bale) tries to organize the boys into a union with this tenacious call to arms, arguing that they ought to fight for the rights they deserve. The song is reprised at the climax of the film when child laborers from all over the city show up at the strike to show their support.

"World without Fences" is the driving "I am" song for the young canine hero in the animated video sequel *Lady and the Tramp II: Scamp's Adventure* (2001). Melissa Manchester and Norman Gimbel wrote the passionate song of yearning sung by the puppy Scamp (singing voice of Roger Bart) who has been chained up in the backyard and aches for a life in the world outside his yard.

"The World's Greatest Criminal Mind" is the waltzing tribute to the villain, the rat Professor Ratigan (voice of Vincent Price), in the animated adventure movie *The Great Mouse Detective* (1986). Ratigan sings to his henchmen that all his glorious crimes of the past are nothing compared to the caper he is planning, and his mouse henchmen celebrate the plot with this cheerful ditty about their boss, the world's finest villain. The music hall–like number was written by Henry Mancini (music), Larry Grossman, and Ellen Fitzhugh (lyric).

"Wouldn't Change a Thing" is the pop-rock love song introduced in the made-for-TV film *Camp Rock 2: The Final Jam* (2010). When teenagers Mitchie (Demi Lovato) and Shane (Joe Jonas) find themselves in an argument about their priorities, they sing this duet about how different they are, admitting they wouldn't change each other because their differences are what make their relationship special. The powerful duet was written by Adam Anders, Nikki Hassman, and Peer Astrom.

"Wringle Wrangle" is the square dance number written by Stan Jones for the adventure film *Westward Ho, the Wagons!* (1956). After the pioneers on the Oregon Trail put their wagons in a circle for the night, they dance by the light of the campfire to this western hoedown number with a happy nonsense lyric.

"Written in the Stars," written by Elton John (music) and Tim Rice (lyric), is the moving song of parting for the two lovers in the Broadway musical *Aida* (2000). The Nubian slave Aida (Heather Headley) convinces the

Egyptian captain Radames (Adam Pascal) to forget her and go ahead with his wedding to the princess Amneris, arguing that their future is not fated to survive. Elton John recorded the number with LeAnn Rimes before the musical opened on Broadway, and later versions were recorded by Rhonda Vincent and Tom Michael.

"Wunderkind" is the sad song of longing written by Alanis Morissette for the fantasy film *The Chronicles of Narnia: The Lion, the Witch and the Wardrobe* (2005). The haunting number takes the point of view of the young Lucy Pevensie (Georgie Henley) who is a "wunderkind," German for a child prodigy. The lyric questions if she is able to meet the formidable task set before her: to overcome obstacles and become one of the queens of Narnia. Morissette sings the ballad over the closing credits of the film, saying the title word with an English pronunciation rather than the German one.

"Wynken, Blynken and Nod" is the operetta-like title song from the 1938 Silly Symphony movie short based on the poem of the same name by Eugene Field. An unidentified solo female voice is heard singing the dreamy song as the three tots of the title travel through the sky in their magic shoe, navigating the skies and fishing for starfish. Leigh Harline wrote the flowing music and the magical lyric, inspired by the first few stanzas of Field's poem.

"Yaller, Yaller Gold" is the rustic folk song by George Bruns (music) and Tom W. Blackburn (lyric) from *Davy Crockett and the River Pirates* (1956) that compares the yellow hair of a pretty girl to shiny gold. The song is first sung by an old peddler in a tavern, then is reprised by a studio chorus on the soundtrack while Davy Crockett (Fess Parker) and his cohorts pretend to transport gold as a decoy to catch some river pirates.

"Yankee Doodle Spirit" is the patriotic march song Oliver Wallace wrote for the wartime film short *The New Spirit* (1942), a Donald Duck cartoon that encouraged Americans to pay their taxes on time to help the war effort. Cliff Edwards sings the cheerful song celebrating the spirit of America over the credits of the clever propaganda film.

"Yo Ho! (A Pirate's Life for Me)" is the simple, repetitive, and easily recalled theme song for the theme park attraction Pirates of the Caribbean, which opened at Disneyland in 1967 and was later re-created at the other parks. George Bruns (music) and Xavier Attencio (lyric) wrote the sea chantey, a cheerful drinking song filled with boasting about looting and pillaging, that is heard throughout the theme park ride. The lusty but silly recording by an all-male chorus is as memorable as the attraction itself. The Jonas Brothers recorded the number in 2006. The song can be heard briefly in the feature film *Pirates of the Caribbean: The Curse of the Black Pearl* (2003) and its sequels.

"Yodel-Adle-Eedle-Idle-Oo" is the silly western yodeling number for the villain Alameda Slim (voice of Randy Quaid), also known as Mr. Y. O'Del, in the animated film *Home on the Range* (2004). Alan Menken (music) and Glenn Slater (lyric) wrote the comic number, filled with vigorous yodeling (provided by Randy Erwin and Kerry Christensen) and sly lyrics about Slim's ample girth. The cattle rustler Alameda sings it to hypnotize cows, making it easier to lead them to his hideaway in the mountains. Slim's sidekicks, the witless Willie Brothers (David Burnham, Jason Graae, and Gregory Jbara), join in singing the jolly number.

"You Are the Music in Me" is the recurring pop love song by Jamie Houston that is used throughout the television sequel *High School Musical 2* (2007). The gentle number, about music starting when you are near the one you love, is first played on the piano by teenage composer Kelsi Nielsen (Olesya Rulin), who has written the song for sweethearts Troy (Zac Efron) and Gabriella (Vanessa Anne Hudgens) to sing at the summer talent show. The couple then gives it a quiet and heartfelt rendition. The song is reprised at a faster and less sincere tempo by the drama queen Sharpay (Ashley Tisdale), who steals the song (and Troy) for her own use. Near the

The surprise television hit *High School Musical* (2006) not only became a phenomenon, spawning equally popular sequels and stage productions, but it began a trend for teen musicals on screen. Pictured (left to right) in the foreground are Ashley Tisdale, Zac Efron, Vanessa Anne Hudgens, and Lucas Grabeel, who became overnight stars after the first broadcast. (Walt Disney/Photofest)

end of the film, the ballad is sung again by Troy and Gabriella as they are reunited after being separated by Sharpay.

"You Belong to My Heart" is the hit ballad that Mexican singing star Dora Luz sings to Donald Duck in the part-animation, part-live-action travel film *The Three Caballeros* (1944). The alluring serenade is based on the Mexican song "Solamente Una Vez," by Augustin Lara, and was given an English lyric by Ray Gilbert for the movie. The ballad immediately caught on and has been frequently recorded, the most popular disc being one by Bing Crosby with Xavier Cugat's Orchestra. Paula Kelly and the Modernaires also recorded it, Andy Russell made versions in English and Spanish, years later Engelbert Humperdinck had a top-selling version of the number, and Spanish opera singer José Carreras also made a disc. The song is featured in the Disney short *Pluto's Blue Note* (1947), Tito Guizar sings it in the Roy Rogers movie *The Gay Ranchero* (1948), and Ezio Pinza sings it in his film debut in *Mr. Imperium* (1951).

"You Can Always Be Number One" is the pop anthem by Dale Gonyea about enjoying a sport for the fun of it and making even the poorest athlete feel good about the game. The number was written as a theme song to be played on the soundtrack of a series of shorts featuring Goofy bungling all sorts of athletics. The fun list song, sometimes titled "Sport Goofy Theme," debuted on the 1983 Disney album *Mickey Mouse Splashdance*, where it was performed by Lora Mumford of the Disney rock band Halyx.

"You Can Do It" is the insistent rhythm number written by Stanley A. Smith and Jilien Manges for the film comedy *Jungle 2 Jungle* (1997), about teenager Mimi-Siku (Sam Huntington), raised in the Venezuelan jungle, going to New York City with his dad (Tim Allen). In Manhattan, Mimi-Siku comes across a street band, complete with steel drums, and the music so enthralls the teen that he uses it to teach his uptight father how to relax and dance. The Sha Shees provided the vocals for the pulsating number.

"You Can Fly, You Can Fly, You Can Fly" is the exhilarating song by Sammy Fain (music) and Sammy Cahn (lyric) that is used so effectively in the animated movie *Peter Pan* (1953). After Peter (voice of Bobby Driscoll) sprinkles the fairy dust on them, Wendy (Kathryn Beaumont), Michael (Paul Collins), and John (Tommy Luske) rhythmically repeat the lyric that Peter sings. Once the foursome fly out the window and over Victorian London, a chorus is heard singing the joyous number on the soundtrack. The song is reprised at the end of the movie. The number is also used in the Peter Pan's Flight attraction at Disneyland and Disney World. A recording was made by David Anderson, Anne Lloyd, Mitch Miller, and Dan Ocko and the Sandpipers, a disc was made by Joe Reisman and His Orchestra, Susan Egan made a standout recording of the song in 1996, and there was also a playful version by Andrew Samonsky and Ashley Brown in 2005 with a quartet comprised of Meredith Inglesby, Andy Karl, Tyler Maynard, and Keewa Nurullah. The song was also heard in the made-for-video film *Tinker Bell* (2008).

"You Have It All" is the turbulent song sung by King Saul (Martin Vidnovic) in the Broadway concert-pageant *King David* (1997). Jonathan (Roger Bart) hints to the king that the masses have stopped following him and instead are drawn to the young David (Marcus Lovett). The king responds with this bitter number about the young upstart, written by Alan Menken (music) and Tim Rice (lyric).

"You Know I Will" is the eager pop-folk song by Gordon Kennedy that is used to illustrate the friendship between the canine Copper and the fox Tod in the made-for-video animated sequel *The Fox and the Hound 2* (2006). Lucas Grabeel sings the number on the soundtrack, proudly proclaiming that two friends can take on the world as long as they can depend on each other.

"You'll Always Find Your Way Back Home" is the song of self-acceptance that is the grand finale of *Hannah Montana: The Movie* (2009). The jubilant ditty, performed by Miley Cyrus as Hannah Montana, tells us that you can do all kinds of things to change your appearance and personality but, in the end, you always have to be true to yourself. The life-affirming number was written by Taylor Swift and Martin Johnson.

"You'll Be in My Heart" is the Oscar-winning up-tempo ballad by Phil Collins from the animated film *Tarzan* (1999). The gorilla Kala (voice of Glenn Close) sings the tender song, about how love is a bond that cannot be broken, to the infant Tarzan, and the number is picked up by Collins on the soundtrack. In the 2006 Broadway version of *Tarzan*, Merle Dandridge played Kala and sang the song with the ensemble. The adult Tarzan (Josh Strickland) and Kala reprise the number later in the show when he decides to join the human world. Collins's recording of the ballad was very popular, and it was also recorded by Teddy Geiger, Steve Tyrell,

Drew Seeley, Michael Crawford, Usher Raymond, and, in a duet version, Andrew Samonsky with Ashley Brown.

"Your Crowning Glory" is the disco-flavored number written by Larry Grossman (music) and Lorraine Feather (lyric) for the film sequel *The Princess Diaries 2: Royal Engagement* (2004). Queen Clarissa (Julie Andrews) sings the tribute to her granddaughter Mia (Anne Hathaway) at a pajama party, stating that Mia's heart of gold will be the crowning glory of her reign. Mia's friend Asana (Raven-Symoné) joins the queen in the song, and soon all the girls are dancing to it.

"Your Heart Will Lead You Home" is the memorable folk song Kenny Loggins wrote with Richard M. and Robert B. Sherman for the animated film *The Tigger Movie* (2000). Over the closing credits of the movie, Loggins and a chorus sing the number, about thinking of your friends so you will always feel like you are home. The Loggins recording enjoyed some popularity, and versions were made by Michael Crawford in 2001 and Natalie Toro in 2003.

"Your Mother and Mine" is the lilting lullaby Wendy (voice of Kathryn Beaumont) sings to the Lost Boys in the animated fantasy movie *Peter Pan* (1953). Sammy Fain (music) and Sammy Cahn (lyric) wrote the tender number about a mother's love, which Wendy sings inside Peter's hideout while Captain Hook and the pirates quietly surround them. The song makes her brothers Michael and John homesick, while outside the pirate Smee weeps as he remembers his own mother. Doris Day made a distinctive recording of the ballad with Paul Weston's Orchestra.

"You're an Ocean" is the driving rock song that Fastball wrote and sang on the soundtrack of the television movie *Motocrossed* (2001). During the opening credits for the film about teen motorcycle riders, Fastball sings about a girl whose emotions are so stormy and wild she might as well be an ocean unto herself.

"You're My Favorite Song" is the romantic duet sung by Mitchie (Demi Lovato) and Nate (Joe Jonas) as they share a day of fun together in *Camp Rock 2: The Final Jam*, the 2010 TV-movie sequel to *Camp Rock*. The sugary song, performed as a make up after a squabble between the two teens, was composed by Jeannie Lurie, Aris Archontis, and Chen Neeman. It was sung during a montage of Mitchie and Nate paddling a boat around the lake.

"You're Nothin' but a Nothin'" is the taunting number written by Frank Churchill and Bert Lewis for the Silly Symphony film short *The Flying Mouse* (1934). When a mouse is magically given the power to fly, he finds that he is rejected by both the birds and the other mice and is mocked by a bunch of bats, who sing this creepy song belittling the poor fellow. The memorable little ditty was published and enjoyed some popularity for a time.

"You're Only Second Rate" is the daffy old-time duet two genies sing in the made-for-video animated film *The Return of Jafar* (1994). Randy Petersen and Kevin Quinn wrote the vaudeville-like number for the wizard-turned-genie Jafar (voice of Jonathan Freeman) and the good Genie (Dan Castellaneta) as they list their credentials and argue over who is better.

"You've Got a Friend in Me" is the Oscar-nominated song Randy Newman wrote for *Toy Story* (1995), the first fully computer-generated animated feature film. Over the opening credits of the movie, Newman sings the bluesy number about the power of friendship as the boy Andy plays with his favorite toy, the cowboy Woody. A duet version by Newman and Lyle Lovett is heard during the end credits of the film. The song is reprised by the toy penguin Wheezy (Robert Goulet) at the end of the movie sequel *Toy Story 2* (1999), and Tom Hanks is heard singing it during the final credits of that film. A playful duet version of the song was recorded by Brian Sutherland and Kaitlin Hopkins, as well as a duo version by Steve Tyrell and Dr. John.

Z

"The Zeke and Luther Theme" is the frantic theme song for the goofy Disney sitcom *Zeke and Luther* (2009). The show follows the title characters, who are two teenagers with very little on their mind other than what their next great skateboard trick will be. The song, which is basically a meandering map of a teenager's mind and its ever-changing focus, is performed by series stars Hutch Dano, Daniel Curtis Lee, and Adam Hicks. The purposely directionless piece features music and lyrics by Christopher Brady and David Howard.

"Zero to Hero" is the pulsating mock rhythm-and-blues song by Alan Menken (music) and David Zippel (lyric) that is used to chronicle the young athlete's rise to fame in the animated movie *Hercules* (1997). The six Greek Muses (voices of Lilias White, Tawatha Agee, Cheryl Freeman, La Chanze, Roz Ryan, and Vanessa Thomas) sing the comic tribute filled with anachronistic slang, outrageous puns, and a slick Motown sound.

"Zip-a-Dee-Doo-Dah" is the Oscar-winning song of contentment by Allie Wrubel (music) and Ray Gilbert (lyric) that is featured in the groundbreaking film *Song of the South* (1946), which mixed animation and live action so effectively. As storyteller Uncle Remus (James Baskett) begins to relate the first story to the youth Johnny (Bobby Driscoll), the movie moves into animation for the first time with a live-action Uncle Remus walking along a road singing to and being joined by cartoon animals. At the end of the film, Johnny and Ginny (Luana Patten) reprise the happy number with a soundtrack chorus as they walk into the sunset. While the song has a lazy Southern flavor to it, the number moves along both musically and lyrically. Johnny Mercer's recording with the Pied Pipers was a best seller, and there were also successful records by Sammy Kaye and His Orchestra and the Modernaires with Paula Kelly. The song remained popular in the 1950s because it was heard on the Disney television show, then it was on the charts again in 1962 with a best-selling record by Bob B. Sox and the Blue Jeans. A hip version by Ric Ocasek in the 1990s was also a hit, and in 2000 Earl Rose made a jazz rendition of the number. Louis Armstrong, Bing Crosby, Jennifer Warnes, Miley Cyrus, Aly & AJ, Barbara Hendricks and the Abbey Road Ensemble, and Stevie Brock are among the other artists to record the song.

"Zorro" is the rousing theme song for the 1957 television series *Zorro*, presented on the weekly *Disneyland* show, and a memorable ballad that became very familiar to viewers during the two years the series ran. George Bruns (music) and Norman Foster (lyric) wrote the narrative number that celebrated the Robin Hood–like swordsman who fights the wealthy and powerful in Latin America. A male chorus sings the catchy song while a montage shows the masked Zorro riding through the night and fighting his adversaries, leaving his "Z" mark everywhere he goes. The ballad is also used in the film *The Sign of Zorro* (1958), which is a compilation of eight of the television episodes. The song is sometimes listed as the "Theme from *Zorro*."

APPENDIX A: ALTERNATE SONG TITLES

Song titles vary from the published sheet music to the record label to the listing in a playbill to a movie or television show's screen credits. Some songs have even been published over the years with different song titles. The following are alternate titles for some of the songs discussed in the entries. The alternate title is followed by the title used in this book.

The Ark Brought into Jerusalem	Entry into Jerusalem
The Ballad of John Colter	John Colter
The *Big Red* Theme	Mon Amour Perdu
Cal-I-For-Nee Gold	California Gold
The Caterpillar Song	A-E-I-O-U
Christmas Scat	One More Sleep Till Christmas
Cinder-elly	The Work Song
Come Little Children	Sarah's Theme
The Dwarfs' Marching Song	Heigh-Ho
The Dwarfs' Washing Song	Bluddle-Uddle-Um-Dum
The Elephant Song	Colonel Hathi's March
Emotional Commotion	The Motion Waltz
Endless Sky	Athena's Song
Expotition March	Sing Ho for the Life of a Bear
Find My Way	Leaving Home
He Lives in You	They Live in You

The Heave Ho Song	The Pooh Will Soon Be Free
Hi-Ho	Heigh-Ho
I Bring You a Song	Looking for Romance
I Gotta Get Outa Kansas	Kansas
I'm Just a Little Black Rain Cloud	A Little Black Rain Cloud
Isn't This a Silly Song?	The Dwarfs' Yodel Song
Jack's Obsession	Something's Up with Jack
Jim's Theme	I'm Still Here
Kill the Beast	The Mob Song
The Kim Possible Song	Call Me, Beep Me
The Land of the Old Countree	Savage Sam and Me
Love Theme from *Pocahontas*	If I Never Knew You
Lullaby of the Wildwood	And Now to Sleep
Madellaine's Love Song	I'm Gonna Love You
The Magic Song	Bibbidi-Bobbidi-Boo
March of the Lost Boys	Following the Leader
The Merrily Song	Merrily on Our Way
The Mickey Mouse Club Theme	The Mickey Mouse Club March
The Moon Pilot Song	Seven Moons of Beta-Lyrae
Now Is the Time	The Best Time of Your Life
Nowhere in Particular	Merrily on Our Way
Pavement Artist	Chim Chim Cher-ee
The Piglet Song	If I Wasn't So Small
Put It Together	Bibbidi-Bobbidi-Boo
Round-Up Rodeo	Talent Round-Up Day
Send Me on My Way	On My Way
The Silly Song	The Dwarfs' Yodel Song
Sing, Sweet Nightingale	Oh Sing, Sweet Nightingale
Sing to the Song of Life	The Song of Life
Spin It!	TaleSpin Theme
Sport Goofy Theme	You Can Always Be Number One
Stoutness Exercise	Up, Down, Touch the Ground
Tee Dum–Tee Dee	Following the Leader
Theme from *Brother Bear*	No Way Out
Theme from *Zorro*	Zorro
This Is the Night	Bella Notte
Today Is Tuesday	Guest Star Day
The Vulture Song	That's What Friends Are For
The Washing Song	Bluddle-Uddle-Um-Dum
Watercolor of Brazil	Brazil

Welcome to Our Family	Welcome
What Do You Do?	In the Name of the Hundred Acre Wood
When Love Is Found	When Love Is Gone
When You Find Yourself	Find Yourself
Who Will Rescue Me?	The Journey
You Ain't Home on the Range	Home on the Range
You Ain't Never Had a Friend Like Me	Friend Like Me
Zoom Zoom Zoom	Super Nova Girl

APPENDIX B: SONGWRITERS DIRECTORY

Following the name of each songwriter is a list of productions or attractions to which the composer and/or lyricist contributed songs included in this book.

Adams, Bryan
  The Three Musketeers
Abbott, Michael
  *Pooh's Grand Adventure: The
    Search for Christopher Robin*
de Abreu, Zequinha
  Saludos Amigos
Adair, John
  The Suite Life of Zack and Cody
  Wizards of Waverly Place
Adair, Tom
  Paul Bunyan
  The Mickey Mouse Club
  Sleeping Beauty
  The Rainbow Road to Oz
  Third Man on the Mountain
Alexander, Jessi
  Hannah Montana: The Movie

Alkenas, Johan
  Pair of Kings
Allan, Mitch
  Camp Rock 2: The Final Jam
Anders, Adam
  Camp Rock
  Camp Rock 2: The Final Jam
  Hannah Montana: The Movie
  *High School Musical 3: Senior
    Year*
Anders, Nikki
  Hannah Montana: The Movie
Anderson, Lyrica
  Camp Rock 2: The Final Jam
Archontis, Aris
  Camp Rock 2: The Final Jam
  Good Luck Charlie
  The Muppets

Armato, Antonina
  Camp Rock
  Camp Rock 2: The Final Jam
  High School Musical 2
Ashman, Howard
  Aladdin
  Beauty and the Beast
  The Little Mermaid
  Oliver & Company
Astrom, Peer
  Camp Rock 2: The Final Jam
Attencio, Xavier
  Country Bear Jamboree
  The Haunted Mansion
  Pirates of the Caribbean
Baker, Buddy
  The Haunted Mansion
  The Rainbow Road to Oz
  Swamp Fox
Ballard, Glen
  Hannah Montana: The Movie
Barnes, Rawanna M.
  The Cheetah Girls
Baron, Phillip
  Dumbo's Circus
Barroso, Ary
  Saludos Amigos
  The Three Caballeros
Belland, Bruce
  The Barefoot Executive
  The Boatniks
  *The Computer Wore Tennis
    Shoes*
Belle, Joleen
  Austin & Ally
Benenate, Bridget
  Cinderella III: A Twist in Time
Benenate, Lisa
  Zenon: Z3

Benjamin, Bennie
  Fun and Fancy Free
  Melody Time
Bennett, Chico
  The Lizzie McGuire Movie
Bettis, John
  Empty Nest
  Nurses
Black, Don
  *Beauty and the Beast: The
    Enchanted Christmas*
Blackburn, Tom
  *Davy Crockett and the River
    Pirates*
  *Davy Crockett, King of the Wild
    Frontier*
  Johnny Tremain
  Westward Ho, the Wagons!
Blackton, Jay
  *Snow White and the Seven
    Dwarfs*
Blondheim, George
  Life-Size
Bluth, Don
  The Small One
Bowling for Soup
  Phineas and Ferb
Bradford, Michael
  *Cinderella II: Dreams Come
    True*
Brady, Christopher
  Zeke and Luther
Breer, Sabelle
  *Zenon: Girl of the 21st
    Century*
Bremers, Beverly
  Mousercise
Brooke, Jonatha
  Return to Never Land

Brunner, Robert F.
  The Barefoot Executive
  The Boatniks
  *The Computer Wore Tennis
    Shoes*
  The Strongest Man in the World
Bruns, George
  *The Adventures of Bullwhip
    Griffin*
  Babes in Toyland
  *Davy Crockett and the River
    Pirates*
  *Davy Crockett, King of the Wild
    Frontier*
  The Fighting Prince of Donegal
  Goliath II
  In the Bag
  Johnny Tremain
  The Mickey Mouse Club
  Paul Bunyan
  Perri
  Pirates of the Caribbean
  Robin Hood
  The Saga of Andy Burnett
  The Saga of Windwagon Smith
  Sleeping Beauty
  Tonka
  Westward Ho, the Wagons!
  Zorro
Buckley, Paul
  Smart Guy
Bunch, Tyler
  Bear in the Big Blue House
Burke, Sonny
  Adventures in Music: Melody
  Lady and the Tramp
  Toot, Whistle, Plunk and Boom
Butler, Daws
  In the Bag

Butron, Lukas McGuire
  *Confessions of a Teenage Drama
    Queen*
Cahn, Sammy
  Peter Pan
Cameron, Al
  Make Mine Music
Canute, Chris
  *The Hunchback of Notre Dame
    II*
Carling, Foster
  Song of the South
Cavallo, Rob
  Brother Bear
Cham, Ray and Greg
  The Cheetah Girls
  The Cheetah Girls 2
  High School Musical
Childs, James
  Kick Buttowski
Christy, Brandon
  The Muppets' Wizard of Oz
Churchill, Frank
  *The Adventures of Ichabod and
    Mr. Toad*
  Bambi
  Dumbo
  The Flying Mouse
  Funny Little Bunnies
  The Golden Touch
  Peter Pan
  The Reluctant Dragon
  The Robber Kitten
  Santa's Workshop
  *Snow White and the Seven
    Dwarfs*
  The Tortoise and the Hare
  The Three Little Pigs
  Who Killed Cock Robin?

Clarke, Stanley
  Hull High
Cochran, Karl
  I'm in the Band
Coda, John
  That's So Raven
Cohen, Adam
  The Muppets' Wizard of Oz
Colcord, Ray
  The Torkelsons
Colina, Michael
  My Science Project
Collins, Phil
  Brother Bear
  Tarzan
  Tarzan II
Connors, Carol
  The Rescuers
Cook, Joe
  *Snow White and the Seven
    Dwarfs*
Cooksey, Jon
  So Weird
Cortazar, Ernesto
  The Three Caballeros
Coslow, Sam
  Song of the South
Crow, Sheryl
  Cars
Cyrus, Billy Ray
  Hannah Montana: The Movie
Cyrus, Miley
  Bolt
  Hannah Montana: The Movie
Daniel, Eliot
  Fun and Fancy Free
  Make Mine Music
  Melody Time
  So Dear to My Heart
  Song of the South

Darby, Ken
  Make Mine Music
  Song of the South
Daring, Mason
  Wild Hearts Can't Be Broken
David, Mack
  Alice in Wonderland (1951)
  Cinderella
  *Cinderella II: Dreams Come
    True*
Davidovitch, Niv
  Stuck in the Suburbs
Davis, Julian Michael
  Kickin' It
de Paul, Gene
  *The Adventures of Ichabod and
    Mr. Toad*
  Alice in Wonderland (1951)
  So Dear to My Heart
De Vol, Frank
  Herbie Goes Bananas
De Vries, Marius
  Meet the Robinsons
Denver, John
  The Bears and I
DeRemer, Patrick
  The Mighty Ducks
  101 Dalmatians: The Series
Derby, David
  Hannah Montana: The Movie
DeRemer, Patrick
  A Goofy Movie
  The Mighty Ducks
DeSalvo, Russ
  *Disney Princesses Enchanted
    Tales: Follow Your Dreams*
Deschanel, Zooey
  Winnie the Pooh
DioGuardi, Kara
  Camp Rock

Camp Rock 2: The Final Jam
Confessions of a Teenage Drama
  Queen
Hannah Montana: The Movie
Herbie Fully Loaded
Ice Princess
Disney, Walt
  Mickey's Follies
Dodd, Andy
  Camp Rock
  Camp Rock 2: The Final Jam
  High School Musical
  High School Musical 2
  High School Musical 3: Senior
    Year
  Stuck in the Suburbs
Dodd, Jimmie
  The Mickey Mouse Club
Dominguez, Armando
  Destino
Drake, Ervin
  Saludos Amigos
Drewe, Anthony
  Mary Poppins
Dudley, Aaron
  Camp Rock 2: The Final Jam
Dunham, By
  Third Man on the Mountain
Dunn, Tamara
  Hannah Montana: The Movie
Dye, Ian
  Teamo Supremo
Eastman, Tish
  The Tree of Life
Edwards, Lawrence
  Hull High
Elfman, Danny
  Alice in Wonderland (2010)
  Meet the Robinsons
  The Nightmare before Christmas

Elizondo, Mike
  Prince of Persia: The Sands of
    Time
Elliott, Jack
  Toot, Whistle, Plunk and Boom
Elliott, Ted
  Pirates of the Caribbean: At
    World's End
Erskine, Martin
  The Lion King 1½
Esperon, Manuel
  The Three Caballeros
Etheridge, Melissa
  Brother Bear 2
Fain, Sammy
  Alice in Wonderland (1951)
  Peter Pan
  The Rescuers
  Sleeping Beauty
Fastball
  Motorcrossed
Farrés, Osvaldo
  Make Mine Music
Feather, Lorraine
  The Jungle Book 2
  Pooh's Heffalump Halloween
    Movie
  The Princess Diaries 2: Royal
    Engagement
Feldman, Jack
  A Goofy Movie
  The Lion King 2: Simba's
    Pride
  Newsies
  Oliver & Company
Fidel, Stan
  The Fox and the Hound
Finn, William
  The Adventures of Tom Thumb
    and Thumbelina

Fitzgerald, Colleen
  Hannah Montana: The Movie
Fitzhugh, Ellen
  The Great Mouse Detective
Flansburgh, John
  Higglytown Heroes
Foster, Lewis
  Swamp Fox
Foster, Norman
  The Sign of Zorro
  Zorro
Fox, Charles
  Good Morning, Miss Bliss
Frank, Debra
  The Muppets' Wizard of Oz
Frederick, Jason
  The Replacements
Freeland, Roy
  A Goofy Movie
Freeman, Ticker
  So Dear to My Heart
Friedman, David
  Aladdin and the King of Thieves
  Bambi II
Friedman, Seth J.
  The Lion King 1½
Gabriel, George
  Kim Possible
Gabriel, Peter
  WALL-E
Gad, Toby
  Camp Rock
  Camp Rock 2: The Final Jam
  Jessie
Gannon, Kim
  Melody Time
Garvey, Linda
  Doug's First Movie
Giacchino, Michael
  Up

Geissman, Grant
  Winnie the Pooh: Springtime with Roo
George, Gil
  The Light in the Forest
  The Mickey Mouse Club
  Old Yeller
  Perri
  Tonka
Gerrard, Matthew
  Brother Bear 2
  Camp Rock
  The Cheetah Girls 2
  Cinderella III: A Twist in Time
  Cory in the House
  The Fox and the Hound 2
  Hannah Montana
  Herbie Fully Loaded
  High School Musical
  High School Musical 2
  High School Musical 3: Senior Year
  Ice Princess
  The Lizzie McGuire Movie
  The Pacifier
  The Princess Diaries 2: Royal Engagement
  Stuck in the Suburbs
  Zenon: Z3
Giacchino, Michael
  The Muppets' Wizard of Oz
  Ratatouille
Gibb, Richard
  101 Dalmatians II: Patch's London Adventure
Gilbert, Ray
  The Adventures of Ichabod and Mr. Toad
  Make Mine Music
  Melody Time

Song of the South
The Three Caballeros
Gilkyson, Terry
The Aristocats
The Jungle Book
The Moon-Spinners
Run, Cougar, Run
Savage Sam
The Scarecrow of Romney
Marsh
Swiss Family Robinson
The Three Lives of Thomasina
Gimbel, Norman
Lady and the Tramp II: Scamp's
Adventure
20,000 Leagues under the Sea
Gleed, Jason
Kickin' It
Gonevea, Dale
Mickey Mouse Splashdance
The Return of Jafar
Gordon, Mack
Cinderella
Grabowsky, Paul
The Jungle Book 2
Gray, Trevor and Howard
101 Dalmatians II: Patch's
London Adventure
Green, Kat
American Dragon: Jake Long
Greenberg, Faye
The Cheetah Girls 2
High School Musical
High School Musical 2
Greene, Mike
Bill Nye, the Science Guy
Groce, Larry
Mousercise
Grossman, Larry
The Great Mouse Detective

Pocahontas II: Journey to a New
World
The Princess Diaries 2: Royal
Engagement
Gurley, Michael
American Dragon: Jake Long
Haenni, G.
Third Man on the Mountain
Hajian, Chris
My Date with the President's
Daughter
Hamlisch, Marvin
The Devil and Max Devlin
Hampton, Steve
The Suite Life of Zack and Cody
Wizards of Waverly Place
Harline, Leigh
The Cookie Carnival
Fun and Fancy Free
Funny Little Bunnies
The Grasshopper and the Ants
The Night before Christmas
The Old Mill
Peculiar Penguins
Pinocchio
Snow White and the Seven
Dwarfs
The Wise Little Hen
Wynken, Blynken and Nod
Harper, Don
Tarzan and Jane
Hartley, David
The Emperor's New Groove
Hartman, Dan
Oliver & Company
Hartman, Jamie Alexander
Confessions of a Teenage Drama
Queen
Harwell, Steve
The Pacifier

Hassman, Nikki
  Camp Rock
  Camp Rock 2: The Final Jam
  *High School Musical 3: Senior
    Year*
Hawkins, Jay
  Hocus Pocus
Hayes, Steve L.
  The Muppets' Wizard of Oz
Healey, Bruce
  Fantasmic!
Heath, Hy
  Song of the South
Hee, T.
  The Reluctant Dragon
Held, Bob
  My Science Project
Heller, Bill
  My Science Project
Hendrickson, Kevin
  Jake and the Never Land Pirates
Hewitt, Jennifer Love
  The Hunchback of Notre Dame II
Hiatt, John
  The Country Bears
Hibler, Winston
  Perri
  Peter Pan
  Sleeping Beauty
Hilliard, Bob
  Alice in Wonderland (1951)
Hirschhorn, Joel
  Freaky Friday
  Hot Lead and Cold Feet
  Pete's Dragon
Hoffman, Al
  Alice in Wonderland
  Cinderella
  *Cinderella II: Dreams Come
    True*

  20,000 Leagues under the Sea
Hohfeld, Brian
  Pooh's Heffalump Movie
Ho'omalu, Mark Keali'i
  Lilo and Stitch
Horner, James
  Hocus Pocus
  Mighty Joe Young
Hoskins, Loren
  Jake and the Never Land Pirates
Houston, James
  Life Is Ruff
Houston, Jamie
  Camp Rock
  The Cheetah Girls
  The Cheetah Girls 2
  High School Musical
  High School Musical 2
  *High School Musical 3: Senior
    Year*
  Tiger Cruise
Howard, David
  Zeke and Luther
Howard, James Newton
  Atlantis: The Lost Empire
Howard, Paul Mason
  A Cowboy Needs a Horse
Huddleston, Floyd
  The Aristocats
  Robin Hood
Hummon, Marcus
  Bambi II
  The Fox and the Hound 2
Irving, Robert
  Goof Troop
Jackson, Michael
  Captain EO
James, Tim
  Camp Rock
  Camp Rock 2: The Final Jam

High School Musical 2
Jarre, Maurice
　The Last Flight of Noah's Ark
Jennings, Will
　Mighty Joe Young
John, Elton
　Aida
　The Lion King
　The Lion King 1½
Johnson, Martin
　Hannah Montana: The Movie
Johnston, Arthur
　Song of the South
Johnston, Richard O.
　The Fox and the Hound
Jonas, Nick, Joe Jonas, and Kevin
Jonas
　JONAS
Jones, Mick
　Confessions of a Teenage Drama
　Queen
Jones, Stan
　The Great Locomotive Chase
　Ten Who Dared
　Texas John Slaughter
　Westward Ho, the Wagons!
Journey
　Tron
Junge, Alexa
　Lilo and Stitch 2: Stitch Has a
　Glitch
　Mulan II
Kahn, George
　Chip 'n' Dale Rescue Rangers
Kamen, Michael
　The Three Musketeers
Kaplan, Michael B.
　I'm in the Band
Kasha, Al
　Freaky Friday

Hot Lead and Cold Feet
　Pete's Dragon
Kavanaugh, John
　Winnie the Pooh: Springtime
　with Roo
Kaye, Buddy
　Fun and Fancy Free
　Song of the South
Kelly, Ray
　Peter Pan
Kennedy, Gordon
　The Fox and the Hound 2
Kennon, Walter Edgar
　The Hunchback of Notre Dame
　II
Kent, Walter
　Melody Time
Kiley, Rilo
　Bolt
Koftinoff, Gary
　Life with Derek
Kollmorgen, Stuart
　JoJo's Circus
Kostal, Irwin
　Mickey's Christmas Carol
Kotch, Michael
　Hannah Montana: The Movie
Krieger, Stu
　Zenon: The Zequel
LaBour, Fred
　Buzz Lightyear of Star
　Command: The Adventure
　Begins
La Marca, Perry
　American Dragon: Jake Long
Lamhene, Boualem
　Ratatouille
Lampert, Diane
　Toby Tyler, or Ten Weeks with a
　Circus

Lara, Augustín
  The Three Caballeros
Lange, Johnny
  Melody Time
  Song of the South
Lange, Robert John
  The Three Musketeers
Larkin, Bill
  The Princess Diaries 2: Royal Engagement
Lavigne, Avril
  Alice in Wonderland (2010)
  The Princess Diaries 2: Royal Engagement
Lawrence, David
  The Cheetah Girls 2
  High School Musical
  High School Musical 2
Lawrence, Jack
  Peter Pan
  Sleeping Beauty
Lee, Peggy
  Lady and the Tramp
Lembeck, Michael
  The Santa Clause 3: The Escape Clause
Lenox, Carl
  The Doodlebops
Lerios, Cory
  Kim Possible
Leven, Mel
  The Adventures of Bullwhip Griffin
  Babes in Toyland
  It's Tough to Be a Bird
  The Litterbug
  101 Dalmatians
  101 Dalmatians II: Patch's London Adventure

Lewis, Bert
  The Flying Mouse
Lewis, Michelle
  Bambi II
Licera, Char
  The Cheetah Girls 2
Light, Kate
  Mulan II
Lincoln, Billy
  American Dragon: Jake Long
Lindsey, Hillary
  Hannah Montana: The Movie
Linnell, John
  Higglytown Heroes
Livingston, Jerry
  Alice in Wonderland (1951)
  Cinderella
  Cinderella II: Dreams Come True
Lodin, Jeffrey
  Doug's First Movie
Loggins, Kenny
  The Tigger Movie
Lopez, Kristen Anderson
  Winnie the Pooh
Lopez, Robert
  Winnie the Pooh
Loring, Richard
  Toby Tyler, or Ten Weeks with a Circus
Lubin, Joe
  Teacher's Pet
Lurie, Jeannie
  Camp Rock 2: The Final Jam
  Good Luck Charlie
  The Muppets
  The Muppets' Wizard of Oz
Lurye, Peter
  The Emperor's New Groove 2: Kronk's New Groove

Stanley
Teacher's Pet
M, Lebo
The Lion King
Mabe, Jon
Hannah Montana:
The Movie
MacGimsey, Robert
Song of the South
Malotte, Albert Hay
Ferdinand the Bull
Manchester, Melissa
The Great Mouse
Detective
Lady and the Tramp II:
Scamp's Adventure
Mancina, Mark
Brother Bear
The Lion King
Tarzan and Jane
Mancini, Henry
The Great Mouse Detective
Manges, Jilien
Jungle 2 Jungle
Manilow, Barry
Oliver & Company
Mann, Barry
Muppet Treasure Island
Oliver & Company
Markowitz, Donny
Zenon: The Zequel
Marks, Franklyn
Third Man on the Mountain
Marley, Ziggy
Muppet Treasure Island
Marx, Richard
Bambi II
Masters, Blair
The Fox and the Hound 2

McCrary, Joel
The Princess Diaries 2: Royal
Engagement
McGarity, Mike
Austin & Ally
McKennitt, Loreena
Tinker Bell
McKenzie, Bret
The Muppets
McKinley, Richard
The Shaggy D.A.
Treasure of Matecumbe
McKuen, Rod
Scandalous John
McNeely, Joel
The Jungle Book 2
Mulan II
Mellencamp, John
America's Heart and Soul
Melonas, Dennis
Mousercise
Menken, Alan
Aladdin
Beauty and the Beast
Enchanted
Hercules
Home on the Range
The Hunchback of Notre Dame
King David
The Little Mermaid
Newsies
Pocahontas
Tangled
Who Discovered Roger
Rabbit?
Mercer, Johnny
Robin Hood
Meuller, Mark
Good Morning, Miss Bliss

Michaels, Julia
  Austin & Ally
Midnight, Charlie
  The Lizzie McGuire Movie
  Oliver & Company
Miller, Dan
  Higglytown Heroes
Miller, Roger
  Robin Hood
Miller, Sidney
  The Mickey Mouse Club
Mills, Billy
  A Cowboy Needs a Horse
Minkoff, Robert
  Oliver & Company
Molinder, Nicolas
  Pair of Kings
Montade, Annmarie
  So Weird
Morey, Larry
  The Adventures of Ichabod and
    Mr. Toad
  Bambi
  Ferdinand the Bull
  The Reluctant Dragon
  Snow White and the Seven
    Dwarfs
  So Dear to My Heart
Morissette, Alanis
  The Chronicles of Narnia: The
    Lion, the Witch and the
    Wardrobe
  Prince of Persia: The Sands of
    Time
Mueller, Mark
  Chip 'n' Dale Rescue Rangers
  DuckTales
Myvette, Kovasciar
  Camp Rock
  Camp Rock 2: The Final Jam

Nazareth, Ernesto
  Melody Time
Neeman, Chen
  Camp Rock 2: The Final Jam
  Good Luck Charlie
  The Muppets
Neill, Roger
  The Weekenders
Nelson, Steve
  Darkwing Duck
Nervo, Miriam
  Hannah Montana: The Movie
Nervo, Olivia
  Hannah Montana: The Movie
Nevil, Robbie
  Brother Bear 2
  The Cheetah Girls 2
  Camp Rock
  Cory in the House
  Hannah Montana
  High School Musical
  High School Musical 2
  High School Musical 3: Senior
    Year
  The Pacifier
  Stuck in the Suburbs
Newman, Fred
  Disney's Doug
  Doug's First Movie
  PB&J Otter
Newman, Randy
  A Bug's Life
  Cars
  James and the Giant Peach
  Monsters, Inc.
  The Princess and the
    Frog
  Toy Story
  Toy Story 2
  Toy Story 3

Newman, Thomas
  WALL-E
Ne-Yo
  The Princess and the Frog
Nichols, C. August
  The Saga of Windwagon Smith
Nilsson, Harry
  Popeye
Noble, Ray
  Fun and Fancy Free
Noko
  *101 Dalmatians II: Patch's
    London Adventure*
Orrall, Robert Ellis
  Hannah Montana: The Movie
Osborn, Kristyn
  Doug's First Movie
Ottestad, Boots
  Stuck in the Suburbs
Paisley, Brad
  Cars
Panzer, Marty
  *Pocahontas II: Journey to a New
    World*
Parker, Fess
  Westward Ho, the Wagons!
Patch, Jeffrey
  The Fox and the Hound
Penner, Ed
  The Reluctant Dragon
Penner, Erdman
  Peter Pan
  Sleeping Beauty
Perrso, Joacim
  Pair of Kings
Petersen, Randy
  Aladdin and the King of Thieves
  Goof Troop
  A Goofy Movie
  High School Musical

High School Musical 2
*The Hunchback of Notre Dame
  II*
The Lion King 1½
Mickey's House of Villains
Mickey's Magical Christmas
The Return of Jafar
Teacher's Pet
Petralia, Mickey
  Holes
Petty, Daniel
  Bambi II
Pitchford, Dean
  Bambi II
  Disney Afternoon
  The Lizzie McGuire Movie
  Oliver & Company
  *101 Dalmatians II: Patch's
    London Adventure*
Plum, Edward H.
  Bambi
Pola, Eddie
  Lambert, the Sheepish Lion
Portman, Rachel
  *Beauty and the Beast: The
    Enchanted Christmas*
Potter, Grace
  Tangled
Powers, Amy
  *Disney Princesses Enchanted
    Tales: Follow Your Dreams*
Proulx, Ron
  Life with Derek
Quenzer, Arthur
  Fun and Fancy Free
Quinn, Kevin
  Aladdin and the King of Thieves
  A Goofy Movie
  Goof Troop
  High School Musical

The Hunchback of Notre Dame II
The Lion King 1½
Mickey's House of Villains
Mickey's Magical Christmas
The Return of Jafar
Teacher's Pet
Rafaelson, Peter
  Stuck in the Suburbs
Rappaport, Ron
  I'm in the Band
Raye, Don
  The Adventures of Ichabod and
    Mr. Toad
  Alice in Wonderland (1951)
  So Dear to My Heart
Rex, Kristian
  Zenon: Girl of the 21st Century
Rice, Tim
  Aida
  Aladdin
  Beauty and the Beast
  King David
  The Lion King
  The Lion King 1½
Rich, Richard
  The Fox and the Hound
  The Small One
Ridel, Stefanie
  Hannah Montana: The Movie
Rifkin, Jay
  The Lion King
Rinker, Al
  The Aristocats
Rivas, Fernando
  Handy Manny
Robbins, Ayn
  The Rescuers
Robins, Lindy
  The Cheetah Girls
  Jessie

Robinson, Will
  The Cheetah Girls 2
  The Fox and the Hound 2
Rocha, Ron
  Oliver & Company
Roeman, Paul
  The Muppets
Rogel, Randy
  Cinderella II: Dreams Come
    True
  101 Dalmations II: Patch's
    London Adventure
  Return to Never Land
  Winnie the Pooh: Springtime
    with Roo
Rogers, Frank
  Cars
Rogers, Tom
  Winnie the Pooh: Springtime
    with Roo
Ronell, Ann
  The Three Little Pigs
Rosman, Mark
  Life-Size
Rossio, Terry
  Pirates of the Caribbean: At
    World's End
Rushton, Steve
  Camp Rock 2: The Final Jam
Russell, Bob
  Rascal
  Smith!
Rzeznik, John
  Treasure Planet
Sack, Al
  Make Mine Music
Sager, Carole Bayer
  The Devil and Max Devlin
Sahanaja, Darian
  The Replacements

Sandell, Geraldo
  Pair of Kings
Sauter, Eddie
  Make Mine Music
Savigar, Kevin
  The Cheetah Girls
Sawyer, Dan
  Disney's Doug
  Doug's First Movie
  PB&J Otter
Schwartz, Stephen
  Enchanted
  Geppetto
  The Hunchback of Notre Dame
  Johnny and the Sprites
  Pocahontas
Scoggin, James Houston
  Camp Rock 2: The Final Jam
Scott, Ed
  Charley and the Angel
Scott, Oz
  The Cheetah Girls
Searles, Frederick
  Mickey's Christmas Carol
Sears, Ted
  Alice in Wonderland (1951)
  Peter Pan
  Sleeping Beauty
Seeley, Andrew
  High School Musical
Shanks, John
  Cars
  Hannah Montana: The Movie
  Herbie Fully Loaded
Sharp, Thomas Richard
  Darkwing Duck
Sherman, Richard M. and Robert B.
  The Absent-Minded Professor
  *The Adventures of Bullwhip
    Griffin*

The Aristocats
Bedknobs and Broomsticks
Big Red
Bon Voyage!
Carousel of Progress
The Enchanted Tiki Room
Follow Me, Boys!
The Gnome-Mobile
The Happiest Millionaire
The Horsemasters
In Search of the Castaways
It's a Small World
Johnny Shiloh
The Jungle Book
The Legend of Lobo
Mary Poppins
Meet the World
*The Misadventures of Merlin
  Jones*
*The Miracle of the White
  Stallions*
Monkeys, Go Home!
The Monkey's Uncle
Moon Pilot
*The One and Only, Genuine,
  Original Family Band*
The Parent Trap
Summer Magic
The Sword in the Stone
That Darn Cat!
Those Calloways
The Tigger Movie
*Walt Disney's Wonderful World
  of Color*
*Winnie the Pooh and the
  Blustery Day*
*Winnie the Pooh and the Honey
  Tree*
*Winnie the Pooh: Seasons for
  Giving*

Sheyne, Pam
  Camp Rock
Siegel, Ralph Maria
  Make Mine Music
Silversher, Patty and Michael
  Adventures of the Gummi Bears
  Belle's Magical World
  Boo to You Too! Winnie the Pooh
  Chip 'n' Dale Rescue Rangers
  DuckTales
  *The Little Mermaid II: Return to
    the Sea*
  *Pooh's Heffalump Halloween
    Movie*
  TaleSpin
  The Return of Jafar
  *Winnie the Pooh: A Valentine for
    You*
  *Winnie the Pooh: A Very Merry
    Pooh Year*
  *Winnie the Pooh: Seasons of
    Giving*
Silvestri, Alan
  Hannah Montana: The Movie
  Lilo and Stitch
Simon, Carly
  Piglet's Big Movie
  Pooh's Heffalump Movie
Skarbek, Sacha
  *Confessions of a Teenage Drama
    Queen*
Slater, Glenn
  Home on the Range
  The Little Mermaid
  Tangled
  Who Discovered Roger Rabbit?
Smith, Michael
  Hannah Montana: The Movie
Smith, Paul J.
  Fun and Fancy Free

The Light in the Forest
Perri
Pinocchio
*Snow White and the Seven
  Dwarfs*
Song of the South
Westward Ho, the Wagons!
Smith, Stanley A.
  Jungle 2 Jungle
Snow, Tom
  Disney Afternoon
  A Goofy Movie
  *The Lion King 2: Simba's
    Pride*
  Oliver & Company
Sondheim, Stephen
  Dick Tracy
Spektor, Regina
  *The Chronicles of Narnia: Prince
    Caspian*
Squier, William
  Doug's First Movie
Stafford, Jim
  The Fox and the Hound
Stalling, Carl
  Mickey's Follies
Steinkellner, Cheri
  Teacher's Pet
Stiles, George
  Mary Poppins
Sting
  The Emperor's New Groove
Straus, Billy
  Little Einsteins
Sturges, Thomas
  Camp Rock 2: The Final Jam
Sturmer, Andy
  Kick Buttowski
Sussman, Bruce
  Oliver & Company

Swift, Taylor
Hannah Montana:
The Movie
Tately, Chuck
TaleSpin
Tatum, Shane
The Apple Dumpling Gang
The Biscuit Eater
Charley and the Angel
The Shaggy D.A.
Superdad
Treasure of Matecumbe
Tavera, Michael
The Emperor's New School
Taylor, Irving
So Dear to My Heart
Taymor, Julie
The Lion King
Tesori, Jeanine
The Emperor's New Groove 2:
Kronk's New Groove
Lilo and Stitch 2: Stitch Has a
Glitch
The Little Mermaid: Ariel's
Beginning
Mulan II
Theodore, Ali Dee
Kickin' It
The Muppets
Theory, Juliana
Motorcrossed
They Might Be Giants
Return to Never Land
Thomas, Rob
Meet the Robinsons
Tipton, George Aliceson
Empty Nest
Nurses
Torimiro, Dapo
Camp Rock 2: The Final Jam

Torme, Mel
So Dear to My Heart
Tosti, Blaise
Pocahontas II: Journey to a New
World
Travolta, John
Bolt
Tumes, Michelle
Tinker Bell
Van Tongeren, John
The Cheetah Girls
Verbinski, Gore
Pirates of the Caribbean: At
World's End
Vincent, Jeffrey
Stuck in the Suburbs
Wainwright, Rufus
Meet the Robinsons
Wallace, Oliver
Alice in Wonderland (1951)
Darby O'Gill and the Little
People
Der Fuehrer's Face
Dumbo
Fun and Fancy Free
The New Spirit
Old Yeller
Peter Pan
Walsh, Brock
Hocus Pocus
Hull High
Walsh, William
Fun and Fancy Free
Warrander, Scott
The Lion King 2: Simba's Pride
Warren, Diane
Atlantis: The Lost Empire
Washington, Ned
Dumbo
Fun and Fancy Free

Pinocchio
Saludos Amigos
Watkin, Lawrence Edgar
  Darby O'Gill and the Little People
  The Great Locomotive Chase
  The Light in the Forest
  Ten Who Dared
Watters, Mark
  Bonkers
  Pooh's Heffalump Halloween Movie
Watts, Adam
  Camp Rock
  Camp Rock 2: The Final Jam
  High School Musical
  High School Musical 2
  High School Musical 3: Senior Year
  Stuck in the Suburbs
Webster, Paul Francis
  Adventures in Music: Melody
Wechter, David and Julius
  Midnight Madness
Weeks, Sarah
  Pooh's Grand Adventure: The Search for Christopher Robin
Weems, Ted
  Make Mine Music
Weil, Cynthia
  Muppet Treasure Island
Weiner, Michael
  Cinderella II: Dreams Come True
  Cinderella III: A Twist in Time
Weiss, George
  Fun and Fancy Free
  Melody Time
Wells, Greg
  Camp Rock

Wells, Robert
  So Dear to My Heart
Wenger, Brahm
  Air Bud: Golden Receiver
Whedon, Joss
  The Lion King 2: Simba's Pride
Widelitz, Stacy
  Pocahontas II: Journey to a New World
Wilde, David
  I'm in the Band
Wilde, Stacy
  I'm in the Band
Wilder, Alec
  Make Mine Music
Wilder, Matthew
  Hannah Montana: The Movie
  The Lizzie McGuire Movie
  Mulan
Williams, Paul
  The Muppet Christmas Carol
  A Muppets Christmas: Letters to Santa
Willis, Allee
  The Devil and Max Devlin
Winans, Sam
  Lizzie McGuire
Wolcott, Charles
  The Adventures of Ichabod and Mr. Toad
  Make Mine Music
  The Reluctant Dragon
  Saludos Amigos
  Song of the South
  The Three Caballeros
Wolff, Jonathan
  Smart Guy
Woodbury, Brian
  Teacher's Pet

Worth, Bobby
  Fun and Fancy Free
  Make Mine Music
  Melody Time
Wright, Ralph
  Perri
Wrubel, Allie
  Make Mine Music
  Melody Time
  Song of the South
Wyle, George
  *Lambert, the Sheepish
   Lion*
Yaeger, Jordan
  Kickin' It

Zachary, Alan
  *Cinderella II: Dreams Come
   True*
  Cinderella III: A Twist in Time
Zaslove, Diana
  Chip 'n' Dale Rescue Rangers
Zimmer, Hans
  The Lion King
  *Pirates of the Caribbean: At
   World's End*
  *Pirates of the Caribbean: The
   Curse of the Black Pearl*
Zippel, David
  Hercules
  Mulan

APPENDIX C: SOURCES AND SONGS

The Absent-Minded Professor
(1961, film)
Medfield Fight Song

Adventures in Music: Melody
(1953, film)
The Bird and the Cricket and the
    Willow Tree

**The Adventures of Bullwhip
Griffin** (1967, film)
The Ballad of Bullwhip Griffin
California Gold
Girls of San Francisco
Whoever You Are

**The Adventures of Ichabod and
Mr. Toad** (1949, film)
The Headless Horseman
Ichabod
Katrina
Merrily on Our Way

**The Adventures of Tom Thumb
and Thumbelina** (2002, video)
I Am So Alone
1–2–Cha-Cha-Cha
A Perfect Day
Welcome to My Hole

Aida (2000, Broadway)
Another Pyramid
Dance of the Robe
Easy as Life
Elaborate Lives
Enchantment Passing Through
Every Story Is a Love Story
Fortune Favors the Brave
The Gods Love Nubia
How I Know You
I Know the Truth
Like Father, Like Son
My Strongest Suit
Not Me

The Past Is Another Land
A Step Too Far
Written in the Stars

Air Bud: Golden Receiver (1998, film)
One Moment

Aladdin (1992, film)
Arabian Nights
Friend Like Me
One Jump Ahead
Prince Ali
A Whole New World

Aladdin and the King of Thieves
(1995, video)
Are You In or Out?
Father and Son
Out of Thin Air
There's a Party Here in Agrabah
Welcome to the Forty Thieves

Alice in Wonderland (1951, film)
A-E-I-O-U
Alice in Wonderland
All in a Golden Afternoon
Beware the Jabberwock
Beyond the Laughing Sky
The Caucus Race
Everything Has a Useness
How D'Ye Do and Shake Hands
I'm Late
I'm Odd
In a World of My Own
March of the Cards
Old Father William
Painting the Roses Red
'Twas Brillig
The Un-Birthday Song
Very Good Advice
The Walrus and the Carpenter

We'll Smoke the Blighter Out

Alice in Wonderland (2010, film)
Alice
Alice's Theme

Almost Home see *The Torkelsons*

American Dragon: Jake Long
(2005, television)
American Dragon
The Chosen One

America's Heart and Soul (2004, film)
The World Don't Bother Me None

The Apple Dumpling Gang
(1975, film)
The Apple Dumpling Gang

The Aristocats (1970, film)
The Aristocats
Ev'rybody Wants to Be a Cat
Scales and Arpeggios
Thomas O'Malley Cat

Atlantis: The Lost Empire (2001, film)
Where the Dream Takes You

Austin & Ally (2011, television)
Without You

Babes in the Woods (1932, film)
Babes in the Woods

Babes in Toyland (1961, film)
The Forest of No Return
Slowly He Sank into the Sea
The Workshop Song

Bambi (1942, film)
Let's Sing a Gay Little Spring Song
Little April Shower

Looking for Romance
Love Is a Song

Bambi II (2006, video)
First Sign of Spring
The Healing of a Heart
There Is Life
Through Your Eyes

The Barefoot Executive (1971, film)
He's Gonna Make It

Bear in the Big Blue House (1997, television)
Bear in the Big Blue House Theme Song
Goodbye Song

The Bears and I (1974, film)
Sweet Surrender

Beauty and the Beast (1991, film)
Be Our Guest
Beauty and the Beast
Belle
Gaston
The Mob Song (Kill the Beast)
Something There

Beauty and the Beast (1994, Broadway)
A Change in Me
Home
Human Again
If I Can't Love Her
Maison de Lunes
Me
No Matter What

Beauty and the Beast: The Enchanted Christmas (1997, video)

As Long as There's Christmas
A Cut Above the Rest
Don't Fall in Love
Stories

Bedknobs and Broomsticks (1971, film)
The Age of Not Believing
The Beautiful Briny
Eglantine
Nobody's Problems for Me
The Old Home Guard
Portobello Road
A Step in the Right Direction
Substitutiary Locomotion
With a Flair

Belle's Magical World (1998, video)
Listen with Our Hearts
A Little Thought

Big Red (1962, film)
Mon Amour Perdu

Bill Nye, the Science Guy (1993, television)
Bill Nye, the Science Guy

The Biscuit Eater (1972, film)
Moreover and Me

The Boatniks (1970, film)
The Boatniks

Bolt (2008, film)
Barking at the Moon
I Thought I Lost You

Bon Voyage! (1962, film)
Bon Voyage

Bonkers (1993, television)
Bonkers

Boo to You Too! Winnie the Pooh (1996, television)
I Am Not Afraid
I Wanna Scare Myself

Brother Bear (2003, film)
Great Spirits
Look Through My Eyes
No Way Out
On My Way
Transformation
Welcome (to Our Family)

Brother Bear 2 (2006, video)
Feels Like Home
It Will Be Me
Welcome to the Day

A Bug's Life (1998, film)
The Time of Your Life

Bunnytown (2007, television)
Bunnytown

Buzz Lightyear of Star Command: The Adventure Begins (2000, video)
To Infinity and Beyond

Camp Rock (2008, television)
Gotta Find You
Hasta La Vista
Here I Am
Our Time Is Here
Play My Music
Start the Party
This Is Me
Too Cool
2 Stars
We Rock
What It Takes
Who Will I Be?

Camp Rock 2: The Final Jam (2010, television)
Brand New Day
Can't Back Down
Fire
Heart & Soul
Introducing Me
It's On
Tear It Down
This Is Our Song
Wouldn't Change a Thing
You're My Favorite Song

Captain EO (1986, theme park film)
Another Part of Me
We Are Here to Change the World

Carousel of Progress (1964, theme park)
The Best Time of Your Life
There's a Great Big Beautiful Tomorrow

Cars (2006, film)
Behind the Clouds
Find Yourself
Our Town
Real Gone

Charley and the Angel (1973, film)
Livin' One Day at a Time

The Cheetah Girls (2003, television)
Cheetah Sisters
Cinderella
End of the Line
Girl Power
Together We Can

The Cheetah Girls 2 (2006, television)

A La Nanita Nana
Amigas Cheetahs
Cherish the Moment
Dance with Me
It's Over
The Party's Just Begun
Step Up
Strut

Chip 'n Dale Rescue Rangers
(1989, television)
Chip 'n Dale Rescue Rangers
  Theme Song
Fat Cat Stomp
The Stage Blight Opera

**The Chronicles of Narnia:
The Lion, the Witch and the
Wardrobe** (2005, film)
Wunderkind

**The Chronicles of Narnia:
Prince Caspian** (2008, film)
The Call

Cinderella (1950, film)
Bibbidi-Bobbidi-Boo
Cinderella
Cinderella Work Song
Dancing on a Cloud
A Dream Is a Wish Your Heart
  Makes
I'm in the Middle of a Muddle
Oh Sing, Sweet Nightingale
So This Is Love
The Work Song

**Cinderella II: Dreams Come
True** (2002, video)
Follow Your Heart
It's What's Inside That Counts
The World Is Looking Up to You

Cinderella III: A Twist in Time
(2007, video)
Anastasia's Theme
At the Ball
I Still Believe
More Than a Dream
Perfectly Perfect

**The Computer Wore Tennis
Shoes** (1969, film)
The Computer Wore Tennis Shoes

**Confessions of a Teenage Drama
Queen** (2004, film)
Ready

The Cookie Carnival (1935,
film)
The Sweetest One of All

Cory in the House (2007,
television)
Cory in the House

The Country Bears (2002, film)
Can Love Stand the Test
Just the Goin'
Kick It into Gear
Let It Ride
Straight to the Heart of Love

Country Bear Jamboree (1971,
theme park)
Bear Band Serenade

A Cowboy Needs a Horse (1956,
film)
A Cowboy Needs a Horse

**Darby O'Gill and the Little
People** (1959, film)
Pretty Irish Girl
The Wishing Song

Darkwing Duck (1991, television)
Darkwing Duck Theme

Davy Crockett (1954, television)
The Ballad of Davy Crockett

Davy Crockett and the River Pirates (1956, film)
King of the River
Yaller, Yaller Gold

Davy Crockett, King of the Wild Frontier (1955, film)
Farewell

Der Fuehrer's Face (1942, film)
Der Fuehrer's Face

Destino (2003, film)
Destino

The Devil and Max Devlin (1981, film)
Any Fool Can See
Roses and Rainbows

Dick Tracy (1990, film)
Back in Business
Live Alone and Like It
More
Sooner or Later
What Can You Lose

The Disney Afternoon (1990, television)
Disney Afternoon Theme

Disney Princess Enchanted Tales: Follow Your Dreams (2007, video)
I've Got My Eyes on You
Keys to the Kingdom
Peacock Princess

Disney Records (recordings)
Bug-A-Boo
Happy, Happy Birthday
Mickey, She's Got a Crush on You
Mousercise
Tall Paul
You Can Always Be Number One

Disney's Adventures in Wonderland (1992, television)
Adventures in Wonderland

Disney's Adventures of the Gummi Bears (1985, television)
Gummi Bears Theme
Gummiberry Juice
The Rough, Tough, Burly Sailor Song

Disney's Doug (1998, television)
Doug's Theme

The Doodlebops (2005, television)
The Doodlebops
Get on the Bus

Doug's 1st Movie (1999, film)
Deep Deep Water
Someone Like Me

DuckTales (1987, television)
The Boogie Beagle Blues
Bubba Duck Theme
DuckTales Theme

Dumbo (1941, film)
Baby Mine
Casey Junior
Look Out for Mr. Stork
Pink Elephants on Parade
Song of the Roustabouts
When I See an Elephant Fly

Dumbo's Circus (1985, television)
Dumbo's Circus
Gotta Fly

The Edison Twins (1984, television)
The Edison Twins

The Emperor's New Groove (2000, film)
My Funny Friend and Me
Perfect World

The Emperor's New Groove 2: Kronk's New Groove (2005, video)
Be True to Your Groove
Feel Like a Million

The Emperor's New School (2006, television)
The Emperor's New School Theme

Empty Nest (1988, television)
Life Goes On

Enchanted (2007, film)
Ever Ever After
Happy Working Song
So Close
That's How You Know
True Love's Kiss

The Enchanted Tiki Room (1963, theme park)
The Tiki Tiki Tiki Room

An Extremely Goofy Movie (2000, video)
Don't Give Up
Nowhere to Run

Fantasmic! (1992, theme park)
Fantasmic

Ferdinand the Bull (1938, film)
Ferdinand the Bull

The Fighting Prince of Donegal (1966, film)
The Drinking Song

The Flying Mouse (1934, film)
I Would Like to Be a Bird
You're Nothin' but a Nothin'

Follow Me, Boys! (1966, film)
Follow Me, Boys!

The Fox and the Hound (1981, film)
Appreciate the Lady
Best of Friends
Goodbye May Seem Forever
A Huntin' Man
Lack of Education

The Fox and the Hound 2 (2006, video)
Blue Beyond
Friends for Life
Good Doggie, No Bone!
Hound Dude
We Go Together
We're in Harmony
You Know I Will

Freaky Friday (1976, film)
I'd Like to Be You for a Day

Fun and Fancy Free (1947, film)
Fee Fi Fo Fum
Fun and Fancy Free
I'm a Happy-Go-Lucky Fellow
Lazy Countryside
My Favorite Dream
My, What a Happy Day

Say It with a Slap
Too Good to Be True

Funny Little Bunnies (1934, film)
See the Funny Bunnies

Geppetto (2000, television)
And Son
Bravo, Stromboli!
Empty Heart
Just Because It's Magic
Pleasure Island
Satisfaction Guaranteed
Since I Gave My Heart Away
Toys

The Gnome-Mobile (1967, film)
The Gnome-Mobile
In Me Jaunting Car

The Golden Girls (1985,
television)
Miami, You've Got Style

The Golden Touch (1935, film)
The Golden Touch

Goliath II (1960, film)
The Elephant March

Good Luck Charlie (2010,
television)
Hang in There, Baby

Good Morning, Miss Bliss (1987,
television)
These Are the Best of Times

Goof Troop (1992, television)
Goof Troop

A Goofy Movie (1995, film)
After Today
I 2 I
Lester's Possum Park

Nobody Else but You
On the Open Road
Stand Out

The Grasshopper and the Ants
(1934, film)
The World Owes Me a Living

The Great Locomotive Chase
(1956, film)
Sons of Old Aunt Dinah

The Great Mouse Detective
(1986, film)
Goodbye So Soon
Let Me Be Good to You
The World's Greatest Criminal
  Mind

Handy Manny (2006, television)
Handy Manny Theme Song

Hannah Montana (2006,
television)
Best of Both Worlds

Hannah Montana: The Movie
(2009, film)
Back to Tennessee
Butterfly Fly Away
The Climb
Crazier
Don't Walk Away
Dream
Hoedown Throwdown
Let's Get Crazy
You'll Always Find Your Way Back
  Home

The Happiest Millionaire (1967,
film)
Are We Dancing?
Bye-Yum Pum Pum

Detroit
Fortuosity
I'll Always Be Irish
It Won't Be Long 'Til Christmas
Let's Have a Drink on It
Strengthen the Dwelling
There Are Those
Valentine Candy
Watch Your Footwork
What's Wrong with That?

The Haunted Mansion (1969, theme park)
Grim Grinning Ghosts

Herbie: Fully Loaded (2005, film)
First

Herbie Goes Bananas (1980, film)
I Found a New Friend
Look at Me

Hercules (1997, film)
Go the Distance
The Gospel Truth
I Won't Say I'm in Love
One Last Hope
A Star Is Born
Zero to Hero

Higglytown Heroes (2004, television)
Here in Higglytown

High School Musical (2006, television)
Bop to the Top
Breaking Free
Get'cha Head in the Game
Start of Something New
Stick to the Status Quo

We're All in This Together
What I've Been Looking For
When There Was Me and You

High School Musical 2 (2007, television)
All for One
Bet on It
Everyday
Fabulous
Gotta Go My Own Way
Humuhumunukunukuapua'a
I Don't Dance
What Time Is It?
Work This Out
You Are the Music in Me

High School Musical 3: Senior Year (2008, film)
The Boys Are Back
Can I Have This Dance?
High School Musical
I Want It All
Just Wanna Be with You
A Night to Remember
Now or Never
Right Here, Right Now
Scream
Walk Away

Hocus Pocus (1993, film)
I Put a Spell on You
Sarah's Theme

Holes (2003, film)
Dig It

Home on the Range (2004, film)
Anytime You Need a Friend
Home on the Range
Little Patch of Heaven
Wherever the Trail May Lead

Will the Sun Ever Shine Again?
Yodel-Adle-Eedle-Idle-Oo

The Horsemasters (1961, television)
The Strummin' Song

Hot Lead and Cold Feet (1978, film)
May the Best Man Win
Something Good Is Bound to Happen

Hull High (1990, television)
Laws of Motion
Once in a Lifetime
Team Sandwich
Undeniably Yours

The Hunchback of Notre Dame (1996, film)
The Bells of Notre Dame
The Court of Miracles
God Help the Outcasts
A Guy Like You
Heaven's Light/Hellfire
Out There
Someday
Topsy Turvy

The Hunchback of Notre Dame II (2002, video)
Fa La La La Fallen in Love
I'd Stick with You
I'm Gonna Love You
Le Jour d'Amour
An Ordinary Miracle

Ice Princess (2005, film)
Reach

I'm in the Band (2009, television)
Weasel Rock You

In the Bag (1956, film)
Humphrey Hop

In Search of the Castaways (1962, film)
The Castaways Theme
Enjoy It
Grimpons

It's a Small World (1964, theme park)
It's a Small World (After All)

It's Tough to Be a Bird (1969, film)
It's Tough to Be a Bird
When the Buzzards Return to Hinckley Ridge

Jake and the Never Land Pirates (2011, television)
Jake and the Never Land Pirates Theme

James and the Giant Peach (1996, film)
Eating the Peach
Family
Good News
My Name Is James
That's the Life

Jessie (2011, television)
Hey, Jessie

Johnny and the Sprites (2005, television)
Johnny and the Sprites

Johnny Shiloh (1963, television)
Johnny Shiloh

Johnny Tremain (1957, film)
Johnny Tremain
The Liberty Tree

JoJo's Circus (2003, television)
JoJo's Circus Theme Song

JONAS (2009, television)
Live to Party

The Jungle Book (1967, film)
The Bare Necessities
Colonel Hathi's March
I Wan'na Be Like You
My Own Home
That's What Friends Are For
Trust in Me

The Jungle Book 2 (2003, video)
Jungle Rhythm
Right Where I Belong
W-I-L-D

Jungle 2 Jungle (1997, film)
You Can Do It

Kick Buttowski (2010, television)
Kick Buttowski

Kickin' It (2011, television)
Kickin' It with You

Kim Possible (2002, television)
Call Me, Beep Me

King David (1997, Broadway concert)
Absalom, My Absalom
The Death of Saul
Enemy Within
Entry into Jerusalem
Goliath of Gath
How Are the Mighty Fallen
Hunted Partridge on the Hill
Israel and Saul
The Long, Long Day
Never Again
Psalm 8

Samuel Anoints David
Saul Has Slain His Thousands
Sheer Perfection
This New Jerusalem
Warm Spring Night
When in Love
You Have It All

Lady and the Tramp (1955, film)
Bella Notte
He's a Tramp
La La Lu
Peace on Earth
The Siamese Cat Song
What Is a Baby?

Lady and the Tramp II: Scamp's Adventure (2001, video)
Always There
I Didn't Know I Could Feel This Way
Junkyard Society Rag
Welcome Home
World without Fences

Lambert, the Sheepish Lion (1952, film)
Lambert, the Sheepish Lion

The Last Flight of Noah's Ark (1980, film)
Half of Me

The Legend of Lobo (1962, film)
The Legend of Lobo

Life Is Ruff (2005, television)
It's a Dog

Life with Derek (2005, television)
Life with Derek Theme Song

Life-Size (2000, television)
Be a Star

The Light in the Forest (1958, film)
I Asked My Love a Favor
The Light in the Forest

Light Magic Parade (1997, theme park)
Light Magic Theme

Lilo and Stitch (2002, film)
Hawaiian Roller Coaster Ride

Lilo and Stitch 2: Stitch Has a Glitch (2005, video)
Always

The Lion King (1994, film)
Be Prepared
Can You Feel the Love Tonight?
Circle of Life
Hakuna Matata
I Just Can't Wait to Be King

The Lion King (1997, Broadway)
Chow Down
Endless Night
The Madness of King Scar
The Morning Report
One by One
Shadowland
They Live in You/He Lives in You

The Lion King 1½ (2004, video)
Digga Tunnah
That's All I Need

The Lion King 2: Simba's Pride (1998, video)
Love Will Find a Way
My Lullaby
One of Us

Upendi
We Are One

The Litterbug (1961, film)
The Litterbug

Little Einsteins (2005, television)
Little Einsteins Theme

The Little Mermaid (1989, film)
Daughters of Triton
Fathoms Below
Kiss the Girl
Les Poissons
Part of Your World
Poor Unfortunate Souls
Under the Sea

The Little Mermaid (1992, television)
Daring to Dance
Edge of the Edge of the Sea
Home Is
In Harmony
In My Blue Backyard
Just a Little Love
Never Give Up
Sing a New Song

The Little Mermaid (2008, Broadway)
Beyond My Wildest Dreams
Human Stuff
I Want the Good Times Back
If Only
Positoovity
She's in Love
The World Above

The Little Mermaid: Ariel's Beginning (2008, video)
Athena's Song (Endless Sky)
I Remember

I Will Sing
Jump in the Line
Just One Mistake

The Little Mermaid II: Return to the Sea (2000, video)
Down to the Sea
For a Moment
Here on the Land and Sea
Tip and Dash

Lizzie McGuire (2001, television)
Lizzie McGuire Theme Song

The Lizzie McGuire Movie (2003, film)
Girl in the Band
What Dreams Are Made Of
Why Not?

Main Street Electrical Parade (1972, theme park)
Main Street Electrical Parade

Make Mine Music (1946, film)
All the Cats Join In
Blue Bayou
Casey, the Pride of Them All
Johnny Fedora and Alice Blue Bonnet
Make Mine Music
The Martins and the Coys
Two Silhouettes
Without You

Mary Poppins (1964, film)
Chim Chim Cher-ee
Feed the Birds
Fidelity Fiduciary Bank
I Love to Laugh
Jolly Holiday
Let's Go Fly a Kite
The Life I Lead

A Man Has Dreams
The Perfect Nanny
Sister Suffragette
A Spoonful of Sugar
Stay Awake
Step in Time
Supercalifragilisticexpialidocious

Mary Poppins (2004 London stage)
Anything Can Happen (If You Let It)
Being Mrs. Banks
Brimstone and Treacle
Cherry Tree Lane
Practically Perfect
Temper, Temper

Meet the Robinsons (2007, film)
Another Believer
The Future Has Arrived
Little Wonders
The Motion Waltz
Where Is Your Heart At?

Meet the World (1983, theme park)
Meet the World

Melody see *Adventures in Music: Melody*

Melody Time (1948, film)
The Apple Song
Blame It on the Samba
Blue Shadows on the Trail
Little Toot
The Lord Is Good to Me
Melody Time
Once Upon a Wintertime
Pecos Bill
The Pioneer Song

The Mickey Mouse Club (1955–1959, television)
Anything Can Happen Day
    (Wednesday)
Circus Day (Thursday)
Encyclopedia
Fun with Music Day (Monday)
Guest Star Day (Tuesday)
I'm No Fool
Mickey Mouse Club Alma Mater
Mickey Mouse Club March
    (Mickey Mouse Club Theme)
Mouseketeer Roll Call
Spin and Marty Theme
Stop, Look and Listen
Talent Round-Up Day (Friday)

Mickey's Christmas Carol (1983, film)
Oh, What a Merry Christmas Day

Mickey's Follies (1929, film)
Minnie's Yoo-Hoo

Mickey's House of Villains (2001, video)
It's Our House Now

Mickey's Magical Christmas (2001, video)
The Best Christmas of All

Mickey's Toontown Fair (1996–2011, theme park)
Mickey's the Mouse for Me
Welcome to Toontown

Midnight Madness (1980, film)
Midnight Madness

The Mighty Ducks (1996, television)
The Mighty Ducks Theme

Mighty Joe Young (1998, film)
Windsong

Miracle of the White Stallions (1963, film)
Just Say Auf Wiedersehen

The Misadventures of Merlin Jones (1964, film)
Merlin Jones

Monkeys, Go Home! (1967, film)
Joie de Vivre

The Monkey's Uncle (1965, film)
The Monkey's Uncle

Monsters, Inc. (2001, film)
If I Didn't Have You

The Moon Pilot (1962, film)
Seven Moons of Beta-Lyrae
True Love Is an Apricot
The Void

The Moon-Spinners (1964, film)
The Moon-Spinners Song

Motocrossed (2001, television)
We're at the Top of the World
You're an Ocean

Mousercise (1983, television)
Bug-A-Boo
Mousercise

Mulan (1998, film)
A Girl Worth Fighting For
Honor to Us All
I'll Make a Man Out of You
Reflection
True to Your Heart

Mulan II (2005, video)
Here Beside Me
Lesson Number One
Like Other Girls

The Muppets (2011, film)
Let's Talk about Me
Life's a Happy Song
Man or Muppet
Me Party
Pictures in My Head

The Muppet Christmas Carol
(1992, film)
Bless Us All
It Feels Like Christmas
Marley and Marley
One More Sleep Till Christmas/
   Christmas Scat
Scrooge
A Thankful Heart
When Love Is Gone/When Love Is
   Found

*A Muppets Christmas: Letters to
Santa* (2008, television)
Delivering Christmas
I Wish I Could Be Santa Claus
It's All about Heart
My Best Christmas Yet

Muppet Treasure Island (1996,
film)
Boom Shakalaka
Cabin Fever
Love Led Us Here
Love Power
A Professional Pirate
Sailing for Adventure
Shiver My Timbers
Something Better

The Muppets' Wizard of Oz
(2005, television)
Calling All Munchkins
Good Life
Kansas
When I'm With You
The Witch Is in the House

*My Date with the President's
Daughter* (1998, television)
My Date with the President's
   Daughter

My Science Project (1985, film)
My Science Project

The New Spirit (1942, film)
Yankee Doodle Spirit

Newsies (1992, film)
Carrying the Banner
High Times, Hard Times
King of New York
My Lovey-Dovey Baby
Once and For All
Santa Fe
Seize the Day
The World Will Know

The Night Before Christmas
(1933, film)
The Night Before Christmas

*The Nightmare Before
Christmas* (1993, film)
Jack's Lament
Kidnap the Sandy Claws
Making Christmas
Oogie Boogie's Song
Poor Jack
Sally's Song

Something's Up with Jack
This Is Halloween
Town Meeting
What's This?

Nurses (1991, television)
Here I Am

The Old Mill (1937, film)
The Old Mill

Old Yeller (1957, film)
Old Yeller

Oliver & Company (1988, film)
Good Company
Once Upon a Time in New York
    City
Perfect Isn't Easy
Streets of Gold
Why Should I Worry?

*The One and Only, Genuine,
Original Family Band* (1968, film)
'Bout Time
Dakota
Drummin' Drummin' Drummin'
The Happiest Girl Alive
Let's Put It Over with Grover
Oh, Benjamin Harrison
The One and Only, Genuine,
    Original Family Band
Ten Feet off the Ground

*One Hundred and One
Dalmatians* (1962, film)
Cruella De Vil
Dalmatian Plantation
Kanine Krunchies Commercial

101 Dalmatians: The Series
(1997, television)
101 Dalmatians

*101 Dalmatians II: Patch's
London Adventure* (2003, video)
I See Spots
One of a Kind
Try Again

The Pacifier (2005, film)
Everyday Super Hero

Pair of Kings (2011, television)
Top of the World

The Parent Trap (1961, film)
For Now, For Always
Let's Get Together
The Parent Trap

Paul Bunyan (1958, film)
Paul Bunyan

PB&J Otter (1998, television)
PB&J Otter Theme

Peculiar Penguins (1934, film)
The Penguin Is a Very Funny
    Creature

Perri (1957, film)
And Now to Sleep
Break of Day
Together Time

Peter Pan (1953, film)
The Elegant Captain Hook
Following the Leader (Tee Dum–
    Tee Dee)
Never Smile at a Crocodile
The Pirate Song
A Pirate's Life (for Me)
The Second Star to the Right
What Makes the Red Man Red?
You Can Fly, You Can Fly, You
    Can Fly
Your Mother and Mine

Pete's Dragon (1977, film)
Bill of Sale
Boo Bop Bobbop Bop (I Love You, Too)
Brazzle Dazzle Day
Candle on the Water
Every Little Piece
The Happiest Home in These Hills
I Saw a Dragon
It's Not Easy
Passamaquoddy
There's Room for Everyone

Phineas and Ferb (2007, television)
Today Is Going to Be a Great Day

The Pied Piper (1933, film)
The Pied Piper

Piglet's Big Movie (2003, film)
Comforting to Know
If I Wasn't So Small
The More I Look Inside
The More It Snows (Tiddely-Pom)
Mother's Intuition
Sing Ho for the Life of a Bear
With a Few Good Friends

Pinocchio (1940, film)
Give a Little Whistle
Hi-Diddle-Dee-Dee (An Actor's Life for Me)
I've Got No Strings
Little Woodenhead
When You Wish Upon a Star

Pirates of the Caribbean (1967, theme park)
Yo Ho! (A Pirate's Life for Me)

Pirates of the Caribbean: At the World's End (2007, film)
Hoist the Colours

Pirates of the Caribbean: The Curse of the Black Pearl (2003, film)
Pirates of the Caribbean Main Theme

Pocahontas (1995, film)
Colors of the Wind
If I Never Knew You
Just Around the Riverbend
Mine, Mine, Mine
Savages
Steady as the Beating Drum
The Virginia Company

Pocahontas II: Journey to a New World (1998, video)
Between Two Worlds
Things Are Not What They Appear
Wait Till He Sees You
What a Day in London
Where Do I Go from Here?

Pooh's Grand Adventure: The Search for Christopher Robin (1997, video)
Adventure Is a Wonderful Thing
Everything Is Right
Forever and Ever
If It Says So
Wherever You Are

Pooh's Heffalump Halloween Movie (2005, video)
As Long as I'm Here with You
Brave Together
Trick or Treating with Our Friends

Pooh's Heffalump Movie (2005, film)
The Horribly Hazardous Heffalumps

In the Name of the Hundred Acre
 Wood
Little Mr. Roo
The Name Game
Shoulder to Shoulder

Popeye (1980, film)
Blow Me Down
Children
Everything Is Food
He Needs Me
He's Large
I Am What I Am
I'm Mean
It's Not Easy Bein' Me
Sail with Me
Swee'pea's Lullaby
Sweethaven

**Prince of Persia: The Sands of
Time** (2011, film)
I Remain

**The Princess Diaries 2: Royal
Engagement** (2004, film)
Breakaway
Genovia Anthem
Your Crowning Glory

The Princess and the Frog (2009,
film)
Almost There
Dig a Little Deeper
Down in New Orleans
Friends on the Other Side
Gonna Take You There
Ma Belle Evangeline
Never Knew I Needed
When We're Human

The Rainbow Road to Oz (1957,
television)

The Oz-Kan Hop
The Patchwork Girl
The Rainbow Road to Oz

Rascal (1968, film)
Summer Sweet

Ratatouille (2007, film)
Le Festin

The Reluctant Dragon (1941,
film)
I'm a Reluctant Dragon
Oh Fleecy Cloud
Radish So Red
'Tis Evening
To an Upside Down Cake

The Replacements (2006,
television)
The Replacements Theme Song

The Rescuers (1977, film)
The Journey (Who Will Rescue
 Me?)
Rescue Aid Society
Someone's Waiting for You
Tomorrow Is Another Day

The Return of Jafar (1994, video)
Forget about Love
I'm Looking Out for Me
Nothing in the World (Quite Like
 a Friend)
You're Only Second Rate

Return to Never Land (2002, film)
Here We Go, Another Plan
I'll Try
So to Be One of Us

The Robber Kitten (1935, film)
Dirty Bill

Robin Hood (1973, film)
Love
Not in Nottingham
Oo-De-Lally
The Phony King of England
Whistle-Stop

Rolie Polie Olie (1998, television)
Rolie Polie Olie

Run, Cougar, Run (1972, film)
Let Her Alone

The Saga of Andy Burnett (1957, television)
Ladies in the Sky
The Saga of Andy Burnett

The Saga of Windwagon Smith (1961, film)
The Saga of Windwagon Smith

Saludos Amigos (1942, film)
Brazil
Saludos Amigos
Tico-Tico (No Fubá)

The Santa Clause 3: The Escape Clause (2006, film)
Come Meet Santa

Santa's Workshop (1932, film)
Santa's Workshop

Savage Sam (1963, film)
Savage Sam and Me

Scandalous John (1971, film)
Pastures Green

The Scarecrow of Romney Marsh (1964, television)
Scarecrow

The Shaggy D.A. (1976, film)
The Shaggy D.A.

Sleeping Beauty (1959, film)
Hail the Princess Aurora
I Wonder
Once Upon a Dream
The Skumps
Sleeping Beauty Song

The Small One (1976, film)
A Friendly Face
The Merchants' Song
Small One

Smart Guy (1997, television)
Smart Guy Theme Song

Smith! (1969, film)
The Ballad of Smith and Gabriel Jimmyboy

Snow White and the Seven Dwarfs (1937, film)
Bluddle-Uddle-Um-Dum
The Dwarfs' Yodel Song
Heigh-Ho
I'm Wishing
One Song
Some Day My Prince Will Come
Whistle While You Work
With a Smile and a Song

Snow White and the Seven Dwarfs (1979, Radio City Music Hall)
Here's the Happy Ending
Welcome to the Kingdom
Will I Ever See Her Again?

So Dear to My Heart (1949, film)
County Fair
It's Whatcha Do with Whatcha Got
Lavender Blue (Dilly Dilly)
Ol' Dan Patch

So Dear to My Heart
Stick-to-it-ivity

So Weird (2001, television)
In the Darkness

Song of the South (1946, film)
Everybody Has a Laughing Place
How Do You Do?
Let the Rain Pour Down
Song of the South
Sooner or Later
That's What Uncle Remus Said
Who Wants to Live Like That?
Zip-a-Dee-Doo-Dah

SpectroMagic Parade (1991,
theme park)
SpectroMagic

Stanley (2001, television)
Stanley Theme Song

The Strongest Man in the World
(1975, film)
Instant Muscle

Stuck in the Suburbs (2004,
television)
Good Life
Make a Wish
More Than Me
On Top of the World
Over It

The Suite Life of Zack and Cody
(2005, television)
Here I Am

Summer Magic (1963, film)
Beautiful Beulah
Femininity
Flitterin'
On the Front Porch

The Pink of Perfection
Summer Magic
The Ugly Bug Ball

Superdad (1973, film)
Los Angeles
These Are the Best Times
When I'm Near You

Swamp Fox (1959, television)
Swamp Fox Theme

Swiss Family Robinson (1960,
film)
My Heart Was an Island

The Sword in the Stone (1963,
film)
Higitus Figitus
The Legend of the Sword in the
    Stone
Mad Madame Mim
A Most Befuddling Thing
That's What Makes the World Go
    Round

TaleSpin (1990, television)
Friends for Life
Home Is Where the Heart Is
I'm Gone
Monkey in Your Tank
TaleSpin Theme

Tangled (2010, film)
I See the Light
I've Got a Dream
Mother Knows Best
Something That I Want
When Will My Life Begin?

Tapestry of Nations Parade
(2000, theme park)
Tapestry of Dreams

Tarzan (1999, film)
Son of Man
Strangers Like Me
Trashin' the Camp
Two Worlds
You'll Be in My Heart

Tarzan (2006, Broadway)
Different
Everything That I Am
For the First Time
I Need to Know
No Other Way
Sure as the Sun Turns to Moon
Waiting for This Moment
Who Better Than Me

Tarzan II (2005, video)
Who Am I?
Leaving Home (Find My Way)

Tarzan and Jane (2002, video)
The Song of Life

Teacher's Pet (2000, television)
Teacher's Pet

Teacher's Pet (2004, film)
A Boy Needs a Dog
I, Ivan Frank
I Wanna Be a Boy
I'm Moving On
Small But Mighty
Take the Money and Run
A Whole Bunch of World

Teamo Supremo (2004, television)
Teamo Supremo Theme

Ten Who Dared (1960, film)
Jolly Rovers
Roll Along

Texas John Slaughter (1958, television)
Texas John Slaughter

That Darn Cat (1965, film)
That Darn Cat

That's So Raven (2003, television)
That's So Raven

Third Man on the Mountain (1959, film)
Climb the Mountain
Good Night Valais

Those Calloways (1965, film)
The Cabin Raising Song
Rhyme-Around

The Three Caballeros (1945, film)
Baia
Mexico
The Three Caballeros
You Belong to My Heart

The Three Little Pigs (1933, film)
Who's Afraid of the Big Bad Wolf?

The Three Lives of Thomasina (1964, film)
Thomasina

The Three Musketeers (1993, film)
All for Love

Tiger Cruise (2004, television)
My Hero Is You

The Tigger Movie (2000, film)
How to Be a Tigger
Pooh's Lullabee
Round My Family Tree
Someone Like Me Lullabee
The Whoop-de-Dooper Bounce

Your Heart Will Lead You Home

Tinker Bell (2008, video)
Fly to Your Heart
To the Fairies They Draw Near

Toby Tyler (1960, film)
Biddle-Dee-Dee

Tonka (1958, film)
Tonka

Toot, Whistle, Plunk and Boom
(1953, film)
A Toot and a Whistle and a Plunk
    and a Boom

The Torkelsons (1991, television)
The Torkelsons Theme Song

The Tortoise and the Hare
(1935, film)
Slow but Sure

Toy Story (1995, film)
I Will Go Sailing No More
Strange Things
You've Got a Friend in Me

Toy Story 2 (1999, film)
When She Loved Me
Woody's Roundup

Toy Story 3 (2010, film)
We Belong Together

Treasure of Matecumbe (1976,
film)
Matecumbe

Treasure Planet (2002, film)
Always Know Where You Are
I'm Still Here

The Tree of Life (1998, theme
park)

It's Tough to Be a Bug
The Tree of Life Theme

Tron (1982, film)
Only Solutions

20,000 Leagues Under the Sea
(1954, film)
A Whale of a Tale

Up (2009, film)
The Spirit of Adventure

WALL-E (2008, film)
Down to Earth

**Walt Disney's Wonderful
World of Color** (1954–1990,
television)
Although I Dropped $100,000 (I
    Found a Million Dollars in Your
    Smile)
The Boogie Woogie Bakery Man
Charleston Charlie
I'm Blue for You, Boo-Boo-Boo-
    Boo-Boo
I'm Professor Ludwig Von Drake
Puppy Love Is Here to Stay
Rutabaga Rag
The Spectrum Song
The Wonderful World of Color

The Weekenders (2000,
television)
The Weekenders Theme

Westward Ho, the Wagons!
(1956, film)
I'm Lonely, My Darlin'
John Colter
Pioneer's Prayer
Westward Ho, the Wagons!
Wringle Wangle

Who Discovered Roger Rabbit?
(c. 1990, unfinished film)
This Only Happens in the
   Movies

Who Killed Cock Robin? (1935,
film)
Somebody Rubbed Out My
   Robin
Who Killed Cock Robin?

Wild Hearts Can't Be Broken
(1991, film)
Weren't So Bad What Used to Be

Winnie the Pooh (2011, film)
The Backson Song
Everything Is Honey
It's Gonna Be Great
A Pooh Bear Takes Care of His
   Tummy
So Long
A Very Important Thing to Do
The Winner Song

*Winnie the Pooh: A Valentine
for You* (1999, television)
Girls Are Like Boys
Places in the Heart
When the Love Bug Bites

*Winnie the Pooh: A Very Merry
Pooh Year* (2002, video)
Happy Pooh Year
Hunny, No Not for Me
Snow Snows

*Winnie the Pooh and the
Blustery Day* (1968, film)
The Heffalumps and Woozles
Hip-Hip-Pooh-Ray!
The Rain, Rain, Rain Came Down,
   Down, Down

What a Rather Blustery Day
The Wonderful Thing about
   Tiggers

*Winnie the Pooh and the Honey
Tree* (1966, film)
A Little Black Rain Cloud
The Pooh Will Soon Be Free
Rumbly in My Tumbly
Up, Down, Touch the Ground
Winnie the Pooh

*Winnie the Pooh: Seasons of
Giving* (1999, video)
Berrily We Roll Along
Hooray Hooray!
Our Thanksgiving Day
Seasons of Giving
The Turkey Song

*Winnie the Pooh: Springtime
with Roo* (2004, video)
Easter Day with You
The Grandest Easter of Them All
Sniffly Sniff
The Way It Must Be Done
We're Huntin' Eggs Today

The Wise Little Hen (1934,
film)
Help Me Plant My Corn

Wizards of Waverly Place (2007,
television)
Everything Is Not What It Seems

Wynken, Blynken and Nod
(1938, film)
Wynken, Blynken and Nod

Zeke and Luther (2011,
television)
The Zeke and Luther Theme

Zenon: Girl of the 21st Century
(1999, television)
Super Nova Girl

Zenon: The Zequel (2001,
television)
The Galaxy Is Ours

Zenon: Z3 (2004, television)
Out of This World

Zorro (1957, television)
Zorro

APPENDIX D: GUIDE TO RECORDINGS, VIDEOS, AND DVDS

SOUNDTRACKS, VIDEOS, AND DVDS

Most Disney productions have been preserved on LP, audiocassette, VHS cassette, CD, or DVD. If the word "soundtrack" is used below, the company released a recording of the songs. If that recording was put on CD, it is listed at the end of the entry. The same is true for VHS videotapes; most shows were put on tape before the advent of DVDs. If the production was put on DVD, that is also indicated. The following list is meant as a guide to let readers know what recordings, videotapes, and DVDs were made, though some may not be easy to locate today. Records and VHS tapes can be found in used record stores and through online services. Old records, movies, and videos currently only available on vinyl and VHS are continually being rereleased on CD and DVD, so it is hoped that some of the hard-to-find items below will be more accessible by the time you read this.

The Absent-Minded Professor
Film (1961) With Fred MacMurray, Nancy Olson, Tommy Kirk, Keenan Wynn. DVD

Adventures in Music: Melody
Film (1953) Walt Disney Treasures: Disney Rarities. DVD

Paperback with four records.

The Adventures of Bullwhip Griffin
Film soundtrack (1967) With Roddy McDowall, Suzanne Pleshette, Harry Guardino, Karl Malden. Story with songs.

The Adventures of Ichabod and Mr. Toad
Film soundtrack (1949) With (the voices of) Bing Crosby, Eric Blore, Basil Rathbone. DVD

Adventures of the Gummi Bears
Television series (1985) Seasons 1, 2, and 3. DVD
Soundtrack (1990) Selection from Disney Afternoon shows. CD

The Adventures of Tom Thumb and Thumbelina
Video film (2002) With (the voices of) Elijah Wood, Jennifer Love Hewitt, Peter Gallagher. DVD

Aida
Original Broadway cast (1999) With Heather Headley, Adam Pascal, Sherie Rene Scott. CD
Studio recording (1999) With Elton John, Heather Headley, Tina Turner. CD

Air Bud: Golden Receiver
Film (1998) With Kevin Zegers, Cynthia Stevenson, Tim Conway, Dick Martin. DVD

Aladdin
Film soundtrack (1992) With (the voices of) Robin Williams, Brad Kane, Lea Salonga. CD, DVD

Aladdin and the King of Thieves
Video soundtrack (1996) With (the voices of) Robin Williams, Liz Callaway, Jerry Orbach, Merwin Foard. CD, DVD
Aladdin Sing-Along (2007) CD

Alice in Wonderland
Film soundtrack (1951) With (the voices of) Kathryn Beaumont, Jerry Colonna, Stanley Holloway, Ed Wynn. CD, DVD
Film soundtrack (2010) With Mia Wasikowska, Johnny Depp, Helena Bonham Carter, Anne Hathaway; (the voices of) Michael Sheen, Stephen Fry, Alan Rickman, Avril Lavigne. CD, DVD

America's Heart and Soul
Film soundtrack (2004) With George Woodard, Charles Jimmie Sr., Vasquez Brothers. CD, DVD

The Apple Dumpling Gang
Film (1975) With Bill Bixby, Susan Clark, Don Knotts, Tim Conway, Harry Morgan. DVD

The Aristocats
Film soundtrack (1969) With (the voices of) Phil Harris, Eva Gabor, Scatman Crothers, Maurice Chevalier. CD, DVD
Songs from *The Aristocats* (2002) CD

Atlantis: The Lost Empire
Film soundtrack (2001) With (the voices of) Michael J. Fox, Jim Varney, James Garner, Claudia Christian, Corey Burton. CD, DVD.

Babes in the Woods
Film short (1932) Walt Disney Treasures: Silly Symphonies. DVD

Babes in Toyland
Film soundtrack (1961) With Annette Funicello, Tommy Sands, Ray Bolger, Ed Wynn. DVD

Bambi
Film soundtrack (1942) With
(the voices of) Bobette Audrey,
Hardie Albright, Peter Behn, Stan
Alexander, Margaret Lee, Joan
Sutherland. CD, DVD

Bambi II
Video soundtrack (2006) With (the
voices of) Patrick Stewart, Cree
Summer, Keith Ferguson. CD,
DVD

The Barefoot Executive
Film (1971) With Kurt Russell,
Cesar Romero, Joe Flynn, Eve
Arden, Wally Cox. DVD

The Bears and I
Film (1974) With Patrick Wayne,
Chief Dan George, Michael
Ansara. DVD

Beauty and the Beast
Film soundtrack (1991) With (the
voices of) Paige O'Hara, Angela
Lansbury, Jerry Orbach. CD, DVD
Original Broadway cast (1994) With
Susan Egan, Terrence Mann, Tom
Bosley, Gary Beach. CD
Original Australian cast (1995)
With Rachel Peck, Michael
McCormick, Hugh Jackman. CD
Original London cast (1997) With
Julie-Alanah Brighten, Alasdair
Harvey. CD
Beauty and the Beast Read-Along
(2002) DVD

*Beauty and the Beast: The
Enchanted Christmas*
Video soundtrack (1997) With
(the voices of) Paige O'Hara,

Angela Lansbury, Jerry Orbach,
Bernadette Peters, Tim Curry. CD,
DVD

Belle's Magical World
Video (1998) With (the voices of)
Paige O'Hara, Robby Benson, Jerry
Orbach, Jim Cummings. DVD

Bedknobs and Broomsticks
Film soundtrack (1971) With
Angela Lansbury, David
Tomlinson. CD, DVD

Big Red
Film (1962) With Walter Pidgeon,
Gilles Payant, Emile Genest,
Janette Bertrand. DVD

Bill Nye, the Science Guy
Television series (1993) With Bill
Nye. Interactive DVD, five-disc
collection, DVD.

The Biscuit Eater
Film (1972) With Dorothy
McGuire, Chuck Connors, Earl
Holliman, Fess Parker, Lew Ayres,
Pat Crowley. DVD

The Boatniks
Film (1970) With Robert Morse,
Stefanie Powers, Norman Fell, Phil
Silvers. DVD

Bolt
Film soundtrack (2008) With (the
voices of) John Travolta, Miley
Cyrus. CD, DVD

Bon Voyage!
Film (1962) With Fred
MacMurray, Jane Wyman, Tommy
Kirk, Michael Callan, Deborah
Walley. DVD

Bonkers
Television series (1993) Selected
episodes on VHS.

*Boo to You Too! Winnie the
Pooh*
Television special (1996) With (the
voices of) Jim Cummings, John
Fiedler, Peter Cullen, Michael
Gough.

Brother Bear
Film soundtrack (2003) With (the
voices of) Joaquin Phoenix, Jeremy
Suarez, Jason Raize, Rick Moranis,
Phil Collins, Tina Turner. CD,
DVD

Brother Bear 2
Video (2006) With (the voices of)
Jeremy Suarez, Patrick Dempsey,
Mandy Moore, Rick Moranis,
Melissa Etheridge. DVD

A Bug's Life
Film soundtrack (1998) With (the
voices of) Jonathan Harris, Dave
Foley, Brad Garrett, Phyllis Diller,
Bonnie Hunt, Randy Newman.
DVD

Bunnytown
Television series (2007) Selected
episodes. DVD

*Buzz Lightyear of Star
Command: The Adventure
Begins*
Video (2000) With (the voices of)
Tim Allen, Ed Bradley, William
Shatner, Lesley Stahl, Bill O'Reilly.
DVD

Camp Rock
Television film soundtrack (2008)
With Jonas Brothers, Demi Lovato,
Meaghan Jette Martin. CD, DVD
Disney Karaoke Series: Camp
Rock. CD

Camp Rock 2: The Final Jam
Television film soundtrack (2010)
With Jonas Brothers, Demi
Lovato, Daniel Cash, Daniel
Fathers, Meaghan Martin, Maria
Canals-Barrera, Chloe Bridges.
CD, DVD

Captain EO
Theme park film (1986) With
Michael Jackson, Anjelica Huston.
DVD
Songs on Michael Jackson CDs
Bad (1987) and *Dangerous* (1991).

Cars
Film soundtrack (2006) With (the
voices of) Paul Newman, Owen
Wilson, Bonnie Hunt. CD, DVD

Charley and the Angel
Film (1973) With Fred
MacMurray, Cloris Leachman,
Harry Morgan, Kurt Russell.

The Cheetah Girls
Television film (2003) With Raven-
Symoné, Adrienne Bailon, Kiely
Williams, Sabrina Bryan. DVD

The Cheetah Girls 2
Television film (2006) With
Raven-Symoné, Adrienne Bailon,
Kiely Williams, Sabrina Bryan.
DVD

Chip 'n' Dale Rescue Rangers
Television series (1989) Two
volumes of episodes. DVD

**The Chronicles of Narnia:
The Lion, the Witch and the
Wardrobe**
Film soundtrack (2005) With Tilda
Swinton, Georgie Henley, Anna
Popplewell, William Moseley,
Skandar Keynes. CD, DVD

**The Chronicles of Narnia:
Prince Caspian**
Film soundtrack (2008) With
Liam Neeson, Ben Barnes, Alicia
Borrachero, Cornell John. CD, DVD

Cinderella
Film soundtrack (1950) With (the
voices of) Ilene Woods, James
MacDonald, Eleanor Audley,
Verna Felton. CD, DVD
Read-Along book and CD

**Cinderella II: Dreams Come
True**
Video (2002) With (the voices of)
Jennifer Hale, Tress MacNeille,
Rob Paulsen, Corey Burton. DVD

Cinderella III: A Twist in Time
Video (2007) With (the voices of)
Jennifer Hale, Tress MacNeille,
Christopher Daniel Barnes, Russi
Taylor. DVD

**The Computer Wore Tennis
Shoes**
Film (1969) With Kurt Russell,
Cesar Romero, Joe Flynn, Alan
Hewitt. DVD

**Confessions of a Teenage Drama
Queen**
Film soundtrack (2004) With
Lindsay Lohan, Megan Fox,
Adam Garcia, Glenne Headly. CD,
DVD

The Cookie Carnival
Film short (1935) With Silly
Symphony: Mickey's Magic Hat
Walt Disney Treasures: Silly
Symphonies. DVD

Cory in the House
Television series (2007) With Kyle
Massey, Jason Dolley. Selected
episodes. DVD

The Country Bears
Film soundtrack (2002) with Haley
Joel Osment, Diedrich Bader,
Candy Ford, John Hiatt. CD,
DVD

A Cowboy Needs a Horse
Film short (1956) Disney Tall
Tales: Cartoon Classics, Vol. 12

**Darby O'Gill and the Little
People**
Film (1959) With Albert Sharpe,
Janet Munro, Sean Connery,
Jimmy O'Dea. DVD
Story with songs.

Darkwing Duck
Television series (1991) Selected
episodes in two volumes. DVD

Davy Crockett
Television series (1954) With
Fess Parker. Disney Treasures:

Complete Davy Crockett Television Series. DVD
Songs from Disney's Davy Crockett.

Davy Crockett and the River Pirates
Film (1956) With Fess Parker, Buddy Ebsen, Jeff York, Kenneth Tobey. DVD

Davy Crockett, King of the Wild Frontier
Film (1955) With Fess Parker, Buddy Ebsen, Basil Ruysdael, Hans Conried. DVD

Der Fuehrer's Face
Film short (1942) With (the voice of) Clarence Nash. Walt Disney Treasures: On the Front Line. DVD.
Music Depreciation by Spike Jones. CD

Destino
Film short (2003) Walt Disney Treasures: Disney Rarities. DVD.

The Devil and Max Devlin
Film (1981) With Elliott Gould, Bill Cosby, Susan Anspach, Adam Rich. DVD

Dick Tracy
Film soundtrack (1990) With Madonna, Mandy Patinkin. CD, DVD

Disney Princess Enchanted Tales: Follow Your Dreams
Video (2007) With (the voices of) Erin Torpey, Linda Larkin, Lea Salonga. DVD

Disney's Doug
Television series (1998) With (the voices of) Billy West, Fred Newman, Constance Shulman. Seasons 1 and 2. DVD

Doug's First Movie
Film (1999) With (the voices of) Thomas McHugh, Fred Newman, Constance Shulman, Chris Phillips. DVD

DuckTales
Television series (1987) With (the voices of) Alan Young, Russi Taylor, Terence McGovern, Joan Gerber. Vols. 1, 2, and 3. DVD

Dumbo
Film soundtrack (1941) With (the voices of) Betty Noyes, Sterling Holloway. CD, DVD

The Edison Twins
Television series (1984) With Andrew Sabiston, Marnie McPhail, Sunny Thrasher. Season 1.

The Emperor's New Groove
Film soundtrack (2000) With (the voices of) David Spade, John Goodman, Eartha Kitt, Patrick Warburton. CD, DVD

The Emperor's New Groove 2: Kronk's New Groove
Video (2005) With (the voices of) Patrick Warburton, Tracy Ullman, Eartha Kitt, David Spade. DVD

Enchanted
Film soundtrack (2007) With Amy Adams, Patrick Dempsey, James Marsden. CD, DVD

The Enchanted Tiki Room
Theme park soundtrack (1963)
With the Jungle Cruise.

An Extremely Goofy Movie
Video (2000) With (the voices of)
Bill Farmer, Jason Marsden, Jim
Cummings. DVD

Ferdinand the Bull
Film short (1938) Disney's
Timeless Tales, Vol. 2. DVD
Film short (1938) Walt Disney
Treasures: Disney Rarities. DVD

The Fighting Prince of Donegal
Film (1966) With Peter McEnery,
Susan Hampshire, Tom Adams,
Gordon Jackson. DVD

The Flying Mouse
Film short (1934) Walt Disney
Treasures: Silly Symphonies. DVD
Story and songs with other tales.

Follow Me, Boys!
Film (1966) With Fred
MacMurray, Vera Miles, Lillian
Gish, Charles Ruggles. DVD

The Fox and the Hound
Film soundtrack (1981) With
(the voices of) Mickey Rooney,
Kurt Russell, Pearl Bailey, Jack
Albertson. DVD

The Fox and the Hound 2
Video soundtrack (2006) With
(the voices of) Jeff Bennett, Jonah
Bobo, Reba McIntire. CD, DVD

Freaky Friday
Film (1976) With Jodie Foster,
Barbara Harris, John Astin, Patsy
Kelly. DVD

Fun and Fancy Free
Film soundtrack (1947) With Edgar
Bergman, (the voice of) Dinah
Shore. DVD

Funny Little Bunnies
Film short (1934) Walt Disney
Treasures: Silly Symphonies.
DVD

Geppetto
Television film soundtrack (2000)
With Drew Carey, Julia Louis-
Dreyfus, Brent Spiner, Rene
Auberjonois. CD, DVD

The Gnome-Mobile
Film soundtrack (1967) With
Walter Brennan, Matthew Garber,
Karen Dotrice, Richard Deacon.
DVD

The Golden Girls
Television (1985) With Beatrice
Arthur, Betty White, Rue
McClanahan, Estelle Getty.
Complete series. DVD

The Golden Touch
Film short (1935) Disney Tall
Tales: Cartoon Classics, Vol. 12.
DVD
Walt Disney Treasures: Silly
Symphonies. DVD

Goliath II
Film short (1960) Walt Disney
Treasures: Disney Rarities. DVD

Goof Troop
Television series (1992) With
(the voices of) Bill Farmer, Rob
Paulsen, Jim Cummings, Dana Hill.
Selected episodes. DVD

A Goofy Movie
Film (1995) With (the voices of)
Wayne Allwine, Dante Basco, Klee
Bragger, Pat Buttram. DVD

The Grasshopper and the Ants
Film short (1934) Walt Disney
Treasures: Silly Symphonies. DVD
Story and song.

The Great Mouse Detective
Film soundtrack (1986) With
(the voices of) Vincent Price,
Barrie Ingham, Val Bettin, Candy
Candido, Susanne Pollatschek. CD,
DVD

The Great Locomotive Chase
Film (1956) With Fess Parker,
Jeffrey Hunter, John Lupton, Jeff
York. DVD

Handy Manny
Television series soundtrack (2006)
Seasons 1 and 2. CD, DVD

Hannah Montana
Television series soundtrack (2006)
With Miley Cyrus, Emily Osment,
Jason Earles, Billy Ray Cyrus,
Mitchel Musso, Moises Arias,
Lucas Till. CD, DVD

Hannah Montana: The Movie
Film soundtrack (2009) With Miley
Cyrus, Taylor Swift, Steve Rushton,
Billy Ray Cyrus. DC, DVD

The Happiest Millionaire
Film soundtrack (1967) With Fred
MacMurray, Tommy Steele, Greer
Garson, Lesley Ann Warren, John
Davidson. CD, DVD

The Haunted Mansion
Theme park soundtrack (1969) CD
The Haunted Mansion: Haunted
Hits (2003) CD

Herbie Fully Loaded
Film soundtrack (2005) With
Lindsay Lohan, Michael Keaton,
Cheryl Hines. CD, DVD

Herbie Goes Bananas
Film (1980) With Stephen W.
Burns, Cloris Leachman, Charles
Martin Smith, John Vernon. DVD

Hercules
Film soundtrack (1997) With
(the voices of) Tate Donovan,
Josh Keaton, Roger Bart, Danny
DeVito. CD, DVD
Hercules Sing-Along (1997)

Higglytown Heroes
Television series (2004) On the
Move; To the Rescue; Playhouse
Disney Holiday. DVDs

High School Musical
Television film soundtrack (2006)
With Zac Efron, Vanessa Anne
Hudgens, Ashley Tisdale, Lucas
Grabeel. CD, DVD

High School Musical 2
Television film soundtrack (2007)
With Zac Efron, Vanessa Anne
Hudgens, Ashley Tisdale, Lucas
Grabeel. CD, DVD

**High School Musical 3: Senior
Year**
Film soundtrack (2008) With Zac
Efron, Vanessa Anne Hudgens,

Ashley Tisdale, Lucas Grabeel. CD, DVD

Hocus Pocus
Film (1993) With Bette Midler, Sarah Jessica Parker, Kathy Najimy. DVD

Holes
Film soundtrack (2003) With Shia LaBeouf, Sigourney Weaver, Tim Blake, Jon Voight. CD, DVD

Home on the Range
Film soundtrack (2004) With (the voices of) Roseanne Barr, Judi Dench, Steve Buscemi, Carole Cook, G. W. Bailey. CD, DVD

Hot Lead and Cold Feet
Film (1978) With Jim Dale, Darren McGavin, Karen Valentine, Don Knotts. DVD

The Hunchback of Notre Dame
Film soundtrack (1996) With (the voices of) Tom Hulce, Heidi Mollenhauer, Demi Moore, Jason Alexander, Tony Jay. CD, DVD
The Hunchback of Notre Dame Read-Along (1996)

The Hunchback of Notre Dame II
Video soundtrack (2002) With (the voices of) Tom Hulce, Jason Alexander, Jennifer Love Hewitt, Haley Joel Osment. CD, DVD

Ice Princess
Film soundtrack (2005) With Michelle Trachtenberg, Kim

Cattrall, Trevor Blumas, Joan Cusack. CD, DVD

In Search of the Castaways
Film (1962) With Hayley Mills, Maurice Chevalier, George Sanders, Wilfred Hyde-White. DVD

It's a Small World
Theme park soundtrack (1964) CD Illustrated book and record.

It's Tough to Be a Bird
Film short (1969) Included with *The Ranger of Brownstone*.

James and the Giant Peach
Film soundtrack (1996) With Paul Terry, Pete Postlethwaite; (the voices of) Simon Callow, Susan Sarandon, David Thewlis. CD, DVD

Johnny and the Sprites
Television series soundtrack (2005) With John Tartaglia. Selected episodes. CD, DVD

Johnny Shiloh
Television series (1963) With Kevin Corcoran, Brian Keith, Darryl Hickman, Skip Homeier.

Johnny Tremain
Film (1957) With Hal Stalmaster, Luana Patten, Richard Beymer, Jeff York. DVD

JoJo's Circus
Television series (2003) With (the voices of) Madeleine Martin, Robert Smith. DVD

The Jungle Book
Film soundtrack (1967) With (the voices of) Bruce Reitherman, Phil Harris, Sebastian Cabot, Louis Prima. CD, DVD

The Jungle Book Sing-Along (2007) CD

The Jungle Book 2
Video soundtrack (2003) With (the voices of) John Goodman, Johnny Hall, Smash Mouth. CD, DVD

Jungle 2 Jungle
Film soundtrack (1997) With Tim Allen, Luis Avalos, Joan Copeland, Bob Dishy, Lolita Davidovich. CD, DVD

Kim Possible
Television series (2002) With (the voices of) Christy Carlson Romano, Will Friedle, Nancy Cartwright. Seasons 1 to 4. CD, DVD

Lady and the Tramp
Film soundtrack (1955) With (the voices of) Barbara Luddy, Larry Roberts, Peggy Lee, Bill Thompson, George Givot. CD, DVD
Lady and the Tramp: Songs and Story (1992)

Lady and the Tramp II: Scamp's Adventure
Video film (2006) With (the voices of) Scott Wolf, Alyssa Milano, Chazz Palminteri, Don Knotts. DVD

Lambert, the Sheepish Lion
Film short (1952) Walt Disney Treasures: Disney Rarities. DVD

The Last Flight of Noah's Ark
Film (1980) With Elliott Gould, Genevieve Bujold, Rick Schroder, Vincent Gardenia. DVD

The Legend of Lobo
Film (1962) With (the voices of) Rex Allen, Sons of the Pioneers. DVD

Life-Size
Television film (2000) With Lindsay Lohan, Jere Burns, Marie Ann DeLuise, Garwin Sanford. DVD

Life with Derek
Television series (2005) With Michael Seater, Ashley Leggat, Jordan Tododey. Seasons 1, 2, and 3. DVD

The Light in the Forest
Film (1958) With James MacArthur, Fess Parker, Wendell Corey, Joanne Dru, Jessica Tandy.

Lilo and Stitch
Film soundtrack (2002) With (the voices of) Tia Carrere, Daveigh Chase, John DeMita, Zoe Caldwell. CD, DVD

Lilo and Stitch 2: Stitch Has a Glitch
Video soundtrack (2005) With (the voices of) Tia Carrere, Dakota Fanning, Holliston Coleman, Paul Vogt. CD, DVD

The Lion King
Film soundtrack (1994) With (the voices of) Matthew Broderick, Nathan Lane, Jim Cummings,

Jeremy Irons, Jonathan Taylor Thomas. CD, DVD

Rhythm of the Pride Lands: Music Inspired by *The Lion King* (1995) CD

Original Broadway cast (1997) With Samuel E. Wright, Jason Raize, John Vickery, Heather Headley, Max Casella. CD

Disney World: The Festival of the Lion King (2001) CD

Disney's Karaoke: *The Lion King* (2003) CD

The Lion King Read-Along (2003) CD

The Lion King 1½

Video soundtrack (2004) With (the voices of) Nathan Lane, Ernie Sabella, Matthew Broderick. CD, DVD

The Lion King 2: Simba's Pride

Video soundtrack (1998) With (the voices of) Matthew Broderick, Moira Kelly, Liz Callaway, Neve Campbell. CD, DVD

Return to the Pride Lands: Music Inspired by *The Lion King II* (1998) CD

Little Einsteins

Television series soundtrack (2005) Selective episodes in three volumes. CD, DVD

The Little Mermaid

Film soundtrack (1989) With (the voices of) Jodi Benson, Pat Carroll, Samuel Wright. CD, DVD

The Little Mermaid: Songs from the Sea (1992)

The Little Mermaid Read-Along (2001)

Disney's Karaoke: *The Little Mermaid* (2006) CD

Broadway soundtrack (2007) With Sierra Boggess, Sean Palmer, Sherie Rene Scott. CD

The Little Mermaid: Splash Hits from the TV series (1995)

Little Mermaid and Friends (2006) Songs from the series and the original film. CD

The Little Mermaid II: Return to the Sea

Video soundtrack (2000) With (the voices of) Jodi Benson, Samuel E. Wright. CD, DVD

The Little Mermaid: Ariel's Beginning

Video film (2008) With (the voices of) Jodi Benson, Samuel E. Wright, Kari Wahlgren, Jim Cummings. DVD

Lizzie McGuire

Television series soundtrack (2001) With Hilary Duff, Adam Lamberg, Jake Thomas. Episodes in four volumes. CD, DVD

The Lizzie McGuire Movie

Film soundtrack (2003) With Hilary Duff, Adam Lamberg, Clayton Snyder. CD, DVD

Make Mine Music

Film soundtrack (1946) With (the voices of) Nelson Eddy, Dinah Shore, Andrews Sisters. DVD

Mary Poppins
Film soundtrack (1964) With Julie
Andrews, Dick Van Dyke, David
Tomlinson, Glynis Johns. CD,
DVD
Let's Fly with Mary Poppins: Louis
Prima and His New Orleans Gang
(1998) CD
Disney's Karaoke: *Mary Poppins*
(2004) CD
Original London cast (2004) With
Laura Mitchell, Gavin Lee, Linzi
Hateley. CD
Duke Ellington Plays *Mary
Poppins* (2005) CD
Sing-Along *Mary Poppins* (2006)
CD

Meet the Robinsons
Film soundtrack (2007) With (the
voices of) Daniel Hansen, Jordan
Fry, Matthew Josten, Stephen
Anderson, CD, DVD

Melody Time
Film soundtrack (1948) With (the
voices of) the Andrews Sisters,
Dennis Day. DVD

Mickey Mouse Club
Television series (1955) With
Jimmie Dodd, Annette Funicello,
Darlene Gillespie, Tommy Cole,
Don Grady. Selected episodes.
DVD
Songs from the Mickey Mouse
Club TV Show.

Mickey's Christmas Carol
Film short soundtrack (1983) With
(the voices of) Alan Young, Wayne

Allwine, Hal Smith, Will Ryan.
DVD

Mickey's House of Villains
Video (2001) With (the voices of)
Wayne Allwine, Russi Taylor, Tony
Anselmo, Bill Farmer. DVD

Mickey's Magical Christmas
Video (2001) With (the voices of)
Wayne Allwine, Alan Young, Hal
Smith, Will Ryan. DVD

Midnight Madness
Film (1980) With David Naughton,
Debra Clinger, David Damas,
Michael J. Fox. DVD

Mighty Joe Young
Film soundtrack (1998) With Bill
Paxton, Charlize Theron, Rade
Serbedzija, Regina King. CD, DVD

Miracle of the White Stallions
Film (1963) With Robert Taylor,
Lilli Palmer, Curt Jurgens, Eddie
Albert. DVD

**The Misadventures of Merlin
Jones**
Film (1964) With Tommy Kirk,
Annette Funicello, Leon Ames,
Stuart Erwin, Alan Hewitt. DVD

Monkeys, Go Home!
Film (1967) With Dean Jones,
Maurice Chevalier, Yvette
Mimieux, Bernard Woringer. DVD

The Monkey's Uncle
Film (1965) With Tommy Kirk,
Annette Funicello, Leon Ames,
Arthur O'Connell. DVD

Monsters, Inc.
Film soundtrack (2001) With
(the voices of) Billy Crystal, John
Goodman, Steve Buscemi, Jennifer
Tilly. CD, DVD

Moon Pilot
Film (1962) With Tom Tryon,
Brian Keith, Edmond O'Brien,
Dany Saval. DVD

The Moon-Spinners
Film soundtrack (1964) With
Hayley Mills, Peter McEnery, Eli
Wallach, Pola Negri. DVD

Mousercise
Television series soundtrack (1983)

Mulan
Film soundtrack (1998) With (the
voices of) Ming-Na, Lea Salonga,
Eddie Murphy, B. D. Wong,
Miguel Ferrer. CD, DVD

Mulan II
Video soundtrack (2005) With (the
voices of) Ming-Na, B. D. Wong,
Isabelle Griffiths, Judy Kuhn. CD,
DVD

The Muppet Christmas Carol
Film soundtrack (1992) With
Michael Caine; (the voices of)
Dave Goelz, Steve Whitmire,
Donald Austin. CD, DVD

Muppet Treasure Island
Film soundtrack (1996) With
Tim Curry, Kevin Bishop, Billy
Connolly; (the voices of) Frank Oz,
Dave Goelz, Steve Whitmire. CD,
DVD

The Muppets
Film soundtrack (2011) With Jason
Segel, Amy Adams, Jim Parsons;
(the voices of) Steve Whitmire,
Peter Linz, Eric Jacobson. CD,
DVD

*A Muppets Christmas: Letters to
Santa*
Television film soundtrack
(2009) With (the voices of) Steve
Whitmire, Dave Goelz, Eric
Jacobson, Bill Barretta. CD, DVD

The Muppets' Wizard of Oz
Television film soundtrack (2005)
With Ashanti, Queen Latifah;
(the voices of) Dave Goelz, Bill
Barretta, Brian Henson. CD,
DVD

*My Date with the President's
Daughter*
Television movie (1998) With Will
Friedle, Elizabeth Harnois, Dabney
Coleman.

My Science Project
Film (1985) With John Stockwell,
Danielle von Zerneck, Fisher
Stevens, Raphael Sbarge. DVD

Newsies
Film soundtrack (1992) With
Christian Bale, David Moscow,
Bill Pullman, Robert Duvall, Ann-
Margret. CD, DVD

The Night before Christmas
Film short (1933) Walt Disney
Treasures: More Silly Symphonies.
DVD

**The Nightmare before
Christmas**
Film soundtrack (1993) With
(the voices of) Chris Sarandon,
Danny Elfman, William Hickey,
Ken Page, Catherine O'Hara. CD,
DVD

The Old Mill
Film short (1937) Walt Disney
Treasures: Silly Symphonies. DVD

Old Yeller
Film (1957) With Tommy Kirk,
Jeff York, Dorothy Malone, Fess
Parker, Kevin Corcoran. DVD

Oliver & Company
Film soundtrack (1988) With (the
voices of) Joseph Lawrence, Billy
Joel, Cheech Marin, Bette Midler.
CD, DVD

**The One and Only, Genuine,
Original Family Band**
Film soundtrack (1968) With
Walter Brennan, Buddy Ebsen,
John Davidson, Lesley Ann
Warren, Janet Blair. DVD

101 Dalmatians
Film soundtrack (1962) With (the
voices of) Rod Taylor, Ben Wright,
Lisa Davis, Betty Lou Gerson. CD,
DVD

**101 Dalmatians II: Patch's
London Adventure**
Video (2003) With (the voices of)
Jason Alexander, Jodi Benson,
Barry Bostwick, Maurice
LaMarche. DVD

The Pacifier
Film (2005) With Vin Diesel, Denis
Akiyama, Tate Donovan, Anne
Fletcher. DVD

The Parent Trap
Film soundtrack (1961) With
Hayley Mills, Brian Keith,
Maureen O'Hara. DVD

Paul Bunyan
Film short (1958) American
Legends, Vol. 2. DVD
Walt Disney Treasures: Disney
Rarities. DVD

Peculiar Penguins
Film short (1934) Walt Disney
Treasures: Silly Symphonies. DVD

Perri
Film (1957) Walt Disney's Legacy
Collection: True Life Adventures,
Vol. 4. DVD
Story with songs. With Jimmie
Dodd and Disneyland Chorus and
Orchestra.

Peter Pan
Film soundtrack (1953) With (the
voices of) Bobby Driscoll, Kathryn
Beaumont, Hans Conried. CD,
DVD
100 Years of *Peter Pan* (2004) CD

Pete's Dragon
Film soundtrack (1977) With
Helen Reddy, Sean Marshall, Jim
Dale, Mickey Rooney. CD, DVD

Phineas and Ferb
Television series (2007) Selected
episodes on three volumes. DVD

The Pied Piper
Film short (1933) Walt Disney
Treasures: More Silly Symphonies.
DVD

Piglet's Big Movie
Film soundtrack (2003) With
(the voices of) John Fielder, Jim
Cummings, Carly Simon. CD, DVD

Pinocchio
Film soundtrack (1940) With
(the voices of) Dickie Jones, Cliff
Edwards, Walter Catlett. CD, DVD
Pinocchio Read-Along (1993)

**Pirates of the Caribbean: The
Curse of the Black Pearl**
Film soundtrack (2003) With
Johnny Depp, Keira Knightley,
Orlando Bloom, Geoffrey Rush.
CD, DVD

**Pirates of the Caribbean: At
World's End**
Film soundtrack (2007) With
Johnny Depp, Keira Knightley,
Orlando Bloom, Geoffrey Rush.
CD, DVD

Pocahontas
Film soundtrack (1995) With (the
voices of) Irene Bedard, Judy
Kuhn, Linda Hunt, Mel Gibson,
Jim Cummings. CD, DVD

**Pocahontas II: Journey to a New
World**
Video (1998) With (the voices of)
Irene Bedard, Jim Cummings,
Linda Hunt, Finola Hughes, Donal
Gibson. DVD

**Pooh's Grand Adventure: The
Search for Christopher Robin**
Video soundtrack (1997) With
(the voices of) Jim Cummings,
John Fiedler, Ken Sansom, Andre
Stojka, Peter Cullen. CD, DVD

Pooh's Heffalump Movie
Film soundtrack (2005) With (the
voices of) Jim Cummings, John
Fiedler, Nikita Hopkins, Kath
Soucie, Ken Sansom. CD, DVD

**Pooh's Heffalump Halloween
Movie**
Video (2005) With (the voices of)
Jimmy Bennett, Jim Cummings,
John Fiedler, Peter Cullen. DVD

Popeye
Film soundtrack (1980) With Robin
Williams, Shelley Duvall, Ray
Walston, Paul Dooley. DVD

**Prince of Persia: The Sands of
Time**
Film soundtrack (2010) With Jake
Gyllenhaal, Gemma Arterton, Ben
Kingsley, Alfred Molina. CD, DVD

The Princess and the Frog
Film soundtrack (2009) With
(the voices of) Anika Noni Rose,
Bruno Campos, Keith David, Jim
Cummings, Jenifer Lewis, Peter
Bartlett, Michael-Leon Wooley.
CD, DVD

**The Princess Diaries 2: Royal
Engagement**
Film soundtrack (2004) With
Anne Hathaway, Julie Andrews,

Callum Blue, Hector Elizondo.
CD, DVD

Rascal
Film (1968) With Steve Forrest,
Bill Mumy, Elsa Lanchester,
Pamela Toll. DVD

Ratatouille
Film soundtrack (2007) With (the
voices of) Patton Oswalt, Ian Holm,
Lou Romano, Brian Dennehy,
Peter O'Toole. CD, DVD

The Reluctant Dragon
Film (1941) With (the voices of)
Robert Benchley, Frances Gilford,
Buddy Pepper. DVD

The Rescuers
Film (1977) With (the voices
of) Eva Gabor, Bob Newhart,
Michelle Stacy, Geraldine Page.
DVD
Story and song.

Return of Jafar
Video (1994) With (the voices
of) Jonathan Freeman, Gilbert
Gottfried, Jason Alexander, Scott
Weinger, Linda Larkin. DVD

Return to Never Land
Film soundtrack (2002) With
(the voices of) Harriet Owen,
Corey Burton, Blayne Weaver,
Jill Bennett, Kath Soucie. CD,
DVD

The Robber Kitten
Film short (1935) Walt Disney
Treasures: Silly Symphonies.
DVD

Robin Hood
Film (1973) With (the voices of)
Brian Bedford, Monica Evans, Phil
Harris, Andy Devine, Roger Miller.
DVD
Story with songs.

Rolie Polie Olie
Television series (1998) Selected
episodes. DVD

Run, Cougar, Run
Film (1972) With Frank Aletter,
Harry Carey Jr., Alfonso Arau,
Lonny Chapman.

The Saga of Windwagon Smith
Film short (1961) Disney Tall Tales:
Carton Classics, Vol. 12. DVD
Walt Disney treasures: Disney
Rarities. DVD
American Legends, Vol. 2. DVD

Saludos Amigos
Film (1942) With (the voices
of) Pinto Colvig, José Oliveira,
Clarence Nash. DVD

*The Santa Clause 3: The Escape
Clause*
Film (2006) With Tim Allen,
Elizabeth Mitchell, Eric Lloyd,
Martin Short. DVD

Santa's Workshop
Film short (1932) Walt Disney
Treasures: More Silly Symphonies.
DVD

Savage Sam
Film (1963) With Brian Keith,
Tommy Kirk, Kevin Corcoran, Jeff
York, Dewey Martin. DVD

Scandalous John
Film (1971) With Brian Keith,
Alfonso Arau, Michele Carey,
Harry Morgan.

The Shaggy D.A.
Film (1976) With Dean Jones,
Tim Conway, Suzanne Pleshette,
Keenan Wynn. DVD

Sleeping Beauty
Film soundtrack (1959) With (the
voices of) Mary Costa, Bill Shirley,
Eleanor Audley, Taylor Holmes,
Bill Thompson. CD, DVD

The Small One
Film short (1976) With (the
voices of) Sean Marshall, William
Woodson. Classic Cartoon
Favorites, Vol. 9. DVD

Smith!
Film (1969) With Glenn Ford,
Nancy Olson, Dean Jagger, Keenan
Wynn, Warren Oates, Chief Dan
George.

**Snow White and the Seven
Dwarfs**
Film soundtrack (1937) With (the
voices of) Adriana Caselotti, Harry
Stockwell, Billy Gilbert, Lucille La
Verne, Pinto Colvig, Roy Atwell.
CD, DVD
Story and Song: *Snow White and
the Seven Dwarfs* (1992)

So Dear to My Heart
Film (1949) With Burl Ives, Bobby
Driscoll, Beulah Bondi, Luana
Patten.

Song of the South
Film soundtrack (1946) With James
Baskett, Bobby Driscoll, Hattie
McDaniel, Luana Patten, Ruth
Warrick. DVD

**The Story of Robin Hood and
His Merrie Men**
Film (1952) With Richard Todd,
Joan Rice, Peter Finch, James
Hayter, Martita Hunt. DVD

The Strongest Man in the World
Film (1975) With Kurt Russell, Joe
Flynn, Eve Arden, Cesar Romero,
Dick Van Patten, Phil Silvers. DVD

The Suite Life of Zack and Cody
Television series (2005) Seasons 1,
2, and 3. DVD

Summer Magic
Film soundtrack (1963) With
Hayley Mills, Burl Ives, Dorothy
McGuire, Deborah Walley, Eddie
Hodges. DVD

Superdad
Film (1973) With Bob Crane,
Kathleen Cody, Kurt Russell, Joe
Flynn, Dick Van Patten. DVD

Swamp Fox
Television series (1959) Walt
Disney Treasures: Legendary
Heroes. DVD

Swiss Family Robinson
Film (1960) With John Mills,
Dorothy McGuire, James
MacArthur, Janet Munro, Tommy
Kirk, Kevin Corcoran. DVD
Story and song.

The Sword in the Stone
Film soundtrack (1963) With (the voices of) Rickie Sorenson, Karl Swenson, Sebastian Cabot, Martha Wentworth. DVD

TaleSpin
Television series (1990) With (the voices of) Ed Gilbert, Sally Struthers, Jack Angel, Michael Bell, Kenneth Mars. Vols. 1 and 2. DVD

Tangled
Film soundtrack (2010) With (the voices of) Mandy Moore, Donna Murphy, Zachary Levi, Ron Perlman, Jeffrey Tambor. CD, DVD

Tarzan
Film soundtrack (1999) With Glenn Close, Tony Goldwyn, Minnie Driver. CD, DVD
Original Broadway cast (2006) With Josh Strickland, Jenn Gambatese, Shuler Hensley. CD

Tarzan II
Video film (2005) With (the voices of) Harrison Chad, George Carlin, Brad Garrett, Ron Perlman. DVD

Tarzan and Jane
Video film (2002) With (the voices of) Greg Ellis, Tara Strong, Michael T. Weiss, Jim Cummings. DVD

Teacher's Pet
Film (2004) With (the voices of) Nathan Lane, Kelsey Grammer. CD, DVD

Ten Who Dared
Film (1960) With Brian Keith, Ben Johnson.

Texas John Slaughter
Television series (1958) With Tom Tryon, Darryl Hickman.

That Darn Cat
Film soundtrack (1965) With Hayley Mills, Dean Jones, Roddy McDowall. DVD

That's So Raven
Television series (2003) With Raven-Symoné, Orlando Brown, Jesse McCartney. Four volumes. CD, DVD
Disney's Karaoke Series: *That's So Raven*. CD

Third Man on the Mountain
Film (1959) With James MacArthur, Janet Munro. DVD

Those Calloways
Film (1965) With Brian Keith, Vera Miles, Ed Wynn, Walter Brennan. DVD

The Three Caballeros
Film (1945) With Aurora Miranda, Carmen Molina. DVD

The Three Little Pigs
Film short soundtrack (1933) With (the voices of) Billy Bletcher, Pinto Colvig, Dorothy Compton. DVD
Walt Disney Treasures: Silly Symphonies. DVD
Disney's Timeless Tales, Vol. 1. DVD

The Three Lives of Thomasina
Film (1964) With Patrick
McGoohan, Susan Hampshire. DVD

The Three Musketeers
Film soundtrack (1993) With
Charlie Sheen, Kiefer Sutherland,
Chris O'Donnell, Tim Curry. CD,
DVD

The Tigger Movie
Film soundtrack (2000) With (the
voices of) Jim Cummings, Nikita
Hopkins. CD, DVD

Tinker Bell
Video film soundtrack (2008) With
(the voices of) Mae Whitman,
Kristin Chenoweth, America
Ferrera. CD, DVD

**Toby Tyler, or Ten Weeks with
a Circus**
Film (1960) With Kevin Corcoran,
Henry Calvin. DVD

Tonka
Film (1958) With Sal Mineo, Philip
Carey, Jerome Courtland.

Toot, Whistle, Plunk and Boom
Film short (1953) Walt Disney
Treasures: Disney Rarities. DVD

The Tortoise and the Hare
Film short (1935) Disney's
Timeless Tales, Vol. 1. DVD
Walt Disney Treasures: Silly
Symphonies. DVD

Toy Story
Film soundtrack (1995) With (the
voices of) Tom Hanks, Tim Allen,

Don Rickles, Annie Potts, Randy
Newman. DVD, CD

Toy Story 2
Film soundtrack (1999) With (the
voices of) Tim Allen, Tom Hanks,
Jodi Benson, Joan Cusack, Kelsey
Grammer. DVD, CD

Toy Story 3
Film soundtrack (2010) With (the
voices of) Randy Newman, Chic,
Gary Wright, Gipsy Kings. CD,
DVD

Treasure of Matecumbe
Film (1976) With Robert
Foxworth, Joan Hackett, Peter
Ustinov. DVD

Treasure Planet
Film soundtrack (2002) With (the
voices of) Joseph Gordon-Levitt,
Patrick McGoohan, Corey Burton,
Roscoe Lee Browne. CD, DVD

Tree of Life
Theme park soundtrack (1998)
Animal Kingdom Songs. CD

Tron
Film soundtrack (1982) With Jeff
Bridges, Bruce Boxleitner. CD,
DVD

20,000 Leagues under the Sea
Film soundtrack (1954) With James
Mason, Kirk Douglas, Peter Lorre.
DVD

Up
Film soundtrack (2009) With (the
voices of) Edward Asner, Jordan

Nagai, Christopher Plummer, Bob Peterson, Craig Copeland. CD, DVD

Victory through Air Power
Film (1943) With (the voice of) Clarence Nash. Walt Disney Treasures: Disney on the Front Lines. DVD

WALL-E
Film soundtrack (2008) With (the voices of) Ben Burtt, Jeff Garlin, Fred Willard. DVD, CD

Westward Ho, the Wagons!
Film (1956) With Fess Parker, Kathleen Crowley, Jeff York, Sebastian Cabot.

Who Killed Cock Robin?
Film short (1935) Walt Disney Treasures: Silly Symphonies. DVD

Wild Hearts Can't Be Broken
Film (1991) With Gabrielle Anwar, Michael Schoeffling, Cliff Robertson. DVD

Winnie the Pooh
Film soundtrack (2011) With (the voices of) Jim Cummings, Craig Ferguson, Bud Luckey, Travis Oates, Tom Kenny, Zooey Deschanel. CD, DVD

Winnie the Pooh: A Valentine for You
Television film (1999) With (the voices of) John Fiedler, Jerome Beidler, Peter Cullen, Jim Cummings. DVD

Winnie the Pooh and the Honey Tree
Film soundtrack (1966) With (the voices of) Sterling Holloway, Sebastian Cabot, Barbara Luddy, John Fiedler. CD, DVD

Winnie the Pooh: A Very Merry Pooh Year
Video (2002) With (the voices of) Jim Cummings, Ken Sansom, Bob Joles, Michael Gough. DVD

Winnie the Pooh and the Blustery Day
Film soundtrack (1968) With (the voices of) Sterling Holloway, John Fiedler, Sebastian Cabot, Barbara Luddy. CD, DVD

Winnie the Pooh: Seasons of Giving
Video (1999) With (the voices of) Jim Cummings, John Fiedler, Gregg Berger, Brady Bluhm. DVD

Winnie the Pooh: Springtime with Roo
Video (2004) With (the voices of) Jimmy Bennett, Jim Cummings, Kath Soucie. DVD

The Wise Little Hen
Film short (1934) Walt Disney Treasures: Silly Symphonies. DVD

Wizards of Waverly Place
Television series (2007) With Selena Gomez, David Henrie. Two volumes. DVD

Wynken, Blynken and Nod
Film short (1938) Walt Disney
Treasues: Silly Symphonies. DVD

Zorro
Television series (1957) With Guy
Williams. Season 1. DVD

RECORDINGS WITH DISNEY SONGS

Some of these compilation albums use the original versions of the songs from the film or video soundtrack. Others include all or several Disney songs with new recordings. The recordings that are not indicated as CD were released only on vinyl or audiocassette and hopefully will be reissued on the CD format someday.

And the Winner Is: A Collection of Honored Disney Classic Songs (1995)
Animated Classics: 101 Strings Orchestra (2002) CD
Barbara Cook: The Disney Album (1988) CD
Barbara Hendricks and the Abbey Road Ensemble Sings Disney (1996) CD
Believe: The Songs of the Sherman Brothers (2003) CD
Best Wishes: Relaxing Magic of Disney Songs (2003) CD
Classic Disney: 60 Years of Musical Magic (2003) CD
Color, Rhythm and Magic: Favorite Songs from Disney Classics (2000) CD
Cruella's Favorite Villain Songs (2001) CD
Disney Baby Lullaby: Favorite Sleepytime Songs for Baby and You (1991) CD
The Disney Collection: Best-Loved Songs from Disney Motion Pictures, Television Shows and Theme Parks (1991)
Disney Princesses: The Ultimate Song Collection (2004) CD
Disney's Fairy Tale Weddings (2005) CD
Disney's Greatest Hits (2005) CD
Disney's Greatest Love Songs (2008) CD
Disney's Greatest Vol. 1 (2001) CD
Disney's Greatest Vol. 2 (2001) CD
Disney's Greatest Vol. 3 (2002) CD
Disney's Happiest Celebration on Earth (2005) CD
Disney's Hero Songs (1996) CD
Disney's Instrumental Impressions: 14 Classic Disney Love Songs (1998)
Disney's Love Songs (2006) CD

Disney's On the Record (2005) CD

Disney's Princesses Collection: The Music of Hopes, Dreams and Happy Endings (2007) CD

Disney's Superstar Hits (2002) CD

Dixie Magic: Bibbidi Bobbidi Boo (2000) CD

Faith, Trust and Pixie Dust: Kerry Butler (2008) CD

Got No Strings: Michelle Shocked (2005) CD

Heigh Ho Banjo: Bluegrass Salutes Favorite Disney Songs (1998) CD

Heigh Ho Mozart: Favorite Disney Tunes in the Style of Great Classical Composers (1995) CD

The Jazz Networks: Beauty and the Beast (1992) CD

Julie Andrews Selects Her Favorite Disney Songs (2005) CD

Louis Armstrong: Disney Songs the Satchmo Way (1968) CD

Mannheim Steamroller Meets the Mouse: Unique Musical Creations Based on Disney Songs (1999) CD

Michael Crawford: The Disney Album (2001) CD

Michael Feinstein: Pure Imagination (1992) CD

Music Behind the Magic: 50 Songs Celebrating 50 Years of Disney Magic (2006) CD

The Music of Disney: A Legacy in Song (1996) CD

My First Disney Songs: Japanese (2003) CD

My First Sing-Along: My First Princess Songs (2004) CD

Part of Your World: Debbie Shapiro Gravitte Sings Alan Menken (1994) CD

Reel Imagination: Classic Songs: Michelle Nicastro (1994) CD

Return to Pride Rock: Songs Inspired by Disney's The Lion King II: Simba's Pride (1998) CD

Sing Your Favorite Walt Disney Songs (2007) CD

Take My Hand: Songs from the Hundred Acre Wood (1995) CD

Ten Disney Favorites: Songs from the Sea and Inspired by The Little Mermaid (2006) CD

Toonful: Michelle Nicastro (1993) CD

Toonful Too: Michelle Nicastro (1995) CD

Twelve Disney Favorites: Doggone Fun Songs (1999) CD

Walt Disney's Fun with Music: 30 Favorite Disney Songs (1964)

Walt Disney's Happiest Songs (1967)

Walt Disney's Merriest Songs (1968)

When You Wish Upon a Star: A Salute to Walt Disney (1994) CD

Winnie the Pooh: Silly Old Bear Songs (1998)

Winnie the Pooh: Tiggerific Songs (1998)

You'll Be in My Heart: The Essential Disney Love Song Collection (2009) CD

Zip-A-Dee-Doo-Dah (1992) CD

DISNEY SONG VHS AND DVDS

Although some of the songs included in these short videos are not from Disney sources, most are—and all are enlivened by Disney characters and scenes from Disney movies and theme parks.

Canta Con Nostros: Nuestro Húesped (Sing-Along Songs: Be Our Guest) Spanish (1994) VHS

Canta Con Nostros: Un Amigo Fiel (Sing-Along Songs: Friend Like Me) Spanish (1995) VHS

Disney's Brother Bear Sing-Along Songs (2003) DVD

Sing a Song with Tigger (2000) VHS

Sing-Along Songs: The Bare Necessities (2006) DVD

Sing-Along Songs: Be Our Guest (1994) VHS

Sing-Along Songs: Beach Party at Walt Disney World (2005) DVD

Sing-Along Songs: Brother Bear (2003) DVD

Sing-Along Songs: Colors of the Wind (1995) VHS

Sing-Along Songs: Disneyland Fun (2005) DVD

Sing-Along Songs: En Español (1995) VHS

Sing-Along Songs: Flik's Musical Adventure (2005) DVD

Sing-Along Songs: Friend Like Me (1994) VHS

Sing-Along Songs: Happy Haunting (2006) DVD

Sing-Along Songs: Heigh-Ho (1994) VHS

Sing-Along Songs: Home on the Range (2004) DVD

Sing-Along Songs: Honor to Us All (1998) VHS

Sing-Along Songs: I Love to Laugh (2006) DVD

Sing-Along Songs: Pongo and Perdita (2006) DVD

Sing-Along Songs: Topsy-Turvy (1996) VHS

Sing-Along Songs: Under the Sea (1994) VHS

Sing-Along Songs: You Can Fly! (2006) DVD

DISNEY DVD ANTHOLOGY COLLECTIONS

Many of the television programs and animated shorts found in this book can be located in DVD collections, which are usually easier to locate than original videotapes or individual DVDs. Here is a list of anthologies followed by the titles of their contents.

Fun and Fancy Free (1947)
   Mickey and the Beanstalk • Bongo

Make Mine Music (1946)
   The Martins and the Coys • Blue Bayou • All the Cats Join In • Without You • Casey at the Bat • Two Silhouettes • Peter and the Wolf • After You've Gone • Johnnie Fedora and Alice Blue Bonnet • The Whale Who Wanted to Sing at the Met

Melody Time (1948)
   Once Upon a Wintertime • Bumble Boogie • The Legend of Johnny Appleseed • Little Toot • Trees • Blame it on the Samba • Pecos Bill

Walt Disney Treasures: Disney on the Front Lines
   Victory Through Air Power • Donald Gets Drafted • The Army Mascot • The Vanishing Private • Sky Trooper • Der Fuehrer's Face • Education for Death • Private Pluto • Fall Out • Reason and Emotion • Victory Vehicles • The Old Army Game • Home Defense • Chicken Little • How to Be a Good Sailor • Commando Duck

Walt Disney Treasures: Disney Rarities—Celebrated Shorts, 1920s–1960s
   Alice's Wonderland • Ben and Me • Alice Gets in Dutch • Football, Now and Then • Alice's Wild West Show • Toot, Whistle, Plunk and Boom • Alice in the Jungle • Pigs Is Pigs • Alice's Egg Plant • Social Lion • Alice's Mysterious Mystery • A Cowboy Needs a Horse • Alice the Whaler • Hooked Bear • Ferdinand the Bull • In the Bag • Chicken Little • Jack and Old Mac • The Pelican and the Snipe • The Story of Anyburg, U.S.A. • The Truth about Mother Goose • The Brave Engineer • Paul Bunyan • Morris, the Midget Moose • Noah's Ark • Lambert, the Sheepish Lion • Goliath II • The Little House • The Saga of Windwagon Smith • Adventures in Music: Melody • A Symposium on Popular Songs

Walt Disney Treasures: Disneyland—Secrets, Stories & Magic
   The Secrets, Stories, and Magic of Disneyland • Operation Disneyland • People and Places

Walt Disney Treasures: Silly Symphonies
   The Skeleton Dance • More Mice • Flowers and Trees • Three Little Pigs • The Old Mill • Cookie Carnival • The Ugly Duckling (1931) • Wood-

land Café • Who Killed Cock Robin? • Music Land • The Wise Little Hen • The Tortoise and the Hare • The Grasshopper and the Ants • The Three Little Pigs • Wynken, Blynken and Nod • Babes in the Woods • Elmer Elephant • The Flying Mouse • The Golden Touch • The Robber Kitten • Lullaby Land • Mother Goose Melodies • The Big Bad Wolf • Three Little Wolves • Toby Tortoise Returns • Water Babies • The Practical Pig • Mother Pluto • Peculiar Penguins • The Old Mill • Funny Little Bunnies • The Ugly Duckling (1939) • Father Noah's Ark • Birds of a Feather • The Busy Beavers • Just Dogs • Music Land • The China Plate • Egyptian Melodies • Farmyard Symphony

Walt Disney Treasures: More Silly Symphonies (1929–1938)

Arctic Antics • Autumn • The Bears and the Bees • The Bird Store • Birds in the Spring • Broken Toys • Bugs in Love • Cannibal Capers • The Cat's Out (also known as The Cat's Nightmare) • The China Shop • The Clock Store • Cock O' the Walk • El Terrible Toreador • The Fox Hunt • Frolicking Fish • The Goddess of Spring • Hell's Bells • King Neptune • Little Hiawatha • Merbabies • The Merry Dwarfs • Midnight in a Toy Shop • Monkey Melodies • More Kittens • The Moth and the Flame • Mother Goose Goes Hollywood • Night • The Night Before Christmas • Old King Cole • The Pied Piper • Playful Pan • Santa's Workshop • The Spider and the Fly • Springtime • Summer • Three Blind Mouseketeers • Three Orphan Kittens • Winter

OTHER COLLECTIONS OF INTEREST (DVDS)

Walt Disney Treasures: Mickey Mouse in Black and White, Volume One
Walt Disney Treasures: Mickey Mouse in Black and White, Volume Two
Walt Disney Treasures: Mickey Mouse in Living Color, Volume One
Walt Disney Treasures: Mickey Mouse in Living Color, Volume Two
Walt Disney Treasures: The Chronological Donald, Volume One (1934–1941)
Walt Disney Treasures: The Chronological Donald, Volume Two (1942–1946)
Walt Disney Treasures: The Chronological Donald, Volume Three (1947–1950)
Walt Disney Treasures: The Complete Goofy
Walt Disney Treasures: The Complete Pluto, Volume One
Walt Disney Treasures: The Complete Pluto, Volume Two

Walt Disney Treasures: Mickey Mouse Club

Walt Disney Treasures: The Adventures of Spin & Marty—The Mickey Mouse Club

Walt Disney Treasures: The Mickey Mouse Club Featuring the Hardy Boys

Walt Disney Treasures: Your Host, Walt Disney

Walt Disney Treasures: Behind the Scenes at the Walt Disney Studio

Walt Disney Treasures: Disneyland USA

Walt Disney Treasures: Tomorrowland: Disney in Space and Beyond

Walt Disney Treasures: The Complete Davy Crockett Televised Series

Walt Disney Treasures: Elfego Baca and The Swamp Fox—Legendary Heroes

APPENDIX E: ACADEMY AWARDS FOR DISNEY SONGS AND SCORES

All of the Disney songs and scores nominated for an Academy Award are listed below. The year given is that of the awards ceremony, not the release date of the film, and the winners are in bold type.

1937
Best Score: *Snow White and the Seven Dwarfs*

1940
Best Song: **"When You Wish upon a Star"** (*Pinocchio*)
Best Score (Original): ***Pinocchio***

1941
Best Song: "Baby Mine" (*Dumbo*)
Best Score: ***Dumbo***

1942
Best Song: "Love Is a Song" (*Bambi*)
Best Score: *Bambi*

1943
Best Song: "Saludos Amigos" (*Saludos Amigos*)
Best Score: *Saludos Amigos, Victory through Air Power*

1945
Best Score: *The Three Caballeros*

1947
Best Song: **"Zip-a-Dee-Doo-Dah"** (*Song of the South*)
Best Score: *Song of the South*

1949
Best Song: "Lavender Blue" (*So Dear to My Heart*)

1950
Best Song: "Bibbidi-Bobbidi-Boo" (*Cinderella*)
Best Score: *Cinderella*

1951
Best Score: *Alice in Wonderland*

1957
Best Score: *Perri*

1959
Best Score: *Sleeping Beauty*

1961
Best Score: *Babes in Toyland*

1963
Best Score: *The Sword in the Stone*

1964
Best Song: **"Chim Chim Cher-ee"** (*Mary Poppins*)
Best Score (Original): **Mary Poppins**
Best Score (Adapted): *Mary Poppins*

1967
Best Song: "The Bare Necessities" (*The Jungle Book*)

1971
Best Song: "The Age of Not Believing" (*Bedknobs and Broomsticks*)
Best Score: *Bedknobs and Broomsticks*

1973
Best Song: "Love" (*Robin Hood*)

1977
Best Song: "Candle on the Water" (*Pete's Dragon*), "Someone's Waiting for You (*The Rescuers*)
Best Score: *Pete's Dragon*

1989
Best Song: "Kiss the Girl" (*The Little Mermaid*), **"Under the Sea"** (*The Little Mermaid*)
Best Score: **The Little Mermaid**

1990
Best Song: **"Sooner or Later"** (*Dick Tracy*)

1991
Best Song: **"Beauty and the Beast"** (*Beauty and the Beast*), "Belle" (*Beauty and the Beast*), "Be Our Guest" (*Beauty and the Beast*)
Best Score: **Beauty and the Beast**

1992
Best Song: "Friend Like Me" (*Aladdin*), **"Whole New World"** (*Aladdin*)
Best Score: **Aladdin**

1994
Best Song: **"Can You Feel the Love Tonight"** (*The Lion King*), "Circle of Life" (*The Lion King*), "Hakuna Matata" (*The Lion King*)
Best Score: **The Lion King**

1995
Best Song: **"Colors of the Wind"** (*Pocahontas*), "You've Got a Friend in Me" (*Toy Story*)
Best Score: **Pocahontas**, *Toy Story*

1996
Best Score: *The Hunchback of Notre Dame, James and the Giant Peach*

1997
Best Song: "Go the Distance" (*Hercules*)

1998
Best Score: *Mulan, A Bug's Life*

1999
Best Song: **"You'll Be in My Heart"** (*Tarzan*), "When She Loved Me" (*Toy Story 2*)

2000
Best Song: "My Funny Friend and Me" (*The Emperor's New Groove*)

2001
Best Song: **"If I Didn't Have You"** (*Monsters, Inc.*)
Best Score: *Monsters, Inc.*

2006
Best Song: "Our Town" (*Cars*)

2007
Best Song: "Happy Working Song" (*Enchanted*), "So Close" (*Enchanted*), "That's How You Know" (*Enchanted*)
Best Score: *Ratatouille*

2009
Best Song: "Down to Earth" (*WALL-E*)
Best Score: *WALL-E*

2010
Best Song: "Almost There" (*The Princess and the Frog*), "Down in New Orleans" (*The Princess and the Frog*)
Best score: ***Up***

2011
Best Song: "I See the Light" (*Tangled*)

GLOSSARY OF SONG TERMS

ballad A term with many different meanings in music and literature, in modern popular music a ballad is a sentimental or romantic song, usually with the same melody for each stanza. Ballads have often been the big sellers, the songs that could move listeners without benefit of plot or character. Most ballads since World War II have a fox trot (4/4) base, but there are many exceptions to that generalization over the decades. A *narrative ballad* is more like poetry's definition of the term (a poem that tells a story), and narrative songs often show up in Disney productions, such as "The Ballad of Davy Crockett" and "The Bells of Notre Dame."

character song Any musical number that is concerned with revealing a character's personality or reaction to the events of the plot can be considered a character number. A person's first character song is often his or her "I am" song. Character songs often do not travel outside the context of the story as easily as ballads do, yet there have been several popular ones over the years, such as "Who's Afraid of the Big Bad Wolf?" and "Whistle While You Work."

charm song A musical number that is less about character development than it is about utilizing the character's warmth and/or comic entertainment value has been termed a charm song. Although charm songs are often expendable to the plot, they have sometimes been audience favorites, as in the case of "A Spoonful of Sugar" and "The Dwarfs' Yodel Song."

chorus A group of characters that sing or dance together is the definition of chorus as used in this book. A musical number can be performed by a vocal chorus of singers or a dancing chorus of dancers. A *chorus number* is one that emphasizes the group over the individual, though many songs are sung by principals accompanied by a chorus. In many films, an omniscient chorus can be heard on the soundtrack, sometimes reflecting the thoughts of a character or providing exposition. This often occurs during the opening credits of a movie. *Chorus* is also another term for the refrain of a song, although, for the sake of clarification, that definition is not used in this book.

dubbing The adding or replacing of an actor's singing and/or speaking voice on a live-action film or television soundtrack is known as dubbing. All voices in an animated production are, in a sense, dubbed. Even when a performer does his or her own singing in a filmed or videotaped production, the songs are usually recorded beforehand, so in a way most actors are dubbing on screen, even if it is their own voice. The parenthetical phrase "singing voice of" is used throughout the book to indicate when one person dubbed the singing for another actor who provided the speaking voice for a character.

"I am" song Often a solo, but any song that introduces a character or a group of characters by revealing their wishes, dreams, confusions, and so on, is termed an "I am" song. These songs usually occur early in a production, helping to establish major characters by letting them express themselves. Sometimes called an "I wish" song, they became requisite in musical theatre with the advent of the integrated musical in the 1940s. The "I am" song has been very important and memorable in many stage and screen works over the decades, as in the Disney songs "Go the Distance" and "Part of Your World."

interpolation A song added to a production that was not written by the songwriters who wrote the rest of the score is said to be interpolated into the show. More common in films and television than in the theatre, interpolations serve the same purpose in all media: to improve a weak score or take advantage of a popular song by adding it to the production. Throughout the book, interpolations are included if they were written for a Disney product. Classical music, such as those used in the two *Fantasia* films, and song *standards*, such as the 1918 favorite "After You've Gone" interpolated into *Make Mine Music* (1946), are not included.

list song Any song, whether serious or comic, that is structured as a list of examples or a series of items is termed a list song. They are sometimes called "laundry list" songs, although the result is intended to be much more interesting than that. Memorable Disney list songs include "The Bare Necessities," "When I See an Elephant Fly," and "Under the Sea."

lyric A line from a song (or the entire set of lines written for a song) is considered a lyric. A lyric is written by a lyricist, as opposed to the author, who writes the unsung words in a script. The plural form *lyrics* refers to the words to all the songs a lyricist has written for a score; one writes a *lyric* for a song and the *lyrics* for a score. In this book, when a songwriter is not referred to specifically as a lyricist or a composer, it can be assumed that he or she wrote both music and lyric for the song. When a song is listed as being written by two or more songwriters with no distinction made about who wrote what, it means that the artists wrote both music and lyrics together, as in the case of all the songs by Richard M. and Robert B. Sherman.

pastiche song Any musical number that echoes the style, either musically or lyrically, of an earlier era is said to pastiche the past. Such songs can be written to spoof the past, as in "Prince Ali" (which spoofs a Las Vegas–like production number) and "Happy Working Song" (poking fun at the famous song "Whistle While You Work"), or to recapture the period for the setting of the new work, as with "Step in Time" (which pastiches British music hall) and "Be Our Guest" (a delightful version of a French *Folies Bergère* number).

refrain The main body of a song is the refrain. It is the section that follows the *verse* and repeats itself with the same melody and/or lyric. The most familiar part of a popular song is usually the refrain. The refrain is sometimes called the *chorus*, but the latter term is too often confused with a group of singers, so it is not used in this book.

release A section of the *refrain* that departs from the repeated melody is said to be a release from the expected and explores a new musical line that may or may not have been suggested in the main melody. The release (also sometimes called the *bridge*) helps keep a song from being too predictable or monotonous.

reprise When all or part of a song is repeated later in a production, it is said to be reprised. Reprises may be sung by the same characters who sang the number originally or by different ones, and often a reprise has a different lyric from the first. A song that is reprised in a film, theatre production, or television show is more likely to be remembered by an audience, so songwriters often try to have their best numbers reprised in a musical.

soliloquy A solo in which a character is alone and reveals his or her thoughts and concerns in the form of a song is considered a musical soliloquy. The most effective soliloquies are songs that show a character debating two sides of an issue or trying to come to a decision, as in "Reflection" and "The Madness of King Scar." A later development of the soliloquy on film and television is having the character's thoughts only sung on the soundtrack. Thus, it is possible to have a soliloquy when the character is with other people.

song form or **structure** Although there are no set rules for writing a song, songwriters know what works and what the public likes to hear, so over the years a formula for structuring a song was developed. Most songs of the past consisted of a *verse* and a *refrain*, sometimes going back and forth between the two. In later years verses became less prevalent, but they have far from disappeared. The most standard form for the refrain of a song is AABA; that is, the first two stanzas are musically identical, the third is a variation on it or a separate *release*, then the final stanza repeats the initial melody of the first two sections. For many years thirty-two measures was considered the traditional length for a popular song, but musical numbers written for stage and films often broke away from this pattern.

standard A song that remains popular over a number of years is classified as a standard. In many cases a song finds little success at first and only reaches the rank of standard years later. There are also standards that fell out of favor after some years, then found a new audience and popularity decades later. Examples of song standards that come from Disney productions include "Some Day My Prince Will Come," "Baby Mine," "When You Wish Upon a Star," and "Zip-a-Dee-Doo-Dah."

theme song When a song is repeated during each episode of a television series, it is identified as the theme song for the show. Usually this song is heard at the beginning of each episode, often combined with the opening credits. In some cases, a movie theme song is heard in more than one film in a series, such as the rousing theme from *Pirates of the Caribbean* feature films.

torch song In popular music, a torch song is usually a sentimental number involving unrequited love. Torch songs may be comic or sarcastic as well as serious, and some torch songs involve a character's yearning for a place as well as a person, as in "Mexico" and "Home on the Range."

verse The introductory section of a song is referred to as the verse. The melody is usually distinct from that of the *refrain* that follows, and verses tend to be shorter. Although most songs are better known for their refrains than their verses, the verse can be very important in setting up the song's ideas or images. Many songs achieve their full potency because of a well-written verse. Sometimes verses are written for a song but are cut from a film or video for various reasons, usually having to do with length. For example, "When You Wish Upon a Star" has a lovely verse that was deleted from *Pinocchio* (1940) and has rarely been heard.

BIBLIOGRAPHY

Agay, Denes. *Best Loved Songs of the American People*. Garden City, NY: Double-day, 1975.

Altman, Rick. *The American Film Musical*. Bloomington: Indiana University Press, 1987.

Benjamin, Ruth, and Arthur Roseblatt. *Movie Song Catalog*. Jefferson, NC: McFarland, 1993.

Bloom, Ken. *Hollywood Song: The Complete Film and Musical Companion*. New York: Facts On File Publications, 1995.

Burton, Jack. *The Blue Book of Hollywood Musicals*. Watkins Glen, NY: Century House, 1975.

Cotter, Bill. *The Wonderful World of Disney Television*. New York: Hyperion, 1999.

Ewen, David. *American Songwriters*. New York: H. W. Wilson, 1987.

———. *The Life and Death of Tin Pan Alley: The Golden Age of American Popular Music*. New York: Funk & Wagnalls, 1964.

Fehr, Richard, and Frederick G. Vogel. *Lullabies of Hollywood: Movie Music and the Movie Musical, 1915–1992*. Jefferson, NC: McFarland, 1993.

Fordin, Hugh. *The World of Entertainment: Hollywood's Greatest Musicals*. New York: Avon, 1975.

Freeman, Graydon Lavern. *The Melodies Linger On*. Watkins Glen, NY: Century House, 1951.

Furia, Philip. *The Poets of Tin Pan Alley*. New York: Oxford University Press, 1990.

Furia, Philip, and Michal Lasser. *America's Songs: The Stories behind the Songs of Broadway, Hollywood, and Tin Pan Alley*. New York: Routledge, 2006.

Gammond, Peter. *The Oxford Companion to Popular Music.* New York: Oxford University Press, 1991.

Green, Stanley. *Encyclopedia of Musical Film.* New York: Oxford University Press, 1981.

———. *Hollywood Musicals, Year by Year.* 2nd ed. Milwaukee: Hal Leonard, 1990.

Hemming, Roy. *The Melody Lingers On: The Great Songwriters and Their Movie Musicals.* New York: Newmarket Press, 1986.

Hirschhorn, Clive. *The Hollywood Musical.* New York: Crown, 1981.

Hischak, Thomas S. *The American Musical Film Song Encyclopedia.* Westport, CT: Greenwood Press, 1999.

———. *The American Musical Theatre Song Encyclopedia.* Westport, CT: Greenwood, 1995.

———. *The Tin Pan Alley Song Encyclopedia.* Westport, CT: Greenwood, 2002.

Hollis, Richard, and Brian Sibley. *The Disney Studio Story.* New York: Crown, 1988.

Hollis, Tim, and Greg Ehrbar. *Mouse Tracks: The Story of Walt Disney Records.* Jackson: University Press of Mississippi, 2006.

Hyland, William G. *The Song Is Ended: Songwriters and American Music, 1900–1950.* New York: Oxford University Press, 1995.

Jacobs, Dick, and Harriet Jacobs. *Who Wrote That Song?* Cincinnati: Writer's Digest Books, 1994.

Jasen, David A. *Tin Pan Alley: The Composers, the Songs, the Performers, and Their Times.* New York: Donald I. Fine, 1988.

Katz, Ephraim. *The Film Encyclopedia.* 3rd ed. New York: HarperCollins, 1998.

Lassell, Michael. *Disney on Broadway.* New York: Disney Editions, 2002.

Lax, Roger, and Frederick Smith. *The Great Song Thesaurus.* 2nd ed. New York: Oxford University Press, 1989.

Lissauer, Robert. *Lissauer's Encyclopedia of Popular Music in America: 1888 to the Present.* New York: Paragon House, 1991.

Lynch, Richard Chigley. *Movie Musicals on Record.* Westport, CT: Greenwood, 1989.

Maltin, Leonard. *The Disney Films.* 4th ed. New York: Disney Editions, 2000.

Marmorstein, Gary. *Hollywood Rhapsody: Movie Music and Its Makers, 1900 to 1975.* New York: Schirmer, 1997.

Paymer, Marvin E., gen. ed. *Facts behind the Songs: A Handbook of Popular Music from the Nineties to the '90s.* New York: Garland, 1993.

Schickel, Richard. *The Disney Version.* New York: Simon & Schuster, 1985.

Sherman, Robert B., and Richard M. Sherman. *Walt's Time.* Santa Clarita, CA: Camphor Press, 1998.

Smith, Dave. *Disney A to Z: The Official Encyclopedia.* 3rd ed. New York: Disney Editions, 2006.

Spaeth, Sigmund. *A History of Popular Music in America.* New York: Random House, 1971.

Thomas, Tony. *Music for the Movies.* New York: A. S. Barnes, 1973.

Tietyen, David. *The Musical World of Walt Disney.* Milwaukee: Hal Leonard, 1990.

White, Mark. *You Must Remember This: Popular Songwriters, 1900–1980.* New York: Charles Scribner's Sons, 1985.

Wilder, Alec. *American Popular Song: The Great Innovators, 1900–1950.* New York: Oxford University Press, 1972.

Williams, John R. *This Was Your Hit Parade.* Camden, ME: John R. Williams, 1973.

INDEX

Note: Page numbers in bold refer to illustrations.

The A Teens, 224

Abbey Road Ensemble, 4, 17, 18, 21, 35, 38, 41, 49, 61, 166, 191, 225, 239, 241, 247, 259

Abbott, Michael, 1, 57, 65, 101, 240

Abraham, F. Murray, 214

Abreu, Zequinha, 215

The Absent-Minded Professor, 140

Adair, John, 83

Adair, Tom, 57, 67, 73, 78, 164, 167, 176, 188

Adams, Amy, 80, 129, 140, 190, 209, 220

Adams, Bryan, 3

Adams, Nancy, 134

Adkins, Seth, 6, 187

Adler, Bruce, 8

Adventures in Music: Melody, 21–22

The Adventures of Bullwhip Griffin, 12, 31, 70, 242

The Adventures of Ichabod and Mr. Toad, 81, 99, 118, 141

The Adventures of Spin and Marty, 196

Adventures of the Gummi Bears. See Disney's Adventures of the Gummi Bears

Adventures of Tom Thumb and Thumbelina, 91, 162, 168, 230

Africk, Michael, 192

Agee, Tawatha, 74, 258

Aguilera, Christine, 177

Aida, 7, 42, 51, 52, 53, 55, 65, 71, 88–89, 94, 129, 150, 154, 166, 199, 250

Air Bud: Golden Receiver, 161

Akers, Karen, 196

Aladdin, 8, 31, 46, 66, 154, 160, 174, 215, 242

Aladdin and the King of Thieves, 8, 9, 60, 164, 211, 231

Albee, Edward, 243

Albert, Eddie, 116

Albertson, Jack, 90

Alderfer, Julie, 12

Alexander, Jason, 59, 77, 123

Alexander, Jessi, 38
Alford, Kenneth, 38
Alice in Wonderland (1951), 2, 3, 4, 20, 34, **56**, 88, 103, 104, 105, 138, 156, 165, 184, 221, 223, 225, 228, 232
Alice in Wonderland (2010), 3
Alice's Adventures in Wonderland, 3
Alkenas, Johan, 218
All American Rejects, 67
All 4 One, 192
Allan, Mitch, 26
Allen, Barbara Jo, 188–89
Allen, Betty, 24
Allen, Rex, 123, 180
Allen, Tim, 254
Allison, Brooke, 21, 64, 110, 249
Allister, Claude, 155, 176, 216
Almost Home, 218
Alvin, Farah, 12
Aly & AJ, 259
American Dragon: Jake Long, 5, 36
America's Heart and Soul, 249
Amoral, Nestor, 12
Anastacia, 191
Anders, Adam, 32, 86, 222, 250
Anders, Nikki, 86
Anderson, David, 235, 255
Anderson, Lyrica, 63, 109, 208
Anderson, Michael, Jr., 76
Anderson-Lopez, Kristen, 12, 57, 109, 172, 225, 244
Andrews, Julie, 12, 16, 35, 61, 94, 114, 127, **128**, 197, 198, 199, 203, 256
Andrews Sisters, 24, 113, 132, 214, 215
Ann-Margret, 85, 149
Apollo 440, 161
The Apple Dumpling Gang, 8
The Apple Dumpling Gang Rides Again, 8
Archontis, Aris, 79, 169, 256
Aristocats, The, 9, 58, 183, 214
Armato, Antonina, 19, 33, 81, 163, 235

Armstrong, Louis, 13, 14, 21, 25, 35, 82, 208, 238, 239, 259
Arnold, Eddy, 13
Arterton, Gemma, 95
Arthur, Beatrice, 141
Ashanti, 39, 72, 118, 237
Ashe, Rosemary, 27
Ashman, Howard, 8, 14, 17, 18, 31, 44, 61, 66, 68, 89, 120, 123, 144, 159, 160–61, 165–66, 173, 174, 186, 193, 224,
Astrom, Peer, 250
Atkinson, Rowan, 93, 108
Atlantis: The Lost Empire, 240
Atomic Kitten, 130
Attencio, Xavier, 15, 75–76, 252
Atwell, Roy, 22
Auberjonois, René, 123, 182
Audley, Eleanor, 189
Austin, Alana, 232
Austin & Ally, 247

B5, 69, 187, 243
Babes in the Woods,
Babes in Toyland, 65, 189, 243, 248
Baby Einstein, 131
Back Porch Majority, 8
Baddeley, Hermione, **37**, 101, 188
Bader, Diedrich, 201
Baha Men, 79, 108, 197
Bailey, Pearl, 8, 19, 121
Bailon, Adrienne, 2, 5, 34, 36, 43, 54, 69, 109, 166, 199, 202, 217
Bakalyan, Richard, 110
Baker, Buddy, 75–76, 164, 167, 176, 203
Bale, Christian, 159, 182, 250
Ballard, Glen, 28
Bambi, 127, 131, 134, 135
Bambi II, 63, 81, 127, 135, 211, 214
Banks, Tyra, 14
Barber, Sandy, 15
Barclay, Betty, 195

The Barefoot Executive, 84
Barenaked Ladies, 76
Barnes, Christopher Daniel, 169
Barnes, Rawanna M., 69
Barnes, Scott, 9, 231
Baron, Phillip, 49, 74
Barrett, Maxine, 215
Barretta, Bill, 237
Barroso, Ary, 12, 26
Barrowman, John, 32, 132
Bart, Roger, 5, 44, 71, 93, 250, 255
Baskett, James, 194–95, 241, 258
Baskin, Derrick, 98, 204
Bathing Beauty, 215
Baum, L. Frank, 166, 176
Bayardelle, Jeanette, 98
Bayless, John, 32, 38
The Beach Boys, 39, 148, 232
Beach, Gary, 14, 89, 193
Beal, John, 190
Bear in the Big Blue House, 16, 73
The Bears and I, 204
Beaumont, Kathryn, 20, 56, 88, 105,
    156, 223, 225, 232, 254, 256
Beauty and the Beast, 14, 16–17, 18,
    34, 68, 86, 89, 100, 137, 139, **143**,
    144, 152, 193
*Beauty and the Beast: The Enchanted
    Christmas*, 9, 41, 47, 200
Beddingfield, Daniel, 49
Bedknobs and Broomsticks, 2, 16, 52,
    153, 156, 199, 202, 246
Belafsky, Marty, 223
Belinda, 2, 43
Bell, Brendyn, 86
Bell, Kristen, 126, 207
Belland, Bruce, 23, 39, 85
Belle, Joleen, 247
Belle, Regina, 242
Belle's Magical World, 130, 132
Beneke, Tex, 119
Benenate, Bridget, 27, 96
Benenate, Lisa, 164

Benjamin, Bennie, 67, 140
Bennett, Chico, 69
Bennett, Jeff, 5, 9, 84, 230
Bennett, Jimmy, 26, 51, 220
Benoit, David, 49, 156
Benson, Jodi, 5, 42, 43, 48, 52, 64, 87,
    95, 96, 105, 106, 115–16, 151, 152,
    165, 173, 188, 224, 230
Benson, Robby, 130, 193
Bentinck, Tim, 96
Bernie, Ben, 243
Berry, John, 135
Bertrand, Janette, 144
Bettis, John, 83, 127
Beu Sisters, 8, 84
The Big Bad Wolf, 243
Big Little Town, 229
Big Red, 144
Bill Nye the Science Guy, 21
Billy Vera and the Beaters, 217
The Biscuit Eater, 146
Bishop, Kevin, 174, 181, 192
Black, Don, 9, 41, 47, 200
Blackburn, Tom, 13, 112, 113, 120,
    127, 233, 252
Blackton, Jay, 84, 231, 244
Blair, Janet, 126, 160, 208, 233
Blakeslee, Susan, 169
Blanchard, Terence, 238
Blankenship, Beth, 130
Bletcher, Billy, 46, 71, 241
Bleu, Corbin, 25, 93, 222
Blevins, Tim, 87
Blind Boys of Alabama, 230
Bliss, Lucille, 155
Blondheim, George, 14
Blonsky, Nikki, 49
Blore, Eric, 141
The Blue Jeans, 259
Bluhm, Brady, 163, 171
Bluth, Don, 140, 189
The Boatniks, 23
Bob B. Sox, 259

Bogardus, Stephen, 107, 181, 186
Boggess, Sierra, 20, 89, 101, 162, 166, 249
Bolt, 14, 96
Bolton, Michael, 49, 71
Bon Voyage!, 23
Bondi, Beulah, 122
Bonkers, 24, 46
Bonney, Betty, 11
Boo to You Too! Winnie the Pooh, 91, 97
Boskovich, Ann Marie, 166
Bosley, Tom, 152
Boston Pops, 35
Bottoms Up, 243
Bowling for Soup, 14, 216
Bowne, Richard, 84, 244
Boyz II Men, 154
Bradford, Don, 231
Bradford, Michael, 21
Brady, Christopher, 258
Brady, Wayne, 219
Brand Spanking New Doug, 47
Braun, Meredith, 237
Braun, Trevor, 186
Braxton, Toni, 34
Brazil, 26
Breaux, Marc, 199
Breer, Sabelle, 202–203
Bremers, Beverly, 148
Brennan, Walter, 30, 49, 70–71, 106, 126, 160, 178, 208
The Bridge on the River Kwai, 38
Bridges, Chloe, 106
Brock, Stevie, 259
Broderick, Matthew, 78
Brooke, Jonatha, 102
Brother Bear, 75, 134, 153, 157, 219, 230
Brother Bear 2, 61–62, 107, 231
Brown, Alexandra, 79
Brown, Ashley, 7, 11, 28, 34, 49, 61, 84, 105, 114, 116, 122, 126, 166, 174, 177, 191, 197, 203, 255, 256

Brown, Jim, 14, 35, 41, 58, 66, 82, 97, 131, 163
Brown, Les, 11, 195
Brown, Orlando, 203, 209
Browning, Robert, 170
Brubeck, Dave, 191
Bruce, Virginia, 26
Brunner, Robert F., 23, 39, 85, 106
Bruns, George, 6, 12–13, 27, 49, 53, 60, 65, 78, 90, 98, 103, 112, 113, 120, 121, 127, 134, 167, 180, 188, 189, 200, 205, 217, 233, 248, 252, 259
Bryan, Sabrina, 2, 5, 34, 36, 43, 54, 69, 109, 166, 199, 202, 217
Bryson, Peabo, 10, 17, 242
Buchanan, Jim, 32
Buckley, Paul, 190
Budd, Julie, 7, 179
A Bug's Life, 215
Bulgarian Women's Choir, 219
Bulifant, Joyce, 28
Bunch, Tyler, 16, 73
Bunnytown, 28
Burgess, Bobby, 167, 176
Burgess, Tituss, 101, 120, 224
Burke, Sonny, 17, 21, 84, 121, 167, 187, 218, 234
Burnham, David, 9, 253
Burns, Stephen W., 93, 133
Burton, Corey, 10, 84, 169
Burton, Lukas McGuire, 177
Burton, Tim, 3
Butler, Daws, 90
Butler, Kerry, 11, 14, 31, 39, 71, 102, 108, 144, 184, 214, 237
Buttons, Red, 55
Buzz Lightyear of Star Command: The Adventure Begins, 216
Buzzi, Ruth, 238

Cahn, Sammy, 53, 184, 235, 254, 256
Cahoon, Kevin, 15, 36

Caillat, Colbie, 120
Caine, Michael, 107, 184, 208, 237
Callas, Charlie, 24
Callaway, Liz, 61, 65, 135, 154, 164, 211
Callea, Anthony, 81
Callow, Simon, 52, 59, 209
Calvin, Henry, 152, 189
Cameron, Al, 139
Camille, 123
Camp Rock, 74, 80, 83, 163, 171, 198, 213, 217, 222, 229, 235, 242
Camp Rock 2: The Final Jam, 26, 33, 63, 81, 107, 109, 207, 213, 250, 256
Campbell, Trevin, 96, 197
Campos, Bruno, 238
Canute, Chris, 103
Captain EO, 6–7, 229
Captain Stubby and the Buccaneers, 122
Carey, Drew, 6, 53, 116, 182, 187, 219
Carling, Foster, 125, 241
Carr, Darleen, 150
Carr, Jane, 35
Carreras, José, 254
Carroll, Lewis, 2, 3, 20, 56, 88, 104, 156, 221, 228
Carroll, Pat, 173
Cars, 17, 62, 163, 177
Carson, Ken, 40, 110, 200
Carter, Aaron, 94
Casella, Max, 32, 78, 120, 215
Caselotti, Adriana, 105, 191, 240, 246
Castellaneta, Dan, 154, 257
Catlett, Walter, 85
Catucci, John, 69
Cecada, Jon, 100
Chad, Harrison, 131
Cham, Greg, 69
Cham, Ray, 43, 69
Chan, Jackie, 101
Chapman, Tracy Nicole, 15, 36
Charendoff, Tara, 64, 215

Charley and the Angel, 133
Chase, David, 14, 35, 41, 58, 66, 82, 97, 131, 163
Cheetah Girls, 99, 100, 191
The Cheetah Girls, 34, 36, 54, 69, 217
The Cheetah Girls 2, 2, 5–6, 34–35, 43, 109, 166, 199, 202
Cherie, 177
Chet Baker Trio, 191
Chevalier, Maurice, 9, 54, 76, 114
Childs, James, 119
Chip 'n Dale: Rescue Rangers, 36, 60, 197
Christensen, Kerry, 253
Christy, Brandon, 72, 118
The Chronicles of Narnia: The Lion, the Witch and the Wardrobe, 251
Chronicles of Narnia: Prince Caspian, 31
Churchill, Frank, 11, 22, 33, 46, 50, 71, 82, 99, 105, 127, 131, 134, 135, 141, 152, 162, 170, 171, 181, 185, 189, 191, 192, 194, 240, 241, 243, 246, 257
Cinderella, 20–21, 36, 43, 48, 103, 155, 191, **246**, 248
Cinderella II: Dreams Come True, 21, 64, 110, 249
Cinderella III: A Twist in Time, 6, 10, 96, 146, 169
Clark, Buddy, 140
Clark, Cam, 229
Clarke, Stanley, 159
Clarkson, Kelly, 27
Clegg, Johnny, 46
Cliff Adams Singers, 13
Cliff, Jimmy, 78
Clooney, Rosemary, 3, 195, 208, 223
Close, Glenn, 255
Clough, Mary Jay, 59
Cochran, Karl, 230
Coda, John, 209
Cody, Kathleen, 212

Coffing, Barry, 240
Cohen, Adam, 237, 245
Colcord, Ray, 218
Coleman, Monique, 3
Colina, Michael, 150
Collins, Paul, 64, 254
Collins, Phil, 45, 57–58, 65, 75, 94,
    123, 129, 134, 153, 157, 194, 201,
    203, 219, 222, 227, 230, 241, 255
Collins, Stephen, 12
Colonna, Jerry, 33, 56, 223
Colvig, Pinto, 23, 204, 249
Como, Perry, 21, 49
The Computer Wore Tennis Shoes, 39
Conaway, Jeff, 21, 79
*Confessions of a Teenage Drama
    Queen*, 177
Connery, Sean, 174
Connick, Harry, Jr., 14
Connors, Carol, 115, 177, 192, 217
Cook, Barbara, 11, 17, 49, 70, 103, 122,
    170, 191, 192, 195, 236, 239, 247
Cook, Joe, 84, 231, 244
The Cookie Carnival, 204
Cooksey, Jon, 106
Cooper, Chris, 127
Cooper, Gladys, 210
Copacabana, 215
Copeland, Craig, 197, 213
Cortazar, Ernesto, 214
Corti, Jesse, 68
Cory in the House, 39
Coslow, Sam, 194
Costa, Mary, 98, 159
Cotton, Billy, 13
Cotton, Bryan, 46
Coulthard, Raymond, 237
The Country Bears, 32, 116, 119, 125,
    200
Courtland, Jerome, 121, 157, 180
A Cowboy Needs a Horse, 40
Crawford, Michael, 11, 32, 38, 39, 94,
    98, 100, 177, 185, 212, 237, 239, 256

Crosby, Bing, 23, 81, 99, 102, 118–19,
    214, 254, 259
Crothers, Scatman, 58
Crow, Sheryl, 177
Crowley, Kathleen, 103
Crystal, Billy, 100
Cugat, Xavier, 26, 215, 254
Cullen, Peter, 18, 88, 188, 220, 245–46
Cullum, Jamie, 240
Cummings, Jim, 15, 18, 51, 57, 65, 66,
    72, 80, 87, 88, 89, 90, 97, 106, 108,
    136, 146, 163, 171, 172, 179, 188,
    190, 192, 198, 220, 221, 232, 238,
    242, 244, 245, 247
Curry, Tim, 47, 135, 174, 181
Cusack, Joan, 237, 248
Cyrus, Billy Ray, 12, 28, 177
Cyrus, Miley, 19, 28, 38, 47, 48, 86, 96,
    125, 166, 255, 259

D-Tent Boyz, 46
Daily, E. G., 201
Dale, Jim, 55, 166, 193
Dali, Salvador, 45, 170
Damiano, Tami Tappan, 146, 169
Dandridge, Merle, 58, 153, 203, 255
Daniel, Eliot, 23, 33, 122, 137, 167,
    183, 200, 210, 217
Danieley, Jason, 164
Dano, Hutch, 258
Darby, Ken, 33, 125, 137, 241
Darby O'Gill and the Little People,
    174, 245
Darin, Bobby, 208
Daring, Mason, 233
Darkwing Duck, 43, 46
Darling, Helen, 135
Darwell, Jane, 61
Davalos, Elyssa, 133
David, Keith, 67
David, Mack, 21, 36, 43, 49, 56, 103,
    155, 191, 223, 225, 246, 248
Davidovitch, Niv, 146

Davidson, John, 9, 25, 42, 45, 126, 233
Davis, Chip, 233
Davis, Julian Michael, 119
Davis, Miles, 191
Davy Crockett, 13
Davy Crockett and the River Pirates, 13, 120, 252
Davy Crocket, King of the Wild Frontier, 13, 60
Day, Dennis, 8, 134, 170
Day, Doris, 184, 195, 225, 247, 256
Daye, Irene, 111
de Oliveira, Aloysio, 26, 215
de Paul, Gene, 20, 81, 99, 110, 118, 221
De Vol, Frank, 93, 133
De Vries, Marius, 6
De Wilde, Brandon, 178
de Tagle, Anna Maria Perez, 33
Debussy, Claude, 23
Dees, Michael, 139
Dempsey, Patrick, 190, 209
Denver, John, 204
Depp, Johnny, 86
Der Fuehrer's Face, 44, **117**
Derby, David, 125
DeRemer, Patrick, 96, 143, 160, 197
DeSalvo, Russ, 111, 119, 167
Deschanel, Zooey, 191, 245
Destino, 45
The Devil and Max Devlin, 7, 179
DeVito, Danny, 161
Devo 2.0, 145
Dick, Andy, 149
Dick Tracy, 11–12, 132, 145, 195, 234
Dinning Sisters, 22, 67
DioGuardia, Kara, 26, 48, 63, 171, 177, 229
Dion, Celine, 17
The Disney Afternoon, 46
Disney Princess Enchanted Tales, 111, 119, 167
Disney, Roy E., 45

Disney, Walt, 43, 45, 61, 75, 144, 176, 180, 201, 206, 217, 246
Disneyland, 13, 113, 121, 164, 166, 176, 183, 203, 208, 259
Disney's Adventures in Wonderland, 2
Disney's Adventures of the Gummi Bears, 46, 76–77, 179
Disney's Doug, 47
Dodd, Andy, 74, 117, 164, 213, 235
Dodd, Jimmie, 7, 38, 57, 67, 76, 104, 142, 205, **206**
Doherty, Katherine, 168
Dominguez, Armando, 45
Donald Duck in Nutzi Land, 44
The Doodlebops, 47, 69
Dooley, Paul, 57
Dorsey, Jimmy, 26
Dotrice, Karen, 16, 35, 70, 94, 106, 114, 126, 168
Doug, 47
Douglas, Kirk, 233
Douglas, Mike, 43, 191
Doug's First Movie, 44, 47, 192
Doyle, Aaryn, 235
Dr. John, 48, 257
Dragon, Carmen, 17
Drake, Ervin, 215
Drew Davis Band, 83
Drewe, Anthony, 7, 17, 27, 35, 173, 208
Dreyfuss, Richard, 52, 60, 209
Driscoll, Bobby, 40, 122, 156, 168, 254, 258
Driscoll, Ryan, 126
The Drummonds, 239
Drury, James, 178
Duchin, Eddy, 26
DuckTales, 24, 28, 46, 49
Dudley, Aaron, 81
Duff, Haylie, 187
Duff, Hilary, 69, 187, 215, 234, 243
Dumbo, 11, 33, 82, 122, 134, 170, 194, 236

Dumbo's Circus, 49, 74, 114
Duncan, Glen, 14, 35, 41, 58, 66, 82, 97, 131, 163
Duncan, Sandy, 8
Dunham, By, 38
Dunn, Tamara, 12
Duran, Chuck, 230
Durang, Christopher, 12
Duvall, Shelley, 81, 85, 181
Dworsky, Sally, 32
Dye, Ian, 207

Eastman, Tish, 220
Eberle, Bob, 26
Ebersole, Christine, 2
Ebsen, Buddy, 120, 126, 160, 208, 233
The Eddy Duchin Story, 26
The Edison Twins, 52
Edwards, Cliff, 54, 67, 70, 102, 104, 200, 236, 239, 252
Edwards, Lawrence, 159
Efron, Zac, 3, 20, 25, 27, 32, 56, 69, 74, 117, 154, 178, 184, 198, 200, 227–28, 232, 235, 238, **253**
Egan, John Treacy, 124
Egan, Susan, 5, 18, 34, 86, 93, 98, 100, 140, **143**, 193, 196, 239, 255
Elfman, Danny, 3, 67, 112, 119–20, 138, 163, 172, 181, 193, 213, 219, 235
Elizondo, Mike, 95
Elliott, Jack, 218
Elliott, Ted, 86
Ellis, Loren, 83
The Emperor's New Groove, 53, 148, 169
The Emperor's New Groove 2: Kronk's New Groove, 15, 61
The Emperor's New School, 53
Empty Nest, 83, 127
En Vogue, 162, 191
Enchanted, 55, 80, 190, 209, 220, 241

Enriquez, Joy, 18
Erskine, Martin, 46
Erwin, Randy, 253
Esperón, Manuel, 214
Etheridge, Melissa, 62, 107, 231
Evans, Linda, 30, 178
Evans, Tiffany, 241
Everlife, 177, 201

Fab 5, 231
Fagerbakke, Bill, 115
Fahn, Harrison, 232
Fain, Sammy, 3, 4, 20, 34, 53, 103, 104, 105, 138, 159, 165, 184, 192, 228, 235, 254, 256
Fan 3, 108
Fanning, Dakota, 5
Fantasia, 23
Farao, Massimo, 243
Farmer, Bill, 153, 157
Farrell, Skip, 102
Farrés, Osvaldo, 247
Fastball, 256
Faughnan, Katheryn, 168
Feather, Lorraine, 9, 115, 178, 243, 256
Fein, Donna, 143
Feinstein, Michael, 3, 62, 103, 113, 208, 223, 239
Feldman, Jack, 2, 33, 85, 120, 135, 149, 153, 158, 159, 161, 168, 182, 185, 229, 249
Felton, Verna, 20, 38, 138, 188
Ferdinand the Bull, 62
Ferguson, Craig, 12
Fidel, Stan, 19
Fiedler, John, 88, 91, 100, 188, 220, 221, 245
Field, Eugene, 251
Field, Sally, 116
Fierstein, Harvey, 70
The Fighting Prince of Donegal, 49
Findley, Matthew, 63, 208

Finn, William, 91, 162, 168, 230
Fisher, Eddie, 13
Fitzgerald, Colleen, 125
Fitzhugh, Ellen, 73, 250
Flack, Roberta, 10
Flansburgh, John, 83
Fleming, Shaun, 25, 104, 205
Flint, Shelby, 115, 192, 217
The Flying Mouse, 99, 257
Foard, Merwin, 9, 60, 231
Ford, Candy, 32
Ford, Tennessee Ernie, 13
Foster, Jodi, 99
Foster, Lewis, 203
Foster, Norman, 259
Follow Me, Boys!, 63
Four Hits, 225
Four Mosquitoes, 13
Four Seasons, 145
Fowler, Beth, 17, 86, 87, 89, 193
The Fox and the Hound, 8, 19, 73, 90, 121
The Fox and the Hound II, 23, 66, 72, 88, 229, 232, 255
Fox, Charles, 212
Francis, Jordan, 80, 198
Frank, Debra, 31, 245
Freaky Friday, 99
Frederick, Jason, 177
Freeland, Roger, 213
Freeland, Roy, 96, 197
Freeman, Cheryl, 74, 198, 258
Freeman, Jonathan, 174, 257
Freeman, Ticker, 190
Frees, Paul, 4, 34, 102, 104, 179, 196
Freeze, James, 14, 35, 41, 58, 66, 82, 97, 131, 163
Fried, Paul, 32
Friedman, David, 9, 164, 211, 231
Friedman, Seth J., 46
Froman, Jane, 11, 236
Fun and Fancy Free, 61, 67, 102, 122, 148, 150, 183, 218

Funicello, Annette, 49, 125–26, 141, 145, 165, 176, 189, 202, 206, 249
Funny Little Bunnies, 185
Furst, Stephen, 215

Gabor, Eva, 58, 177, 183
Gabriel, George, 31
Gabriel, Peter, 48
Gad, Toby, 80, 85, 109, 208, 217
Gaines, Rosie, 96
Galasso, Frankie J., 57, 65
Galde, Anthony, 1
Gallagher, Peter, 230
Galloway, Jenny, 35
Galway, James, 17, 32
Gambatese, Jenn, 45, 65, 129, 201, 227
The Gang's All Here, 26
Gannon, Kim, 8, 134, 170
Garay, Joaquin, 214
Garber, Matthew, 16, 35, 62, 70, 94, 106, 114, 126, 168
Garrett, Brad, 110, 201
Garson, Greer, 107
Garvey, Linda, 44
The Gay Ranchero, 254
Geiger, Teddy, 255
Geissman, Grant, 75, 228
Gellman, Yani, 234
Genest, Emile, 144
George, Gil, 129, 157, 200, 205, 217
Geppetto, 6, 26, 53, 111, 116, 172, 182, 187, 219, 239
Gerrard, Matthew, 3, 19, 25, 27, 40, 56, 61, 85, 93, 96, 97, 107, 137, 152, 154, 159, 164, 166, 177, 198, 199, 232, 235, 242, 243
Getty, Estelle, 141
Giacchino, Michael, 31, 123, 196, 237, 245
Gibb, Richard, 161, 221
Gibson, Mel, 100, 143, 226
Gilbert, Billy, 61
Gilbert, Ed, 66, 102

Gilbert, Ray, 4, 12, 22, 23, 33, 55, 113, 141, 160, 195, 214, 221, 247, 254, 258

Gilkyson, Terry, 13, 124, 145, 149, 182, 183, 214

Gill, Florence, 82

Gillespie, Darlene, 164, 176

Gimbel, Norman, 5, 92, 115, 230, 233, 250

Gipsy Kings, 111

Givot, George, 17

Gleed, Jason, 119

Glockner, Eleanor, 89

The Gnome-Mobile, 70, 106

Godt, Heidi, 12

Goelz, Dave, 98, 108, 139, 192, 237

Go-Gos, 126

Goldberg, Jesse, 131

Goldberg, Whoopi, 15

The Golden Girls, 141

The Golden Touch, 71

Goldsboro, Bobby, 212

Goliath II, 53

Gomez, Selena, 41, 57, 63

Gonyea, Dale, 154, 254

Gonzalez, Mandy, 130

Good Luck Charlie, 79

Good Morning, Miss Bliss, 212

Goodman, Benny, 4

Goodman, John, 14, 100, 149, 243

Goof Troop, 74

A Goofy Movie, 2, 96, 124, 153, 157, 197

Gordon, Anita, 148, 150

Goris, Parker, 115

Gottfried, Gilbert, 65, 104, 167, 211

Gottschall, Ruth, 28

Gould, Elliott, 7, 179

Goulet, Robert, 257

Goz, Michael, 181

Graae, Jason, 66, 86, 202, 203, 253

Grabeel, Lucas, 3, 25, 59, 71, 90, 93, 97, 117, 200, 232, 235, **253**, 255

Grabowsky, Paul, 115, 243

Gracin, Joshua, 88, 232

Graeme, James, 100

Grammer, Kelsey, 93, 104

The Grasshopper and the Ants, 249

Gravitte, Debbie Shapiro, 17, 161, 162, 166, 173, 182, 185

Gray, Trevor and Howard, 161

Grayson, Carly, 45

Great Jazz Trio, 191

The Great Locomotive Chase, 194

The Great Mouse Detective, 73, 125, 250

Green, Kat, 36

Greenberg, Faye, 34–35, 59, 90, 109, 199

Greene, Mike, 21

Gregory, Chester, II, 194, 219, 241

Groce, Larry, 28

Grossman, Larry, 73, 212, 227, 234, 239, 250, 256

Guillaume, Robert, 224

Guizar, Tito, 26, 254

Gumley, Matthew, 168

Gurley, Michael, 36

Gyllenhaal, Jake, 95

Haenni, G., 73

Haig, David, 35, 126, 128, 138

Haines, Guy, 234

Hajian, Chris, 148

Hale, Jennifer, 64

Hall Johnson Choir, 125, 210, 236

Hall, Jonnie, 191

Halyx, 254

Hamlisch, Marvin, 7, 179

Hammerstein, Oscar, 45

Hampton, Steve, 57, 83

Handy Manny, 79

Hanks, Tom, 248, 257

Hannah Montana, 19

Hannah Montana: The Movie, 12, 19, 28, 38, 40, 47, 48, 86, 125, 255

Hansel and Gretel, 11
The Happiest Millionaire, 9, 28, **37**, 45, 66, 101, 107, 126, 201, 210, 225, 228, 236
Harajuku, 39
Harline, Leigh, 70, 82, 85, 102, 111, 132, 152, 157, 168, 170, 185, 204, 239, 249, 251
Harmon, Steve, 233
Harnell, Jess, 9, 115
Harnois, Elisabeth, 2
Harper, D. J., 191
Harper, Don, 194
Harriet, Judy, 206
Harris, Barbara, 99
Harris, Phil, 13, 58, 97, 169, 214
Harrison, Rex, 236
Hartley, David, 148, 169
Hartman, Dan, 243
Hartman, Jamie Alexander, 177
Harwell, Steve, 56
Hassman, Nikki, 32, 222, 250
Hateley, Linzi, 17, 35, 126
Hathaway, Anne, 27, 69, 256
The Haunted Mansion, 76
Having Wonderful Time, 82
Hawkins, Jay, 94
Hawn, Goldie, 233
Haydn, Richard, 2
Hayes, Bill, 13
Hayes, Steve L., 31, 237, 245
Haymes, Dick, 239
Haynes, Henry D., 15
Headley, Heather, 32, 42, 51, 52, 53, 71, 89, 129, 137, 150, 154, 166, 185, 199, 247, 250
Healey, Bruce, 60
Heath, Hy, 210
Hee, T., 102, 155, 176, 216
Heidt, Horace, 82
Held, Bob, 150
Heller, Bill, 150

Hendricks, Barbara, 4, 17, 18, 21, 35, 38, 41, 49, 61, 103, 166, 191, 225, 239, 241, 259
Hendrickson, Kevin, 112
Henley, Don, 32, 201
Henley, Georgie, 251
Hensley, Shuler, 153, 203
Herbert, Victor, 65, 189, 248
Herbie Fully Loaded, 63
Herbie Goes Bananas, 93, 133
Hercules, 71, 74, 99, 143, 161, 198, 258
Hewitt, Jennifer Love, 91, 103, 162, 230
Hiatt, John, 32, 116, 119, 125, 200–201
Hibbard, David, 208
Hibler, Winston, 6, 27, 64, 98, 217, 231
Hickok, John, 7, 129
Hicks, Adam, 258
Higglytown Heroes, 83
High School Musical, 25, 27, 69, 122, 159, 198, 200, 207, 232, 235, 238, **253**
High School Musical 2, 3, 19, 56, 59, 74, 90, 93, 235, 248
High School Musical 3: Senior Year, 25, 32, 85, 97, 117, 152, 154, 178, 183–84, 227, 232
Hill, Dru, 53
Hilliard, Bob, 3, 4, 20, 34, 103, 104, 105, 165, 184, 228
Hirschhorn, Joel, 21, 24, 27, 32, 55, 80, 95, 99, 109, 139, 166, 193, 211
Ho, Don, 90
Hocus Pocus, 94, 182
Hodges, Eddie, 63, 157, **158**, 170, 202, 228
Hodges, Henry, 168
Hoffman, Al, 20–21, 36, 43, 49, 56, 103, 155, 191, 223, 225, 233, 246, 248
Hohlfeld, Brian, 88, 151
Holes, 46

Holloway, Sterling, 104, 122, 131, 134, 221, 224, 233
Holmes, Taylor, 188
Home on the Range, 8, 87, 131, 240, 244, 253
Hong, James, 70
Ho'omalu, Mark Keali'i, 80–81
Hooven, Marilyn, 202
Hopkins, Kaitlin, 39, 84, 100, 105, 159, 162, 164, 173, 174, 191, 242, 244, 257
Hopkins, Nikita, 88, 89, 131, 151, 188
Horne, Lena, 191
Horner, James, 182, 244
The Horsemasters, 202
Hoskins, Loren, 112
Hot Lead and Cold Feet, 139, 193
The House at Pooh Corner, 146
Houston, Jamie, 5, 27, 34, 56, 83, 108, 149, 178, 183, 202, 227, 238, 253
Howard, Clint, 38
Howard, David, 258
Howard, James Newton, 240
Howard, Paul Mason, 40
Hoyle, Geoff, 94, 146
Huddleston, Floyd, 58, 134
Hudgens, Vanessa Anne, 3, 27, 32, 39, 56, 74, 117, 154, 178, 198, 200, 227, 232, 235, 238, **253**
Hudson, Lord Tim, 210
Hughes, Buddy, 67
Hughes, Marjorie, 49
Hulce, Tom, 40, 77, 81, 99, 123, 163, 164, 218
Hull High, 122, 159, 207, 223
Hummon, Marcus, 66, 72, 81, 229
Humperdinck, Englebert, 254
The Hunchback of Notre Dame, 18, 40, 71, 77, 81, 163, 164, 192, 218
The Hunchback of Notre Dame II, 59, 99, 103, 123, 163
Hunt, Linda, 130
Huntington, Sam, 254

Huss, Toby, 32, 201
Huston, Angelica, 6, 229

Ian and Sylvia, 124
Ice Princess, 177
I'm in the Band, 230
In Search of the Castaways, 33, 54, 76
In the Bag, 89
Inglesby, Meredith, 18, 58, 94, 99, 124, 126, 144, 173, 174, 187, 191, 193, 215, 224, 228, 255
Irby-Ranniar, Scott, 36, 78, 94, 147, 212
Irons, Jeremy, 15, 108
Irving, Robert, 74
Isaacs, Sonya, 187
It's Tough to Be a Bird, 110, 237–38
It's Tough to Be a Bug, 110
Ives, Burl, 35, 55, 122, 126, 156, 157, 197, 223, 243

Jackson, Janet, 94
Jackson, Michael, 6, 229
Jacobson, Eric, 98, 108, 140, 237, 245
Jake and the Never Land Pirates, 112
Jam Session, 26
James and the Giant Peach, 51, 59, 73, 149, 209
James, Harry, 239
James, Tim, 19, 33, 81, 163, 235
Jarre, Maurice, 79
Jay, Tony, 82
Jazz Networks, 14, 17, 35, 58, 84, 120, 187, 191, 224, 239
Jbara, Gregory, 53, 87, 263
Jefferson, Brenden, 46
Jenkins, Daniel, 35, 126, 128, 138
Jennings, Will, 244
Jerome, Timothy, 130
Jessie, 85
Jillian, Ann, 65
Joel, Billy, 239, 243

John, Elton, 7, 15, 32, 36, 37, 42, 51, 52, 53, 55, 65, 71, 78, 88, 94, 129, 136, 146, 150, 154, 166, 199, 209, 250–51
Johnny and the Sprites, 113
Johnny Shiloh, 113
Johnny Tremain, 113, 127
Johns, Glynis, 126, 127, 188
Johnson, Ben, 178
Johnson, Martin, 255
Johnston, Arthur, 194
Johnston, Richard O., 19
JoJo's Circus, 114
JONAS, 133
JONAS L.A., 133
Jonas Brothers, 5, 33, 97, 133, 172, 173, 252
Jonas, Joe, 74, 81, 133, 171, 198, 213, 250, 256
Jonas, Kevin, 81, 133
Jonas, Nick, 81, 133
Jones, Dean, 114, 185
Jones, Dickie, 70, 85, 111
Jones, Mick, 177
Jones, Spike, 45
Jones, Stan, 114, 178, 194, 208, 250
Jones, Tom, 168
Jones, Vanessa A., 52
Journey, 162, 229
Joyce, Bob, 39
Jump 5, 17, 81
Junge, Alexa, 5, 70, 124, 130
The Jungle Book, 13, 38, 66, 97, 102–103, 150, 210, 221
The Jungle Book 2, 14, 39, 97, 115, 178, 243
Jungle Cubs, 14
Jungle 2 Jungle, 254

Kahn, George, 197
Kamen, Michael, 3
Kandel, Paul, 9, 18, 40, 123, 218, 231
Kane, Brad, 60, 65, 154, 161, 162, 164, 211, 231, 242
Kane, Helen, 34
Kansas City Kitty, 215
Kaplan, Michael B., 230
Karl, Andy, 18, 58, 94, 99, 124, 126, 144, 173, 174, 187, 191, 193, 215, 224, 228, 255
Kasch, Max, 46
Kasha, Al, 21, 24, 27, 32, 55, 80, 95, 99, 109, 139, 166, 193, 211
Kavanaugh, John, 51, 190, 232
Kaye, Buddy, 183, 217
Kaye, Sammy, 122, 195, 259
Keating, Roan, 38
Keats, Ele, 159
Keir, Andrew, 49
Keith, Brian, 30
Kelley, Elijah, 212
Kelly, Josh, 62
Kelly, Laura Michelle, 7, 28, 35, 61, 114, 174, 197, 203
Kelly, Paula, 254, 259
Kelly, Ray, 171
Kelly, Wynton, 191
Ken Darby Chorus, 23
Ken Peplowski Quartet, 239
Kennedy, Gordon, 23, 255
Kennon, Walter Edgar, 59, 99, 163
Kent, Walter, 8, 134, 170
Kentucky Headhunters, 13
Kick Buttowski, 119
Kickin' It, 119
Kiley, Rilo, 14
Killam, Taran, 72, 137, 146, 159
Kim Possible, 31
Kimbrough, Charles, 59, 77, 123
Kimmel, Bruce, 234
King David, 1, 44, 54, 71, 88, 90, 107, 133, 151, 174, 181, 182, 186, 213, 228, 237, 255
King's Men, 139
Kirk, Tommy, **92**, 141, 145
Kitt, Eartha, 61
Kline, Kevin, 40

Knightley, Keira, 86
Koftinoff, Gary, 128
Kolfi, 120
Kollmorgen, Stuart, 114
Korbich, Eddie, 89, 173
Kostal, Irwin, 156
Kotch, Michael, 125
Krakowski, Jane, 196
Krauss, Alison, 211
Kravitz, Lenny, 129
Krieger, Stu, 68
Krupa, Gene, 67, 111
Kuhn, Judy, 20, 39, 90, 100, 116, 130, 151, 186, 234, 239
Kusatu, Clyde, 9
Kyser, Kay, 119

L. L. Cool J., 243
La Chanze, 74, 198, 258
LaBour, Fred, 216
LaBeouf, Shia, 46
Ladden, Cassidy, 119
Lady and the Tramp, 17, 84, 121, 167, 187, 234
Lady and the Tramp II: Scamp's Adventure, 18, 93, 115, 230, 250
Lalaine, 41
LaMarca, Perry, 5
Lambert the Sheepish Lion, 121, 134
Lamberts, Heath, 89, 193
Lamhene, Boualem, 123
Lampert, Diane, 21
Lanchester, Elsa, 188
Lane, Nathan, 25, 32, 46, 78, 96, 104, 205, 209
lang, k. d., 131
Lange, Johnny, 23, 167, 210
Lange, Robert John, 3
Langford, Frances, 160
Lansbury, Angela, 2, 9, 16, 52, 153, 173, 193, 199, 202, 246
Lara, Augustin, 254
Larkin, Bill, 68

Larkin, John, 30
The Last Flight of Noah's Ark, 79
Lavigne, Avril, 3, 27
Lawrence, David, 2, 34, 59, 90, 109, 199
Lawrence, Eula, 233
Lawrence, Jack, 152, 159
Lawrence, Joseph, 9
Lawrence, Vicki, 232
Le Loka, Tsidii, 38, 212
Lebo M, 37, 46, 54, 78, 160, 185, 212, 244
Lee, Bill, 41, 216
Lee, Daniel Curtis, 258
Lee, Gavin, 35, 114, 128, 138
Lee, Johnny, 55, 88
Lee, Peggy, 17, 84, 121, 167, 187, 235
Leeves, Jane, 52, 60, 209
The Legend of Lobo, 123
Leggat, Ashley, 128
Lembeck, Michael, 39
Lennox, Lisa, 47, 69
Lenox, Carl, 47, 69
Lerios, Cory, 31
Les Misérables, 104
Leven, Mel, 12, 40, 42, 65, 110, 118, 130, 161, 189, 237, 248
Levering, Kate, 208
Levi, Zachary, 95
Lewis, Bert, 11, 99, 257
Lewis, Huey, 159
Lewis, Jenifer, 46
Lewis, Jenny, 14
Lewis, Michelle, 63
Lewis, Norm, 101, 249
Lewis, Ted, 4
Licera, Char, 43
Lichine, David, 221
Life Is Ruff, 108
Life-Size, 14
Life with Derek, 128
The Light in the Forest, 92, 129
Light, Kate, 83

Lilo and Stitch, 80

Lilo and Stitch 2: Stitch Has a Glitch, 5, 81

Lincoln, Billy, 36

Lindsey, Hillary, 47

Linnell, John, 83

Linz, Peter, 129, 138

The Lion King, **15**, 32, 36, 37–38, 46, 54, 78, 93–94, 108, 136, 147, 160, 185, 209, 212, 215

The Lion King 1½, 32, 38, 46, 78, 94, 209, 212

The Lion King 2: Simba's Pride, 135, 149, 161, 224, 229

The Lion King's Timon and Pumbaa, 78

The Litterbug, 130

Little Einstens, 131

The Little Mermaid, 20, 43, 44, 52, 60–61, 83, 87, 89, 97, 101, 105, 106, 115, 120, 123–24, 151, 165–66, 173, **186**, 188, 204, 224, 249

The Little Mermaid: Ariel's Beginning, 10, 95, 98, 115, 116, 162

The Little Mermaid II: Return to the Sea, 48, 64, 84, 166, 215

Little Shop of Horrors, 166

Livingston, Jerry, 21, 36, 43, 49, 56, 103, 155, 191, 223, 225, 246, 248

Lizzie McGuire, 133

The Lizzie McGuire Movie, 69, 234, 243

Lloyd, Anne, 235, 255

Locke, Kimberly, 49

Lodin, Jeffrey, 192

Logan, Rick, 39

Logan, Stacey, 89

Loggins, Kenny, 256

Lohan, Lindsay, 14, 63

Lohr, Aaron, 2, 153, 158

Loper, Don, 215

Lopez, Robert, 12, 57, 109, 172, 225, 244

Loptata, Gail, 142

Loring, Richard, 21

Lou, Gracie, 152

Louis-Dreyfus, Julia, 116, 187

Lovato, Demi, 26, 33, 163, 209, 213, 241, 250, 256

Lovett, Lyle, 257

Lovett, Marcus, 1, 71, 88, 90, 133, 151, 175, 181, 182, 186, 213, 228, 237, 255

Lowell, Tom, 70

Lubin, Joe, 207

Luckey, Bud, 108, 244

Luddy, Barbara, 189

Luker, Rebecca, 17, 35, 64, 126

Lurie, Jeannie, 72, 79, 118, 169, 237, 245, 256

Lurye, Peter, 15, 96, 197

Luske, Tommy, 64, 254

Luz, Dora, 45, 254

Lynch, Ross, 247

Lynn, Vera, 122

Mabe, Jon, 38

Mac, Christie, 54

Macalush, Crysta, 149

MacArthur, James, 38, **92**

MacDonald, James, 90, 248

MacGimsey, Robert, 88

MacMurray, Fred, **37**, 63, 101, 107, 126, 133, 201, 236

MacNeal, Noel, 16, 74

MacRae, Gordon, 21

Madonna, 12, 145, 195, 234

The Madness of King George, 136

Maeda, Guy, 39

Maione, Gia, 35, 61, 114, 126, 198, 203

Make Mine Music, 4, 23, 33, 113, 137, 139, 221, 247

Malotte, Albert Hay, 62

Manche, Daniel, 57, 94, 241

Manchester, Melissa, 5, 92, 115, 125, 230, 250

Mancina, Mark, 94, 185, 194, 212
Mancini, Henry, 73, 250
Manges, Jilien, 254
Manhattan Jazz Quintet, 191
Manilow, Barry, 168
Mann, Barry, 24, 30, 135, 159, 174,
    181, 187, 192
Mann, Terrence, 100, 193
Mannheim Steamroller, 13
Marano, Laura, 247
Margherita, Lesli, 6, 169
Margolyes, Miriam, 52, 60, 209
Marin, Cheech, 15
Markowitz, Donny, 68
Marks, Franklyn, 38
Marley, Ziggy, 135
Marsden, James, 220
Marshall, Sean, 21, 24, 27, 66, 109,
    141, 189, 211
Martin, Jesse L., 44
Martin, Mary, 21, 82, 103, 105, 122,
    134, 162, 191, 239, 241, 247
Martin, Meaghan, 208, 217, 222
Martin, Millicent, 202
Marx, Richard, 214
Mary Poppins, 7, 15, 16, 17, 27–28, 35,
    37, 61, 62, 94, 114, 126, 127, **128**,
    138, 144, 168, 173, 188, 197, 198,
    199, 203, 208
Marylee, 18
Massey, Kyle, 39–40, 108
Masters, Blair, 23
Mathers, Jimmy, 16, **158**, 202, 223
Mathis, Johnny, 239
Mathis, Stanley Wayne, 15, 36
Mavin, 36
Maynard, Tyler, 58, 94, 98, 99, 124,
    126, 144, 173, 174, 187, 191, 193,
    204, 215, 224, 228, 255
McBride, Martina, 214, 237
McCartney, Jesse, 72, 102, 184
McClanahan, Rue, 141
McCrary, Joel, 68

McDaniel, Hattie, 194, **195**
McDermott, Sean, 52
McDowall, Roddy, 12
McElroy, Donna, 49
McEnery, Peter, 49
McEntire, Reba, 72, 232
McFerrin, Bobby, 21, 187
McGarity, Mike, 247
McGraw, Tim, 240
McGuire, Dorothy, 16, **92**, 149, **158**,
    202
McKennitt, Loreena, 216
McKenzie, Bret, 127, 128, 138, 140
McKinley, Richard, 139, 185
McKuen, Rod, 166
McLachlan, Sarah, 237
McLaughlin, Jon, 190
McNamara, Chad, 47, 69
McNeely, Joel, 83, 178
Meet the Robinsons, 6, 67, 132, 147,
    240
Mellencamp, John, 249
Mellowmen, 82, 165, 167
Melody Time, 8, 22, 23, 132, 134, 140,
    160, 167, 170,
Melonas, Dennis, 148
Mendler, Bridgit, 79
Menken, Alan, 1, 8, 14, 17, 18, 20, 31,
    33, 34, 39, 40, 44, 54, 55, 61, 66,
    68, 71, 72, 74, 77, 80, 81, 83, 85, 86,
    87, 88, 89, 90, 95–96, 97, 99, 100,
    101, 107, 111, 116, 120, 123, 130,
    131, 133, 137, 140, 143, 144, 147,
    149, 151, 152, 159, 160, 161, 162,
    164, 165–66, 173, 174, 175, 181,
    182, 183, 185, 186, 190, 192, 193,
    198, 204, 209, 213, 218, 220, 224,
    226, 228, 237, 238–39, 240, 242,
    244, 249, 253, 255, 258
Mercer, Johnny, 169, 259
Merrill, Larry, 228
Meuller, Mark,
Michael, Tom, 251

Michaels, Julia, 247
Mickey Mouse Club, 7, 38, 54, 57, 67, 76, 104, 142, 148, 196, 200, 205, **206**,
Mickey Mouse, Splashdance, 80, 142, 254
Mickey's Christmas Carol, 156
Mickey's Follies, 144
Mickey's House of Villains, 109, 213
Mickey's Magical Christmas, 19
Midler, Bette, 11, 71, 95, 168
Midnight Madness, 143
Midnight, Charlie, 69, 243
The Mighty Ducks, 143
Mighty Joe Young, 244
Milano, Alyssa, 86, 93
Miles, Vera, 178
Milian, Christina, 31
Miller, Dan, 83
Miller, Gene, 135
Miller, Glenn, 239
Miller, Mitch, 152, 235, 255
Miller, Roger, 153–54, 162, 240
Miller, Sidney, 67
Mills, Billy, 40
Mills, Hayley, 16, 33, 54, 62, 63, 64, 76, 92, 125–26, **158**, 170, 202, 212
Mills, John, **92**
Milne, A. A., 146, 172, 179, 224, 245
Mineo, Sal, 217
Minkoff, Robert, 72
Minnelli, Liza, 12
Miracle of the White Stallions, 116
Miranda, Carmen, 26, 30, 215
The Misadventures of Merlin Jones, 141, 145
Modernaires, The, 254, 259
Molinder, Nicolas, 218
Mollenhauer, Heidi, 71
Monkeys, Go Home!, 114
The Monkey's Uncle, 145
Monroe, Vaughn, 23
Monsters, Inc., 100

Montade, Annmarie, 106
Montan, Nils, 191
The Moon Pilot, 185, 220, 226
The Moon-Spinners, 145
Moore, Clement, 152
Moore, Crista, 49, 184
Moore, Mandy, 95, 111, 194, 222, 238
Morehead, Paige, 11
Morey, Larry, 22, 50, 62, 82, 105, 122, 127, 131, 134, 135, 141, 162, 189, 191, 200, 240, 246, 249
Morgan, Cass, 61
Morgan, Gary, 21, 79
Morgan, Harry, 133
Moriarty, Cathy, 115
Morissette, Alanis, 95, 251
Mormon Tabernacle Choir, 239, 243
Moscow, David, 159, 185
Moses, Burke, 68, 137, 140, 144
Motorcrossed, 232, 256
The Mouse Factory, 144
Mousercise, 28, 148
Mower, Mike, 32
Mowry, Tahj, 190
Mr. Imperium, 254
Mueller, Mark, 36, 49, 212
Mulan, 70, 87, 101, 177, 220
Mulan II, 70, 83, 124, 130
Mumford, Lora, 238, 254
Mumy, Bill, 189
Munro, Janet, 38, **92**, 174
The Muppet Christmas Carol, 22, 107, 139, 161, 184, 208, 237
Muppet Treasure Island, 24, 30, 135, 174, 181, 187, 192
The Muppets, 217, 128, 138, 140, 169
A Muppets Christmas: Letters to Santa, 44, 98, 108, 148
The Muppets' Wizard of Oz, 31, 72, 118, 237, 245
Murphy, Donna, 147
Musso, Mitchell, 100, 218
My Best Friend's Wedding, 32

My Date with the President's Daughter, 148
My Science Project, 150
Mya, 240
Myers, Melinda, 161
Myvette, Kovasciar, 80, 109, 208

'N Sync, 219, 239
Najimy, Kathy, 95
Nakasone, Kahorn, 35
Nash, Clarence, 44, 130, 214
Naughton, James, 132–33
Nazareth, Ernesto, 22
Neeman, Chen, 79, 169, 256
Neill, Roger, 230
Nelson, Jerry, 22, 107, 139, 161
Nelson, Steve, 43
Nervo, Miriam, 125
Nervo, Olivia, 125
Nevil, Robbie, 3, 19, 25, 40, 56, 61, 85, 93, 97, 107, 137, 152, 154, 159, 166, 198, 199, 232, 235, 242
The New Adventures of Winnie the Pooh, 91
New Christie Minstrels, 35
The New Mickey Mouse Club, 142
The New Spirit, 252
Newhart, Bob, 177
Newman, Fred, 47, 167
Newman, Randy, 4, 46, 48, 51, 59, 67, 72, 73, 98, 100, 136, 150, 163, 201, 210, 215, 229, 237, 238, 248, 257
Newman, Thomas, 48
Newsies, 33, 85, 120, 149, 159, 182, 185, 249
Ne-Yo, 152
Nichols, C. August, 180
The Night Before Christmas, 152
The Nightmare Before Christmas, 112, 119, 137–38, 163, 172, 181, 193, 213, 219, 235
Nilsson, Harry, 22, 35, 57, 81, 85, 91, 104, 109, 181, 204

98 Degrees, 220
Nixon, Marni, 87
No Secrets, 120
Noble, Ray, 148, 150
Noko, 161
Nolan, Bob, 23
Nolan, Jeanette, 73
Noll, Christiane, 116
Nolte, Bille, 72
Novis, Donald, 134, 135, 152
Noyes, Betty, 11
Nurses, 83
Nurullah, Keewa, 18, 58, 94, 99, 124, 126, 144, 173, 174, 187, 191, 193, 215, 224, 228, 255
Nuss, Hubert, 61
Nye, Bill, 21

O'Callaghan, Cindy, 2, 16, 173, 202
Ocasek, Rick, 259
Ocko, Dan, 235, 255
O'Connell, Helen, 26
O'Dea, Jimmy, 245
O'Donnell, Rosie, 219
O'Hara, Catherine, 120, 181
O'Hara, Maureen, 64
O'Hara, Paige, 9, 17, 18, 41, 130, 132, 193, 200
The Old Mill, 157
Old Yeller, 157, 182
Oliveira, José, 214, 215
Oliver & Company, 72, 159, 168, 201, 243
Oliver Twist, 159, 168, 201, 243
O'Malley, J. Pat, 38, 88, 141, 156, 210, 228
The One and Only, Genuine, Original Family Band, 25, 42, 49, 79, 126, 155, 160, 208, 233
One by One, 160
One Flew South, 67
101 Dalmatians, 40, 42, 118,
101 Dalmatians: The Series, 160

101 Dalmatians II: Patch's London Adventure, 41, 42, 96, 118, 161, 221
Operation Dumbo Drop, 236
Orbach, Jerry, 9, 14, 41, 193
Orrall, Robert Ellis, 40
Ortega, Kenny, 69, 97, 122, 207
Osborn, Kristyn, 44
Osment, Haley Joel, 14, 99, 115, 116–17, 125
Osmond, Donny, 101
Ottestaad, Boots, 72
Oury, Alet, 12
Owen, Harriet Kate, 102
Oz, Frank, 22, 25, 135

PB&J Otter, 167
The Pacifier, 56
Pacino, Al, 145
Page, Bobbi, 191
Page, Geraldine, 210
Page, Ken, 163
Paige, Jennifer, 119
Pair of Kings, 218
Paisley, Brad, 17, 62
Palmer, Keke, 177, 221
Palmer, Sean, 61, 83, 101
Panabaker, Danielle, 72
Panettiere, Hayden, 41, 96, 149
Panzer, Marty, 212, 227, 229, 234, 239
The Parent Trap, 64, 125, 165
Parker, Barnett, 102, 216
Parker, Fess, 13, 60, 103, 112, 180, 252
Parker, Sarah Jessica, 95, 182
Parsons, Jim, 138
Pascal, Adam, 7, 51, 52, 53, 65, 89, 129, 154, 199, 251
Patch, Jeffrey, 73
Patinkin, Mandy, 132, 234
Patten, Luana, 122, 156, 168, 259
Paul Bunyan, 167
Paul, Les, 26
Paulette Sisters, 152

Pauley, Wilbur, 87
Paulsen, Rob, 9, 10, 48, 169, 249
Pawk, Michelle, 209
Paxton, Sara, 32
Payant, Gilles, 144
Peculiar Penguins, 168
Pendleton, Diane, 24
Penner, Erdman, 102, 155, 171, 176, 188, 216
Perkins, Damian, 89, 154
Perri, 6, 27, 216
Perry, William, 87
Persson, Joacim, 218
Peter Pan, 20, 53, 63, 64, 152, 171, 184, 216, 235, 254, 256
Peters, Bernadette, 10, 196
Peters, Caleigh, 177
Petersen, Randy, 9, 19, 25, 60, 74, 93, 103, 104, 109, 123, 124, 189, 205, 224, 242, 248, 257
Peterson, Paul, 228
Pete's Dragon, 21, 24, 27, 32, 55, 79, 95, 109, 166, 211
Petralia, Mickey, 46
Petty, Daniel, 63
Phillips, Mackenzie, 106
Phineas and Ferb, 216
Phoenix, Joaquin, 153
Piaf, Edith, 113
The Pied Piper, 169
The Pied Pipers, 259
Piglet's Big Movie, 39, 100, 146, 147, 188, 245
Pimental, Brian, 127
Pinchot, Bronson, 115
Pinocchio, 70, 85, 102, 111, 132, 239
Pinza, Ezio, 254
Pirates of the Caribbean,
Pirates of the Caribbean: At the World's End, 86
Pirates of the Caribbean: The Curse of the Black Pearl, 171, 252
Pitchford, Dean, 47, 201, 214, 221, 234

Plain White T's, 236
Plasscharet, Kelly, 148
Pleshette, Suzanne, 70, 149, 242
Pluto's Blue Note, 254
Pocahontas, 39, 100, 116, 130, 143, 183, 198, 226
Pocahontas II: Journey to a New World, 20, 212, 227, 234, 239
Pointer, Ruth, 201
Pola, Eddie, 121
Ponce, Carlos, 18
Pooh's Grand Adventure: The Search for Christopher Robin, 1, 57, 65, 101, 240
Pooh's Heffalump Halloween Movie, 9, 26, 82, 91, 97, 220
Pooh's Heffalump Movie, 82, 88, 106, 131, 151, 187
Popeye, 22, 35, 57, 81, 85, 91, 104, 109, 181, 204
Portman, Rachel, 9, 41, 47, 200
Potter, Grace, 193
Powers, Amy, 111, 119, 167
Poynton, Bob, 168
The Practical Pig, 243
Press, Brian, 89
Price, Kelly, 71
Price, Paul B., 214
Price, Vincent, 73, 250
Prima, Louis, 35, 61, 97, 114, 126, 198, 203
The Prince of Persia – The Sands of Time, 95
The Princess and the Frog, 4, 46, 48, 67, 72, 136, 152, 238
The Princess Diaries 2: Royal Engagement, 27, 68, 256
Proctor, Phil, 213
Proulx, Ron, 128
Pruitt, Jordan, 55, 237
Pullman, Bill, 120, 159
Putting It Together, 12, 132, 195

Quaid, Randy, 253
Quenzer, Arthur, 61
Quinn, Kevin, 9, 19, 25, 60, 74, 93, 104, 109, 123, 124, 189, 205, 224, 242, 248, 257

Rafaelson, Peter, 146
Rafferty, Kevin, 66
The Rainbow Road to Oz, 164, 166, 176
Raines, Ron, 100
Raitt, Bonnie, 32, 201, 244
Raize, Jason, 32, 54, 78, 212
Ramirez, Carlos, 141
Ramirez, Sara, 39
Rappaport, Ron, 230
Rascal, 202
Raskin, Kenny, 68, 137
Ratatouille, 122
Raven-Symoné, 2, 5, 34, 36, 43, 54, 69, 109, 166, 199, 202, 209, 217, 221, 224, 256
Ravenscroft, Thurl, 75–76, 167
Raye, Don, 20, 81, 99, 110, 118, 221
Raymond, Usher, 172, 256
Reddy, Helen, 21, 27, 32–33, 109, 211
Reisman, Joe, 152, 255
Reitherman, Bruce, 12, 38–39, 150, 210
The Reluctant Dragon, 102, 155, 176, 216
The Replacements, 177
The Rescuers, 115, 177, 192
Reser, Harry, 253
Return of Jafar, 65, 103, 154, 257
Return to Never Land, 84, 102, 191
Reubens, Paul, 119
Rex, Kristian, 202–203
Rhys, Phillip, 68, 164, 203
Rhythmaires, 81, 99
Riabouchinska, Tatiana, 221

Rice, Tim, 1, 7, 15, 32, 34, 36, 37, 42, 44, 51, 52, 53, 54, 55, 65, 66, 71, 72, 78, 86, 88, 90, 94, 100, 107, 129, 133, 136, 137, 140, 146, 150, 151, 152, 154, 166, 174, 181, 182, 186, 199, 209, 213, 228, 237, 242, 250, 255
Rich, Richard, 66, 73
Richards, Jasmine, 33, 83
Richie Family, 26
Ridel, Stefanie, 125
Riders in the Sky, 248
Rifkin, Jay, 54, 212
Rimes, LeAnn, 251
Rinker, Al, 58
Ripley, Alice, 173, 228, 237
The Ritz, 214
Rivas, Fernando, 79
Road to Rio, 26
The Robber Kitten, 46
Robbins, Ayn, 115, 177, 192, 217
Robbins, Tom Alan, 32, 78
Robin Hood, 134, 153, 162, 169, 240
Robins, Lindy, 36, 85
Robinson, Andrea, 10
Robinson, Will, 5, 88, 232
Rocha, Ron, 72
Rocks, Victoria, 119
Rogel, Randy, 75, 84, 96, 110, 228, 249
Rogers, Frank, 17
Rogers, Roy, 23, 26, 40, 168, 254
Rogers, Tom, 190
Rolie Polie Olie, 178
Romano, Christy Carlson, 39, 207
Romberg, Sigmund, 49
Ronell, Ann, 243
Ronstadt, Linda, 49, 239
Rooney, Mickey, 8, 21, 27, 95, 115, 129
Root, Stephen, 201
Rose, Anika Noni, 4, 48, 238
Rose, Earl, 17, 18, 32, 39, 71, 184, 191, 192, 224, 242, 259

Rosman, Mark, 14
Rossio, Terry, 86
Rub, Christian, 132
Rulin, Olesya, 117, 253
Run, Cougar, Run, 124
Rupert, Michael, 12
Rupp, Debra Jo, 104
Rush, Geoffrey, 86
Rushton, Steve, 81
Russell, Andy, 247, 254
Russell, Bob, 13, 26, 202
Russell, Bryan, 31
Russell, Kurt, 208, 212
Rutherford, Alex, 57, 94, 241
Ryan, Debbie, 85
Ryan, Roz, 74, 198, 258
Rzeznik, John, 5, 105

S-Club, 32
Sabella, Ernie, 32, 78
Sablon, Jean, 243
Sack, Al, 221
A Safe Place, 122
The Saga of Andy Burnett, 121, 180
The Saga of Windwagon Smith, 180
Sager, Carole Bayer, 179
Sahanaja, Darian, 177
Salerno, Mary Jo, 84
Salonga, Lea, 70, 87, 111, 124, 167, 177, 242
Saludos Amigos, 26, 181, 215
Samonsky, Andrew, 49, 58, 94, 97, 99, 164, 201, 224, 242, 255, 256
Samuel, Peter, 44, 87, 107, 181, 231
Sanborn, David, 49, 156
Sandell, Geraldo, 218
Sandpipers, 235, 255
Sands, Tommy, 165, 189, 249
Sansom, Ken, 51, 75, 88, 101, 228, 238
The Santa Clause 3: Escape Clause, 39
Santa's Workshop, 181
Sarandon, Susan, 52, 60, 209

Sauter, Eddie, 4
Savage Sam, 182
Saval, Dany, 185
Saved by the Bell, 212
Savigar, Kevin, 36
Sawyer, Dan, 44, 47, 167
Scandalous John, 166
The Scarecrow of Romney Marsh, 183
Schwartz, Stephen, 6, 18, 26, 39, 40,
    53, 55, 71, 77, 80, 81, 100, 113, 116,
    130, 143, 164, 172, 182, 183, 186,
    187, 190, 192, 198, 209, 218, 219,
    220, 226
Scoggin, James Houston, 107
Scott, Ed, 133
Scott, Jimmy, 239
Scott, Sherie Rene, 55, 94, 97, 150,
    154, 173, 199
Scott, Oz, 54
Searles, Frederick,156
Sears, Ted, 64, 98, 231
Secada, Jon, 100
Seeley, Andrew, 27, 43, 69, 198, 232,
    235, 256
Seeley, Drew, 62
Segal, Jason, 129, 138
The Sha Shees, 254
The Shaggy D. A., 1985
The Shaggy Dog, 1985
Shanice, 100
Shanks, John, 47, 48, 63, 177
Shanti, Oliver, 38
Sharp, Thomas Richard, 43
Sharpe, Albert, 245
Shatner, William, 216
Shaw, Artie, 241
Shaw, Doc, 218
Shaw, Reta, 188
Shedaisy, 44
Sheldon, Gene, 189
Sheldon, Jack, 205
Shepard, Vondra, 240
Sherberg, Jane, 121

Sherman, Al, 4, 102
Sherman, Richard M. and Robert B.,
    2, 4, 9, 16, 19, 23, 24, 25, 28, 30, 31,
    33, 34, 35, 37, 38, 42, 45, 49, 52, 54,
    61, 62, 63, 64, 65–66, 70, 76, 79, 82,
    86, 89, 94, 97, 101, 102, 104, 106,
    107, 113, 114, 116, 123, 125, 126,
    128, 131, 136, 138, 140, 141, 144,
    145, 147, 150, 153, 155, 156, 157,
    158, 160, 165, 168, 170, 172, 173,
    175, 176, 178, 179, 183, 184, 185,
    188, 192, 196, 197, 198, 199, 201,
    202, 203, 206, 208, 210, 211, 215,
    220, 221, 224, 225, 226, 228, 233,
    236, 242, 245, 246, 247, 256
Sheyne, Pam, 80, 217
Shi, Lil Shi, 39
Ship Cafe, 243
Shirley, Bill, 159
Shore, Dinah, 21, 122, 183, 218, 221
Short, Martin, 39
Shrewsbury, Kelli, 12
Shuford, Kujuana, 94
Shutta, Ethel, 243
Siegel, Ralph Maria, 247
The Sign of Zorro, 259
Silversher, Patty and Michael, 18, 24,
    26, 28, 48, 60, 64, 65, 66, 70, 76,
    80, 84, 87, 90, 91, 97, 102, 130, 132,
    142, 145, 154, 163, 171, 179, 190,
    205, 215, 220, 221, 238
Silvestri, Alan, 28, 80
Simard, Jennifer, 145
Simon, Carly, 39, 88, 100, 106, 131,
    146, 147, 151, 187, 188, 245
Simpson, Jessica, 166, 242
Sinatra, Frank, 223, 240
Skarbek, Sacha, 177
Skinner, Emily, 173
Slater, Glenn, 8, 20, 61, 83, 87, 89,
    95–96, 97, 101, 111, 124, 131, 147,
    162, 173, 186, 204, 213, 238–39,
    240, 244, 249, 253

Sleeping Beauty, 43, 78, 98, 159, 188
The Small One, 66, 140, 189
Smart Guy, 190
Smash Mouth, 56, 97
Smith!, 13
Smith, Ethel, 22, 215
Smith, Jack, 122
Smith, Kate, 239
Smith, Michael, 125
Smith, Paul J., 61, 92, 129, 170, 217
Smith, Paul L., 104, 109
Smith, Riley, 232
Smith, Stanley A., 254
Snart, Roy, 2, 16, 173, 202
Snow, Tom, 2, 46–47, 135, 153, 158, 161, 201, 229
Snow White and the Seven Dwarfs, 22, 50, 82, 84, 105, 162, 191, 231, 241, 244, 246
So Dear to My Heart, 40, 110, 122, 156, 190, 200
So Weird, 106
Sondheim, Stephen, 12, 132, 145, 195, 234
Sondheim: A Celebration at Carnegie Hall, 133
Song of the South, 55, 88, 125, 194, **195**, 210, 241, 258
Sons of the Pioneers, 23, 123, 168, 180
Sorenson, Ricky, 210
Soucie, Kath, 131, 188, 220, 246
Soul II Soul, 120
Spade, David, 149, 169
Sparks, Randy, 8
Spektor, Regina, 31
Spencer, Charlotte,
Spice Girls, 150
Spicer, Willie, 45
Spiner, Brent, 26, 187
Squier, William, 192
Stafford, Jim, 8, 90, 121
Stafford, Jo, 21
Stalling, Carl, 144

Stanger, Kyle, 26, 151, 220
Stanley, 197
Stanley, Gordon, 9, 137, 231
Stapleton, Jean, 227
Star Trek, 216
Starr, Ringo, 239
Steele, Tommy, **37**, 66, 101, 126
Steinkellner, Cheri, 93, 104, 205, 242
Stevenson, Robert Louis, 5, 105
Stewart, Rod, 3
Stiers, David Ogden, 9, 41, 143, 183, 189, 193, 213, 226
Stiles, George, 7, 17, 27, 35, 173, 208
Stiller, Jerry, 189
Sting, 3, 7, 148, 169
Stockwell, Harry, 105, 162
Stojka, Andre, 1, 70
Stomp, 248
Stoner, Alyson, 33, 163
Storm, Billy, 175
Stott, Harry, 168
Stout, Mary, 77
Straus, Billy, 131
Straus, Emma, 131
Streisand, Barbra, 111, 159, 191, 239, 243
Strickland, Josh, 45, 57, 65, 201, 222, 255
Stritch, Billy, 12
Stroh, Kaycee, 150
Stroman, Guy, 9, 231
The Strongest Man in the World, 106
Struthers, Sally, 87
Stuart, Chad, 210
Stuck in the Suburbs, 72, 137, 146, 159, 164
Sturges, Thomas, 33
Sturmer, Andy, 119
Suarez, Jeremy, 153
The Suite Life of Zack and Cody, 83
Sullivan, Nicole, 240
Sullivan, Stacy, 49
Sumac, Yma, 98

Summer Magic, 16, 62, 63, 157, **158**, 170, 202, 223
Superdad, 134, 212, 236
Sussman, Bruce, 168
Sutherland, Brian, 97, 98, 100, 124, 159, 164, 184, 237, 257
Sutton, Julia, 61
Swamp Fox, 203
Sweetnam, Skye, 166
Swenson, Karl, 86, 147, 210
Swift, Taylor, 40, 255
Swiss Family Robinson, **92**, 149
The Sword in the Stone, 86, 123, 136, 147, 210

T-Squad, 184
TaleSpin, 66, 87, 102, 145, 205
Tambor, Jeffrey, 110
Tangled, 95, 110, 147, 193, 238
Tappan, Tami, 9
Tartaglia, John, 113
Tarzan, 45, 57, 65, 94, 129, 153, 194, 201, 203, 219, 222, 227, 241, 255
Tarzan II, 94, 123, 194, 241
Tarzan and Jane, 194, 222
Tately, Chuck, 145
Tatum, Shane, 8, 133, 134, 139, 146, 185, 212, 236
Tavera, Michael, 53
Taylor, Ben, 39, 245
Taylor, James, 164
Taylor, Irving, 190
Taylor, Russi, 169
Taylor, Sarah, 2
Taylor-Good, Karen, 198
Taymor, Julie, 54
Tchaikovsky, Peter Ilich, 159
Teacher's Pet, 25, 93, 96, 104, 189, 205, 207, 239, 242
Teagarden, Jack, 239
Teamo Supremo, 207
Ten Who Dared, 114, 178
Terfel, Bryn, 18

Terry, Paul, 51, 59, 149, 209
Tesori, Jeanine, 5, 10, 61, 95, 98, 115, 116, 124, 130
Texas John Slaughter, 208
That Darn Cat, 208
That's So Raven, 40, 209
Theodore, Ali Dee, 119, 127
Theory, Juliana, 232
Thewlis, David, 52, 60, 209
They Might Be Giants, 84, 191
Thigpen, Lynn, 74
Third Man on the Mountain, 38, 73
Thomas, Khleo, 46
Thomas, Rob, 132
Thomas, Vanessa, 74, 198, 258
Thompson, Bill, 21, 34, 89–90, 103, 171, 188, 232
Those Calloways, 30, 178
Thousands Cheer, 215
The Three Caballeros, 12, 22, 141, 214, 254
3D Jamboree, 22
Three Kaydets, 122
The Three Little Pigs, 243
Three Little Wolves, 243
The Three Lives of Thomasina, 214
The Three Musketeers, 3
Through the Looking Glass, 3
Tiger Cruise, 149
The Tigger Movie, 89, 172, 179, 192, 242, 247, 256
Till, Lucas, 48
Tinker Bell, 63, 216, 255
Tipton, George, 83, 217
Tisdale, Ashley, 3, 25, 59, 74, 90, 97, 120, 191, 200, 232, 235, **253**
Toby Tyler, 21
Todd, Hallie, 69, 133
Tomlinson, David, 16, 52, 62, 126, 127, 138, 153, 157, 173, 202, 246
Tondo, Jerry, 70
Tonka, 217
Toot, Whistle, Plunk and Boom, 22, 218

Toppins, Mike, 14, 35, 41, 58, 66, 82, 97, 131, 163
Torimiro, Dapo, 63
Torkelsons, The, 218
Tormé, Mel, 40, 132
Toro, Natalie, 256
Torres, Mitchie, 26
The Tortoise and the Hare, 189
Tosti, Blaise, 20
Toy Story, 98, 201, 257
Toy Story 2, 205, 237, 248, 257
Toy Story 3, 229
Tracey, Doreen, 167, 176
Tran, Myhanh, 72
Travolta, John, 96
Treasure Island, 5, 105
Treasure of Matecumbe, 139
Treasure Planet, 5, 105
Trencher, Philip, 131
Tron, 162
Trotter, John Scott, 45
Troy, Billy, 14, 35, 41, 58, 66, 82, 97, 131, 163
Tryon, Tom, 185, 220
The Tubes, 150
Tumes, Michelle, 63
Turner, Sammy, 122
Turner, Tina, 51, 75, 212
Turner, Wendy, 62
20,000 Leagues Under the Sea, 233
Twillie, Carmen, 37
Tyner, Charles, 21, 79
Tyrell, Steve, 11, 14, 17, 18, 41, 49, 58, 84, 120, 159, 237, 239, 255, 257

Underwood, Carrie, 55
Up, 197
Usher. *See* Raymond, Usher

van der Poll, Anneliese, 33, 164,
Van Dyke, Dick, 16, 35, 62, 94, 114, 127, **128**, 138, 199, 203
Van Tongeren, John, 54, 217

The Vanishing Prairie, 171
Verbinski, Gore, 86
Vickery, John, 15, 136
Vidnovic, Martin, 44, 54, 90, 107, 182, 186, 213, 255
Vincent, Jeffrey, 146
Vincent, Rhonda, 251
Vitamin C, 120

Wagner, Windy, 178
Wainwright, Rufus, 6, 147, 240
Wallace, Oliver, 2, 44, 64, 88, 117, 156, 157, 170, 171, 174, 231, 236, 245, 252
WALL-E, 48
Walley, Deborah, 62
Walsh, Brock, 122, 182, 207, 223
Walsh, William, 148, 150
Walston, Ray, 35, 109
Walt Disney's Wonderful World of Color, 4, 24, 34, 102, 105, 175, 179, 196, 247
Warnes, Jennifer, 259
Warrander, Scott, 149
Warren, Diane, 240
Warren, Lesley Ann, 8, 25, 28, **37**, 45, 79, 101, 126, 160, 208, 225, 233, 236
Washington, Ned, 11, 33, 70, 85, 102, 111, 132, 134, 181, 194, 236
Waters, Oren, 230
Watkin, Lawrence Edgar, 92, 114, 174, 178, 194, 245
Watson, Leo, 241
Watters, Mark, 9, 24
Watts, Adam, 74, 117, 164, 213, 235
Weaver, Jason, 78, 93
Webster, Paul Francis, 21
Wechter, David and Julius, 143
The Weekenders, 230
Weeks, Sarah, 1, 57, 65, 101, 240
Weems, Ted, 139
Weighill, Ian, 2, 16, 173, 202

Weil, Cynthia, 24, 30, 135, 174, 181, 187, 192
Weiner, Michael, 6, 10, 64, 146, 169
Weiss, George, 67, 140
Weiss, Gretchen, 12
Welk, Lawrence, 119
The Wellingtons, 13
Wells, Greg, 171, 229
Wells, Robert, 40
Wendy and the Wombats, 243
Wenger, Brahm, 161
Wentworth, Martha, 136, 192
West, Mae, 192
Westenra, Hayley, 83
Weston, Jack, 214
Weston, Paul, 184, 256
Westward Ho the Wagons!, 103, 112, 170, 233, 250
Wexler, Jonathan, 47
Wheldon, Joss, 149
Whitaker, Johnny, 146
White, Betty, 141
White, Lilias, 74, 198, 258
White, Onna, 95
White, Richard, 18, 68, 144
Whitman, Jerry, 39
Whitman, Mae, 14
Whitmire, Steve, 22, 31, 44, 108, 135, 148, 161, 169, 192, 237
Who Discovered Roger Rabbit?, 214
Who Killed Cock Robin?, 192, 241
Who's Afraid of Virginia Woolf?, 243
Widelitz, Stacy, 20
Wild Hearts Can't Be Broken, 233
Wilde, David, 230
Wilde, Stacy, 230
Wilder, Alec, 4
Wilder, Matthew, 12, 69–70, 87, 101, 177, 220, 234
Wilkof, Lee, 53
Williams, Denise, 229
Williams, Joseph, 32

Williams, Kiely, 2, 5, 34, 36, 43, 54, 69, 109, 166, 199, 202, 217
Williams, Laura, 93
Williams, Paul, 22, 44, 98, 107, 108, 139, 148, 161, 184, 208, 237
Williams, Rhoda, 155
Williams, Robin, 8, 22, 35, 57, 60, 66, 92, 174, 181, 204, 211
Williams, Vanessa, 39
Willis, Allee, 7
Wilson, Don, 62
Winans, Sam, 133
Winchell, Paul, 238, 247
Wingert, Wally, 191
Winnie the Pooh, 12, 57, 109, 172, 191, 225, 244, 245
Winnie the Pooh, a Valentine for You, 70, 171, 238
Winnie the Pooh: A Very Merry Pooh Year, 80, 90, 190
Winnie the Pooh: Seasons of Giving, 18, 87, 163, 184, 221
Winnie the Pooh: Springtime with Roo, 51, 75, 190, 228, 232
Winnie the Pooh and the Blustery Day, 82, 86, 176, 233, 247
Winnie the Pooh and the Honey Tree, 131, 172, 179, 224, 245
Winnie the Pooh and Tigger Too!, 247
Winters, Shelley, 21, 79
The Wise Little Hen, 82
Withers, Jane, 123
Wizards of Waverly Place, 57
Wolcott, Charles, 102, 141, 155, 176, 181, 195, 215, 216, 221
Wolcott, Oliver, 141
Wolf, Scott, 93
Wolff, Jonathan, 190
Wonder, Stevie, 220
Wood, DeeDee, 199
Wood, Gloria, 24, 34, 167

Wood, Lauren, 191
Woodbury, Brian, 96
Woods, Ilene, 21, 43, 48, 155–56, 191
Wooley, Michael-Leon, 238
Worth, Bobby, 23, 122, 160
Wright, Ben, 40, 42
Wright, Ralph, 27, 217
Wright, Samuel E., 48, 84, 115, 120, 147, 151, 186, 212, 224
Wrubel, Allie, 55, 113, 132, 258
Wyle, George, 121
Wynken, Blynken and Nod, 251
Wynn, Ed, 30, 56, 94, 249
Wynn, Nan, 26

Yaeger, Jordan, 119
Yamin, Elliott, 32

Yearwood, Trisha, 23
York, Jeff, 120
York, Rachel, 12, 195
Young, Will, 221

Zachary, Alan, 6, 10, 64, 146, 169
Zane, Billy, 20, 227
Zaslove, Diana, 197
Zeke and Luther, 258
Zenon: Girl of the 21st Century, 202
Zenon: The Zequel, 68, 203
Zenon: Z3, 164
Ziemba, Karen, 196
Zimmer, Hans, 54, 86, 171, 185
Zippel, David, 69, 71, 74, 87, 99, 101, 161, 177, 198, 220, 258
Zorro, 259

ABOUT THE AUTHORS

Thomas S. Hischak is the author of twenty-two books on popular music, theatre, and film, including such titles as *Theatre as Human Action, The Oxford Companion to the American Musical, The Tin Pan Alley Encyclopedia,* and *Through the Screen Door: What Happened to the Broadway Musical When It Went to Hollywood.* Hischak is professor of theatre at the State University of New York College at Cortland. He is also the author of twenty-three published plays.

Mark A. Robinson is a longtime Disney fan who has directed plays and musicals and taught theatre and film in various high schools in Nebraska and New York State. He is the author of *Encyclopedia of Television Theme Songs* and the forthcoming *The World of Musicals.* Robinson graduated from the State University of New York College at Cortland with a BA in Theatre and has published some poetry.